IARIA

AICT 2019

The Fifteenth Advanced International Conference on Telecommunications

July 28 – August 2, 2019

Nice, France

AICT 2019 Editors

Eugen Borcoci, University Politehnica Bucharest, Romania

Toshihiko Kato, University of Electro-Communications, Japan

Abheek Saha, Hughes Systique Corporation, Gurgaon, India

Printed from e-media with permission by:

Curran Associates, Inc.
57 Morehouse Lane
Red Hook, NY 12571

proceedings.com

Some format issues inherent in the e-media version may also appear in this print version.

International Academy, Research, and Industry Association (IARIA)
412 Derby Way
Wilmington, DE 19810

Phone: (408) 893-6407
Fax: (408) 527-6351

petre@iaria.org

Additional copies of this publication are available from:

Curran Associates, Inc.
57 Morehouse Lane
Red Hook, NY 12571 USA
Phone: 845-758-0400
Fax: 845-758-2633
Email: curran@proceedings.com
Web: www.proceedings.com

Table of Contents

AICT 2019

Forward

The Fifteenth Advanced International Conference on Telecommunications (AICT 2019), held between July 28, 2019 and August 02, 2019 in Nice, France, continued a series of events covering a variety of challenging telecommunication topics ranging from background fields like signals, traffic, coding, communication basics up to large communication systems and networks, fixed, mobile and integrated, etc. Applications, services, system and network management issues also received significant attention.

The spectrum of 21st Century telecommunications is marked by the arrival of new business models, new platforms, new architectures and new customer profiles. Next generation networks, IP multimedia systems, IPTV, and converging network and services are new telecommunications paradigms. Technology achievements in terms of co-existence of IPv4 and IPv6, multiple access technologies, IP MPLS network design driven methods, multicast and high speed require innovative approaches to design and develop large scale telecommunications networks.

Mobile and wireless communications add profit to large spectrum of technologies and services. We witness the evolution 2G, 2.5G, 3G and beyond, personal communications, cellular and ad hoc networks, as well as multimedia communications.

Web Services add a new dimension to telecommunications, where aspects of speed, security, trust, performance, resilience, and robustness are particularly salient. This requires new service delivery platforms, intelligent network theory, new telecommunications software tools, new communications protocols and standards.

We are witnessing many technological paradigm shifts imposed by the complexity induced by the notions of fully shared resources, cooperative work, and resource availability. P2P, GRID, Clusters, Web Services, Delay Tolerant Networks, Service/Resource identification and localization illustrate aspects where some components and/or services expose features that are neither stable nor fully guaranteed. Examples of technologies exposing similar behavior are WiFi, WiMax, WideBand, UWB, ZigBee, MBWA and others.

Management aspects related to autonomic and adaptive management includes the entire arsenal of self-ilities. Autonomic Computing, On-Demand Networks and Utility Computing together with Adaptive Management and Self-Management Applications collocating with classical networks management represent other categories of behavior dealing with the paradigm of partial and intermittent resources.

The conference included academic, research, and industrial contributions. It had the following tracks:

- Wireless technologies
- Ad Hoc, autonomic and sensor networks
- Trends on telecommunications features and services
- Architectures and communication technologies for 4G and 5G wireless networks
- New telecommunications technologies
- Future applications and services
- Edge and IoT Application Deployment for 5G Networks

We take here the opportunity to warmly thank all the members of the AICT 2019 technical program committee, as well as all the reviewers. The creation of such a high quality conference program would not have been possible without their involvement. We also kindly thank all the authors who dedicated much of their time and effort to contribute to AICT 2019. We truly believe that, thanks to all these efforts, the final conference program consisted of top quality contributions.

We also thank the members of the AICT 2019 organizing committee for their help in handling the logistics and for their work that made this professional meeting a success.

We hope that AICT 2019 was a successful international forum for the exchange of ideas and results between academia and industry and to promote further progress in the field of telecommunications. We also hope that Nice, France provided a pleasant environment during the conference and everyone saved some time to enjoy the charm of the city.

AICT 2019 Chairs

AICT Steering Committee

Kevin Daimi, University of Detroit Mercy, USA
Eugen Borcoci, University "Politehnica" of Bucharest (UPB), Romania
Carlos Becker Westphall, Federal University of Santa Catarina, Brazil
Tulin Atmaca, Telecom SudParis, France
Mariusz Głąbowski, Poznan University of Technology, Poland
Mario Freire, University of Beira Interior, Portugal
Ioannis Moscholios, University of Peloponnese, Greece
Masayuki Murata, Osaka University Suita, Japan
Wenzhong Li, Nanjing University, China
Ali Houssein Harmouch, Lebanese University, Lebanon

AICT Publicity Chair

Ustijana Rechkoska-Shikoska, University for Information Science and Technology "St. Paul the Apostle" - Ohrid, Republic of Macedonia

AICT Industry/Research Advisory Committee

Mayank Raj, IBM, USA
Sergei Semenov, Huawei Technologies, Lund, Sweden
Dragana Krstic, University of Niš, Serbia
György Kalman, Norwegian University of Science and Technology, Norway
Seema Garg, Nokia, India
Sungsoo Choi, Korea Electrotechnology Research Institute (KERI), South Korea
Motoyoshi Sekiya, Fujitsu Laboratories Limited, Japan

AICT 2019

Committee

AICT Steering Committee

Kevin Daimi, University of Detroit Mercy, USA
Eugen Borcoci, University "Politehnica" of Bucharest (UPB), Romania
Carlos Becker Westphall, Federal University of Santa Catarina, Brazil
Tulin Atmaca, Telecom SudParis, France
Mariusz Głąbowski, Poznan University of Technology, Poland
Mario Freire, University of Beira Interior, Portugal
Ioannis Moscholios, University of Peloponnese, Greece
Masayuki Murata, Osaka University Suita, Japan
Wenzhong Li, Nanjing University, China
Ali Houssein Harmouch, Lebanese University, Lebanon

AICT Publicity Chair

Ustijana Rechkoska-Shikoska, University for Information Science and Technology "St. Paul the Apostle" - Ohrid, Republic of Macedonia

AICT Industry/Research Advisory Committee

Mayank Raj, IBM, USA
Sergei Semenov, Huawei Technologies, Lund, Sweden
Dragana Krstic, University of Niš, Serbia
György Kalman, Norwegian University of Science and Technology, Norway
Seema Garg, Nokia, India
Sungsoo Choi, Korea Electrotechnology Research Institute (KERI), South Korea
Motoyoshi Sekiya, Fujitsu Laboratories Limited, Japan

AICT 2019 Technical Program Committee

Ghulam Abbas, GIK Institute of Engineering Sciences and Technology, Pakistan
Iwan Adhicandra, University of Sydney, Australia
Michele Albano, University of Pisa, Italy
Petre Anghelescu, University of Pitesti, Romania
Kamran Arshad, Ajman University, UAE
Manal Assaad, University of Applied Sciences Emden/Leer, Germany
Tulin Atmaca, Telecom SudParis, France
Nizamettin Aydin, Yildiz Technical University, Turkey
Erdoğan Aydın, Istanbul Medeniyet University, Turkey
Ilija Basicevic, University of Novi Sad, Serbia
Oussama Bazzi, Lebanese University, Lebanon

Matthieu Gautier, IRISA | University of Rennes 1, France
Juraj Gazda, Technical University of Kosice, Slovakia
Andrei Gheorghiu, "Politehnica" University of Bucharest, Romania
Mircea Giurgiu, Technical University of Cluj-Napoca, Romania
Mariusz Głąbowski, Poznan University of Technology, Poland
Teresa Gomes, University of Coimbra & INESC Coimbra, Portugal
Luís Gonçalo Cancela, Instituto Universitário de Lisboa (ISCTE-IUL) & Instituto de Telecomunicações, Portugal
Norton Gonzalez, Luciano Feijão Faculty, Sobral, Ceará, Brazil
Carlos Guerrero, University of Balearic Islands, Spain
Jan Haase, University of Lübeck, Germany
Ali Houssein Harmouch, Lebanese University, Lebanon
Piyush Harsh, Zurich University of Applied Science, Switzerland
Davit Harutyunyan, FBK CREATE-NET, Italy
Zhiyuan Hu, Nokia Shanghai Bell, China
Takeshi Ikenaga, Kyushu Institute of Technology, Japan
Ilias Iliadis, IBM Research - Zurich, Switzerland
Shital Joshi, Oakland University, Michigan, USA
Branislav Jovic, Defence Technology Agency (DTA) | New Zealand Defence Force (NZDF), Auckland, New Zealand
Seifedine Kadry, American University of the Middle East, Kuwait
György Kalman, Norwegian University of Science and Technology, Norway
Alexandros Kaloxylos, University of Peloponnese, Greece
Georgios Kambourakis, University of the Aegean, Greece
Dimitris Kanellopoulos, University of Patras, Greece
Meriem Kassar Ben Jemaa, Ecole Nationale d'Ingénieurs de Tunis, Tunisia
Ahmad Khalil, Laboratoire d'Informatique de la Bourgogne (LIB) - University of Bourgogne Franche Comté, France
Tomotaka Kimura, Doshisha University, Japan
Francine Krief, Bordeaux INP, France
Visnja Krizanovic Cik, Faculty of Electrical Engineering, Computer Science and Information Technology Osijek | Josip Juraj Strossmayer University in Osijek, Croatia
Dragana Krstic, University of Niš, Serbia
Lopamudra Kundu, Intel Corporation, USA
Hoang Le, Google, USA
Gyu Myoung Lee, Liverpool John Moores University, UK
Wenzhong Li, Nanjing University, China
Marco Listanti, University Sapienza of Roma, Italy
Erwu Liu, Tongji University, China
Malamati Louta, University of Western Macedonia, Greece
Juraj Machaj, University of Zilina, Slovakia
Tatiana K. Madsen, Aalborg University, Denmark
Zoubir Mammeri, IRIT - Toulouse, France
Nafees Mansoor, University of Liberal Arts Bangladesh (ULAB), Bangladesh
Alexandru Martian, Politehnica University of Bucharest, Romania
Erik Massarczyk, University of Applied Sciences RheinMain - Wiesbaden Rüsselsheim, Germany
Wojciech Mazurczyk, Warsaw University of Technology, Poland
Natarajan Meghanathan, Jackson State University, USA

Dawit Mengistu, Kristianstad University, Sweden
Amalia Miliou, Aristotle University of Thessaloniki, Greece
Andrea Morichetta, University of Camerino, Italy
Alistair Morris, Trinity College Dublin, Ireland
Ioannis Moscholios, University of Peloponnese, Greece
Juan Pedro Muñoz-Gea, Universidad Politécnica de Cartagena, Spain
Masayuki Murata, Osaka University Suita, Japan
Amor Nafkha, IETR/SCEE CentraleSupélec, France
Paolo Napoletano, University of Milano-Bicocca, Italy
Antonio Navarro, Universidad Complutense de Madrid, Spain
Huan X Nguyen, Middlesex University, London
Petros Nicopolitidis, Aristotle University of Thessaloniki, Greece
Claudia Cristina Oprea, Politehnica University of Bucharest, Romania
Constantin Paleologu, University Politehnica of Bucharest, Romania
Jari Palomäki, Tampere University of Technology, Finland
Danilo Pelusi, University of Teramo, Italy
Cathryn Peoples, The Open University, UK
Maciej Piechowiak, Kazimierz Wielki University, Bydgoszcz, Poland
Padma Pillay-Esnault, Huawei, R&D, USA
Anders Plymoth, MaXentric Technologies LLC / University of California, San Diego, USA
Emanuel Puschita, Tehnical University of Cluj-Napoca, Romania
Mayank Raj, IBM, USA
Adib Rastegarnia, Purdue University, USA
Abolfazl Razi, Northern Arizona University, USA
Maurizio Rebaudengo, Politecnico di Torino, Italy
Ustijana Rechkoska-Shikoska, University for Information Science and Technology "St. Paul the Apostle" - Ohrid, Republic of Macedonia
José Renato da Silva Junior, Universidade Federal do Rio de Janeiro (UFRJ), Brazil
Éric Renault, Institut Mines-Télécom - Télécom SudParis, France
Laura Ricci, University of Pisa, Italy
Neda Rojhani, University of Florence, Italy
Juha Röning, University of Oulu, Finland
Torsten M. Runge, University of Hamburg, Germany
Zsolt Saffer, University of Technology and Economics (BUTE), Budapest, Hungary
Abheek Saha, Hughes Systique Corp., India
Demetrios Sampson, Curtin University, Australia
Vincent Savaux, IRT b<>com, Rennes, France
Motoyoshi Sekiya, Fujitsu Laboratories Limited, Japan
Sergei Semenov, Huawei Technologies, Lund, Sweden
Alex Sim, Lawrence Berkeley National Laboratory, USA
Kajetana Marta Snopek, Warsaw University of Technology, Poland
Celio Marcio Soares Ferreira, LinuxPlace, Brazil
Marco Aurélio Spohn, Federal University of Fronteira Sul, Brazil
Kostas Stamos, University of Patras, Greece
Philipp Svoboda, Vienna University of Technology, Austria
Sándor Szénási, Óbuda University, Budapest, Hungary
Yoshiaki Taniguchi, Kindai University, Japan
António Teixeira, Universidade de Aveiro, Portugal

Copyright Information

A Novel Synchronization Algorithm for Hybrid Inter-Satellite Link Establishment

Alexandru Crisan, Cristian Anghel, Remus Cacoveanu
Telecommunications Department
University Politehnica of Bucharest
Bucharest, Romania
e-mail: alexandru.crisan@ceospacetech.pub.ro; cristian.anghel@upb.ro; remus.cacoveanu@upb.ro

Abstract—**This paper presents a new synchronization algorithm proposed to establish an inter-satellite link in a system with two satellites flying in tandem. The complete system is described, including both the master and the companion satellite. The proposed physical layer is a customization of the one from Long Term Evolution (LTE) telecommunications systems, based on the Orthogonal Frequency Division Multiplexing (OFDM) technology with Time Division Duplexing (TDD) approach. The proposed synchronization algorithm uses two preamble-symbols per radio frame. Simulation results for different frequency deviations are provided.**

Keywords-synchronization; OFDM; preamble; frequency offset; inter-satellite link.

I. INTRODUCTION

When it comes to data relay satellites or constellation and formation flying missions, the Inter-Satellite Link (ISL) is a topic that has been intensively discussed [1]. The ISL is needed not only to support the communication function, but also to enable the formation acquisition and formation control through precise relative positioning using inter-satellite metrology consisting in ranging and Line of Sight (LoS) determination. Having to fulfill the complex requirements of both the selected communication system and the navigation module, the ISL is the key in finding the tradeoff between ensuring the data bandwidth and the data transfer quality on the communication path, and providing the accurate measurements and inputs for the navigation algorithms.

The Hybrid Inter-Satellite Link (H-ISL) is the new terminology used for a system which shall be able to ensure relative navigation (range and LoS estimation) between two spacecraft flying in formation, and also data exchange using the communication link. Thus, the H-ISL system architecture involves two spacecraft, namely the master satellite and the companion satellite. Both the quality of the link, measured as Bit Error Rate (BER), and the accuracy of the Navigation (NAV) commends are highly dependent on the synchronization algorithm results in terms of frequency alignment (for the two clock references used on the two satellites) and time synchronization (the correct radio frame start shall be identified by the receiver). On the other hand, the total cost of the system, the power consumption and the physical dimensions are to be considered as well.

Synchronization techniques for Orthogonal Frequency Division Multiplexing (OFDM) waveforms are based on either received signal autocorrelation or cross-correlation of a training symbol with a local replica. The autocorrelation is robust to large carrier frequency offsets (CFO) and exploits some form of redundancy built in the transmitted signal, for example the cyclic prefix (CP) [2] or a training symbol with two identical halves [3]. The main disadvantage of autocorrelation is that timing synchronization is only coarse and a fine-timing estimation stage is also required. On the other hand, cross-correlation techniques [4] provide accurate timing, but are very sensitive to large CFO values. Thus, the common approach is to have a coarse estimation stage for timing and fractional CFO, followed by a fine estimation stage for timing and integer frequency offset (IFO). Based on this approach, a two-stage synchronization algorithm is presented in [5]. Synchronization for downlink (DL) Long Term Evolution (LTE) is proposed in [6]. Coarse timing and fractional CFO is estimated using the CP technique, then fine timing consists in identifying the specific synchronization signals and a frequency-domain estimation of the IFO. The residual offset is also tracked. The method developed in [7] exploits the properties of constant amplitude zero autocorrelation sequences to achieve synchronization. In [8] a cross-correlation based joint timing and frequency synchronization scheme based on Zadoff-Chu (ZC) sequences is presented. The technique also uses a two-stage approach and optimizes the ZC sequence parameter selection based on the shift of the cross-correlation peak to allow for coarse timing and CFO estimation.

In this context, a novel synchronization algorithm for H-ISL scenario has been proposed. It is based on the one used in the LTE communications systems, with customizations specific to spatial radio link. Our approach has the advantage of achieving fine timing synchronization without the need for a coarse stage and frequency-domain IFO estimation is not required.

The rest of this paper is organized as follows. Section II provides the system description, with both the digital part (including the 3 main modules MAC, PHY and NAV) and the analog part (RF daughter board plus additional analog circuits). Section III describes the proposed synchronization algorithm, highlighting the changes made compared with the one used in the LTE communication systems. Section IV provides the obtained results, exemplifying the time alignment and the frequency corrections generated by the algorithm in real-life conditions. The acknowledgement and conclusions close the article.

II. SYSTEM DESCRIPTION

A. *The hardware platform selection*

The NAV requirements in terms of information input and resolution set mainly the system architecture. The master satellite, the one on which the NAV algorithm runs, has 3 antennas, placed in a square triangle pattern, with the master antenna corresponding to the intersection of the catetes. This solution with 3 antennas allows the master satellite to compute the LoS, i.e., the vector from the companion spacecraft transmitter to the master spacecraft receiver. The navigation module takes into account measurements coming from the triplet of antennas. The 3 antennas create 2 perpendicular antenna baselines and provide path differences measurements on the two baselines. For navigation purposes H-ISL shall use two frequency bands, 100-200 MHz apart. The two frequencies allocated for navigation purposes are used as carrier frequencies for data communication as well.

In this context, the hardware platform selection is restricted by these constraints and requirements. Several solutions were studied, the final decision being based on a Xilinx ZCU102 board [9] for the digital part, called motherboard, and Analog Devices FMComms5 [10] for the RF part, named daughter board.

The digital part includes the Zynq UltraScale XCZU9EG [11] SoC, which contains a Quad-Core ARM Cortex A-53 for the Application Processor Unit (APU), a Dual-Core ARM Cortex R5 for the Real Time Processor Unit (RTPU), and a Xilinx's 16nm FinFET+ programmable logic fabric (specific to Xilinx 7 families).

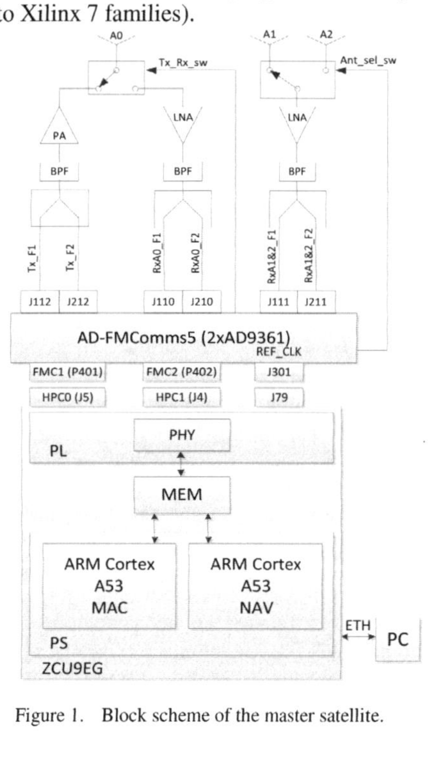

Figure 1. Block scheme of the master satellite.

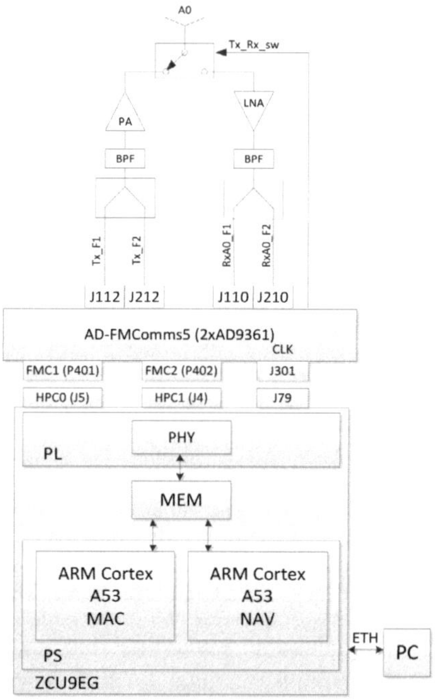

Figure 2. Block scheme of the companion satellite.

This internal structure allows the MAC and NAV modules to run on Processing System (PS), while the PHY is implemented on (Programmable Logic) PL side. The connections between PS and PL is made via AXI interfaces [12], using shared RAMs.

The RF part includes two AD9361 devices [13], each of them supporting 2×2 RF transceivers with integrated 12-bit DACs and ADCs.

The connection between the motherboard and the daughter board is made via two FPGA Mezzanine Cards (FMCs) connectors, as depicted in Figure 1 for the master satellite, respectively Figure 2 for the companion satellite. Additionally, in the two above-mentioned figures, one can observe also the extra analog circuitry needed to support the co-existing of the two used frequencies and the duplexing technique.

B. *The PHY parameters*

In order to clearly describe the proposed synchronization algorithm, the PHY parameters should be first presented. The starting point for their values selection was the LTE standard. We consider a TDD duplexing, with radio frames of 10 ms, the DL and uplink (UL) parts being balanced 1:1. The OFDM technology is used, with 1024 sub-carriers spaced at 15 kHz for a channel of 10 MHz.

Normal CP of 72 samples is added to each OFDM symbol of 1024 samples. The resulted sampling frequency is 15.36 MHz. The maximum throughput computation can be done having in mind that the two OFDM symbols on each DL/UL sub-frame are allocated to the preambles used by the synchronization algorithm. The 1096 samples-long OFDM

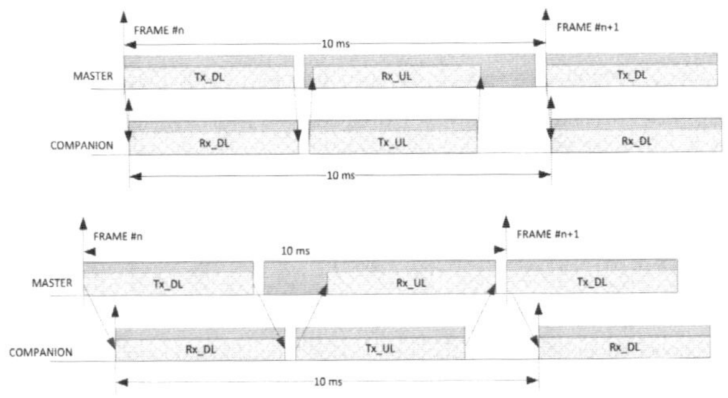

Figure 3. Frame structure for a) short distance between the satelites b) long distance between the satelites

symbol (including the CP) lasts 71.3 us at the indicated sampling frequency, this leading to a targeted number of 64 OFDM symbols per DL/UL. In conclusion, excluding the two symbols for synchronization, a maximum DL/UL throughput of around 2 Mbps can be achieved when BPSK modulation is used, with a channel coding rate of 1/3. The rest of a radio frame is split between the Transmit Time Gap (TTG) and the Receive Time Gap (RTG). Figure 3 depicts the timing expected when the two limit scenarios are considered, i.e, the two satellites being very close to each other, respectively very far.

III. PROPOSED SYNCHRONIZATION ALGORITHM

The first step in establishing the ISL consists in time and frequency synchronization at the companion satellite. Time synchronization is necessary in order to ensure that the receiver window encompasses the entire DL sub-frame and to identify the boundaries of the received OFDM symbols. Frequency synchronization must be performed to eliminate the inter-carrier interference and to prevent loss of sub-carrier orthogonality.

In an Additive White Gaussian Noise (AWGN) channel, the baseband signal received by the companion can be expressed as [2]:

$$y[n]=x[n-n_0]e^{j2\pi n\frac{\Delta f_c}{F_s}}+w[n] \tag{1}$$

where $x[n]$ is the transmitted DL preamble symbol, n_0 is the timing offset in samples, Δf_c is the CFO, F_s is the sampling frequency and $w[n]$ is the AWGN. The training symbol is BPSK-modulated in frequency domain and is constructed as an extension of the Secondary Synchronization Signal (SSS) in LTE.

Firstly, the timing offset must be estimated so that the receiver window can be positioned correctly. To achieve this, the received signal is cross-correlated with a local, time-synchronized replica of the training symbol:

$$R[m]=\sum_{n=0}^{N-1} x^*[n]y[m+n] \tag{2}$$

where N is the Fast Fourier Transform (FFT). The timing offset can by finding the peak of $|R[m]|$:

$$n_0=\arg\max\{|R[m]|\} \tag{3}$$

In practical systems, $R[m]$ is normalized with a factor that depends on the energy of the received signal. Although the cross-correlation provides very accurate timing, it is very sensitive to CFO. For CFO values that are close to or exceed the sub-carrier spacing (15 kHz for LTE signals), the cross-correlation peak can no longer be identified.

In order to overcome this effect, our novel approach consists in performing the cross-correlation between $y[n]$ and a set of training symbols that incorporate certain CFO values untill the cross-correlation peak exceeds a preset threshold. More specifically, at the companion we store seven versions of the training symbol with the following CFOs: 0, ±5, ±10 and ±15 kHz. Moreover, in order to allow for faster computation, the received signal is split into batches of equal length and the cross-correlation theorem is exploited: the spectrum of the batch is multiplied with the spectrum of the complex-conjugated training symbol on a point-to-point basis and then the inverse FFT (IFFT) is computed to obtain the time-domain values.

Our approach ensures fine timing sychronization and allows for joint coarse CFO estimation. The coarse CFO is used to adjust the reference frequency source of the companion satellite. Since there are actually two training symbols in the preamble, the cross-correlation will yield two peaks at n_0 and n_1.

Once timing synchronization has been achieved and the reference frequency has been coarsely adjusted, the remaining, uncorrected frequency offset is estimated using the redundancy of the two training symbols. Let Δf_c^r be the uncorrected offset. The received training symbols in the preamble can be expressed as:

$$y_l[n]=x[n]e^{j2\pi\frac{\Delta f_c^r}{F_s}[n+(l-1)(N+N_{cp})]}+w_l[n] \tag{4}$$

where $l=1,2$ is the symbol index and N_{cp} is the CP length. Δf_c^r can be estimated as follows:

$$\Delta f_c^r=\frac{F_s}{2\pi(N+N_{cp})}angle\left\{\sum_{n=0}^{N-1} y_1^*[n]y_2[n]\right\} \tag{5}$$

Considering the approach presented above, the synchronization steps are detailed in the following paragraphs.

Since the DL preamble is transmitted every radio frame, at the companion 10 ms worth of samples must be processed. This amounts to 153600 samples. The received samples are split into batches of equal length with a 50%

overlap between adjacent batches. The data is processed as follows:

***Step 1**: Set the training symbol CFO index i=0 (corresponding to a training symbol with 0 CFO).*

***Step 2**: The energy of each batch is computed. Store the minimum energy value (corresponding to noise) in $b_{\min}$ and the maximum energy value (corresponding to noise+useful signal) in $b_{\max}$. If the ratio $b_{\max}/b_{\min}>1.5$, then the preamble is located in the set of the 153600 samples. Proceed to step 3.*

If the energy threshold is not met, the current radio frame is discarded. A new set of 153600 samples is recorded and step 2 is repeated.

***Step 3**: Calculate the normalization factor as a weighted difference between $b_{\max}$ and $b_{\min}$:*

$$L=\sqrt{(b_{\max}-b_{\min})\cdot b_x} \quad (6)$$

where b_x is the energy of the reference training symbol $x[n]$. L is designed such that after normalization, the amplitude of the cross-correlation peak varies only with the CFO.

***Step 4**:The cross-correlation between each batch and $x_i[n]$ is calculated (by applying the cross-correlation theorem).*

***Step 5**: Find the peak value for each batch and apply the normalization L. If the normalized peak exceeds the fixed threshold p_{xc}, then store the peak index.*

***Step 6**: If no peaks are identified, increment i and repeat the process starting with step 4. If two peaks have been identified, then adjust the receiver window with the following correction value c_r:*

$$c_r=round\left(\frac{n_0+n_1-N-3N_{cp}-2}{2}\right) \quad (7)$$

The correction c_r is designed such that the receiver window converges towards correct positioning ($c_r=0$) over the course of a few iterations.

***Step 7**: Correct the coarse CFO depending on the current value of i. Proceed to step 8.*

***Step 8**: Estimate the uncorrected CFO Δf_c^r with (5).*

By strategic selection of p_{xc} it can be ensured that:

- The peaks are always identified before exhausting the set of stored training symbols;
- No undesired peaks (not related to the training symbols) are obtained;
- Δf_c^r is limited to ± 5 kHz.

Once timing synchronization and coarse CFO correction has been achieved, then the values of c_r and i should be 0. Δf_c^r is estimated on every received preamble and the reference frequency is readjusted periodically.

Timing resynchronization is necessary due to oscillator drifts and variations in distance between the satellites or if the ISL is lost. In normal functioning conditions, since the reference frequency is adjusted periodically, only the distance variations would cause significant loss of timing. Considering an inter-satellite relative speed of 1 m/s, at the sampling rate of 15.36 MHz a timing error of one sample would occur approximately every 19.53 seconds. In order to compensate this effect, timing resynchronization is carried out once every 10 seconds or immediately after the radio link is interrupted.

IV. OBTAINED RESULTS

Our first set of results is focused on the effect that the proposed normalization coefficient L has on the amplitude of the cross-correlation peak. To this end, the CFO is set to 0 and the Signal to Noise Ratio (SNR) is varied from 0 to 30 dB. The results, plotted in Figure 4, illustrate that the normalized amplitude of the peak is relatively constant across a wide range of SNR values. Therefore, the use of a fixed threshold p_{xc} regardless of operating SNR is justified.

The second set of results is focused on the performances of the synchronization algorithm. The CFO is set to 18 kHz, the threshold p_{xc} is 0.8 and a delay of 1500 samples is added to the transmitted preamble. Table I shows the effect of adjusting the receiver window; over 3 iterations the correction value c_r converges towards 0 and timing synchronization is achieved.

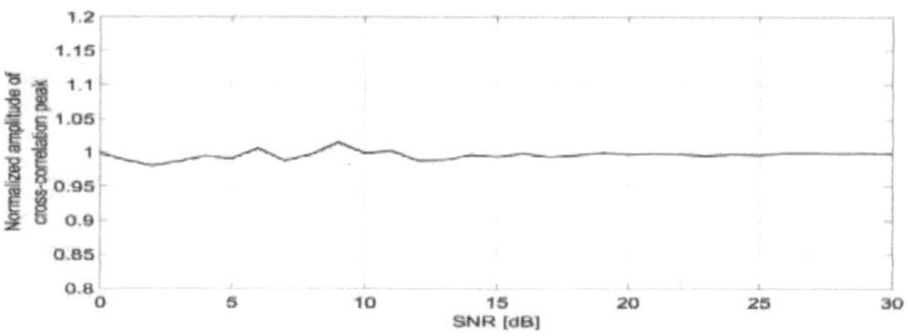

Figure 4. Variation of the normalized peak amplitude vs. SNR

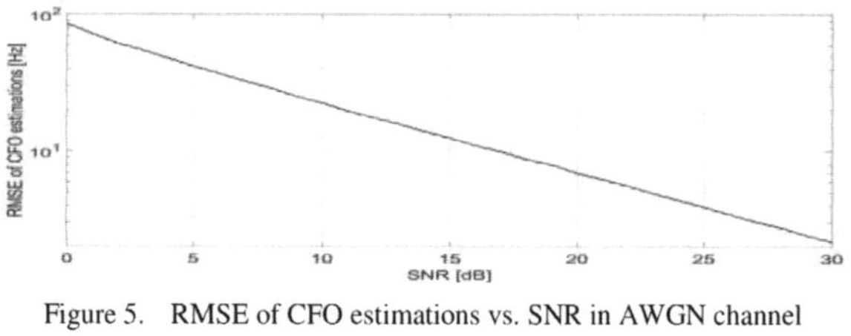

Figure 5. RMSE of CFO estimations vs. SNR in AWGN channel

TABLE I. ADJUSTING THE RECEIVER WINDOW

Iteration	1	2	3
c_r	1226	2394	0

Figure 5 shows the root-mean-square error (RMSE) of the CFO estimations against SNR in an AWGN channel. At 0 dB, the accuracy is approximately 84 Hz.

V. CONCLUSIONS

This paper presented a novel synchronization algorithm proposed to be used in an H-ISL system. The starting point is the model used in the LTE communication systems. The new preamble structure and its positioning in the DL sub-frame, correlated with the new proposed method of computation, provide good results in terms of timing alignment and frequency synchronization. The presented simulation results demonstrate the algorithm performance.

A real test-bench is under preparation and several real test-cases will be executed on the presented setup. The obtained results will be presented in future work.

ACKNOWLEDGMENT

The work has been funded by the European Space Agency through the contract "Hybrid - Inter Satellite Link" with the number 4000121222/17/NL/CBi, subcontracted by UPB through the contract 18/05.10.2017.

REFERENCES

[1] R. Sun, D. Maessen, J. Guo, and E. Gill, "Enabling Inter-Satellite Communication and Ranging for Small Satellites", Small Satellite Systems and Services Symposium (4S), Funchal, Portugal, pp 1 – 15, 31 May – 4 June 2010

[2] J. J. van de Beek, M. Sandell and P. O. Borjesson, "ML estimation of time and frequency offset in OFDM systems," in IEEE Transactions on Signal Processing, vol. 45, no. 7, pp. 1800 - 1805, July 1997.

[3] T. M. Schmidl and D. C. Cox, "Robust frequency and timing synchronization for OFDM," in IEEE Transactions on Communications, vol. 45, no. 12, pp. 1613-1621, Dec. 1997.

[4] C. Wang and H. Wang, "Optimized Joint Fine Timing Synchronization and Channel Estimation for MIMO Systems," in IEEE Transactions on Communications, vol. 59, no. 4, pp. 1089-1098, April 2011.

[5] H. Minn, V. K. Bhargava and K. B. Letaief, "A robust timing and frequency synchronization for OFDM systems," in IEEE Transactions on Wireless Communications, vol. 2, no. 4, pp. 822-839, July 2003.

[6] Q. Wang, C. Mehlfuhrer, and M. Rupp, "Carrier frequency synchronization in the downlink of 3GPP LTE," 21st Annual IEEE International Symposium on Personal, Indoor and Mobile Radio Communications, Instanbul, pp. 939-944, 2010.

[7] J. Meng and G. Kang, "A novel OFDM synchronization algorithm based on CAZAC sequence," 2010 International Conference on Computer Application and System Modeling (ICCASM 2010), Taiyuan, 2010, pp. V14-634-V14-637.

[8] M. M. U. Gul, X. Ma and S. Lee, "Timing and Frequency Synchronization for OFDM Downlink Transmissions Using Zadoff-Chu Sequences," in IEEE Transactions on Wireless Communications, vol. 14, no. 3, pp. 1716-1729, March 2015.

[9] https://www.xilinx.com/products/boards-and-kits/ek-u1-zcu102-g.html, retrieved: June, 2019

[10] https://www.analog.com/en/design-center/evaluation-hardware-and-software/evaluation-boards-kits/eval-ad-fmcomms5-ebz.html, retrieved: June, 2019

[11] https://www.xilinx.com/support/documentation/selection-guides/zynq-ultrascale-plus-product-selection-guide.pdf, retrieved: June, 2019

[12] https://www.xilinx.com/products/intellectual-property/axi.html, retrieved: June, 2019

[13] https://www.analog.com/en/products/ad9361.html, retrieved: June, 2019

A Simple Precoding Scheme for Multi-User MIMO Transmission Over a Shared Channel in a TDD Cellular Network

Abheek Saha
Hughes Systique Corporation,
Gurgaon, India
Email: abheek.saha@hsc.com

***Abstract*—Multi-User Multiple-Input Multiple-Output (MIMO) transmission is one of the key technologies for achieving the ambitious targets for coverage and throughput in modern cellular networks. It allows us to take advantage of the large number of transmission elements possible in the radio-heads or eNodeB and allow users to share a channel. A key challenge in the deployment of multi-user MIMO is the problem of cross-user interference due to mutual non-orthogonality within the shared channel. The transmitter must select an optimal transmit precoding so as to eliminate this cross-user interference, since the receivers cannot coordinate and jointly decode the transmission. In this paper, we propose a novel algorithm for multi-user MIMO precoding over a shared channel. Our algorithm is a combination of ideas both from Dirty Paper Coding as well as the more recent Interference Alignment techniques. We demonstrate that we can achieve better performance than zero-forcing and that our algorithm is practical to implement within the framework of existing 4th and upcoming 5th generation systems, being realizable in linear time.**

Keywords*—*Multi-user MIMO; Dirty Paper Coding; Interference Alignment; Shared channel; Block Cholesky decomposition.

I. INTRODUCTION

Fourth and fifth generation cellular networks are distinguished by the rapid and widespread deployment of multiple antenna systems. These systems can be deployed in various ways; multiple antenna deployed at a single tower, multiple distributed antenna installations under the control of a single centralized Radio Access Node (cRAN), or even multiple cooperating eNodeBs (this is known as a Coordinated Multipoint or CoMP deployment). The initial deployment of multiple antenna transmission was in the single user MIMO systems [1], where a single eNodeB and a single User Terminal (UT) communicate over a dedicated channel using multiple receive and transmit elements. These have been commercially deployed for about a decade, with mixed results ; in practical environments, achieving more than 2 simultaneous streams per channel has proven to be difficult. Advances in radio technology are pushing multi-user MIMO (MuMIMO) as a replacement to single user MIMO. MuMIMO [2] consists of a single eNodeB with a large number of antennas to simultaneously transmit to multiple MIMO-capable UTs each equipped with a smaller number of antennas, over a common shared channel (Figure 1). The promise of MuMIMO is in the increase of the number of simultaneous streams per channel, hence increasing both the throughput and coverage at both cell-center and cell-edge. The primary advantage is that it is easier to put larger numbers of antenna elements on an eNodeB than on a UT (due to the form factor) and independent UTs with geographical separation have a higher spatial diversity than that of large number of antennas on a single receiver. This spatial diversity leads to a corresponding independence in channel matrices which is the basis of the gains of MIMO transmission.

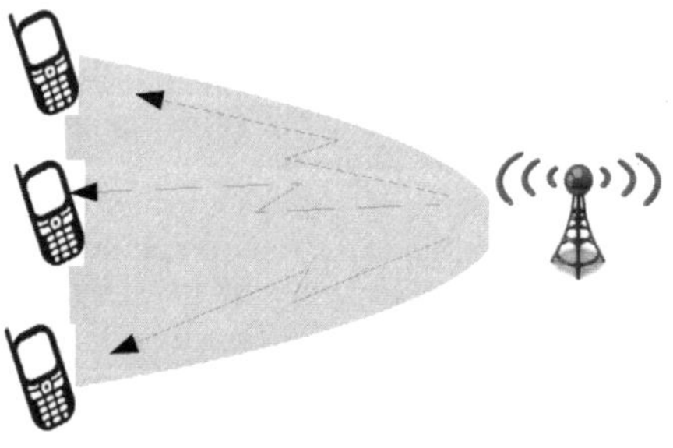

Figure 1. Deployment of MuMIMO

MuMIMO has been supported in 4th generation cellular networks (Long Term Evolution (LTE)) standards since Release 10 and is increasingly seeing commercial deployment. As we move towards the fifth generation, the number of antenna on the wireless network nodes (Remote Radio Heads or eNodeBs) is also increasing manifold (Massive MIMO). More complex modes of deployment, such as cooperative MuMIMO and multi-user CoMP are being proposed, especially to support the cell-edge (Figure 2) [3]. Over the last few years, the 3rd Generation Partnership Project has rapidly pushed the MuMIMO transmission modes into the mainstream of cellular access networks [4], standardizing the relevant operating modes, associated sounding and dedicated reference signals etc. The 5G New Radio standard (5G-NR) recognizes the importance of MuMIMO and has introduced further enhancements to the existing LTE standards to support more complex and efficient deployments [5]. This includes the use of comb-structures and cyclic shifts to support a higher number of orthogonal training signals, to support up to 32 simultaneous layers. The specifications also allow for flexible deployment of training signals, so as to support very low-latency decoding and adaptation for high-doppler environments.

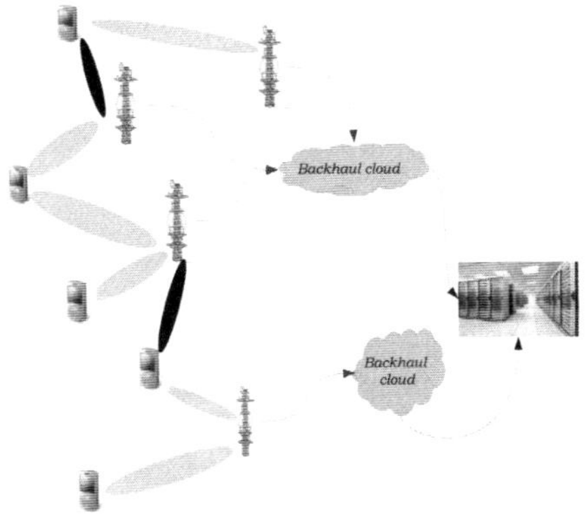

Figure 2. Cooperative MuMIMO

In contrast to the single-user MIMO, where the computation of optimal precoding matrix is well understood, optimal/near-optimal precoding/decoding for MuMIMO is relatively complex and has been the subject of much recent research. MuMIMO performance is limited by co-user interference over a complex shared medium; the individual channels of the individual UTs cause interference between each other in a manner which is tied to the mutual information in the channel. While the network can fully anticipate the cross-user interference, the UTs have only knowledge of their own channel and cannot coordinate with each other. This creates an interesting problem of optimal multi-user encoding at the network, which is the subject of this paper.

The contribution of this paper is as follows. We propose a novel MuMIMO transmit precoding scheme for a transmitter with $N * K, N, K > 1$ antenna transmitting to N receivers, each with K antenna elements. In the existing literature (Section III) there are two main approaches to the MuMIMO precoding problem. The earlier research was based on the technique of Dirty Paper Coding (DPC) [6], which is an elegant approach to solving the *known interference issue*, but is however, difficult to scale to a large number of users due to the need to solve a difficult joint optimization problem. On the other hand, in recent years, much work has taken place using the technique of Interference Alignment(IA) [7], which was primarily designed for the shared cross-channel environment, i.e., K transmitters and K receivers on a single channel. Our Successive interference Compensation (SiC) algorithm is a mixture of both approaches. We use the block diagonalization approach of DPC and join it with the sub-space reduction technique of interference alignment. We show that the resultant algorithm is fast, easy to implement and provides an intuitive outer bound of the K user MuMIMO bounds. We note that the K user MIMO case is relatively less addressed in the interference alignment literature as well as the older DPC literature, in terms of theoretical upper bounds for achievable rate. This shall be described in more detail in Subsection II-B.

The rest of this paper is organized as follows. In Section II, we describe the problem in context of the generic theory of interference channels and provide a survey of previous work, organized in terms of the two main approaches, Dirty Paper Coding (II-A) and Interference Alignment (II-B). In Section III, we give a detailed mathematical framework for our problem, followed by the description of the algorithm in Subsection III-A. In Section IV, we provide some simulation results comparing our approach against the baseline Zero-Forcing approach. Finally, in Section V, we conclude the paper by proposing future directions in our research.

II. MULTI-USER INTERFERENCE CHANNELS - THEORY AND PREVIOUS WORK

Our problem involves the multi-user shared channel in a generic LTE Time Division Duplex (TDD) cellular network. A single eNodeB with $N \times K$ antennas is controlling a cell in which there are N UTs with K receive antennas each. The eNodeB has to transmit simultaneously to all N UTs during each transmission frame over a shared good quality (high Signal to Noise Ratio (SNR)) Gaussian channel, varying stochastically from frame to frame. The eNodeB has perfect Channel State Information (CSI) for all UTs because it is a TDD network. It can also control the exact decoding matrix to be used by each UT, by embedding appropriate reference signals in each frame. The UTs have knowledge only of their own channels. Our aim is to design an algorithm by which the single eNodeB, given the knowledge of the complete set of channels for all N receivers, can near-optimally choose the transmission precoding matrix, so as to maximize the aggregate capacity for the channel. The aggregate capacity is a function of the number of layers transmitted, the number of UTs transmitted to and the Bit Error Rate (BER) for each UT. Because the system is operating in a high SNR environment, the system performance i.e. BER is constrained by the cross-user interference rather than the external noise.

The most generic case of a shared channel is the cross-channel case, which supports K transceiver pairs over a common channel. The broadcast channel case, on the other hand, has a single transmitter with K receivers. The common thread among both these cases is that the system performance (aggregate rate capacity) is limited by co-channel interference and the individual agents are cooperative, as pointed out by the authors in [8]. The problem of rate maximizing for selfish users is an open problem. In the most generic model of the distributed cross channel, neither the receivers nor the transmitters can coordinate with each other in realtime [9]. In other words, the individual receivers and transmitters have to individually process their own signals for precoding/ decoding. In such a system, the individual transmitters and receivers may agree on common parameters such as the precoding/decoding matrices and the operating codebook, but cannot share their processing in real-time; each will have to work on their own copy of the signal (transmit or receive) once the system is activated. Clearly, MuMIMO and Coordinated Multipoint systems are both special cases of the shared channel. MuMIMO is a broadcast channel case where there is a single transmitter, but multiple noncommunicating users. The CoMP case is a variant of the cross-channel, as there are multiple transmitters with limited ability to coordinate with each other.

Interest in the problem of shared channel transmission dates back at least 15 years starting from the two-user broadcast channel. The theoretical background is much older, dating back to the 1970s. The research question is as follows; how do we configure the transmitters and receivers in a shared channel so as to maximize the aggregate transmission rate. There are at least four parameters for optimization. The obvious ones are the transmit and receive filters (precoding/decoding matrices in MIMO terms). Alternately, one can design appropriate code-books, or decompose the code-book into separate subsets and reserve one for each transceiver pair. Finally, there exists user selection/scheduling. An associated problem is the need is to estimate the theoretical achievable rate capacity of such a channel in terms of the covariance between the channel matrices of individual users [10].

Over the years, there have been two major approaches to the shared channel rate optimization problem. The first is the DPC approach [6] as applied to the wireless channel, as is seen in the works of [11] and others. This approach works on the theory of *pre-compensation*; how to adjust the transmit signal so as to null out the effect of the known interference at the receiver. The second, which has garnered enormous interest of late, is the technique of interference alignment [12]. This technique (and its predecessor, Zero-Forcing(ZF)) works on the basis of one-time *optimal precoding*.

A. Dirty Paper Coding

Dirty Paper Coding originated in the work of Costa [6]. It solves the problem of transmitting a signal s to a receiver on top of a known (to the transmitter) interference vector z and a random noise term n. The problem is to construct an encoding operation $\mathcal{T}(z, n)$ based on the knowledge of z and r and a corresponding decoding operation $\mathcal{R}$, which can be used without knowledge of the interference term z. The original paper shows that the problem is solvable by proving the existence of an alphabet to encode s, z jointly and a corresponding pair of operations $\mathcal{T}, \mathcal{R}$, which can be used independently at either end of the channel for the encoding/decoding operations. A simple realization of DPC is Tomlinson Harashima Precoding (THP) [13][14], first introduced to solve a problem of self-interference due to cross-talk in cabled environments. In this work, $\mathcal{T}$ and $\mathcal{R}$ are modulo operations on the transmit symbol.

In the context of wireless and broadband MIMO, the early research in DPC focussed on the two receiver broadcast channel [15].The achievable rate for a two user broadcast channel have been extensively studied [16]–[18], culminating in the Marton's upper bound for two user broadcast channels.

In [15, Slepian Wolf Theorem], it is shown that the rate-capacity of the two user channel is limited only by the mutual information between the two signal-spaces and hence, achievable using a DPC method. The same result has been proven in different contexts by [19] and others.

Yu and Cioffi propose an alternate technique to achieve Marton's rate capacity in a two user broadcast system, using a decision feedback equalizer from the precoder output [11][20]. Published literature on practical DPC techniques for the shared wireless channel is relatively sparse, especially in the multiple user ($N > 2$) case. Much of the available literature uses Tomlinson Harashima precoding (or similar techniques) as a means of constrained interference suppression [21]. In [22], the authors pair the THP approach with a decision feedback filter to meet the power constraints on a per symbol basis. In [23], the authors implement a robust form of the THP for a decision feedback structure. Similar work is presented in [24]–[26].

B. Interference alignment

Interference alignment(IA) [9][12][27] works by decomposing a single channel into multiple sub-spaces, each corresponding to one of the degrees of freedom of each individual user. The key idea is that of trading degrees of freedom for interference [28]. In a standard IA realization, one of the subspaces is selected as the designated 'interference' subspace and all transmitters have to select an encoding such that the interference vector generated by that transmitter lies in the designated interference sub-space. This makes the other sub-spaces available for use for interference-free signal transmission. IA is a more efficient successor for the earlier zero-forcing (ZF) approach [29][30], as ZF requires each user to choose a separate interference sub-space, which is the null-space of the complement channel. The simplest case of IA is a K-user Multiple Input Single Output (MISO) interference channel [8], where K pairs of users sacrifice half the available degrees of freedom for interference free operation. Over the last ten years, an enormous corpus of literature has been created for interference alignment as a interference nulling technique in multiple contexts [7]. The theoretical work on interference alignment addresses the cross-channel case in two modes. In [12][27] we have two transmitters and two receivers sharing a single channel and both the transmitter and the receiver has multiple antenna. A specific subcase of the cross channel case is given in Section 10 of [12], which is the cognitive transmitter case; here, the two transmitters are able to share the transmit message that each intends to transmit to the other. In these enviroments, IA has been proposed as a distributed optimization problem [8][28] extended to the generic multi-antenna case in [31]. The other application of IA is in the K-user MISO cross-channel case [8], where we have a single transmitter transmitting to N users, each equipped with a single antenna. These IA techniques maybe adapted to the K user MuMIMO broadcast channel but are very complex to implement. This is both due to the full CSI requirement as well as the need to implement multiple matrix optimization passes for each frame. Practical algorithms mostly involve some version of ZF using rank-reduction technique [32][33]. Alternately, the somewhat more realizable alternating minimization algorithm in [34] can be used iteratively.

III. Successive Interference Compensation with Block Diagonalization

In this section, we present a simple to implement algorithm for precoding a MuMIMO transmission over a known broadcast channel with N receivers (UTs). The novelty of our solution is in that approaches interference compensation as in the DPC approach, using diagonalization to linearize the problem. It then uses the rank-reduction technique of interference alignment in order to compensate the interference vector without violating the transmit power norm. This idea of trading off between power and degrees of freedom is an adaptation of the theoretical work in [10].

As is standard in LTE cellular networks, the UTs are not aware that they are part of a MuMIMO cohort. They simply obey the eNodeB instructions as encoded in the reference signals to decode the transmitted symbols. In LTE Release 12 and onwards, this is achieved by an appropriately encoded Demodulation Reference Signals (DMRS) embedded in the transmission frame, which can be used both to control both the decoding matrix the UT will use and the number of streams each UT should decode. The UTs can only act as per the subset of information they have and cannot anticipate what the eNodeB is going to do. The eNodeB, however, requires full CSI information for all UTs. In a TDD network, this is directly available from the uplink. In an Frequency Division Duplex (FDD) network, this has to be signaled and has the additional complexity of quantization error. For the purpose of this paper, we assume that the CSI information for all user channels are available at the eNodeB with arbitrarily small error, as is achievable in a standard TDD network.

The SiC algorithm is computationally simple as it is single-pass and only involves matrix operations of size $K \times K$. The inversion of a Hermitian matrix required in the first block diagonalization stage is easily computed from the singular value decomposition. In contrast, the ZF approach requires us to implement Gram-Schmidt orthogonolization of an assymetric $N.(K-1) \times N.K$ matrix, this operation being repeated N times per frame. Standard IA algorithms are even more complex, because the optimal matrix search requires multiple iterative passes, each of which require quadratic operations on the entire $N.K \times N.K$ transmission matrix.

In the rest of the paper, we use the following conventions. We number matrix/vector rows and columns from 1 to N. Variables denoted by capital letters, i.e., $A, B, C...$ are considered to be elements of $\mathcal{M}_{N.K \times N.K}$ the set of matrices of $N.K$ rows and columns. Variables of the form $\tilde{A}_{m,n}, \tilde{B}_{m,n}, \tilde{C}_{m,n}$ represent the sub-matrix of size $K \times K$ of the corresponding matrix A, B, C etc, starting from the row position $(m-1) \times K$ and column position $(n-1) \times K$. Vectors are denoted by lower case letters x, y, etc. Uppercase greek letters (Υ, Γ, etc.) are used exclusively to denote diagonal or block-diagonal matrices and $\tilde{\Upsilon}_{m,n}, \tilde{\Gamma}_{m,n}$ their $K \times K$ size submatrices as defined above. Vector norms are denoted by $|x|$. For the equuivalent matrix norms, we utilize the trace function, which is given by $|X| = \text{Tr}(X)$. x^* and X^* represent the complex transpose of the vector x and the conjugate transpose of the matrix X respectively. The square root of a Hermitian semidefinite matrix S is obtained by taking the Singular Value Decomposition $S = V \Sigma V^*$ and then constructing the root $S^{1/2} = V \Sigma^{1/2} V^*$. S^{-1} is the matrix inverse.

A. Algorithm description

The SiC algorithm is implemented in two steps. In the first step (Subsection III-B), we block diagonalize the channel and hence separate the interference and signal space for each user. In the second step (Subsection III-C), we add a compensating vector for each user to cancel the effect of the causal noise and simultaneously reduce the number of transmitted streams so as to normalize the transmit power.

The interference compensation step can be interpreted both in the DPC sense and in the IA sense. In the DPC sense, we are successively modifying the space of code-words for each user to take into account the code-word transmitted by the previous user. If we see this in the sense of the formulation provided in [10], we are essentially choosing a transmit code-word from a modified dictionary $\mathcal{W}$, which maps to a subset of valid receiver code-words, but can cancel interference without violating the power transmit norm. In the IA sense, we can view the rank reduction step as a tradeoff between the degrees of freedom in the spatial sense to reduce the overlap between the users, without *fully orthonormalizing them*. This trade-off frees up some power so that we can add the additional compensating vector to cancel out interference. Thus, we are considering the combination of power and MIMO spatial sub-channels as a joint resource within which the optimal operating configuration has to be found.

Our algorithm improves upon the performance of standard MIMO IA algorithms, which are completely driven by the condition number of the aggregate channel matrix. If the condition number is large, i.e., the individual channel matrices are strongly correlated, IA algorithms provide poor results for all the UTs. This is because the act of subspace decomposition forces each user into a very poor channel, in order to achieve orthogonalization with respect to the common channel. Consider the worst case where there are two users, both with the exact same channel. The nullspace of one is the nullspace of the other, and neither will achieve any transmission in the IA case. In the SiC algorithm, at least one of the users will get through with no interference whatsover (the one which is encoded first), at the cost of the subsequent users.

B. Block Decomposition of a Composite Channel Matrix

The Block Cholesky decomposition (BLDL) technique has been used for DPC of the MuMIMO channel because it converts a multi-variate optimization problem to an stepwise optimization problem [35][36]. It allows us to decompose each UT's channel into a simple $K \times K$ *effective channel*, independent of the other UTs. For a symmetric matrix, the $K \times K$ block decomposition is computationally simple, because the diagonal matrices can be easily inverted. We let the channel matrix between the eNodeB and the M UTs, each with K antenna be written as a composite $\mathcal{H} \in \mathcal{M}_{MK\times MK}$ as in (1).

$$\mathcal{H} = \begin{bmatrix} \tilde{H}_1 \\ \tilde{H}_2 \\ \dots \\ \tilde{H}_M \end{bmatrix} = \begin{bmatrix} \tilde{H}_{1,1} & \tilde{H}_{1,2} & \dots & \tilde{H}_{1,M} \\ \tilde{H}_{2,1} & \tilde{H}_{2,2} & \dots & \tilde{H}_{2,M} \\ \dots & \dots & \dots & \dots \\ \tilde{H}_{M,1} & \tilde{H}_{M,2} & \dots & \tilde{H}_{M,M} \end{bmatrix} \quad (1)$$

The matrix $\tilde{H}_j$ represents the channel between the j UT and the eNodeB. Each $\tilde{H}_{j,k}$ is a $K \times K$ matrix within the composite matrix, where the diagonal terms represent the interference free channel and the off-diagonal terms represent the covariance between the different UTs. In the first step, we carry out Block Cholesky decomposition composite matrix $\mathcal{H}\mathcal{H}^*$ in the form given in (2), where the size of each sub-matrix is $K \times K$.

$$\begin{aligned} \mathcal{H}\mathcal{H}^* &= \mathcal{G}\Sigma\mathcal{G}^* \\ \Sigma &= \text{diag}[\tilde{S}_1, \tilde{S}_2, \dots, \tilde{S}_M] \\ \mathcal{G} &= \begin{bmatrix} I & 0 & 0 & \dots & 0 \\ \tilde{G}_{2,1} & I & 0 & \dots & 0 \\ \dots & \dots & \dots & 0 & 0 \\ \tilde{G}_{M,1} & \tilde{G}_{M,2} & \dots & I & \end{bmatrix} \\ \tilde{H}_{k,k} &= \sum_{p<k} \tilde{G}_{k,p}\tilde{S}_p\tilde{G}^*_{k,p} + S_{k,k} \\ \tilde{H}_{j,k<j} &= \sum_{p<k} \tilde{G}_{j,p}\tilde{S}_p\tilde{G}^*_{k,p} + \tilde{G}_{j,k}S_{k,k} \end{aligned} \quad (2)$$

Note that $S_k, 1 \leq k \leq N$ is a sequence of symmetric positive semi-definite matrices. We can write the singular value decomposition of S_k as in (3), where U is once again a unitary matrix of size $K \times K$

$$\tilde{S}_k = \tilde{U}_k\tilde{\Delta}_k\tilde{U}^*_k \quad (3)$$

The eNodeB precodes the transmission by the precoding matrix given in (4) choosing λ_k so as to meet the transmit norm $||P|| = 1$.

$$\mathcal{P} = \mathcal{H}^*\mathcal{G} \begin{bmatrix} \tilde{U}_1\lambda_1 & 0 & \dots & 0 \\ 0 & \tilde{U}_2\lambda_2 & 0 & \dots \\ \dots & \dots & \tilde{U}_{M-1}\lambda_{M-1} & 0 \\ \dots & \dots & 0 & \tilde{U}_M\lambda_M \end{bmatrix} \quad (4)$$

The precoding is implemented on an appropriately chosen transmit vector z comprising of a block of K size transmit vectors $\tilde{z}_k$, each k-th block targetted to the k-th receiver (5). λ_k is the power loading term.

$$z = \begin{bmatrix} \tilde{z}_1 & \tilde{z}_2 & \dots & \tilde{z}_M \end{bmatrix} \quad (5)$$

In the rest of this paper, we have assumed that $\lambda_k = \Delta_k^{-1/2}$ which essentially ensures that the eNodeB has a fixed power output $(NK)^2|z|$. The composite signal after passing through the channel is given as the vector r in (8).

A particularly useful feature of the BLDL decomposition is that the amount of interference at each stage (the power norm of the interference vector) is computable step-wise from the sub-matrices of the block diagonalized channel matrix. Further, the total co-channel interference in the Block Diagonalization is upper bounded by $\sum_p |\mathcal{H}_{p,p} - \tilde{S}_{p,p}|$. We can verify this as follows. Assume that the individual transmit blocks $\tilde{z}_k$ are of unit norm. The interference vector for the k-th user is given as i_k from (7). By triangle inequality, we get upper bound of i_k as in (6).

$$\begin{aligned} &|\mathrm{i}_k| \leq \sum_{p\leq k} |G_{k,p-1}\Delta^{1/2}_{p-1}\tilde{z}_p| \leq \sum_{p\leq k} |G_{k,p-1}S_{p-1}G^*_{k,p-1}| \\ &|\sum_{p\leq k} G_{p,p-1}S_{p-1}G_{p,p-1}| = |\tilde{H}_{k,k} - \tilde{S}_{k,k}| \\ &\Rightarrow |\mathrm{i}_k| \leq |\tilde{H}_{k,k} - \tilde{S}_{k,k}| \end{aligned} \quad (6)$$

Intuitively, we can check the result from the fact that each receiver has K antennas and can thus coherently decode K streams. This means that the energy of the K streams can be removed from the interference seen by the system as a whole. Each submatrix $G_{k,j}, k \neq j$ then captures the mutual information between the k-th and the j-th user. If the sum of the off-diagonal terms of $\mathcal{H}\mathcal{H}^*$ were negligible, (i.e., $\sum_p \tilde{H}_{j,p}\tilde{H}_{p,j} \equiv 0$) in (2), then the inter-receiver co-channel interference terms would also vanish.

C. Cancelling the co-channel interference vector

Because of the nature of the precoding, the co-channel interference also takes a particular form, in that each i-th user is only affected by the interference generated by the previous users. We can verify this by formally deriving the interference vector i_k from the structure of the receive vector given in (7).

$$\begin{aligned} y_1 &= \Delta_1^{1/2}\tilde{z}_1 \\ y_2 &= U_2^*G_{2,1}U_1\Delta_1^{1/2}\tilde{z}_1 + \Delta_2^{1/2}\tilde{z}_2 \\ &\dots \\ y_k &= \tilde{U}^*_k \sum_{j<k} G_{k,j}\tilde{\Delta}_j^{1/2}\tilde{U}_j\tilde{z}_j + \tilde{\Delta}_k^{1/2}\tilde{z}_k \\ &= \mathrm{i}_k + \tilde{\Delta}_k^{1/2}\tilde{z}_k \end{aligned} \quad (7)$$

We will now compensate for this interference. To each transmit vector z_m, we shall add an additional compensating vector ζ_m, so that the combination, after precoding will counteract the effect of i_m, the known interference vector *for this, the m-th user.* While this step will cancel the interference vector completely, it may cause the combined output vector $z_m + \zeta_m$ to exceed the power norm. To take care of this, we shall truncate the transmit block as shown in (9). The output vector will have zero co-user interference, but some of the streams will be nulled out. We interpret this as a reduction in the degrees of freedom available for this particular channel. The only impact on the receiver is that it has to discard the last L_k symbols it receives. We repeat

$$r = \mathcal{HP}\hat{z} = \mathcal{HH}^*\mathcal{G}\begin{bmatrix} \tilde{U}_1\Delta_1^{-1/2} & 0 & \dots & 0 \\ 0 & \tilde{U}_2\Delta_2^{-1/2} & 0 & \dots \\ \dots & \dots & \tilde{U}_{M-1}\Delta_{M-1}^{-1/2}\lambda_{M-1} & 0 \\ \dots & \dots & 0 & \tilde{U}_M\Delta_M^{-1/2}\lambda_M \end{bmatrix}\begin{bmatrix} \tilde{z}_1 \\ \tilde{z}_2 \\ \dots \\ \tilde{z}_M \end{bmatrix}$$

$$= \lambda\begin{bmatrix} 1 & 0 & \dots & 0 \\ \tilde{G}_{2,1} & 1 & 0 & \dots \\ \dots & 1 & 0 & \dots \\ \tilde{G}_{M,1} & \tilde{G}_{M-1,1} & 1 & \dots \end{bmatrix}\begin{bmatrix} \tilde{U}_1\tilde{\Delta}_1^{1/2} & 0 & \dots & 0 \\ 0 & \tilde{U}_2\tilde{\Delta}_2^{1/2} & 0 & \dots \\ \dots & \dots & \tilde{U}_{M-1}\tilde{\Delta}_{M-1}^{1/2} & 0 \\ \dots & \dots & 0 & \tilde{U}_M\tilde{\Delta}_M^{1/2} \end{bmatrix}\begin{bmatrix} \tilde{z}_1 \\ \tilde{z}_2 \\ \dots \\ \tilde{z}_M \end{bmatrix} \tag{8}$$

this step successively for the $(k+1)$-th and then the $(k+2)$-th user, as long as the impact of the interference is more than the reduction of throughput due to truncation. We note that the interference vector $(i)_k$ has to be updated after the compensation is completed for the $(k-1)$-th user, because it is dependent on the compensated output as well. For each user, the crucial task, hence, is to minimize the value of L_k, the number of streams that the k-th user has to reduce.

$$\begin{bmatrix} z_{k,1} \\ z_{k,2} \\ \dots \\ z_{k,K-L_k} \\ \dots \\ z_{k,K} \end{bmatrix} \rightarrow \begin{bmatrix} z_{k,1} \\ z_{k,2} + \zeta_{k,2} \\ \dots \\ z_{k,K-L_k} + \zeta_{k,K-L_k} \\ \dots \\ 0 \end{bmatrix} \tag{9}$$

1) Truncation step: We consider the problem of transmission of a vector $\tilde{z}_k$ through a channel with matrix $H_k \in \mathcal{M}_K$ with a known interference vector i_k with norm ε_k. We can find an interference compensating vector ζ_k which we can add to $\tilde{z}_k$ to get $\hat{z}_k$ with $K-L$ non-zero spatial streams, such that $T(\tilde{z}_k, K-L) = T(\hat{z}_k + \mathrm{i}_k), K-L)$, where $T(A,n)$ is the truncation operator. The receive vector y is given by the equation (10), where the eNodeB uses the precoding matrix $V\tilde{\Delta}^{-1}$, where V comes from the SVD of H, $H = U\Delta V^*$.

$$y = U^*\mathrm{i}_k\tilde{\Delta}^{-1} + (x+\zeta) \tag{10}$$

We know that U is a unitary matrix, so $|U^*\mathrm{i}_k| = \varepsilon_k$. If we set $\zeta = \left(-U^*\mathrm{i}_k\tilde{\Delta}^{-1}\right)$ then $y = x$. However, by triangle inequality

$$|x+\zeta| \le |x| + \frac{\varepsilon_k}{|\tilde{\Delta}|} \tag{11}$$

Hence, our modified transmit vector $x+\zeta$ may violate the transmit power norm by an amount up to $\frac{\varepsilon_k}{|\tilde{\Delta}|}$. To solve this problem, we reduce the number of spatial streams from K to $K-L$. Hence we only wish to find a ζ whereby the first $K-L$ entries in y match $K-L$ entries in x. The remaining entries in ζ are set to zero. The equation in (10) is then modified to that of (12), where $T(S,k)$ is the truncation operator when truncates the matrix S to its first k rows and columns.

$$\zeta = -U^*\eta\tilde{\Delta}^{-1}$$

$$y = U^*\mathrm{i}_k\tilde{\Delta}^{-1} + \begin{bmatrix} x_1 \\ x_2 \\ \dots \\ x_{K-L} \\ 0 \\ \dots \\ 0 \end{bmatrix} + \begin{bmatrix} \zeta_1 \\ \zeta_2 \\ \dots \\ \zeta_{K-L} \\ 0 \\ \dots \\ 0 \end{bmatrix} \tag{12}$$

D. Aggregate Rate

We now come to the problem of estimating the aggregate rate we achieve by the SiC algorithm. We recall that for a MIMO transmission, the aggregate rate for a given user is the sum of the eigen-values of the effective channel matrix for that user, corresponding to each stream or layer chosen for transmission. In our case, we have deliberately truncated the effective precoding matrix; this is the cost incurred for mitigating cross-user interference. From the expression in (12) we can estimate the number of streams L_k which the k-th user has to sacrifice in order to achieve the null interference condition. The aggregate simply becomes the throughput of remaining streams, as in (13)

$$\sum_{i\in\mathcal{K}} \log_2\left(1+\alpha\lambda_i/\rho\right) \tag{13}$$

$\mathcal{K}$ is the set of streams which are retained for transmission and ρ is the wide-band Gaussian (non-causal) noise in the system. For a given k-th user facing the interference vector i_k as given in (6), the number of streams which have to be reduced is given by L in the equation (14). Note that if $|\mathrm{i}| \approx |\tilde{\Delta}_k^{1/2}|$, we get $L = K/2$ which is the MISO case.

$$L = K\frac{|\mathrm{i}|}{|\Sigma_k| + |\mathrm{i}|} \tag{14}$$

Consider the vector z_k with known interference vector $\mathfrak{k}$. For each stream that we reduce, we reduce the norm of the interference vector by at least $1/K$. We also allow for the addition of a compensating vector ζ_k of norm $1/K$. To achieve null interference condition, we have to allow the norm of the compensating vector to match the worst case norm of the interference vector. Hence, we get $|\mathrm{i}|(K - L/K) = L/K$. Simplifying for L we get the result above.

From the above result and the overall upper bound on the interference given in (7), we get an upper bound on the total number of streams that have to be sacrificed to achieve the null interference condition. The total number of streams to be reduced over the entire cohort of M receivers is given by

$$\sum_{k=2}^{M} L_k = \sum_{k} \frac{|\tilde{\mathcal{H}}_k - \tilde{S}_k|}{|\tilde{\mathcal{H}}_k - \tilde{S}_k| + |\tilde{S}_k|} \quad (15)$$

E. Optimal ordering

The expression in (2) also gives us a useful heuristic for ordering the UTs prior to the block-diagonalization stage. Let us assume that we are scheduling a set of UTs whose indices are given in U. If we compute the relative orthogonality of the k-th channel to the rest in terms of $\mathcal{R}(k, U) = \min_{k \neq j, j \in U} |H_{j,k} H^*_{j,k}|$, then ordering the UTs in descending order of $\mathcal{R}(k, U)$ improves the aggregate capacity. The initial UTs get the best transmission rate, since their interference vectors are relatively low. The UTs which may interfere with the others are further down the list. We can demonstrate this by a simple example. Consider a 3 UT system, where the UTs have channel matrices H_1, H_2 and $\alpha H_1 + (1-\alpha) H_2$, where H_1 and H_2 are perfectly orthogonal to each other. If we organize the composite channel matrix is $\tilde{H} = \left[\begin{array}{ccc} H_1 & H_2 & \alpha H_1 + (1-\alpha) H_2 \end{array}\right]$, then the cross user interference vectors are 0, 0 and $\alpha^2 + (1-\alpha)^2$. On the other hand, if we flip the positions of the 2nd and the 3rd UTs, i.e., $\tilde{H} = \left[\begin{array}{ccc} H_1 & \alpha H_1 + (1-\alpha) H_2 & H_2 \end{array}\right]$, then the cross user interference vectors are 0, α^2 and 1 respectively. As we can see, the second ordering has lower rate capacity though the first one is less fair. In general, we find the ordering in terms of descending $\mathcal{R}(k, u)$ gives good results as we shall see in Section IV below.

A scheduling algorithm to balance ordering and capacity is currently under study.

IV. Simulation Results and Discussion

In this section, we present some simulation results. We have simulated a system comprising of a single eNodeB with 64 transmit antenna (an 8x8 antenna configuration) and multiple UTs; only the basic downlink shared channel is implemented and the DMRS and other reference signals are communicated directly to the UTs. The entire simulation code is written in C and the key elements of the transmit and receive chain are implemented using the Gnu Scientific Library (GSL). The channel matrices are randomly generated (using the GSL random number generator) with full rank and condition number 0.5. At each frame, the eNodeB creates a transmit vector for transmission to the N users simultaneously, with K symbols per UT, from a standard 16-QAM constellation. All transmit vectors are normalized to a unit norm; hence, the power saved by decimating any of the spatial streams is distributed over the rest of the spatial streams. The channel matrices are then randomly generated and then the algorithm given in is implemented at the simulated eNodeB. The resultant precoded transmit vector is passed through the random composite channel with AWGN noise added to it and handed over to the UTs. At each UT, the decoding chain is implemented using the signaled decoding matrix and SNR computed individually. Figure 3 show the combined bit-rate achieved for four cases; 2 UTs of 32 antenna each, 4 UTs of 16 antenna each, 8 UTs of 8 antenna each, 16 UTs of 4 antenna each and finally, 32 UTs of 2 antenna each. For each configuration, we have run the simulation 500 times. As we can see in Figure 3, as the number of antenna increase, the total bitrate asymptotically approaches the best case performance. The gap in between is equivalent to the *coordination penalty* described by [37].

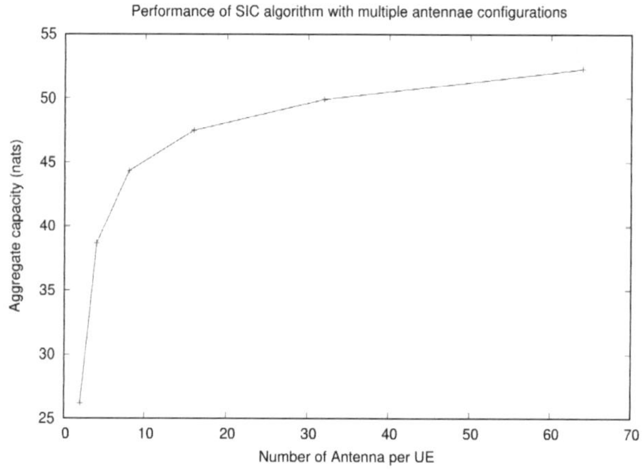

Figure 3. Relative performance of the successive interference cancellation algorithm vs full coordination

In Figure 4, we compare the performance of the system against a reference case. The reference for us is the zero-forcing algorithm as implemented in [29]. Zero-forcing worsk by setting the precoding matrix for each user to $P_i = H_{ii} \tilde{V}_{ii}$, where $\tilde{V}_{i,i}$ lies in the nullspace of the complementary vector ((16).

$$\tilde{H}_{i,i} = \left[\begin{array}{cccccc} H_{i,1} & H_{i,2} & \ldots & H_{i,i-1} & H_{i,i+1} & \ldots \end{array}\right] \quad (16)$$

We chose ZF as the baseline algorithm, because as of now it remains the most practical algorithm in the $N >> 1, K > 2$ case, being implementable in approximately linear time. As mentioned earlier, MuMIMO implementations of existing IA or DPC algorithms, or more sophisticated lattice coding algorithms remain prohibitively expensive to implement since they scale super-linearly in N for large values of K. Further, multi-pass algorithms as suggested in literature are not realizable in current cellular networks, given that the corresponding signaling mechanisms don't exist. As we have previously indicated, the SiC algorithm should substantially outperform the ZF algorithm when the condition number of the aggregate channel matrix is high. The chart in Figure 5 shows the relative performance of the two algorithms for different channel condition numbers.

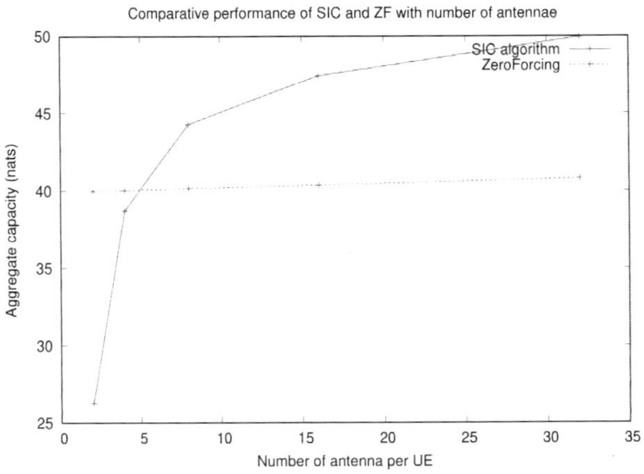

Figure 4. Performance of SIC Algorithm versus ZF

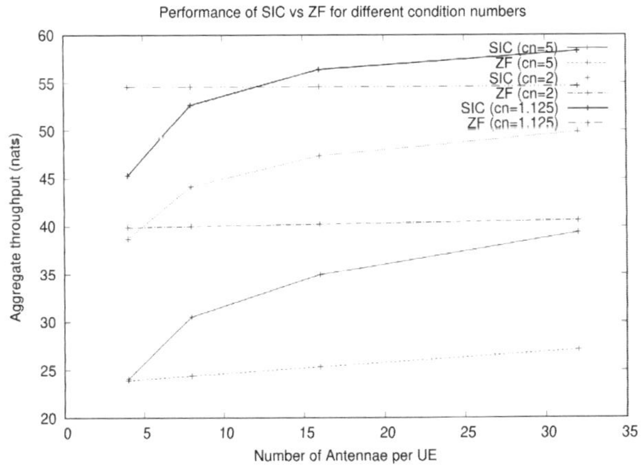

Figure 5. Performance of SIC Algorithm versus ZF with different channel conditions

Our first Figure 3 shows the expected performance of the SIC as the number of users reduce and the number of antenna per user goes up. As the users have larger and larger numbers of receive antenna, the amount of signal energy which gets converted to interference drops off asymptotically. Further, the interference per user is now spread over a larger number of streams and hence is easier to eliminate. Figure 4 shows that there is a substantial gain of the Successive Interference Compensation algorithm versus the standard zero-forcing case. As argued earlier, this is because of the very large penalty in the zero-forcing case due to full orthonormalization of all channels, whereas the SiC algorithm trades off transmit power for overlap. In the last chart, we can see that performance in the ZF case flat-lines at low

V. CONCLUSION

In this paper, we have proposed an algorithm for Mu-MIMO transmission over the shared channel from a single transmitter (eNodeB) to multiple UTs. The SiC algorithm is implementable at the eNodeB of a standard LTE cellular network, operating in TDD mode, using standard linear operations. We have implemented it in cloud RAN settings relatively easily, because the matrix operations are straightforward to implement and all the algorithms are linear, with no requirement for complex iterative optimization procedures. We have demonstrated its performance with respect to the existing standards of zero-forcing. The future extension of the SiC algorithm is to the CoMP case, which has to take into account the limitations of how much information can be shared between the cooperating eNodeBs. We have considered one case where we have two eNodeBs (configured in master-slave mode) and N UTs, where the slave eNodeB is dedicated to generating the interference compensation vector for the block diagonalized transmission of the master . In this case, we have to share just the interference vector (as known to the master) between the two eNodeBs. The slave, based on its own knowledge of the channel can use the interference vector can do interference cancellation. This allows us to extend the successive interference compensation to multiple eNodeBs, without requiring full CSI. This will be further explored in the future. Another area which we are pursuing is the optimal scheduling algorithm for all users, so as to guarantee minimum guaranteed QoS rates, while maintaining maximum aggregate rate capacity. This shall be published in future work.

REFERENCES

[1] A. J. Paulraj, D. A. Gore, R. U. Nabar, and H. Bolcskei, "An overview of mimo communications-a key to gigabit wireless," Proceedings of the IEEE, vol. 92, no. 2, 2004, pp. 198–218.

[2] R. W. H. Jr., T. Wu, Y. H. Kwon, and A. C. K. Soong, "Multiuser mimo in distributed antenna systems with out-of-cell interference," IEEE Transactions on Signal Processing, vol. 59, no. 10, Oct 2011, pp. 4885–4899.

[3] Y.-N. R. Li, J. Li, W. Li, Y. Xue, and H. Wu, "Comp and interference coordination in heterogeneous network for lte-advanced," in Globecom Workshops (GC Wkshps), 2012 IEEE, Dec 2012, pp. 1107–1111.

[4] J. Lee, J.-K. Han, and J. Zhang, "Mimo technologies in 3gpp lte and lte-advanced," EURASIP J. Wirel. Commun. Netw., vol. 2009, Mar. 2009, pp. 3:1–3:10. [Online]. Available: http://dx.doi.org/10.1155/2009/302092

[5] M. Shafi, A. F. Molisch, P. J. Smith, T. Haustein, P. Zhu, P. De Silva, F. Tufvesson, A. Benjebbour, and G. Wunder, "5g: A tutorial overview of standards, trials, challenges, deployment, and practice," IEEE journal on selected areas in communications, vol. 35, no. 6, 2017, pp. 1201–1221.

[6] M. H. M. Costa, "Writing on dirty paper (corresp.)," Information Theory, IEEE Transactions on, vol. 29, no. 3, May 1983, pp. 439–441.

[7] N. Zhao, F. R. Yu, M. Jin, Q. Yan, and V. C. M. Leung, "Interference alignment and its applications: A survey, research issues, and challenges," IEEE Communications Surveys Tutorials, vol. 18, no. 3, thirdquarter 2016, pp. 1779–1803.

[8] V. R. Cadambe and S. A. Jafar, "Interference alignment and degrees of freedom of the$k$-user interference channel," IEEE Transactions on Information Theory, vol. 54, no. 8, Aug 2008, pp. 3425–3441.

[9] M. A. Maddah-Ali, A. S. Motahari, and A. K. Khandani, "Communication over mimo x channels: Interference alignment, decomposition, and performance analysis," IEEE Transactions on Information Theory, vol. 54, no. 8, Aug 2008, pp. 3457–3470.

[10] S. Vishwanath, N. Jindal, and A. Goldsmith, "Duality, achievable rates, and sum-rate capacity of gaussian mimo broadcast channels," Information Theory, IEEE Transactions on, vol. 49, no. 10, Oct 2003, pp. 2658–2668.

[11] W. Yu and J. Cioffi, "Sum capacity of gaussian vector broadcast channels," Information Theory, IEEE Transactions on, vol. 50, no. 9, Sept 2004, pp. 1875–1892.

[12] S. A. Jafar and S. Shamai, "Degrees of freedom region of the mimo x channel," IEEE Transactions on Information Theory, vol. 54, no. 1, Jan 2008, pp. 151–170.

[13] M. Tomlinson, "New automatic equaliser employing modulo arithmetic," Electronics letters, vol. 7, no. 5, 1971, pp. 138–139.

[14] H. Miyakawa and H. Harashima, "Information transmission rate in matched transmission systems with peak transmitting power limitation," in Nat. Conf. Rec., Inst. Electron., Inform., Commun. Eng. of Japan, 1969, pp. 138–139.

[15] T. Cover, "Comments on broadcast channels," IEEE Transactions on Information Theory, vol. 44, no. 6, Oct 1998, pp. 2524–2530.

[16] ——, "Broadcast channels," IEEE Transactions on Information Theory, vol. 18, no. 1, Jan 1972, pp. 2–14.

[17] ——, "An achievable rate region for the broadcast channel," IEEE Transactions on Information Theory, vol. 21, no. 4, Jul 1975, pp. 399–404.

[18] K. Marton, "A coding theorem for the discrete memoryless broadcast channel," IEEE Transactions on Information Theory, vol. 25, no. 3, May 1979, pp. 306–311.

[19] A. E. Gamal and E. van der Meulen, "A proof of marton's coding theorem for the discrete memoryless broadcast channel (corresp.)," IEEE Transactions on Information Theory, vol. 27, no. 1, Jan 1981, pp. 120–122.

[20] W. Yu and J. Cioffi, "Trellis precoding for the broadcast channel," in Global Telecommunications Conference, 2001. GLOBECOM '01. IEEE, 2001, pp. 1344–1348 vol.2.

[21] R. Wesel and J. Cioffi, "Achievable rates for tomlinson-harashima precoding," Information Theory, IEEE Transactions on, vol. 44, no. 2, Mar 1998, pp. 824–831.

[22] K. Kusume, M. Joham, W. Utschick, and G. Bauch, "Efficient tomlinson-harashima precoding for spatial multiplexing on flat mimo channel," in Communications, 2005. ICC 2005. 2005 IEEE International Conference on, May 2005, pp. 2021–2025 Vol. 3.

[23] M. Shenouda and T. Davidson, "A framework for designing mimo systems with decision feedback equalization or tomlinson-harashima precoding," Selected Areas in Communications, IEEE Journal on, vol. 26, no. 2, February 2008, pp. 401–411.

[24] A. Liavas, "Tomlinson-harashima precoding with partial channel knowledge," Communications, IEEE Transactions on, vol. 53, no. 1, Jan 2005, pp. 5–9.

[25] L. Sun and M. Lei, "Quantized csi-based tomlinson-harashima precoding in multiuser mimo systems," Wireless Communications, IEEE Transactions on, vol. 12, no. 3, March 2013, pp. 1118–1126.

[26] W. Yu, D. Varodayan, and J. Cioffi, "Trellis and convolutional precoding for transmitter-based interference presubtraction," Communications, IEEE Transactions on, vol. 53, no. 7, July 2005, pp. 1220–1230.

[27] S. A. Jafar and M. J. Fakhereddin, "Degrees of freedom for the mimo interference channel," IEEE Transactions on Information Theory, vol. 53, no. 7, July 2007, pp. 2637–2642.

[28] K. Gomadam, V. R. Cadambe, and S. A. Jafar, "Approaching the capacity of wireless networks through distributed interference alignment," in IEEE GLOBECOM 2008 - 2008 IEEE Global Telecommunications Conference, Nov 2008, pp. 1–6.

[29] Q. Spencer, A. Swindlehurst, and M. Haardt, "Zero-forcing methods for downlink spatial multiplexing in multiuser mimo channels," Signal Processing, IEEE Transactions on, vol. 52, no. 2, Feb 2004, pp. 461–471.

[30] Q. Spencer, C. Peel, A. Swindlehurst, and M. Haardt, "An introduction to the multi-user mimo downlink," Communications Magazine, IEEE, vol. 42, no. 10, Oct 2004, pp. 60–67.

[31] C. M. Yetis, T. Gou, S. A. Jafar, and A. H. Kayran, "On feasibility of interference alignment in mimo interference networks," IEEE Transactions on Signal Processing, vol. 58, no. 9, Sept 2010, pp. 4771–4782.

[32] L.-U. Choi and R. D. Murch, "A transmit preprocessing technique for multiuser mimo systems using a decomposition approach," IEEE Transactions on Wireless Communications, vol. 3, no. 1, Jan 2004, pp. 20–24.

[33] C. Wang and R. Murch, "Adaptive downlink multi-user mimo wireless systems for correlated channels with imperfect csi," Wireless Communications, IEEE Transactions on, vol. 5, no. 9, September 2006, pp. 2435–2446.

[34] S. W. Peters and R. W. Heath, "Interference alignment via alternating minimization," in 2009 IEEE International Conference on Acoustics, Speech and Signal Processing, April 2009, pp. 2445–2448.

[35] V. Stankovic and M. Haardt, "Generalized design of multi-user mimo precoding matrices," Wireless Communications, IEEE Transactions on, vol. 7, no. 3, 2008, pp. 953–961.

[36] R. Zhang, "Cooperative multi-cell block diagonalization with per-base-station power constraints," Selected Areas of Communication, IEEE Journal on, vol. 28, no. 9, 2010, pp. 1435–1445.

[37] K.Gomadam, V. R. Cadambe, and S. A. Jafar, "A distributed numerical approach to interference alignment and applications to wireless interference networks," IEEE Transactions on Information Theory, vol. 57, no. 6, June 2011, pp. 3309–3322.

Evaluation of the Speech QoE in Voice over LTE services

Manuela Vaser
Dept. of Electronic Engineering
University of Rome "Tor Vergata"
Rome, Italy
email: manuela.vaser@uniroma2.it

Giuseppe Iazeolla
Dept. of Innovation and Information Engineering "Guglielmo Marconi" University, and University of Rome "Tor Vergata"
Rome, Italy
email: giuseppe.iazeolla@uniroma2.it

Abstract – **This work introduces a mathematical relationship linking Quality of Experience (QoE) and Quality of Service (QoS) in Voice over Long Term Evolution (VoLTE) services, validated through an OPNET simulation model. Moreover, a real world test is reported that confirms the simulation validation. Besides its academic interest, knowledge of the relationship can provide Long Term Evolution (LTE) network management a way to predict the QoE offered to VoLTE users, by simply knowing the measurements of the network QoS.**

Keywords – QoE; QoS; User Experience; LTE; VoLTE; OPNET simulation model.

I. INTRODUCTION

In the network management process, it is of interest to the network operator to focus on user satisfaction, by continuously monitoring the user QoE and, if necessary, adjust the QoE by operating on the network QoS.

In order to do this, it is essential to establish a link between QoE perceived by the user and QoS offered by the network. QoS defines the network quality and it is measured by quantitative parameters named Key Performance Indicators (KPI), such as packet loss, delay and jitter [1]-[4]. On the other hand, QoE defines the quality subjectively perceived by the end-user, and gives information on how well the network meets the user's needs. QoE is measured by qualitative parameters, named Key Quality Indicators (KQI), such as "very good", "good", "poor"[5]-[8].

If the relationship between QoE and QoS is known, the network operator may measure the network KPIs and adjust them to obtain satisfactory KQIs for the end-user. So, it is important to make such a relationship known.

The LTE standard assures to deliver high performance and quality IP services, like voice call, but only focuses on the definition of network performance (QoS), without giving its relationship with the QoE [9]-[13].

However, the network operator needs to exploit such a relationship in order to meet the Service Level Agreement (SLA) established with the end-user. By knowing this relationship, the network operator may predict the QoE that can be offered simply based on QoS measurements.

The scope of this paper is thus to mathematically express this relationship in network scenarios delivering VoLTE services.

The paper is organized as follows. Section II introduces the basic mathematics to evaluate the VoLTE QoE. Section III introduces the related works. Section IV introduces proposed relationship between QoE and QoS in VoLTE and Section V validates such a relationship in simulated scenarios.

II. BASIC ANALYTICS FOR THE VOLTE QOE

VoLTE is the voice service delivered in LTE all IP Packet-Switched domain, in which the network operator provides the service by means of its own network, so that he can manage all phases of the service.

VoLTE calls provisioning is made possible by specific architectural elements composing the so called Internet Multimedia Subsystem (IMS), standardized by Third Generation Partnership Project (3GPP) in [14][15].

In considering the User Plane, some remarks are necessary in understanding the VoLTE procedure. For what concerns the protocol stack, the User Equipment (UE) and the IMS entities that terminate the User Plane must use the Real Time Protocol (RTP) at Application Layer [16]. So, voice streams of the same voice call follow the same RTP flow. However, VoLTE is delivered in a packet switched domain, where IP packets of the same RTP flow can reach the destination by means of different network paths, and consequently with different delays.

This phenomenon is measured by a KPI, also known as network jitter or packet delay variation, that can be calculated in real-time as the floating average of differences between the timestamps, contained in the RTP protocol header, of consecutively received packets [17][18].

Jitter can affect heavily the perceived quality of a voice call, and for this reason, at the receiver side, de-jitter buffers are implemented, with the aim of re-establishing the right order of IP packets, by adding to each packet a proper delay.

If the end-to-end delay of a packet is greater than de-jitter buffer dimension, the packet is discarded. The consequence of this operation is a degradation of voice quality [19][20].

Concerning VoLTE QoE, the most relevant KQI is the Mean Opinion Score (MOS), an adimensional subjective parameter for the evaluation of voice call quality, with values in the range between 1 and 5 [19][20].

MOS can be estimated by the E-Model algorithm, whose output is the R-Factor, defined in [21]-[24]. Table I below illustrates the matching between R-factor and MOS values.

The R-factor can be expressed as follows, according to [21]:

$$R = R_0 - I_s - I_d - I_{e,eff} + A. \quad (1)$$

where:
- R_0 is the Signal to Interference Ratio;
- I_s is a combination of impairment factors, occurring simultaneously or not in the voice session;
- I_d is an impairment factor due to talk and listener echo, and delay contributions;
- A is known as Expectation or Advantage Factor, with values from 0 to 20, as shown in table 2/G.107 in [18];
- $I_{e,eff}$ stands for Equipment Factor, and represents the impairment caused by low bit rate CODEC, and packet loss. In the ITU-T G.107 recommendation [21], this parameter has been expressed by:

$$I_{e,eff} = I_e + (95 - I_e)\frac{P_{pl}}{P_{pl}+B_{pl}}. \quad (2)$$

where I_e and B_{pl} are parameters that can assume values as indicated in the recommendation, and P_{pl} is the packet loss, in a range of values between 0 and 1, calculated as:

$$P_{pl} = 1 - \frac{m}{n}. \quad (3)$$

where m is the number of RTP packets received and n is the number of RTP packets sent, with uncorrelated losses [21]. Packet loss is an important KPI to take into account, as seen further on.

III. Related Works

The analysis of User Experience in real time services like Voice over IP (VoIP), VoLTE and Video over LTE (ViLTE) has been the object of several studies in literature, taking into account voice services delivered over an IP core network, and a radio access network that can be LTE access network or Wi-Fi and WiMAX one.

In [25] the impact of QoS parameters (such as packet loss and packet delay) on the QoE of ViLTE is evaluated by using a test-bed integrating the real network with an UE under test.

TABLE I. R-Factor MOS matching [18]

User Satisfaction Level	R-Factor	MOS
Maximum using G.711	93	4.4
Very satisfied	90-100	4.3-5
Satisfied	80-90	4-4.3
Some users satisfied	70-80	3.6-4
Many users dissatisfied	60-70	3.1-3.6
Nearly all users dissatisfied	50-60	2.6-3.1
Not recommended	Less than 50	1-2.6

In [26], the MOS is used to adaptively control the QoE of VoIP services periodically determined by means of a modified version of E-Model.

In [27], by using an OPNET simulation model, MOS, delay and jitter have been observed in a VoIP application, with a network scenario in which the radio access system is either Wi-Fi or WiMAX.

In [28], simulation results are presented that show the improvements that can be obtained in the VoLTE MOS by use of a closed-loop power control algorithm applied to the downlink of the VoLTE radio bearer for an indoor scenario served by small cells.

In [29], the MOS of VoIP services in 3G mobile networks is evaluated in applications like Line and Skype. QoS parameters as jitter and packet loss were measured and the QoE was derived using the QoS versus QoE tables defined by the G.107 ITU-T [21].

In [30], a dynamic adaptation algorithm of joint source-channel code rate is used to improve the VoLTE QoE. The wideband E-Model is used to assess the voice quality.

All mentioned works perform QoE measurements on actual platforms.

Unfortunately, QoE measurements are to be performed on the user devices (rather than on the network), but the measurements of this type need expensive user test equipment.

For this reason, this paper approach is to mathematically derive QoE from QoS, since QoS measurements can be easily obtained directly on the network, by use of standard equipment.

In literature, a series of studies can be found that derive the QoE from QoS by use of a mathematical relationship holding between the two [31]-[33].

However, such studies refer to VoIP services, while in this paper the mathematical relationship holding for VoLTE is derived.

IV. The VoLTE QoE Model

A mathematical relationship between QoS and QoE holding for VoIP has been introduced in [32][33]. This relationship is known as the *IQX Hypothesis (exponential interdependency of Quality of Experience and Quality of Service).*

In such a relationship, QoE depends on only one QoS parameter, and it is expressed as follows:

$$QoE = \alpha e^{-\beta QoS} + \gamma. \quad (4)$$

where α, β and γ in (4) are calculated by means of non-linear regression. An example of regression result is as follows:

$$f(p_L) = 2.861e^{-29.816p_L} + 1.134. \quad (5)$$

where the QoE, in MOS, is indicated with $f(p_L)$ and the QoS parameter is packet loss [32][33].

The IQX hypothesis has been drawn up for an IP context, and it is related to a particular service, the voice call, so it can represent a good starting point in establishing QoE/QoS relationship for VoLTE.

The IQX hypothesis deals with voice application and with a QoE/QoS relationship based on only one QoS parameter (either jitter or packet loss). In this paper, instead, the QoE of voice application is assessed by basing the relationship on two QoS parameters (both jitter and packet loss).

To this scope, in the model presented here, the strict packet loss expression (3) will be replaced by an expression that includes the contribution of packet loss and jitter, known as effective packet loss $P_{pl,eff}$, defined in [31]:

$$P_{pl,eff} = 1 - (1 - P_{pl})(1 - P_{jitter}). \quad (6)$$

where P_{pl} remains the packet loss from (3), and jitter is expressed as a Pareto probability by writing:

$$P_{jitter} = \frac{1}{2}\left(1 - \frac{0.1x}{\sigma}\right)^{20}. \quad (7)$$

where x is the jitter buffer dimension and σ is network jitter delay, both expressed in [ms].

The $P_{pl,eff}$ in (6) can be considered as a further KPI resulting from the combination of two original KPIs, network jitter and packet loss [20].

By replacing (6) in the exponent of (4), the expression for MOS becomes:

$$MOS = \alpha e^{-\beta P_{pl,eff}} + \gamma. \quad (8)$$

Apart from its academic interest, the equation (8) could be useful for the network operator to predict the User Experience starting from the variation of the combined jitter and packet-loss parameters. The next Section provides the necessary validation of (8) in the VoLTE context.

V. VALIDATION OF THE QoE VERSUS QoS RELATIONSHIP FOR VoLTE SERVICES

The use of simulation is the first step for the comprehension of network mechanisms that can affect performances and services. A well done simulation model can help to get the perspective view of the network, without turning to expensive ad hoc experimental solutions, used in real scenarios.

In this research, OPNET Modeler [34] has been used to simulate an LTE network with the IMS section, since OPNET offers a plurality of modules and network nodes compliant with the 3GPP LTE standard. Moreover, OPNET also allows to monitor the network performance by placing probing points on the simulated network.

An OPNET simulation model gives in output KPIs like jitter and packet loss and system KQIs like MOS. These parameters are evaluated at application level.

Simulation parameters such as number of simulation runs or initial bias removal are taken care of internally by OPNET, in order to guarantee the statistical significance of the results.

Figure 1 gives the geographical overview of the simulated scenario. The IMS, (see Sect. II), using Session Initiation Protocol (SIP) application signaling protocol, is responsible for initiating, maintaining and terminating VoLTE call set-up in LTE.

In the model, IMS is physically located in Milan and it is composed of standardized nodes Proxy Call Session Control Function (P-CSCF), Serving Call Session Control Function (S-CSCF) and Interrogating Call Session Control Function (I-CSCF), simulated by means of proxy servers, linked to Gtwy2 by a 1000BaseX link [14][15].

The Gtwy2 and IP_Backbone are linked via the PPP_DS1, and the IP_Backbone is linked to Gtwy1 by a similar link. Gtwy1 and Gtwy2 are simulated by an OPNET Ethernet4_slip8_gtwy, i.e., a router with 4 Ethernet and 8 IP interfaces.

A "Campus Network" node, physically located in Rome, and detailed in Figure 2, is linked to Gtwy1 via a 1000BaseX link. The Campus Network is a LTE network, with physical dimension of 10x10 Km, composed of various OPNET elements:

- An Evolved Packet Core (EPC) node, fully compliant with the standard;
- Two eNodeB nodes.
- Eight mobile workstations (UE_1_1, UE_1_2, UE_1_3_t and UE_1_3_t2 attached to eNB_1; and UE_2_1, UE_2_2, UE_2_3_t, UE_2_3_t2 attached to eNB_2), to represent eight User equipment generating and receiving IP traffic.
- A File Transfer Protocol (FTP) server.
- An Application Definition Node, for the characterization of application parameters.
- A Profile Definition Node, creating the profiles that generate the traffic in a specific temporal order, by means of the applications defined with the Application Definition Node.
- An LTE Configuration Node, setting physical LTE configurations and EPS Bearer specification.
- An IP QoS Node, for the definition of scheduling policies.

The connections between the two eNodeBs and the EPC, and between the EPC and the FTP server simulate a 1000BaseX link (44.736 Mbps).

The propagation settings of the radio interface section between UEs and eNodeBs simulate a typical urban scenario.

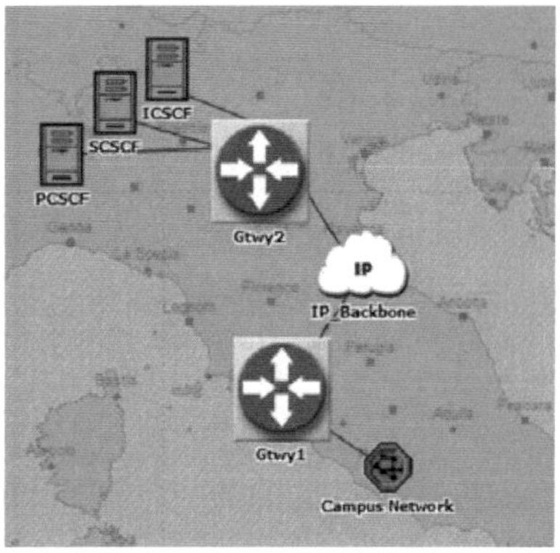

Figure 1. Geographical overview of the simulated scenario.

VI. THE SIMULATED TRAFFIC LOAD

In order to simulate a realistic network scenario, in addition to VoLTE traffic, background traffic has also been generated. It consists of FTP, Voice over IP and Video Streaming applications.

The application protocols taken into account are RTP for VoLTE and VoIP over LTE, and Real Time Streaming Protocol (RTSP) for Video Streaming.

For what concerns FTP, it consists of a file transfer from a server to the UE, so the transport protocol is User Datagram Protocol (UDP).

The characteristics of monitored and background applications are:

- VoLTE (monitored application)
  Codec: RTP Adaptive Multi Rate (AMR) 12.2K
  Frame size: 10 ms
  Code rate: 64 kbps
  Uplink Guaranted Bit Rate: 1 Mbps
  Downlink Guaranted Bit Rate: 1 Mbps
  ToS: Interactive Voice - 6
  QoS Class Identifier (QCI): 1
  Allocation and Retention Priority (ARP) = 1
- FTP application (background traffic)
  Packet dimension: 1000 byte
  FTP get, UE download file from FTP server
  Type of Service (ToS): Best Effort - 0
  ARP = 5
- Voice application (background traffic)
  Codec: RTP AMR 12.2K
  Frame size: 10 ms
  Code rate: 64 kbps
  ToS: Interactive Multimedia - 5
  ARP = 2
- Video Streaming application (background traffic)
  ToS: Interactive Multimedia - 5
  ARP = 4

The simulated run time was for 800 sec. The VoLTE application starts 170 sec after the simulation begins, and it remains active until simulation ends.

The FTP application starts 135 sec after the simulation begins, and it is composed of 2 active blocks of 120 sec each, with an inter-repetition time of 300 sec between the blocks.

The Voice and Video Streaming applications both start 170 sec after the simulation begins, and they remain active until the simulation ends.

The VoLTE application runs between UE_1_1 (the caller) and UE_2_1 (the called).

The FTP application runs between UE_1_2, UE_2_2, and the FTP server.

The Voice application runs between UE_1_3_t (the caller) and UE_2_3_t (the called).

The Video Streaming application runs between UE_1_3_t2 and UE_2_3_t2.

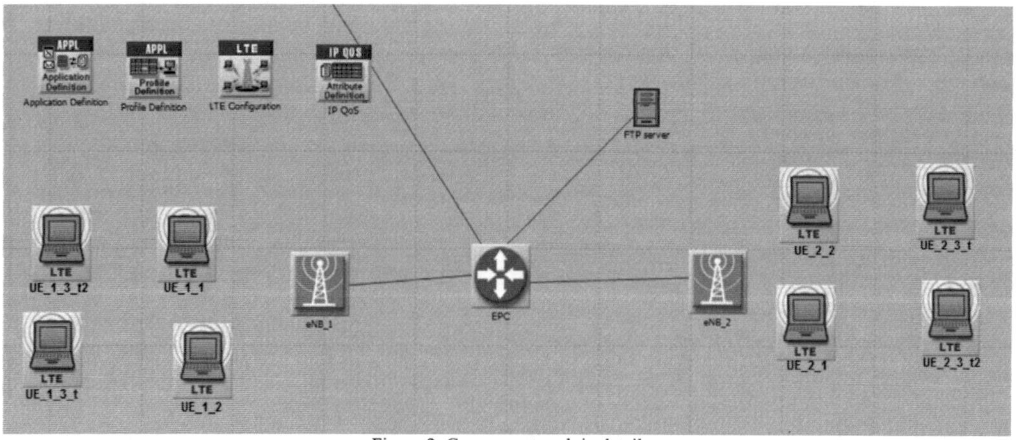

Figure 2. Campus network in detail

VII. ANALYSIS OF THE SIMULATION OUTPUT

OPNET has been used to investigate the trend of the QoE (MOS) versus increasing values of jitter and packet loss. To obtain variations in the VoLTE jitter and packet loss, various changes in the above described four traffic loads have been operated.

By setting the timing of such traffic loads, the VoLTE traffic has been monitored, and performance parameters have been collected.

Several scenarios have been simulated versus increasing values of jitter and packet loss and simulation results have been extracted by means of probes placed on the network nodes and interfaces.

The values of the network KPIs (VoLTE network jitter and VoLTE packet loss) and the KQI (VoLTE MOS) obtained from simulation have been analyzed with the Matlab regression toolbox in order to estimate the α, β and γ parameters holding for VoLTE.

In a first approach, simulation has been used to check under which condition the IQX Hypothesis in (4), originally introduced for VoIP, could also hold for VoLTE. To this purpose, the behavior of the VoLTE MOS was plot versus the network jitter first, and then versus the packet loss P_{pl} defined in (3).

Figure 3 gives the plot of MOS versus network jitter and shows that its mathematical regression (with a coefficient of correlation 0.998) well complies with the exponential behavior of (4). This proves that relationship (4), originally introduced for VoIP, also holds for VoLTE services.

Figure 4 instead shows that no exponential relationship holds between the VoLTE MOS and packet loss. In other words, the IQX Hypothesis can be extended to VoLTE, under condition that the QoS parameter appearing in the exponent of (4) is network jitter, while no extension holds in case the exponent is packet loss P_{pl}.

The question then arises: what happens if, in place of the P_{pl} defined in (3), the $P_{pl,eff}$ defined in (6) is instead used in the exponent, i.e. if a combination of jitter and packet loss is used? In other words, what happens if the VoLTE MOS is expressed by (8)?

Figure 5 shows that the mathematical regression of the simulation MOS versus $P_{pl,eff}$ well complies with the exponential behavior of (8) and this gives the expected validation of formula (8) for the VoLTE context. To strengthen such a proof, the VoLTE MOS produced from simulation was plot versus P_{jitter} defined in (7) and versus the standard packet loss P_{pl} defined in (3), taken separately.

The result can be seen in Figure 6 where the simulation output is compared with the mathematical 3D regression obtained using the two QoS parameters separately. The exponential relationship is shown to hold.

This completes the simulation validation of model (8). Such validation has been confirmed by real world tests performed on the VoLTE national scenario, in cooperation with the TIM telecommunication company, on the occasion of a patent filing [35].

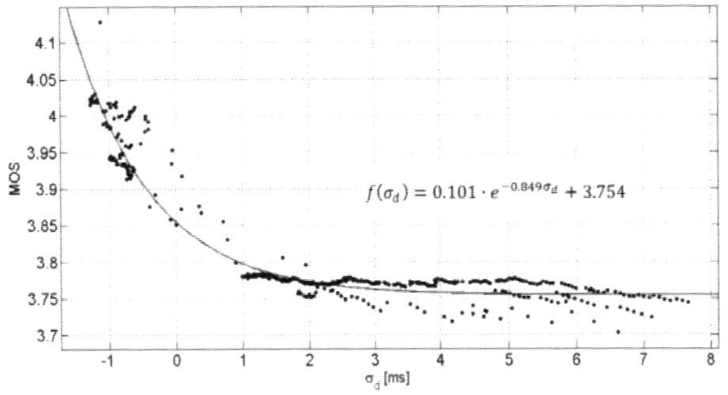

Figure 3. Behavior of VoLTE MOS versus network jitter.

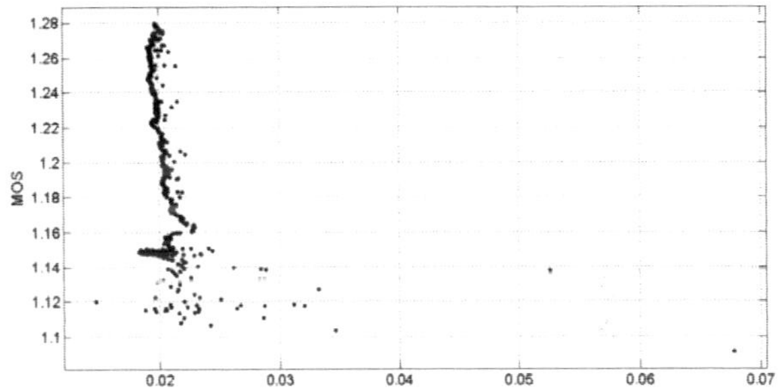

Figure 4. Behavior of VoLTE MOS versus packet loss P_{pl}.

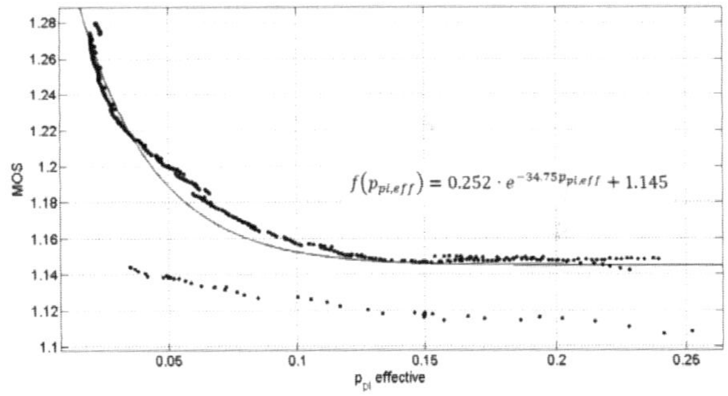

Figure 5. Behavior of VoLTE MOS versus effective packet loss $P_{pl,eff}$.

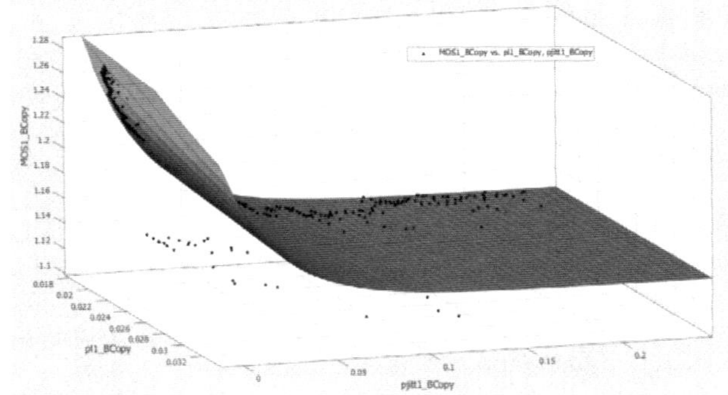

Figure 6. Behavior of VoLTE MOS versus packet loss P_{pl} and P_{jitter}.

VIII. CONCLUSIONS

The LTE standard only focuses on the definition of network QoS, without giving its relationship with the QoE. In this paper, a hypothesis relationship was introduced and proved valid for VoLTE services by use of an OPNET simulation model. Validation was confirmed by real world tests performed in cooperation with the telecommunication company TIM, on the VoLTE national scenario.

Knowing this relationship, the network management can adjust the network KPIs (packet loss and jitter) to continuously meet the QoE expected from the SLA negotiated with the end-user.

ACKNOWLEDGEMENTS

Funding was from the Guglielmo Marconi University Research Strategic Plan on the Performance of Communication Networks, Rome Italy, and from the University of Rome Tor Vergata Project on Next Generation Networks, Rome Italy.

REFERENCES

[1] 3GPP Technical Specification TS 23.207 V10.0.0, "End-to-end Quality of Service (QoS) Concept and Architecture" March 2011.
[2] 3GPP Technical Specification TS 23.107 V11.0.0, "Quality of Service (QoS) Concept and Architecture" June 2012.
[3] 3GPP TS 32.455 version 10.0.0 Release 10 "LTE; Telecommunication management; Key Performance Indicators (KPI) for the Evolved Packet Core (EPC)".
[4] 3GPP TS 32.450 version 8.0.0 Release 8 "Universal Mobile Telecommunications System (UMTS); LTE; Telecommunication management; Key Performance Indicators (KPI) for Evolved Universal Terrestrial Radio Access Network (E-UTRAN): Definitions".
[5] ITU-T Recommendation P.10/G.100, "Vocabulary for performance and quality of service", 2006.
[6] ETSI Technical Report 102 643 V1.0.2."Human Factors (HF); Quality of Experience (QoE) requirements for real-time communication services." October 2010.
[7] S. Barakovi and L. Skorin-Kapov, "Survey and Challenges of QoE Management Issues in Wireless Networks", Journal of Computer Networks and Communications, vol. 2013, 2013.
[8] TeleManagement FORUM, The Open Group, "SLA Management Handbook – Volume 4: Enterprise Perspective", October 2004.
[9] 3GPP TS 36.401, "Evolved Universal Terrestrial Radio Access Network (E-UTRAN) Architecture description"
[10] 3GPP TS 23.002, "Network architecture"
[11] H. Holma and A. Toskala, "LTE for UMTS: Evolution to LTE-Advanced," Chapter 3, April 2011, Wiley.
[12] 3GPP survey of M. Nohborg, "LTE Overview", 3GPP website.
[13] 3GPP survey of F. Firmin, MCC, "The Evolved Packet Core", 3GPP website.
[14] 3GPP Technical Specification TS 23.228 V11.8.0, "IP Multimedia Subsystem (IMS)", June 2013.
[15] 3GPP Technical Specification TS 22.228 V12.6.0, "Service Requirements for the Internet Protocol (IP) Multimedia Core Network Subsystem (IMS)" June 2013.
[16] RFC 3550, "RTP: A Transport Protocol for Real-Time Applications", July 2003.
[17] RFC 3393 "IP Packet Delay Variation Metric for IP Performance Metrics (IPPM)".
[18] RFC 1889, "Audio-Video Transport Working Group, RTP: A Transport Protocol for Real-Time Applications", January 1996.
[19] S. Forconi and M. Vaser, "4G LTE Architectural and Functional Models of Video Streaming and VoLTE Services", the Seventh International Conference on Ubiquitous and Future Networks (ICUFN 2015). Sapporo, Japan, July 2015.
[20] M. Vaser, "Analisi Funzionale del Servizio Voce in LTE e Studio Simulativo delle Relazioni tra QoE e QoS", PhD Thesis, XXVII Cycle.
[21] ITU-T Recommendation G.107, "The E-Model: A Computational Model for Use in Transmission Planning", December 2011.
[22] ITU-T Recommendation P.862, "Perceptual Evaluation of Speech Quality (PESQ): An Objective Method for end-to-end Speech Quality Assessment of Narrowband Telephone Networks and Speech Codecs", February 2001.
[23] ITU-T Recommendation P.862.2, "Wideband extension to Recommendation P.862 for the assessment of wideband telephone networks and speech codecs", November 2007.
[24] ITU-T G.109 Amendment 1, "Definition of Categories of Speech Transmission Quality Amendement 1: New Appendix I – The E-Model Based Quality Contours for Predicting Speech Transmission Quality and User Satisfaction from Time-Varying Transmission Impairments", January 2007.
[25] C. Callegari et al, "Experimental Analysis of ViLTE Service", IEEE Access, published on April 2nd, 2018.
[26] E.Silva et al, "Mean Opinion Score Measurements Based on E-Model During a VoIP call", The Eleventh Advanced International Conference on Telecommunications, 2015.
[27] M.H. Miraz et al, "Simulation and Analysis of Quality of Service (QoS) Parameters of Voice over IP (VoIP) Traffic through Heterogeneous Networks", International Journal of Advanced Computer Science and Applications, Vol. 8, N. 7, 2017.
[28] F.B. Mismar and B.L. Evans, "Q-Learning Algorithm for VoLTE Closed-Loop Power Control in Indoor Small Cells", 2018.
[29] P. Wuttidittachotti and T. Daengsi, "Quality Evaluation of Mobile Networks Using VoIP Applications: A case study with Skype and LINE based-on Stationary Tests in Bangkok", I.J. Computer Network and Information Security, 2015, 12, 28-41.
[30] D. Nguyen and H. Nguyen, "A Dynamic Rate Adaptation algorithm using WB E-Model for voice traffic over LTE network", 2016.
[31] A. Kovac, M. Halas, M. Orgon and M. Voznak, 'E-Model MOS Estimate Improvement through Jitter Buffer Packet Loss Modelling'', Information and Communication Technologies and Services, Vol 9, n. 5, 2011.
[32] M. Fiedler, T. Hossfeld and P. Tran-Gia, Blekinge Inst. of Technol., Karlskrona, Sweden; "A generic quantitative relationship between quality of experience and quality of service ", Network, IEEE (Volume:24 , Issue: 2), 2010.
[33] T. Hossfeld, D. Hock, P. Tran-Gia, K. Tutschku and M. Fielder, "Testing the IQX Hypothesis for Exponential Interdependency between QoS and QoE of Voice Codecs iLBC and G.711", 18th Seminar on Quality Experience, Sweden 2008.
[34] Riverbed Website , Overview of Steel Central characteristics
[35] M. Vaser and G. Maggiore, "Method and System for determining a Quality of Experience during a Real-Time Communication Service", requested for patent on 30th April 2018, number I17220-IT/AD

A Survey on 5G Standardization for Edge Computing and Internet of Things

Harpreet Kaur
Hughes Systique
Gurgaon, India
Email: harpreet.kaur@hsc.com

Abstract— **The networking world is undergoing a radical change to support innovative use cases and new market verticals. International Telecommunication Union (ITU) has defined three categories of these use cases – Enhanced Mobile Broadband (eMBB), Ultra-Reliable and Low Latency Communications (UR-LLC) and Massive Machine Type Communication (mMTC). 5G is considered a harbinger for achieving high data rates, high connection density and ultra-low latency essential to realize these use cases. Emerging technologies, such as Software Defined Networking (SDN), Network Functions Virtualization (NFV) and Multi-Access Edge Computing (MEC), are needed to accomplish the desired performance, scalability and agility. Standardization bodies, like 3rd Generation Partnership Project (3GPP), the Internet Engineering Task Force (IETF), and the European Telecommunications Standards Institute (ETSI) are working in synergy towards defining standards around 5G and these supporting technologies. This survey article summarizes the key enablers added in 5G standards, to support the edge and Internet of Things (IoT) applications. The article also annotates standardization activities around the deployment of virtualization in all segments of the network. Finally, it explores standards around edge deployments and how they leverage these virtualized infrastructures to realize the services envisioned by future 5G Networks, for IoT applications.**

Keywords- Edge Computing; Standardization; 3GPP; Internet of Things.

I. INTRODUCTION

5G is proving to be the next major iteration in cellular technology. 5G promises to offer peak data rate of 20 Gbps in downlink and 10 Gbps in uplink, one way latency at the access side of about 1 millisecond, and connection density of the order of one million device per square km area to support the massive scale of IoT devices expected in the near future [40] [9].

Enterprises and service providers are offering a plethora of applications to end customers, e.g., IoT, Virtual Reality (VR), industrial control, ubiquitous on-demand coverage, as well as the opportunity to meet customized market needs. Each application differs in terms of expected data rates, latency, reliability and availability. Hence, they need different treatments by the underlying cellular networks.

This kind of network transformation involves changes at radio access, core and transport, how network softwarization at each layer helps, how emerging technologies, like Network Function Virtualization and Software defined Networking, help in network softwarization of the cellular network, how innovative ideas, like computing at the edge or network slicing can help improve application performance.

With the enormous number of IoT enabled devices, the amount of data they generate and the latency they expect, cloud computing is no more an option to deliver the promised Quality of Experience (QoE). Edge Computing brings the cloud resources (i.e., compute storage and networking) closer to the user. Compute intensive or latency sensitive applications can be hosted on these edge resources to realize the stringent 5G requirements. 5G networks need to serve a diverse set of applications. Network slicing allows creating multiple, logically isolated, virtual networks over the same physical infrastructure. Each network slice can be configured separately as per the requirements of the application it serves.

In May 2015, the International Telecommunication Union (ITU) conceptualized the International Mobile Communications (IMT)-2020 standard (IMT-2020) [9], to analyze how emerging 5G technologies will interact in future networks, as a preliminary study into the networking innovations required to support the development of 5G systems. The work involved defining requirements from the 5G network, the architecture reference models, the procedures and flows needed in the 5G system, adding network softwarization using NFV/SDN and augmentations, like Edge Computing to realize the desired efficiency.

This is where multiple standardization bodies have stepped in – each one trying to resolve one piece of this 5G puzzle. ITU, 3GPP, ETSI and IETF consortiums have been working cohesively for developing the specifications for IMT - 2020. This article surveys specifications released by these consortiums and how they address some of the practical challenges foreseen when trying to adapt to 5G cellular networks and using them for emerging applications. This article is structured as follows: Section II covers the contributions from ITU and 3GPP who are focusing on the 5G requirements, frameworks, reference architectures, procedural flows, management and control planes. Section III covers the ETSI focus on NFV specifications, NFV being projected as a key technology enabler for many use cases defined in IMT-2020. To cover the use cases from ultra-low latency services to massive Internet of Things, ETSI established MEC Industry Specification Group (ISG), contributing the edge reference architecture, its APIs and use cases. This is covered in Section

IV. Section V discusses a few open source initiatives conceptualized around these specifications, which will work as building blocks for 5G cellular networks. The article finally concludes on the convergence of these activities towards developing standards in 5G for MEC and IoT.

II. 5G STANDARDIZATION UNDER ITU, ETSI AND 3GPP

ITU is responsible for coordinating the international standardization of 5G systems. In 2015, ITU shared a recommendation document ITU-R M.2083-0 [9] stating diverse usage scenarios and applications foreseen in next generation networks. It categorizes the usage scenarios broadly into three categories: Enhanced Mobile Broadband (eMBB), Ultra-Reliable and Low Latency Communications (UR-LLC) and Massive Machine Type Communication (mMTC). Different usage scenarios result in diverse requirements. This ITU recommendation further states the kind of capabilities required to handle these requirements under eight parameters – peak data rate, user experienced data rate, latency, mobility, connection density, energy efficient, spectrum efficiency and area traffic capacity.

ITU recommendation ITU-T Y.3101 [10] states the general principles expected from the 5G networks in terms of service diversity, QoS diversity, diversity of mobility levels, user data types and most crucially in terms of flexibility and programmability needed in such networks. The recommendation, then goes into the detailed requirements from service point of view (eMBB, UR-LLC and mMTC) and from networking point of view. The networking requirements state the need for programmability of network functions, separation of control and user plane, network slicing requirements, interworking among multiple heterogeneous access networks, support the exposure of network capabilities, etc.

3GPP started working on the requirements of IMT-2020/5G and came up with a document 3GPP TS 22.261 [11] summarizing the complete set of requirements that define a 5G system – these high level requirements served as guidance for the architectural study. The requirements focused on the need of network softwarization and a complete re-architecture of cellular networks – to support separation of control and user plane, to leverage SDN and NFV technologies to improve on operational efficiency and increase flexibility, to support network slicing allowing the operators to provide customized networks, to support network capability exposure to trusted 3rd party applications (for instance, MEC applications) in a Service Hosting Environment to improve user experience, to allow Interoperability with legacy 3GPP systems, etc.

The 3GPP specification on system architecture 3GPP TS 23.501 [1], covers the 5G architecture reference models, interworking between 5G system and EPS, architectural enablers for virtualized deployments, support for end to end network slicing and support for Edge Computing. Further, the specification 3GPP TS 23.502 [2] highlights the procedures and Network Function services for the 5G system in terms of end-to-end information flows and the NF service operations of these flows for the communication within the 5G core.

5G system supports a service based representation, where network functions, e.g., Access and Mobility Management Function (AMF), Session Management Function (SMF), User Plane Function (UPF), Network Exposure Function (NEF) and Policy Control Function (PCF), within the Control Plane enable other authorized network functions to access their services. The specification 3GPP TS 23.501 [1] emphasizes on separation of user plane and control plane to allow independent scalability and flexible deployments (e.g., centralized or distributed edge) locations of the network functions. This feature along with the concurrent access support to local/centralized services, enables the flexible deployment of UPF for MEC use cases.

To support virtualized deployments of 5G core, each instance of 5G core network functions need to be deployed as fully distributed, fully redundant, stateless, and fully scalable. The specification 3GPP TS 23.501 [1] explains the kind of interactions executed by the network functions to support the centralization of state information and statelessness of the network functions.

3GPP also highlights the network slicing concepts to serve a particular service category or customer. This is crucial for the MEC and IoT use cases which have different requirements with respect to bandwidth, guaranteed QoS, security level and latency. Specification 3GPP TS 23.501 [1] introduces a new network function "Network Slice Selection Function" which helps in selection of the set of Network Slice instances for a User Equipment (UE). For establishing global interoperability for slicing, this specification introduces Standardized Slice/Service Type (SST) values for eMBB, UR-LLC and mMTC (Massive IoT). The specification also explains the signalling interactions among the 5G core network functions to configure the availability of a Network Slice in a tracking area, on trigger from the operator. Another 3GPP specification 3GPP TR 28.801 [12] explains the management and orchestration of end-to-end network slice by demarcating the slice management at three levels - Communication Service Management Function (service instance layer), Network Slice Management Function (network slice instance layer), Network Slice Subnet Management Function (resource layer).

The specification 3GPP TS 23.501 [1] dedicates a separate section to the MEC enablers in 5G. This includes concurrent access to centralized and local servers using multiple PDU session anchors, Application Function (AF) to trigger UPF (re)selection and traffic routing, session and service continuity for UE and application mobility, support for local area data network and lastly the NEF to provide information or accept configuration from external 3rd party applications (MEC applications or functional entities). This NEF interface can be used by the edge applications to provide policies or trigger traffic routing via the 5G core. The specification 3GPP TS 23.502 [2] details out the procedural flows between AF and other 5G core network functions for handling the AF requests for these traffic routing scenarios. ETSI specification ETSI TS 129 522 [6] introduces the NEF northbound interface between 5G NEF and the AF. It specifies the RESTful APIs (e.g., TrafficInfluence API), leveraged by the AF to access the services and capabilities of the 3GPP network entities. It also defines the data models for each API.

MEC use cases require de-centralization of UPF functions and could lead to an exponential increase in number of UPF instances. In addition, handling massive number of devices could lead to a high demand which is not evenly distributed – thus address allocation in response to the UE demand may exhaust IP Address/Prefixes allocation in one function while low demand elsewhere in the network may leave unused IP Addresses/Prefixes in other functions. Thus, basic SMF allocation methods will not work in these complex cases. The 3GPP specification 3GPP TR 23.726 [13] highlights some of these key issues around the SMF and UPF interactions and suggests corresponding solutions for these issues. For instance, one such solution is the UPF allocating the IPv4 address/IPV6 prefix to be used by a PDU Session over N6 interface, instead of SMF.

III. NFV STANDARDIZATION UNDER ETSI, IETF AND 3GPP

ETSI released new use cases in context of NFV relating to the 5G features, like network slicing and IoT virtualization in its existing specification ETSI GR NFV 001 [16]. The "Network slicing" use case in this specification states how network slicing can leverage virtualization – network functions of the slice may be virtualized, or the network slicing management and orchestration entities may be virtualized. The use case also gives explains the possible realization and provisioning of network slices, explaining the life cycle of the network slice and entities participating in this life cycle. Another use case that the specification introduced is "Virtualization of Internet of Things" – IoT is a leading use case of 5G as per NGMN Alliance [40]. The specification explains how virtualization can help in augmenting efficiency and achieve desired agility for the IoT applications/services. It explains how the IoT service providers can leverage the NFV infrastructure to offer services for collection, storage, management and processing of the IoT data and how one can design more services based on these processed data. It introduces the various actors in this complete ecosystem.

To handle the scalability, resilience and performance requirement of IoT and edge applications, 3GPP specification 3GPP TS 23.501 [1] enlists some design principles for 5G core architecture – separation of control and user plane, modularity, minimal dependencies between AN and CN, stateless network functions, etc. These design principles push towards a cloud-native implementation for the 5G core, the 5G core network functions being implemented as Virtual Network Function (VNFs). ETSI standardized the classification of Cloud Native VNF implementations in ETSI GS NFV-EVE 011 [17]. It states the non-functional parameters for classification of cloud-native VNFs, e.g., resiliency, scaling, VNF design for location independence, use of containers, etc. With each parameter, it states the requirements of that parameter to be considered while designing the VNF as cloud-native. Taking an example, parameter "VNF design for location independence" states a requirement that the components of the cloud-native VNF shall be deployed independent of location if resource constraints (hardware acceleration capabilities) or placement constraints (affinity/anti-affinity rules) are met.

Massive deployment of virtualization technologies in the 5G networks signifies the need of service function chaining in mobile networks. IETF draft [39] discusses the kinds of service functions expected in 4G/5G networks. It also mentions the varied instantiation of 5G protocol stack – different instances can be physically located in different entities of the network based on requirements of the implemented service, the radio characteristics and the transport network capacity. For example, all the VNFs belonging to vehicular communications should be located close to the transmission point to ensure low latency. But the broadband access users can have their network functions in core network. This requires the concurrent execution of different instantiations of the 5G protocol stack on the same physical infrastructure. Service function chaining allows the deployment of different chains across such dynamic cloud infrastructure setups.

Acknowledging the importance of network slicing in 5G deployments handling the edge/IoT applications, ETSI dedicated a separate specification ETSI GR NFV-EVE 012 [18] identifying the changes needed in the NFV systems to support network slicing use cases. This specification mapped NFV and 3GPP network slicing concepts – 3GPP specification 3GPP TR 28.801 [12] states a network slice to be a concatenation of network slice subnets, each having one or more network functions. The ETSI specification ETSI GR NFV-EVE 012 [18] deciphers these network functions as VNFs or PNFs. Thus, NFV defined network service could be regarded as a resource-centric of a 3GPP network slice – each instance of a slice is basically a combination of one or more VNFs. The specification mentions the functional requirements for supporting Network Services over multi-site/multi Network Function Virtualization Infrastructure Point of Presence (NFVI-PoPs), to represent the network slice spanning multiple administrative domains. The specification also mentions the need for a functional interface between NFV Management and Orchestration (NFV-MANO) and Network Slice Management function (NSMF) to support resource orchestration of the network service supporting the network slice, in virtualized deployments. As per the IETF draft specification IETF draft-flinck-slicing-management-00 [19], NSMF is a part of Operational Support Systems / Business Support Systems (OSS/BSS) and sits above the NFV orchestrator (NFVO) of ETSI NFV framework architecture.

IV. MULTI-ACCESS EDGE COMPUTING (MEC) STANDARDIZATION UNDER ETSI

The core objective of Multi-access Edge Computing (MEC) is, to reap the IT cloud like benefits in telco environment, by providing cloud computing benefits within the radio access network. Close proximity to the user and receiving local radio-network contextual information aids in achieving extremely low latency, better QoE optimizations and efficient usage of the network bandwidth. ETSI has a dedicated ISG to develop standards around MEC, to create a standardized, open environment which will allow efficient and seamless integration of applications from vendors, service providers, and third-parties across multi-vendor MEC platforms.

The first relevant specification around this standard, ETSI GS MEC 002 [20] starts with some generic principles for MEC. It mentions the significance of aligning the MEC platforms with existing NFV platforms – MEC is expected to use a virtualization platform for running the user applications at the edge and NFV already provides such a virtualization platform. The specification also defines the MEC framework requirements (MEC system leveraging NFV and its interoperability with the 5G core network), requirements with respect to application lifecycle and its runtime environment, and service requirements in terms of platform services offered to the MEC applications.

A. MEC Service scenarios & Requirements

To support the new era of services in the operator's network, ETSI categorized the applications into three broad categories: consumer-oriented services, Operator and third party services, Network performance and QoE improvements. ETSI GS MEC 002 [20] enlists different use cases under each category and elaborates on the capabilities needed in the MEC system to support those use cases. Latest version of the specification has been augmented with interesting use cases, like 'Factories of the future', 'Flexible deployment with containers', 'Multi-RAT (Radio Access Technology) application computation offloading', etc. One new use case 'MEC System deployment in 5G environment', explores the requirements for interaction with the 5G core network, to support the applications running on a MEC system deployed in a 5G environment.

By providing service delivery at a closer proximity to the actual terminal devices MEC can significantly benefit the IoT applications. ETSI GS MEC-IEG 004 [21] introduces some service scenarios directly related to IoT. The scenario 'Assistance for intensive computation', mentions the use of MEC servers to perform high performance computations on behalf of remote devices – can improve the performance and battery life of low processing power devices/sensors in the IoT domain. The specification also mentions 'IoT gateway service scenario', where the MEC servers can be used to aggregate various IoT device messages connected through the mobile network close to the devices. This will provide an analytics processing capability closer to the devices and a low latency response time.

The use cases identified in ETSI GS MEC 002 [20] and service scenarios defined in ETSI GS MEC-IEG 004 [21] expect MEC to optimize the network and services, reduce latency, and support creating personalized and contextualized services. This requires the identification of metrics for these services/applications which can validate the optimization requirements promised by MEC. The specification ETSI GS MEC-IEG 006 [22] identifies several key performance indicators for these services and applications, based on the 5G service requirements defined by NGMN or 3GPP. Latency, energy efficiency, network throughput, system resource footprint and objective/subjective service dependent/independent quality metrics are the key metrics defined in this specification. It further elaborates on the measurement methodology of each metric – whether it should be computed in a standalone or an integrated environment, what measurement approaches can be taken, should it be done using a dedicated service monitoring tool or using common service monitoring, etc.

B. MEC Framework

Based on the framework requirements mentioned in ETSI GS MEC 002 [20], ETSI defined a framework and reference architecture in ETSI GS MEC 003 [3], which describes a MEC system that enables the MEC applications to run in a multi-access network. It starts with the MEC framework dividing the MEC system into different components - MEC system level management, MEC host level management and the MEC host (containing the MEC platform services, the virtualization infrastructure and the MEC applications running on it). The specification further identifies the different functional elements of each component and the reference points between them. It also mentions the platform services (radio network information, location, bandwidth management) provided by the MEC system. These services are essential to fulfil the use-cases driven requirements defined in ETSI GS MEC 002 [20]. The message flows and the data models for each service is defined in its respective specification - ETSI GS MEC 012 [24] for Radio Network Information service (RNIS), ETSI GS MEC 013 [25] for location service and ETSI GS MEC 015 [26] for Bandwidth Management service.

In continuation to ETSI GS MEC 002 [20] which highlights the need to align the MEC deployments with existing NFV infrastructures, the specifications ETSI GS MEC 003 [3] and ETSI GR MEC 017 [23] elaborate on the deployment of MEC in an NFV environment. This deployment instantiates the MEC applications and the existing/new NFV VNFs on the same virtualization infrastructure. MEC platform and the MEC applications are treated as VNFs and hence the existing ETSI NFV MANO components can be used for MEC management and orchestration. ETSI introduces a functional component, MEC Application Orchestrator (MEAO), responsible for management and orchestration of the MEC applications. MEAO uses a NFV orchestrator (NFVO) for orchestration of MEC application VNFs. Likewise, ETSI GS MEC 003 [3] and ETSI GR MEC 017 [23] define the new reference points for all such interactions between the MEC functional entities and existing NFV MANO components. ETSI GR MEC 017 [23] also identifies the key architectural issues in using a NFV environment for MEC deployments and suggests the normative work required to be performed in ETSI NFV ISG and ETSI MEC ISG to resolve these issues. For instance, using a network service to model Mobile Edge (ME) platform VNFs and ME app VNFs, the network service concept in NFV ISG might require re-work to support the association between each ME app VNF and associated ME platform VNF. This will require changes to the network service descriptor formats.

C. Lifecycle Management of MEC Applications

The specification ETSI GS MEC 010-2 [5] defines the complete lifecycle management of the MEC applications. It starts with the requirements on the reference points between the OSS, the Mobile edge orchestrator and the mobile edge platform manager. It then defines the message flows for application on-boarding, application instantiation and application termination. It defines the information model for application descriptors which includes the application requirement and rules. Based on these requirements and rules, the Mobile edge orchestrator can choose the optimal MEC host and then, the steering of traffic to this MEC host is triggered.

Though the mobile edge orchestrator can choose an optimal host based on the application descriptor, UE mobility in the underlying network might require a need to move the MEC application instance to a different ME host, to respect the optimality constraints. ETSI GR MEC 018 [8] signifies the need to support ME service continuity in such application mobility cases. The specification mentions the detailed message flow between the MEC functional entities for the application instance or application context re-location.

ETSI GR MEC 018 [8] also identifies some key issues in supporting ME mobility cases. For instance, MEC system needs to keep the connectivity between the UE App and the MEC application instance on the MEC host even after there is a change in the UE IP address since the UE is now served by a new UPF in the 5G network. To support this, ETSI GR MEC 018 [8] suggests passing the UE-ID and the UE IP address to the mobile edge platform during the application instantiation. Then, the mobile edge platform can use this UE ID to bind the application instance to the new IP context. Another issue that ETSI GR MEC 018 [8] highlights is the traffic steering to the target mobile edge host after application re-location. ETSI GR MEC 018 [8] indicates multiple options to trigger this traffic steering update. The source mobile edge platform might trigger this update towards the target edge platform based on radio network information it receives from the platform services or based on the trigger from mobile edge application orchestrator.

D. Upcoming initiatives

ETSI Work Programme portal [27] also mentions some in-progress specifications relevant to the MEC and IoT deployments. Work item 'DGR/MEC-0027ContainerStudy' explores the additional support needed in MEC for running applications in containers. Work item 'DGR/MEC-0024NWslicing' will work on support needed in MEC for network slicing. It will identify the new interfaces needed, the data models and changes needed in application descriptors, for the deployment of the MEC functions in combination with network slicing. Lastly, the work item 'DGS/MEC-0033IoTAPI' will define the APIs and the data models needed for device provisioning, configuration of the associated components and applications requiring connection to the IoT and MTC devices in a MEC environment.

V. OPEN INITIATIVES FOR 5G AND MEC AT 5G PPP

The 5G Infrastructure PPP (5G PPP) is a joint initiative between the European Commission and the European Information and Communication Technology (ICT) industry. Its initiatives are divided into three phases: research, deployment/optimization and large scale trials. It aims to deploy 5G around 2020. Phase 1 [28] included 19 projects targeting the research around technical challenges in the 5G deployments to cope up with future demands by year 2020. Some interesting projects of this phase were – 5GNORMA, SEASAME and SONATA.

5G NORMA (5G NOVEL RADIO MULTISERVICE ADAPTATIVE NETWORK ARCHITECTURE) [29] aims to develop a new mobile network architecture using SDN/NFV concepts, leading to flexible base stations, software-based centralized controllers and software-based RAN elements. The multi-service, multi-tenancy and context aware network functions developed by 5G NORMA will be resource efficient and enable dynamic sharing and distribution of network resources between operators.

SEASAME (Small Cell coordination for Multi-tenancy and Edge Services) [32] proposes the concept of Cloud-Enabled Small Cell (CESC), a new multi-operator enabled Small Cell - Light Data Center (Light DC) with low-power processors and hardware accelerators for time critical operations, used to build a highly manageable clustered Edge Computing infrastructure. It leverages logically isolated 'slices' to accommodate multiple operators under the same infrastructure, satisfying the profile and requirements of each operator separately.

Scope of SONATA (Service Programming and Orchestration for Virtualized Software Networks) [33] ranges from programmability of the networks to supporting service function chaining and orchestration. It aims to add a Software Development Kit (SDK) for service development, an orchestration framework and a DevOps model to integrate operators with external networks. Multi-access Edge Computing is one of the key cases focused in this project.

Phase 2 of 5G PPP [34] focused on the 5G architectures, pre-standardizations, applicability of SDN/NFV to Wired and Wireless Networks, including networking Clouds, IoT Services, etc. Some interesting projects of phase 2 are 5G ESSENCE, 5G-Transformer and MATILDA.

5G ESSENCE (Embedded Network Services for 5G Experiences) [35] is particularly focused on Edge Cloud computing and Small Cell-as-a-Service. It defines the interfaces for the provisioning of a cloud-integrated multi - tenant SC network and a programmable Radio Resources Management controller; development of the centralized SD-RAN (Software-Defined Radio Access Network) controller to program the radio resources usage in a unified way for all the CESCs (Cloud-Enabled Small Cells); development of orchestrator's enhancements for the distributed service management, etc.

5G-Transformer (5G Mobile Transport Platform for Verticals) [36] aims to transform the current mobile transport network into a SDN/NFV based Mobile Transport and Computing Platform (MTP). It particularly focuses on 'Network Slicing' paradigm in the mobile transport networks – it introduces a 'vertical slicer' for different verticals to request the creation of their respective transport slices. The project aims to demonstrate in verticals, like Automotive, eHealth and Media & Entertainment.

MATILDA [37] provides a framework for the design, development and orchestration of the 5G-ready applications and network services over sliced programmable infrastructure. It offers multi-site management of the Edge Computing and IoT resources using a multi -site virtualized infrastructure manager. It is particularly useful for Smart City Intelligent Lighting Systems, Remote Control and Monitoring of Automobile Electrical Systems, Industry 4.0 Smart Factory, etc.

Phase 3 of 5G PPP is focused towards Infrastructure projects, automotive projects and advanced 5G validation trials across multiple vertical industries. One interesting project in the phase 3 is 5G EVE (5G European Validation platform for Extensive trials) [38]. The 5G-EVE end-to-end facility, consisting of the interconnection of four 5G-site-facilities, will be used to conduct experiments with Mobile Edge Computing, backhaul, core/service technologies and means for site-interworking and multi-site/domain/technology slicing/orchestration.

VI. CONCLUSION

The 5G standardization process is complex due to its inter-dependence on other emerging technologies, such as Multi-access Edge Computing, Network Function Virtualization and Software Defined Networking. The diverse set of use-cases that the future networks will demand adds to the complexity due to the need for programmability of networks, network slicing and intelligent resource orchestration. Thus, there is a need for the various standardization bodies, as discussed in this paper, to work in close collaboration, to come up with exhaustive standards solving the challenges in future networks. While the scope of 3GPP Release 15 covers 'standalone' 5G, with a new radio system complemented by a next-generation core network, Release 16 would enhance the existing LTE and 5G RATs towards achieving the goals of IMT-2020.

REFERENCES

[1] 3GPP TS 23.501 V15.5.0 (2019-03), "System Architecture for the 5G System; Stage 2 (Release 15) "

[2] 3GPP TS 23.502 V15.5.0 (2019-03), "Procedures for the 5G System; Stage 2 (Release 15) "

[3] ETSI GS MEC 003 V2.1.1 (2019-01), "Mobile-Edge Computing (MEC); Framework and Reference Architecture"

[4] 3GPP TS 23.503 V15.5.0 (2019-03), "Policy and Charging Control Framework for the 5G System; Stage 2 (Release 15) "

[5] ETSI GS MEC 010-2 V1.1.1 (2017-07), "Mobile Edge Management; Part 2: Application lifecycle, rules and requirements management"

[6] ETSI TS 129 522 V15.0.0 (2018-07), "5G; 5G System; Network Exposure Function Northbound APIs; Stage 3 (3GPP TS 29.522 version 15.0.0 Release 15) "

[7] ETSI White Paper No. 28, "MEC in 5G networks" : https://www.etsi.org/images/files/ETSIWhitePapers/etsi_wp28_mec_in_5G_FINAL.pdf [Retrieved: 06/2019]

[8] ETSI GR MEC 018 V1.1.1 (2017-10), "Mobile Edge Computing (MEC); End to End Mobility Aspects"

[9] ITU-R M.2083-0 (09/2015), "IMT Vision - Framework and overall objectives of the future development of IMT for 2020 and beyond"

[10] ITU-T Y.3101 (01/2018), "Requirements of the IMT-2020 network"

[11] 3GPP TS 22.261 V15.7.0 (2018-12), "Service requirements for the 5G system"

[12] 3GPP TR 28.801 V15.1.0 (2018-01), "Study on management and orchestration of network slicing for next generation network"

[13] 3GPP TR 23.726 V16.0.0 (2018-12), "Study on Enhancing Topology of SMF and UPF in 5G Networks"

[14] TR 21.915 V1.0.0 (2019-03), "Summary of Rel-15 Work Items"

[15] ITU-T Y Suppl. 44 (07/2017), "Standardization and open source activities related to network softwarization of IMT-2020"

[16] ETSI GR NFV 001 V1.2.1 (2017-05), "Network Functions Virtualisation (NFV); Use Cases"

[17] ETSI GS NFV-EVE 011 V3.1.1 (2018-10), "Specification of the Classification of Cloud Native VNF implementations"

[18] ETSI GR NFV-EVE 012 V3.1.1 (2017-12), "Report on Network Slicing Support with ETSI NFV Architecture Framework"

[19] IETF draft-flinck-slicing-management-00 (July 3, 2017), "Network Slicing Management and Orchestration"

[20] ETSI GS MEC 002 V2.1.1 (2018-10), "Multi-access Edge Computing (MEC); Phase 2: Use Cases and Requirements"

[21] ETSI GS MEC-IEG 004 V1.1.1 (2015-11), "Mobile-Edge Computing (MEC); Service Scenarios"

[22] ETSI GS MEC-IEG 006 V1.1.1 (2017-01), "Mobile Edge Computing; Market Acceleration; MEC Metrics Best Practice and Guidelines"

[23] ETSI GR MEC 017 V1.1.1 (2018-02), "Mobile Edge Computing (MEC); Deployment of Mobile Edge Computing in an NFV environment"

[24] ETSI GS MEC 012 V1.1.1 (2017-07), "Mobile Edge Computing (MEC); Radio Network Information API"

[25] ETSI GS MEC 013 V1.1.1 (2017-07), "Mobile Edge Computing (MEC); Location API"

[26] ETSI GS MEC 015 V1.1.1 (2017-10), "Mobile Edge Computing(MEC); Bandwidth Management API"

[27] https://portal.etsi.org/home.aspx [Retrieved: 06/2019]

[28] The 5G Infrastructure Public Private Partnership (5G PPP): First Wave of Research & Innovation Projects, https://5g-ppp.eu/wp-content/uploads/2015/10/5GPPP-brochure-final-web.pdf [Retrieved: 06/2019]

[29] https://5g-ppp.eu/5G-norma/ [Retrieved: 06/2019]

[30] https://5g-ppp.eu/fantastic-5g/ [Retrieved: 06/2019]

[31] https://5g-ppp.eu/metis-ii/ [Retrieved: 06/2019]

[32] https://5g-ppp.eu/sesame/ [Retrieved: 06/2019]

[33] https://5g-ppp.eu/sonata/ [Retrieved: 06/2019]

[34] The 5G Infrastructure Public Private Partnership (5G PPP): Second Wave of Research & Innovation Projects, https://5g-ppp.eu/wp-content/uploads/2017/11/5GPPP-brochure-phase2-final-web.pdf [Retrieved: 06/2019]

[35] https://5g-ppp.eu/5G-ESSENCE/ [Retrieved: 06/2019]

[36] https://5g-ppp.eu/5G-Transformer/ [Retrieved: 06/2019]

[37] https://5g-ppp.eu/matilda/ [Retrieved: 06/2019]

[38] https://5g-ppp.eu/5g-eve/ [Retrieved: 06/2019]

[39] IETF draft-aranda-sfc-dp-mobile-04Service (July 01, 2017), "Function Chaining Dataplane Elements in Mobile Networks"

[40] https://www.ngmn.org/fileadmin/ngmn/content/images/news/ngmn_news/NGMN_5G_White_Paper_V1_0.pdf [Retrieved: 06/2019]

AI Based Beam Management for 5G (mmWave) at Wireless Edge: Opportunities and Challenges

Chitwan Arora
Hughes Systique Corporation
Gurgaon, India
e-mail: chitwan.arora@hsc.com

Abstract—**Fast and efficient beam management mechanism is the key enabler in 5G (millimeter wave) to achieve low latency and high data rate requirements. Recent advances in Artificial Intelligence (AI) have shown that Machine Learning (ML) and Deep Learning (DL) based techniques can play a significant role in efficient beam management. These techniques can continuously learn and adapt themselves based on the highly varying traffic and channel conditions. For effective operation, it is essential that the ML and DL based beam management algorithm should be deployed at the place in network where all the relevant input parameters needed for beam management are available continuously, as well as the output of the beam management can be applied instantly. In this paper, advantages along with challenges of deploying ML and DL based beam management techniques at the wireless edge of 5G networks are explored.**

Keywords-mmWave; beam management; artifical intelligence; wireless edge.

I. Introduction

The millimeter wave (mmWave) frequencies offer the availability of huge bandwidths to provide unprecedented data rates to meet the demand for Fifth Generation (5G) applications. However, mmWave links are highly susceptible to rapid channel variations and suffer from severe free space pathloss and atmospheric absorption. To address these challenges, base stations and mobile terminals use highly directional antennas to achieve enough link budget in wide area networks. Directional links, however, require fine alignment of the transmitter and receiver beams, achieved through a set of operations known as **beam management**. They are fundamental to the performance of a variety of control tasks including (i) **Initial Access (IA)** for idle users, which allows a mobile User Equipment (UE) to establish a physical link connection with a gNB (5G base station), and (ii) **Beam tracking**, for connected users, which enables beam adaptation schemes, or handover, path selection and radio link failure recovery procedures [1][2]. Figure 1 captures the details of the beam management procedure for 5G Stand Alone (SA) scheme. In existing Long-Term Evolution (LTE) systems (using spectrum in 3-5 GHz), these control procedures are performed using omnidirectional signals, and beamforming or other directional transmissions can only be performed after a physical link is established, for data plane transmissions. On the other hand, in the mmWave bands, it is essential to exploit the antenna gains even during initial access and, in general, for control operations. Hence, there is a need for precise alignment of the transmitter and the receiver beams.

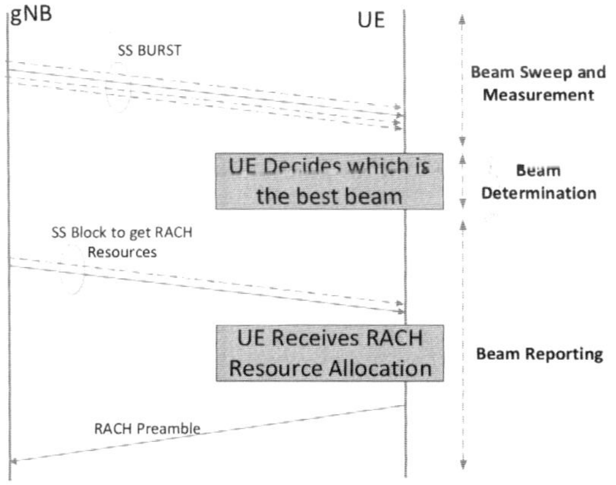

Figure 1. 5G Stand Alone beam management procedure

The initial access in 5G millimeter wave is a time-consuming search to determine suitable directions of transmission and reception. In the cell discovery phase, one approach is sequential beam sweeping by the base station that requires a brute force search through many beam-pair combinations between UE and gNB to find the optimum beam-pair i.e., the one with the highest Reference Received Signal Power (RSRP) level, as shown in Figure 2. The sequential search may result in a large access delay and low initial access efficiency. It also consumes a fair amount of energy in the receiver, which makes it unsuitable for energy constrained receivers, such as Internet of Things (IoT) endpoints.

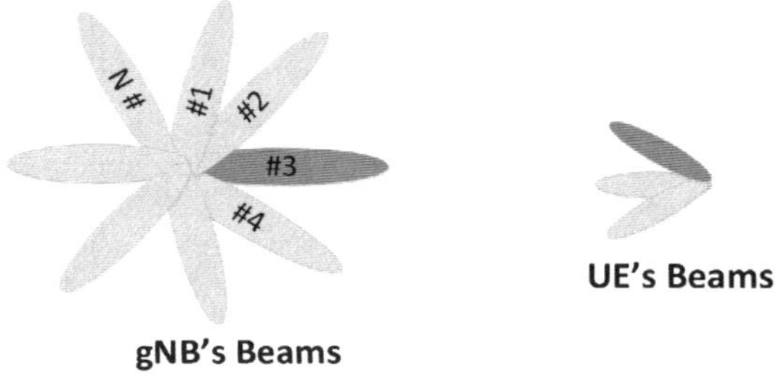

Figure 2. Sequential Beam Sweeping

In existing LTE systems, DL channel quality is estimated from an omnidirectional signal called the Cell Reference Signal (CRS) [3] for beam alignment and selection in connected state. CRS is regularly monitored by each UE in connected state to create a wideband channel estimate that can be used both for demodulating downlink transmissions and for estimating the channel quality [4]. In 5G mmWave networks, in addition to the rapid variations of the channel, CRS-based estimation is challenging due to the directional nature of the communication, thus requiring the network and the UE to constantly monitor the direction of transmission of each potential link. Tracking changing directions can decrease the rate at which the network can adapt and can be a major obstacle in providing robust and ubiquitous service in the face of variable link quality. In addition, UE and gNB may only be able to listen to one direction at a time, thus making it hard to receive the control signaling necessary to switch paths.

From the above description, it is apparent that 5G networks should support a mechanism by which the users and the infrastructure can quickly determine the best directions to establish the mmWave links. These are particularly important issues in 5G networks and motivate the need to extend current LTE control procedures with innovative mmWave-aware beam management algorithms and methods.

In this paper, we explore various traditional as well as upcoming ML and DL based techniques for minimizing the latency and the overhead of the initial communication process. It has been observed that online DL based techniques give better performance than offline DL based techniques. Online DL techniques efficiently adapt themselves to support high mobility in mmWave systems. Deployment strategies for the training of these deep learning algorithms are explored in this paper and we propose that the wireless edge is the appropriate place for the deployment of these DL based algorithm for beam management.

The remainder of this paper is organized as follows. Section II discusses the literature survey of traditional (non-ML/DL) beam management techniques, as well as ML/DL based mean management techniques. Section III discusses in detail different ML/DL based beam management techniques. Section IV discusses the deployment strategy of the deep learning-based beam forming algorithm and Section V presents the conclusions.

II. Literature Survey

In this section, work related to traditional (Non-ML/DL) and ML/DL based beam management is presented.

Traditional (Non-ML/DL) based beam management: Several approaches for directional based schemes have been proposed in the literature to enable efficient control procedures for both the idle and the connected mobile terminals. Most literature on Initial Access and tracking refers to challenges that have been analyzed in the past at lower frequencies in ad hoc wireless network scenarios or, more recently, referred to the 60 GHz IEEE 802.11ad WLAN and WPAN scenarios (e.g., [5]-[7]). However, most of the proposed solutions are unsuitable for next-generation cellular network requirements and present many limitations (e.g., they are appropriate for short range, static and indoor scenarios, which do not match well the requirements of 5G systems). In [8][9], the authors propose an exhaustive method that performs directional communication over mmWave frequencies by periodically transmitting synchronization signals to scan the angular space. The result of this approach is that the growth of the number of antenna elements at either the transmitter or the receiver provides a large performance gain compared to the case of an omnidirectional antenna. However, this solution leads to a long duration of the Initial Access with respect to LTE, and poorly reactive tracking.

Similarly, in [10], measurement reporting design options are compared, considering different scanning and signaling procedures, to evaluate access delay and system overhead. The channel structure and multiple access issues are also considered. The analysis demonstrates significant benefits of low-resolution fully digital architectures in comparison to single stream analog beamforming. More sophisticated discovery techniques are reported in [11][12] to alleviate the exhaustive search delay through the implementation of a multi-phase hierarchical procedure based on the access signals being initially sent in few directions over wide beams, which are iteratively refined until the communication is sufficiently directional. In [13], a low-complexity beam selection method by low-cost analog beamforming is derived by exploiting a certain sparsity of mmWave channels. It is shown that beam selection can be carried out without explicit channel estimation, using the notion of compressive sensing. The issue of designing efficient beam management solutions for mmWave networks is addressed in [14], where the author designs a mobility-aware user association strategy to overcome the limitations of the conventional power-based association schemes in a mobile 5G scenario.

Other relevant papers on this topic include [15], in which the authors propose smart beam tracking strategies for fast mmWave link establishment. The algorithm proposed in [16] takes into account the spatial distribution of nodes to allocate the beam width of each antenna pattern in an adaptive fashion and satisfy the required link budget criterion. Since the proposed algorithm minimizes the collisions, it also minimizes the average time required to transmit a data packet from the source to the destination through a specific direction. In 5G scenarios, papers [8][9][11] give some insights on trade-offs among different beamforming architectures in terms of user communication quality. Articles [17][18] evaluate the mmWave cellular network performance while accounting for the beam training, association overhead and beamforming architecture. The results show that, although employing wide beams, initial beam training with full pilot reuse is nearly as good as perfect beam alignment.

ML/DL based beam management: The recent progress in Machine learning and Deep Learning has raised interest in applying these techniques to communication system related problem [19] – [25]. On the same line of thought as traditional beam management approaches, data-driven Deep Learning-based approaches have been used for efficient beam management. The key idea is that ML/DL is used to make recommendations of promising beam pairs based on the various system parameters as well as past beam measurements.

Papers [26] - [28] propose beam alignment techniques using Machine Learning. Position-aided beam prediction was proposed in [26][27]. Decision tree learning was used in [26], and a learning to rank method was used in [27]. The work in [26] - [28] shows that machine learning is valuable for mmWave beam prediction. A more exhaustive survey is provided in the next section.

III. Insight of ML/DL Based Beam Management Techniques

This section captures the detailed analysis of challenges related to Beam sweeping, Beam alignment and Beam selection using ML/DL based techniques.

A. *Beam Sweeping*

There are various papers which focus on predicting the proposed **Beam sweeping** pattern based on the dynamic distribution of user traffic. In [29], a form of Recurrent Neural Networks (RNNs) called a Gated Recurrent Unit (GRU) has been proposed. In this paper, the spatial distribution of users is inferred from data in Call Detail Records (CDRs) of the cellular network. Results show that the user's spatial distribution and their approximate location (direction) can be accurately predicted based on CDRs data using Gated Recurrent Unit (GRU), which is then used to calculate the sweeping pattern in the angular domain during cell search. In [30] beam sweeping pattern based on GRU is compared with random starting point sweeping to measure the synchronization delay distribution. Results shows that this deep learning beam sweeping pattern prediction enables the UE to initially assess the gNB in approximately 0.41 of a complete scanning cycle with probability 0.9 in a sparsely distributed UE scenario.

Figure 3 shows that, in the sparsely distributed UE scenario, DL based techniques can help to reduce the number of beams to be traversed during beam sweeping. As a result, it will reduce the sweeping time drastically.

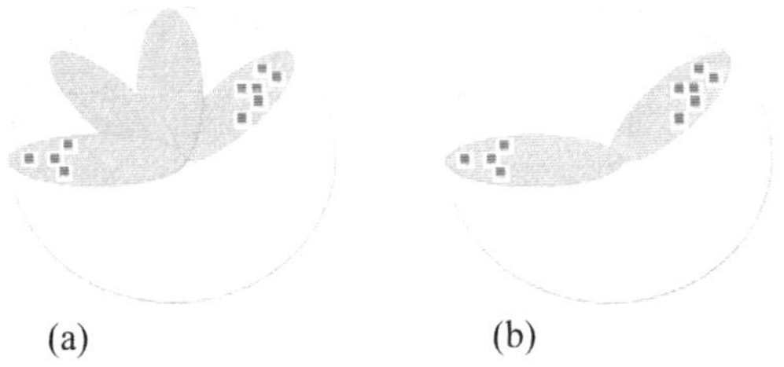

Figure 3. Beam Sweeping in Sparsely distributed UE Scenario

B. *Beam Alignment and Selection*

Position-Aided: Position information may be leveraged for fast beam alignment in mmWave systems. Inverse fingerprinting is one approach to exploit position information [31], which works in Non-Line-of-Sight (NLOS) channels. There are multiple research papers [32]-[34] which focus on using machine learning to propose beam pairs based on the location of the UE position relative to the gNB and past beam measurements. The UE location and past beam measurements can be input into a learning algorithm that learns to rank promising beam directions. By prioritizing beam training in top-ranked directions, the training overhead can be reduced. Figure 4 shows the steps of beam management based on Position Information.

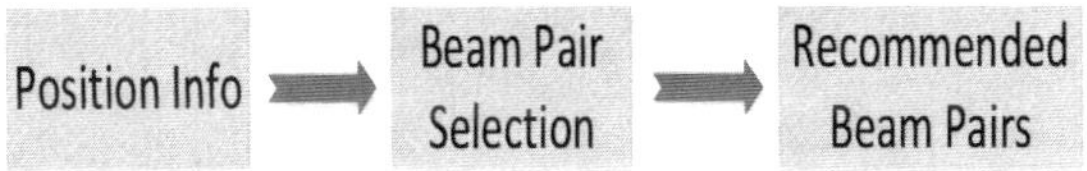

Figure 4. Beam Management based on Position Information

Paper [34] proposes UE positions-based beam alignment in the context of vehicular communication. The authors state that this inverse fingerprinting method is efficient. However, these approaches have some limitations. First, the approach is offline, which means its use is delayed until the database is collected. Second, also due to being offline, its performance depends entirely on the accuracy of the collected database, which may become stale over time. To overcome these shortcoming, online approaches have been proposed. In the online approaches, it has been proposed to keep collecting new observations during operation, making it possible to improve the database.

Situational Awareness: Machine learning tools combined with awareness of the proximity situation have been proposed in [35] to learn the beam information (power, optimal beam index, etc.) from past observations. In this paper, situational awareness that is specific to the vehicular setting including the locations of the receiver and the surrounding vehicles has been considered. The result shows that situational awareness along with machine learning can largely improve the prediction accuracy and the model can achieve throughput with little performance loss and almost zero overhead.

Coordinated Beamforming: A coordinated beamforming solution using deep learning was proposed in [36]. In this paper, the received training signals via omni reception at a set of coordinating Base Stations (BSs) are used as the input to a deep learning model that predicts the beamforming vectors at those BSs to serve a single user. These coordinated beamforming deep learning techniques are based on supervised learning techniques, which assume an offline learning setting and require a separate training data collection phase. However, there are papers which focus on online learning algorithms using the Multi Armed

Bandit (MAB) framework, which is a special class of Reinforcement Learning (RL).

IV. Deployment Strategy at Wireless Edge

From the above studies we can see that ML/DL leverages a large amount of data samples (e.g., radio signals) to acquire accurate knowledge of the RF environment to have optimum beam management. However, the majority of the works presented above focus on centralized ML/DL (as shown in Figure 5), whose goal is to improve the communication performance assuming a well-trained ML model as well as full access to a global dataset. It also assumes massive amounts of storage and computing power are available.

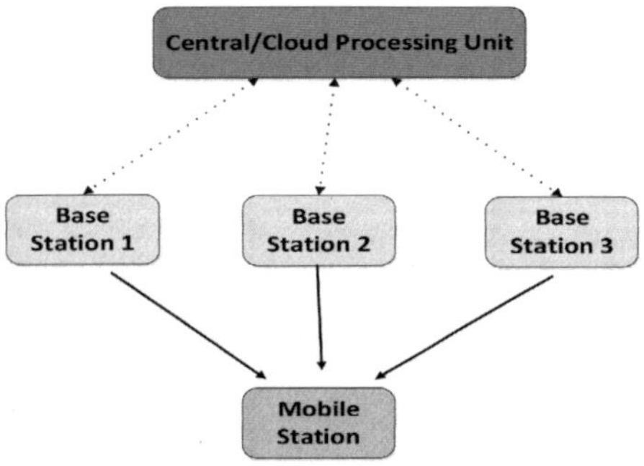

Figure 5. Centralized Deployment of ML/DL Algorithms

However, these approaches have overlooked the additional latency induced by the prior training process and the posterior inference latency. Along with that, for highly varying channel conditions, we need to regularly provide the updated input information to the ML/DL based model.

In this paper, we propose a deployment of ML/DL based algorithm for optimal beam management as a distributed solution, leveraging the Mobile Edge architecture. As we shall show, there will be numerous advantages if we deploy the ML/DL model in a more distributed way (i.e. at Wireless Edge) instead of centralized ML/DL (i.e. at the cloud), as captured in Figure 6.

In this deployment, we have assumed that the Wireless Edge will be present near to gNB. As a result, Wireless Edge will have immediate access to all the relevant data i.e. RF related data, Channel specific data, Cell specific data and User specific data. This will help to use the online learning model which will continuously train itself based on the latest UE and channel information received.

gNBs interact with each other and can have access to relevant information from the neighboring gNBs. These inputs will boost the performance of situational based and coordinated DL/ML model deployed at the wireless edge, as these models can make decisions based on the overall environmental conditions i.e., interference as well as other neighboring gNB parameters. The wireless edge can interact with central/cloud processing unit for exchanging the common information to all the gNBs.

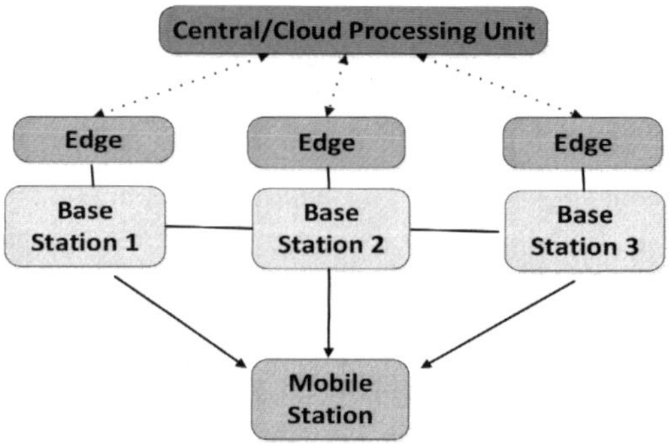

Figure 6. Deployment of ML/DL Algorithms at Wireless Edge

Based on the above description, some of the key advantages of the deployment of a DL\ML based algorithm at wireless edge are as follows:

(i) Performing inference at wireless edge reduces latency and cost of sending data to the cloud for prediction.

(ii) Rather than sending all data to the cloud for performing ML inference, inference is run directly at the wireless Edge device, and data is sent to the cloud only when additional processing is required.

(iii) Every wireless edge entity will have access to a fraction of the data and training and inference are carried out collectively. Moreover, edge devices communicate and exchange their locally trained models, instead of exchanging their private data.

(iv) Since inference results will be available with very low latency, better beam management performance will be achieved in highly mobile and dynamically changing environment conditions.

(v) Since data is present locally at the edge and not going to the cloud, it will enhance the overall reliability as well as privacy.

(vi) Higher inference accuracy can be achieved by training with a wealth of user-generated data e.g., location history, network operational status, etc.

However, there are certain challenges in deploying the ML/DL based algorithms at wireless edge, as follows:

(i) There is a lack of authentic set of data from real communication systems or prototype platforms in actual physical environments. So far, simulations results [32][33][36] prove that the recently proposed DL-based communication algorithms demonstrate a competitive performance. However, due to the lack of standardized data, benchmarking the performance is a real challenge.

(ii) In the wireless edge-based ML/DL deployment, training data might be distributed at different wireless edge nodes and a given wireless edge node might have access to a fraction of the training data. Hence, in wireless edge based deployment, each edge device first trains the local model using its own data samples, and then exchanges the trained local model parameters among other wireless edges. Also, it is difficult to characterize the convergence behavior as well as model performance (i.e., whether the trained model is overfitted or underfitted) due to the distributed nature of the data. As a result, the complexity of networks and training phases will be increased in edge-based ML/DL deployment.

CONCLUSION

From the analysis mentioned above, we can say that emerging DL/ML based techniques can be used for efficient beam management in 5G mmWave. These AI based algorithms deployed at wireless edge can help in providing high performing networks and services that can handle data in a much more secure and faster way for 5G.

REFERENCES

[1] M. Giordani and M. Zorzi, "Improved user tracking in 5G millimeter wave mobile networks via refinement operations," in 16th Annual Mediterranean Ad Hoc Networking Workshop (Med-Hoc-Net), pp. 1-8, June 2017.

[2] M. Polese, M. Giordani, M. Mezzavilla, S. Rangan, and M. Zorzi, "Improved Handover Through Dual Connectivity in 5G mmWave Mobile Networks," IEEE Journal on Selected Areas in Communications, vol. 35, no. 9, pp. 2069–2084, September 2017.

[3] S. Schwarz, C. Mehlfuhrer, and M. Rupp, "Calculation of the spatial preprocessing and link adaption feedback for 3GPP UMTS/LTE," in 6th conference on Wireless advanced (WiAD). IEEE, pp. 1–6, 2010.

[4] M. Giordani, M. Mezzavilla, A. Dhananjay, S. Rangan, and M. Zorzi,"Channel dynamics and SNR tracking in millimeter wave cellular systems," in 22th European Wireless Conference. VDE, pp. 1-8, 2016.

[5] T. Nitsche et al., "IEEE 802.11ad: directional 60 GHz communication for multi-Gigabit-per-second Wi-Fi [Invited Paper]," IEEE Communications Magazine, vol. 52, no. 12, pp. 132–141, December 2014.

[6] J. Wang, "Beam codebook based beamforming protocol for multi-Gbps millimeter-wave WPAN systems," IEEE Journal on Selected Areas inCommunications, vol. 27, no. 8, pp. 1390–1399, October 2009.

[7] R. Santosa, B.-S. Lee, C. K. Yeo, and T. M. Lim, "Distributed Neighbor Discovery in Ad Hoc Networks Using Directional Antennas," in The Sixth IEEE International Conference on Computer and Information Technology, September 2006, pp. 97–97.

[8] C. Jeong, J. Park, and H. Yu, "Random access in millimeter-wave beamforming cellular networks: issues and approaches," IEEE Communications Magazine, vol. 53, no. 1, pp. 180–185, January 2015.

[9] C. N. Barati et al., "Directional cell discovery in millimeter wave cellular networks," IEEE Transactions on Wireless Communications, vol. 14, no. 12, pp. 6664–6678, December 2015.

[10] C. N. Barati et al., "Directional initial access for millimeter wave cellular systems," in 49th Asilomar Conference on Signals, Systems and Computers. IEEE, 2015, pp. 307–311.

[11] V. Desai, L. Krzymien, P. Sartori, W. Xiao, A. Soong, and A. Alkhateeb, "Initial beamforming for mmWave communications," in 48th Asilomar Conference on Signals, Systems and Computers, 2014, pp. 1926–1930.

[12] L. Wei, Q. Li, and G. Wu, "Exhaustive, Iterative and Hybrid Initial Access Techniques in mmWave Communications," in 2017 IEEE Wireless Communications and Networking Conference (WCNC). IEEE, 2017.

[13] J. Choi, "Beam selection in mm-Wave multiuser MIMO systems using compressive sensing," IEEE Transactions on Communications, vol. 63, no. 8, pp. 2936–2947, August 2015.

[14] A. S. Cacciapuoti, "Mobility-Aware User Association for 5G mmWave Networks," IEEE Access, vol. 5, pp. 21 497–21 507, 2017.

[15] J. Palacios, D. De Donno, and J. Widmer, "Tracking mm-Wave channel dynamics: Fast beam training strategies under mobility," in IEEE Conference on Computer Communications (INFOCOM). IEEE, 2017.

[16] K. Chandra, R. V. Prasad, I. G. Niemegeers, and A. R. Biswas, "Adaptive beamwidth selection for contention based access periods in millimeter wave WLANs," in IEEE 11th Consumer Communications and Networking Conference (CCNC). IEEE, 2014, pp. 458–464.

[17] A. Alkhateeb, Y. H. Nam, M. S. Rahman, J. Zhang, and R. W. Heath, "Initial Beam Association in Millimeter Wave Cellular Systems:Analysis and Design Insights," IEEE Transactions on Wireless Communications, vol. 16, no. 5, pp. 2807–2821, May 2017.

[18] Y. Li, J. Luo, M. Castaneda, R. Stirling-Gallacher, W. Xu, and G. Caire,"On the Beamformed Broadcast Signaling for Millimeter Wave Cell Discovery: Performance Analysis and Design Insight," arXiv preprint arXiv:1709.08483, 2017.

[19] S. D¨orner, S. Cammerer, J. Hoydis, and S. ten Brink. "Deep learning-based communication over the air," [Online]. Available: https://arxiv.org/abs/1707.03384, 2017.

[20] U. Challita, L. Dong, and W. Saad, " Proactive resource management in LTE-U systems: A deep learning perspective," https://arxiv.org/abs/1702.07031, 2017.

[21] R. C. Daniels, C. M. Caramanis, and R. W. Heath, "Adaptation in convolutionally coded MIMO-OFDM wireless systems through supervised learning and SNR ordering," IEEE Trans. Veh. Technol., vol. 59, no. 1, pp. 114–126, January 2010.

[22] S. K. Pulliyakode and S. Kalyani, "Reinforcement learning techniques for outer loop link adaptation in 4G/5G systems," https://arxiv.org/abs/1708.00994, 2017.

[23] A. Fehske, J. Gaeddert, and J. H. Reed, "A new approach to signal classification using spectral correlation and neural networks," in Proc. IEEE Int. Symp. New Frontiers in Dynamic Spectrum Access Networks (DYSPAN), 2005, pp. 144–150.

[24] E. E. Azzouz and A. K. Nandi, "Modulation recognition using artificial neural networks," in Proc. Automatic Modulation Recognition of Communication Signals, 1996, pp. 132–176.

[25] M. Ibukahla, J. Sombria, F. Castanie, and N. J. Bershad, "Neural networks for modeling nonlinear memoryless communication channels," IEEE Trans. Commun., vol. 45, no. 7, pp. 768–771, July 1997.

[26] Y. Wang, M. Narasimha, and R. W. Heath Jr, "MmWave beam prediction with situational awareness: A machine learning approach," https://arxiv.org/abs/1805.08912, June 2018, in Proc. of IEEE SPAWC.

[27] V. Va, T. Shimizu, G. Bansal, and R. W. Heath Jr., "Position-aided millimeter wave V2I beam alignment: A learning-to-

rank approach," in Proc. IEEE Int. Symp. on Personal, Indoor and Mobile Radio Commun.,October 2017, pp. 1–5.

[28] A. Alkhateeb, S. Alex, P. Varkey, Y. Li, Q. Qu, and D. Tujkovic, "Deep learning coordinated beamforming for highly-mobile millimeter wave systems," IEEE Access, vol. 6, pp. 37 328–37 348, June 2018.

[29] A. Mazin, M. Elkourdi, and R. D. Gitlin, "Accelerating beam sweeping in mmWave standalone 5G new radios using recurrent neural networks," in 2018 IEEE Vehicular Technology Conference (VTC), 2018. [Online]. Available: https://arxiv.org/abs/1809.01096

[30] A. Mazin, M. Elkourdi, and R. D. Gitlin, "Comparative Performance Analysis of Beam Sweeping Using a Deep Neural Net and Random Starting Point in mmWave 5G New Radio," in 9th IEEE Annual Ubiquitous Computing, Electronic and Mobile communication conference (UEMCON), 2018.

[31] V. Va, J. Choi, T. Shimizu, G. Bansal, and R. W. Heath Jr., "Inverse multipath fingerprinting for millimeter wave V2I beam alignment," IEEE Trans. Veh. Technol., vol. 67, no. 5, pp. 4042–4058, May 2018.

[32] A Klautau, P. Batista, N. Gonzalez-Prelcic, Y. Wang, and R. W. Heath Jr "5G MIMO Data for Machine Learning: Application to Beam-Selection using Deep Learning" Proc of the information theory and application workshop, February 2018.

[33] V.Shimizu, G. Bansal, and R. W. Heath, "Position-aided millimeter wave V2I beam alignment: A learning-to-rank approach", IEEE 28th Annual International Symposium on Personal, Indoor, and Mobile Radio Communications (PIMRC), 2017.

[34] V. Shimizu, G. Bansal and R. W. Heath, "Online Learning for Position-Aided Millimeter Wave Beam Training," in IEEE Access, vol. 7, pp. 30507-30526, 2019.

[35] Y. Wang, M. Narasimha and R. W. Heath, "MmWave Beam Prediction with Situational Awareness: A Machine Learning Approach," 2018 IEEE 19th International Workshop on Signal Processing Advances in Wireless Communications (SPAWC), Kalamata, 2018, pp. 1-5.

[36] A. Alkhateeb, S. Alex, P. Varkey, Y. Li, Q. Qu and D. Tujkovic, "Deep Learning Coordinated Beamforming for Highly-Mobile Millimeter Wave Systems," in *IEEE Access*, vol. 6, pp. 37328-37348, 2018.

5G and Edge Computing as Driving Force behind Autonomous Vehicles

Manu Agrawal
Hughes Systique
Gurgaon, India
E-mail: manu.agrawal@hsc.com

Abstract— **Multi-access Edge Computing (MEC) uses the edge of the network to bring computing closer to consumers and the data generated by applications, which reduces latency and increases connection speeds. 5G is the next generation of mobile networks that promises to have estimated network speeds as fast as 10 Gb/s and ultra-reliable low latency communication. Both MEC and 5G are considered disrupting technologies on their own, but combined, they will become a powerful force in the world of computing. Connected Vehicles and especially Connected Autonomous Driving (CAD) vehicles bring a whole new ecosystem with new requirements on the network architecture to support and to satisfy the real-time service requirements. This paper provides an overview of the automotive use cases, some of the key challenges and how MEC and 5G can play a vital role in overcoming these challenges.**

Keywords-Edge Computing; 5G; Autonomous Vehicles; DSRC; C-V2X.

I. INTRODUCTION

The automotive industry is evolving towards connected and autonomous vehicles that offer many benefits, such as improved safety, less traffic congestion, less environmental impacts and lower capital expenditure. A key enabler of this evolution is vehicle-to-everything (V2X) communication, which allows a vehicle to communicate with other vehicles, pedestrians, road-side equipment and the Internet. With V2X, critical information can be exchanged among vehicles to improve situation awareness and thus avoid accidents. Furthermore, V2X provides reliable access to the vast information available in the cloud. For example, real time traffic, sensor and high-definition mapping data can be made available, which is useful not only for today's drivers, but will be essential for navigating self-driving vehicles in the future.

The paper is organized as follows: Section II provides an overview of the V2X communication and use cases, Section III describes the current status of V2X implementation using the standard IEEE 802.11p. Section IV describes the Cellular V2X and the associated use cases. In Section V, we propose the application of V2X using MEC-based architecture support in the 5G infrastructure. It provides insights into how emerging 5G technologies will accelerate the realization of advanced V2X communication to improve transportation experience and quality of life. For example, 5G-based V2X is expected to enable very high throughput, high reliability, low latency and accurate position determination use cases. Some of the use cases will involve 5G working in tandem with other technologies including cameras, radar and lidar. Cellular V2X Communications Towards 5G [3] describes these use cases, starting with the advanced driving categories identified in 3GPP, including ranging/positioning, extended sensors, platooning and remote driving. The paper conclusion is that a combination of these technologies can be helpful in achieving the strict requirements of the V2X communication. It also summarizes how mobile network operators, vehicle manufacturers, cloud service providers and regulatory bodies can work together to deliver a brand-new experience for drivers, travelers and other road users in the near future.

II. OVERVIEW OF V2X

V2X, which stands for 'vehicle to everything', is the umbrella term for the car's communication system, where information from sensors and other sources travels via high-bandwidth, low-latency, high-reliability links, paving the way to fully autonomous driving.

There are several components of V2X, including vehicle-to-vehicle (V2V), vehicle-to-infrastructure (V2I), vehicle-to-pedestrian (V2P), and vehicle-to-network (V2N) communications. In this multifaceted ecosystem, cars will talk to other cars, to infrastructure such as traffic lights or parking spaces, to smartphone-toting pedestrians and cyclists, and to data centers via cellular networks. Different use cases will have different sets of requirements, which the communications system must handle efficiently and cost-effectively.

Figure 1 illustrates some examples of V2X communication [1]. It is implied that these communications are generally bidirectional.

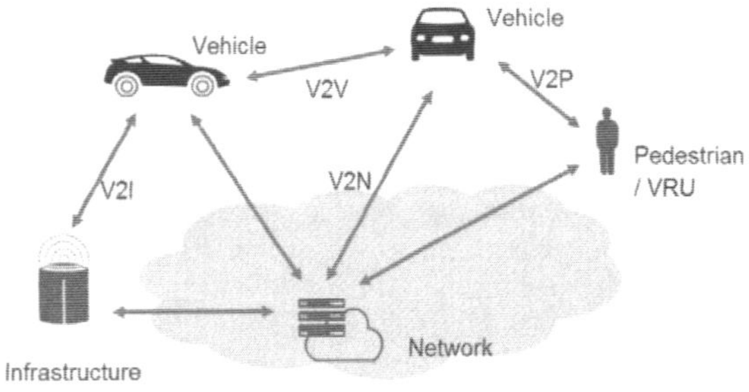

Figure 1. Types of V2X Communication

V2V technology consists of wireless data transmissions between motor vehicles. The primary purpose of this communication is to prevent possible accidents, allowing vehicles in transit to transfer data on their position and their speed within an ad-hoc mesh network. It uses a decentralized connection system, which may provide either a fully connected mesh topology or a partially connected mesh topology.

Depending on how the technology is developed, the driver of a vehicle can receive a warning in the event of an accident risk or the vehicle itself can independently take preventive actions, such as emergency braking, if it is designed to carry out safety interventions.

Unlike the V2V communication model, which allows the exchange of information only among vehicles, the V2I enables vehicles in transit to interface with the road system. These components include RFID readers, traffic lights, cameras, lane markers, street lamps, signage, and parking meters.

V2P involves direct communications between a vehicle and one or multiple pedestrians within close proximity. In addition, communication can be to other vulnerable road users, such as cyclists. V2P is conducted directly or through the use of network infrastructure. It will facilitate warnings to be provided to the pedestrian of an approaching vehicle, and warnings to the vehicle of vulnerable road users.

V2N enables both broadcast and unicast communications to take place between vehicles and the V2X management system and also the V2X AS (Application Server). This is achieved by making use of the Cellular network infrastructure. Vehicles are able receive broadcasted alerts regarding accidents further down the road or warnings of congestion or queues on the planned route.

V2V and V2P transmission are based on primarily broadcast capability between vehicles or between vehicles and vulnerable road users (e.g., pedestrian, cyclist), such as for providing information about location, velocity and direction to avoid accidents.

The 5G Automotive Association (5GAA) categorizes a comprehensive list of connected vehicle applications [1] [2], categorized in four main groups of use cases:

- Safety,
- Convenience,
- Advanced Driving Assistance and
- Vulnerable Road User (VRU).

To maximize the benefit that connected vehicles can bring, fast, secure and reliable wireless communications are required.

Various vehicular communication standards have been proposed over the years with the dominant standard known as IEEE 802.11p. IEEE 802.11p defines only the lower layers of the communication system. The upper layers are defined in separate standards: in the US this is IEEE 1609 while in Europe this is ITS-G5.

III. V2X BASED ON IEEE 802.11P

The original V2X standard is based on a Wi-Fi offshoot, IEEE 802.11p (part of the IEEE's WAVE, or Wireless Access for Vehicular Environments program), running in the unlicensed 5.9GHz frequency band. IEEE 802.11p, which was finalized in 2012, underpins Dedicated Short-Range Communications (DSRC) in the US, and ITS-G5 in the European Cooperative Intelligent Transport Systems (C-ITS) initiative.

V2X communication via 802.11p goes beyond line-of-sight-limited sensors such as cameras, radar and LIDAR, and covers V2V and V2I use cases such as collision warnings, speed limit alerts, and electronic parking and toll payments.

The DSRC system transmits a basic safety message (BSM) between vehicles [3] [4]. The BSM includes information such as exact vehicle location and direction of travel, speed, braking status, and some other useful and relevant data. The driver doesn't see it, but the BSM provides safety warnings and could trigger action such as automatic braking or other collision avoidance maneuvers or warnings. The BSM is updated and transmitted 10 times per second [5] [6].

Another proposed function of DSRC is V2I communications. The vehicle links up with roadside access points that can provide additional useful information, such as traffic or road conditions, weather, construction and traffic light status. A V2N connection is also possible for other services to be determined.

However, DSRC has several limitations. There is no apparent path for continued evolution of the radio standard to meet changing technological and consumer needs. Additionally, as it was designed for rapid transmission of short-range basic safety messages, it is unable to meet the higher bandwidth demands of V2N applications such as autonomous driving, multimedia services. DSRC also doesn't have the bandwidth necessary to transmit the raw vehicle sensor data that will become increasingly common in automated vehicles [3]. DSRC also has limited range: about 300 m.

DSRC would require the deployment of tens of thousands of RoadSide Units (RSUs) embedded or attached to roadway infrastructure to enable an effective network along the nation's roads [3].

In summary, there are several challenges present with DSRC. First, the system relies on RSUs, which are not currently deployed. Secondly, at the physical layer, several inefficiencies arise due to the asynchronous nature of the system, resulting in reduced performance, such as range. The worst packet delay in DSRC is unbounded and it also lacks deterministic Quality of Service (QoS) guarantees. Due to the ad hoc nature of DSRC, it is difficult to bind the worst case CSMA backoff time for MAC scheduling. Finally, there is currently no evolutionary path (or IEEE 802.11 standards activities) to allow for improvements in the DSRC physical/MAC layers with respect to range, robustness and reliability [1].

However, a complementary technology, LTE and 5G cellular systems, has the potential to support existing DSRC use cases [7] [8]. In addition to that, low latency, high reliability and high bandwidth offered by the cellular systems can play a pivotal role in supporting advanced, futuristic and more challenging features and use cases [9] [10].

IV. CELLULAR V2X

A challenger to DSRC for V2X has emerged from the cellular industry: it is called C-V2X and it is designed to complement and extend existing cellular capabilities. Cellular V2X is an umbrella term for 3GPP-defined V2X technologies, encompassing both LTE- and forthcoming 5G-based V2X systems.

LTE cellular networks are already deployed and cover most parts of the world. With the planned deployment of 5G in 2020, it will further enhance the network capabilities.

C-V2X can be used in many possible different ways to improve road safety, while making more efficient use of transport networks and infrastructure. The Intelligent Transportation Systems (TIS) services can be broadly categorized into safety-related services and non-safety related services. This section gives examples of the many use cases in which C-V2X can help to enhance safety and improve user experience [11]:

1) Vehicle Status Warning. The Vehicle Status Warning use case includes vehicle detection of abnormal safety conditions and signaling the associated danger to others

2) Traffic Hazard Warning. The Traffic Hazard Warning use case includes vehicle or road infrastructure alerting other approaching vehicles of immobilized vehicles (e.g., an accident, a breakdown, etc.) or current roadwork. This use case prevents collisions by helping vehicles to avoid a dangerously immobilized vehicle situation or roadwork.

3) Collision Risk Warning. The Collision Risk Warning use case includes informing a vehicle of approaching vehicles intending to turn across traffic. This feature mitigates the risk of collision at an intersection by warning vehicles in the affected area. A RSU detects and alerts two or more vehicles.

4) Traffic Condition Warning. The Traffic Condition Warning use case allows vehicles and roadside stations to signal to other vehicles of current traffic conditions. This function helps drivers to choose the best route and leads to less traffic congestion and brings environmental benefits by reducing energy consumption.

5) Queue warning. Roadside infrastructure can also use C-V2X to warn vehicles of queues or road works ahead of them, so they can slow down smoothly and avoid hard braking. More broadly, the roadside infrastructure can use C-V2X to help vehicles retain a consistent speed and reduce the number of so-called phantom traffic jams caused by the ripple effect caused by sudden braking and lane changes on motorways.

6) Avoiding collisions. Each vehicle on the road could use C-V2X to broadcast its identity, position, speed and direction. An on-board computer could combine that data with that from other vehicles to build its own real time map of the immediate surroundings and determine whether any other vehicle is on a potential collision trajectory. The vehicles involved could then take an evasive action, such as braking or accelerating, that will enable a collision to be avoided. In cases where a human driver is about to cause an accident, the information collected by C-V2X could be used to over-ride the manual controls. For example, if a driver is about to pull out at a junction into the path of another vehicle, the on-board computer could automatically apply the brakes and prevent the car from moving forward.

7) Automated overtake. Fully-automated vehicles will need to perform overtake maneuvers on two-way roads. Such maneuvers may be dangerous as a quickly approaching oncoming vehicle may be out-of-range of vehicle sensors. Vehicles thus need to cooperate to allow a safe overtake without a risk of collision.

See through sensors enable the exchange of video information between a vehicle and the one behind it. For instance, a vehicle behind a truck receives a video stream coming from the camera at the front of the truck. This will give the driver an extended vision of the environment, thus allowing safer decision making (e.g. when the vehicle decides to overtake the truck). Such use cases require a high reliability, availability and data rate, as well as a low latency.

8) High Definition Map (HDMap) download. In fully autonomous driving, the use of usual 2D digital roadmaps is not enough. Indeed, autonomous vehicles require precise information about their complex environment. HDMaps represent a new generation of maps that could be used for this purpose. Such maps have high precision at centimeter level accuracy, but require high data rate to be downloaded by vehicles.

9) Cooperative Adaptive Cruise Control (CACC). The CACC use case uses unicast V2X cooperative awareness messages to obtain lead vehicle dynamics and general traffic ahead of a vehicle.This allows the vehicle to enhance the performances of its existing ACC.

10) Platooning refers to the formation of a convoy in which the vehicles are much closer together than can be safely achieved with human drivers. Such automated convoys make better use of road space, save fuel and make the transport of goods more efficient. C-V2X can be used to enable communications between up to three vehicles in the platoon, so that they all slow down or speed up simultaneously. C-V2X could also be used to signal the presence of the platoon to other vehicles and roadside infrastructure. Platoons will be flexible in that they will typically be established on a motorway, then broken up when a vehicle leaves the motorway. For platoons of more than three vehicles, relaying information between vehicles takes too long to enable synchronous braking. Therefore, platoons of more than three vehicles will also need to make use of the low latency cellular network infrastructure that will be deployed with 5G [12].

11) Out-of-Coverage Operation. C-V2X can operate outside of network coverage using direct communication without requiring provisioning of a Universal Subscriber Identity Module (USIM). To enable USIM-less communication, automobile Original Equipment Manufacturers (OEMs) will pre-configure the vehicle device with parameters necessary for out-of-network operation [4], including:

- Authorization to use V2X.
- A list of authorized application classes and the frequencies to use for them.
- Radio parameters for use on direct links.

- Configuration for receiving V2X messages via cellular broadcast, for example, Multimedia Broadcast/Multicast Service (MBMS).

Direct USIM-less communication allows C-V2X to support critical safety services when network coverage is unavailable or if the vehicle does not have an active cellular subscription. These parameters can also be securely updated, if needed, by the OEM, just like any other updates. Vehicle OEMs and mobile operators can work together to ensure the parameters they each provision are compatible, resulting in harmonious operation of various vehicle devices using the direct link in an area.

There are two modes of LTE V2X operation: direct and via the network [13].

Direct communication uses the LTE PC5 interface, which is based on Release 12's proximity services communications ("ProSe") feature [14]. It also has enhancements to accommodate high speeds/high doppler, high vehicle density, improved synchronization and decreased message transfer latency. This mode is suitable for proximal direct communications (hundreds of meters) and for V2V safety applications that require low latency, for example Advanced Driver Assistance Systems (ADAS), situational awareness, etc. This mode can work both in and out of network coverage.

Network-based communication uses the LTE Uu interface from the UE located in the vehicle and the eNBs. UEs send unicast messages via the eNB to an application server, which, in turn, broadcasts them via evolved Multimedia Broadcast Multicast Service (eMBMS) for all UEs in the relevant geographical area to receive. This mode uses the existing LTE Wide Area Network (WAN) and is suitable for more latency-tolerant use cases (e.g., situational awareness, mobility services).

With widely deployed infrastructure in major countries, LTE has proven its reliability in bandwidth and coverage area. In spite of such convenience, LTE is still only trusted with non-time critical and non-safety critical communication such as hyperlocal weather, road conditions, traffic data, etc. The main concern comes from the centralized LTE architecture. On the data plane, we have eNodeB (eNB), the Serving Gateway (S-Gw), and the Packet Gateway (P-Gw). eNBs are normally distributed across the nation providing radio access to User Equipment (UE), while S-Gw and P-Gw are part of the Evolved Packet Core (EPC) located at highly centralized data centers. Since the P-Gw anchors all UEs IP addresses, all user plane packets must cross a large backbone network to reach P-Gw of EPC before being routed towards their destination. The actual end to end LTE packet delay could be as high as 60-100 ms, exceeding the designed 20 ms user plane latency. Therefore, current cellular networks become unsuitable for time critical safety messaging [15].

To decrease latency, LTE-D2D and LTE-V are developed, where user devices communicate directly to their target rather than going through a base station and the core networks. However, they share similar issues with most distributed communication. If the wireless access channels are managed by the LTE scheduler, we can only communication between two stationary devices under the same cell coverage, otherwise the mobility issue could also be challenging.

Since V2X must be deployed in the near term and should be extended to the future, it must offer the necessary high performance to meet use cases, e.g., intersection movement assistance, emergency electronic brake light, forward collision warning, blind spot warning, lane change warning, etc., while being future proof and scalable to meet the requirements of use cases of tomorrow, e.g., ADAS, where vehicles can cooperate, coordinate and share sensed information, and ultimately CAD.

V. 5G, MEC AND C-V2X

In this section, we propose/analyze an edge-computing architecture based on 5G for C-V2X in light of some of the standard use-cases discussed above.

The stringent latency requirements posed by the V2X system can be satisfied by introducing Multi-access Edge Computing (MEC) technology to the cellular network architecture. Let us consider a MEC-assisted network architecture, in which MEC hosts are collocated with eNBs/gNBs. They can receive and process VRU messages at the edge of the access network. Leveraging its ability to provide processing capabilities at the cellular network's edge, an overlaid MEC deployment is expected to assist vehicles in achieving low packet delays, due to its close proximity to end users. By means of numerical evaluation, it has already been observed that, for some of the investigated system parameterizations, the proposed overlaid deployment of MEC hosts can offer up to 80% average gains in latency reduction as compared to the conventional network architecture [16].

Focusing on the C-V2X technology, the architecture of the cellular network is expected to have a vital impact on the support of delay-intolerant V2X services. This occurs because the End-to-End (E2E) latency of C-V2X signaling is limited by the quality and dimensioning of the cellular infrastructure, i.e., the capacity of backhaul connections, the delays introduced by both the Core Network (CN), as well as the Transport Network (TN). As one would expect, these latency bottlenecks will be more prominent for high loads corresponding to coverage areas of high vehicular/ pedestrian densities. MEC can play an important role in overcoming these challenges and reducing the latency in high density scenarios [16].

Figure 2 illustrates the typical network scenario where MEC and 5G infrastructure will be deployed to support the challenging requirements of C-V2X communication and support the various use cases listed above. Another variant of this network scenario can be where MEC, 5G and 4G infrastructure co-exist. The edge supports some of the core network functionalities that are hosted from the core network. The existing eNB/gNB and/or the RSUs with processing and storage capabilities can also be used to host some of the core network functionalities.

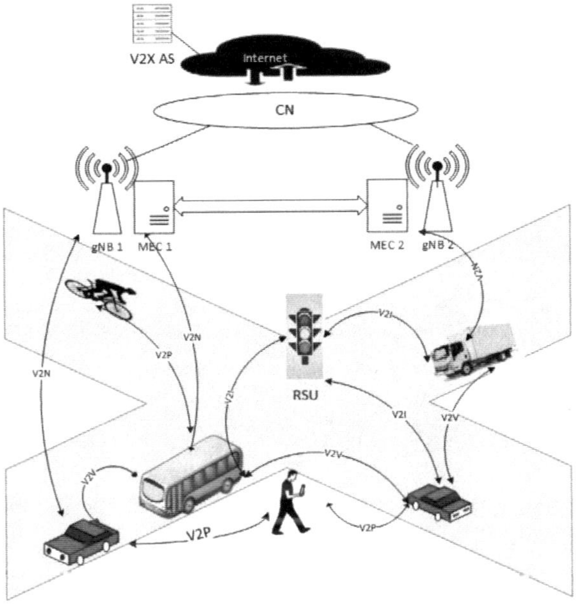

Figure 2. C-V2X Network Architecture with MEC and 5G

5G will support a broad range of V2X and non-V2X use cases [18], including enhanced Mobile Broadband (eMBB), massive Internet of Things (mIoT) and mission-critical services. These use cases have diverse requirements, including high data rates for eMBB, low power consumption and high scalability for mIoT, as well as Ultra-Reliable and Low Latency Communications (URLLC) for mission-critical services [17]-[19].

Network slicing allows network operators to define different types of services and dynamically allocate proper resources to support this end-to-end service by configuring different network segments. By using slicing technology, one physical network can be divided into multiple virtual networks, each supporting different service requirements or even different customers [20].

V2N and communication via the network are typical use cases for network slicing. For instance, autonomous driving or safety/emergency services would require an URLLC network slice. Meanwhile, some auxiliary/comfort or personal mobility services would require either a best effort slice or an eMBB slice in the case of streaming infotainment videos. A given vehicle could access different slices at the same time, with passengers watching an HD movie while a see-through application detects a road hazard and triggers an emergency message for the cars behind or nearby to slow down or stop to prevent an accident.

C-V2X is designed to be fully compatible with 5G, meaning investments in infrastructure and modules today will not become obsolete for a long time to come.

The deployment of commercial 5G networks from 2020 onwards based on the 3GPP standards will enhance C-V2X in several different ways [11]. In the 5G era, C-V2X will be able to support:

- Very precise positioning and ranging to support cooperative and automated driving.
- High throughput and low-latency connectivity to enable the exchange of raw or processed data gathered through local sensors or live video images.
- High throughput to build local, dynamic maps based on camera and sensor data, which can then be distributed at street intersections. For example, C-V2X could be used to supply a driver or an on-board computer with a bird's eye view of an intersection or see-through capability when driving behind a truck.
- Very low latency and high reliability to support high-density platooning [21] [22].

VI. CONCLUSION

In this paper, we have described various V2X use cases, existing DSRC implementation for V2X communication, its advantages and some of the challenges associated with it. Also, we have covered the Cellular V2X, which is entering the vehicular communication space, in competition with the tried and tested DSRC.

Cellular V2X communication has the potential to enhance the traffic safety, comfort and is going to play a crucial role in supporting the future use cases towards autonomous driving. However, under high load conditions, it might not be able to meet the latency requirements for the safety related use cases. The automotive industry, OEMs, standard bodies need to work towards the co-existence of these technologies to leverage the full potential, which will make 802.11p and LTE-A/5G more compatible, and can even consider the option to merge the two, to create a heterogeneous vehicular networking system that leverages the best of both – the ability of 802.11p to support safety-related use-cases, and the ability of LTE-A/5G to support non-safety-related use-cases.

Widespread deployment of Multi-access Edge Computing in 5G networks can help in achieving the latency requirements to support safety-related use-cases and will act as accelerators for autonomous driving cars. Network slicing is also going to play an important role to meet the diverse requirements of a variety of safety related and non-safety related use-cases. However, security and safety aspects will play an important role for V2X communication, be it DSRC, LTE, MEC or 5G.

REFERENCES

[1] V2X Cellular Solutions http://www.5gamericas.org/files/2914/7769/1296/5GA_V2X_Report_FINAL_for_upload.pdf [Retrieved: 06/2019]

[2] "5G Automative Association," http://5gaa.org/ [Retrieved: 06/2019]

[3] "Cellular V2X Communications Towards 5G" http://www.5gamericas.org/files/9615/2096/4441/2018_5G_Americas_White_Paper_Cellular_V2X_Communications_Towards_5G__Final_for_Distribution.pdf [Retrieved: 06/2019]

[4] J. Kenney, "Dedicated Short-Range Communications (DSRC) Standards in the United States". Proceedings of the IEEE. 99. 1162 – 1182, 2011. 10.1109/JPROC.2011.2132790.

[5] K. Abboud, H. A. Omar, and W. Zhuang, “Interworking of DSRC and cellular network technologies for V2X communications: A survey,” IEEE Transactions on Vehicular Technology, vol. 65, no. 12, pp. 9457– 9470, Dec. 2016.

[6] Heterogeneous Vehicular Networks By Kan Zheng, Lin Zhang, Wei Xiang, and Wenbo Wang.

[7] “V2X Communication for ITS - from IEEE 802.11p Towards 5G” https://futurenetworks.ieee.org/tech-focus/march-2017/v2x-communication-for-its [Retrieved: 06/2019]

[8] Z. Mir, and F. Filali, “LTE and IEEE 802.11p for vehicular networking: a performance evaluation” https://jwcn-eurasipjournals.springeropen.com/articles/10.1186/1687-1499-2014-89 [Retrieved: 06/2019]

[9] “C-V2X Enabling Intelligent Transport” https://www.gsma.com/iot/wp-content/uploads/2017/12/C-2VX-Enabling-Intelligent-Transport_2.pdf [Retrieved: 06/2019]

[10] “Cellular V2X as the Essential Enabler of Superior Global Connected Transportation Services” https://futurenetworks.ieee.org/tech-focus/june-2017/cellular-v2x [Retrieved: 06/2019]

[11] ETSI TR 102 638 V1.1.1 (2009-06) Intelligent Transport Systems (ITS); Vehicular Communications; Basic Set of Applications; Definitions

[12] G. Nardini, A. Virdis, C. Campolo, A. Molinaro, and G. Stea, “Cellular-V2X Communications for Platooning: Design and Evaluation” https://www.mdpi.com/1424-8220/18/5/1527 [Retrieved: 06/2019]

[13] “C-V2X Conclusions based on Evaluation of Available Architectural Options” http://5gaa.org/wp-content/uploads/2019/02/5GAA_White_Paper_on_C-V2X_Conclusions_based_on_Evaluation_of_Available_Architectural_Options.pdf [Retrieved: 06/2019]

[14] ETSI TS 123 303 V12.6.0 (2015-10) LTE; Proximity-based Services (ProSe); Stage 2, 3GPP TS 23.303 version 12.6.0 Release 12 https://www.etsi.org/deliver/etsi_ts/123300_123399/123303/12.06.00_60/ts_123303v120600p.pdf [Retrieved: 06/2019]

[15] S. Zhou, P. P. Netalkar, Y. Chang, Y. Xu, and J. Chao, "The MEC-Based Architecture Design for Low-Latency and Fast Hand-Off Vehicular Networking," *2018 IEEE 88th Vehicular Technology Conference (VTC-Fall)*, Chicago, IL, USA, 2018, pp. 1-7. doi: 10.1109/VTCFall.2018.8690790 URL: http://ieeexplore.ieee.org/stamp/stamp.jsp?tp=&arnumber=8690790&isnumber=8690547 [Retrieved: 06/2019]

[16] M. Emara, M. C. Filippou, and D. Sabella, "MEC-Assisted End-to-End Latency Evaluations for C-V2X Communications," *2018 European Conference on Networks and Communications (EuCNC)*, Ljubljana, Slovenia, 2018, pp. 1-9. doi: 10.1109/EuCNC.2018.8442825 URL: http://ieeexplore.ieee.org/stamp/stamp.jsp?tp=&arnumber=8442825&isnumber=8442432 [Retrieved: 06/2019]

[17] “5G Communications for Automation in Vertical Domains” http://www.5gamericas.org/files/1815/4222/3220/5G_Americas_White_Paper_Communications_for_Automation_in_Vertical_Domains_November_2018.pdf [Retrieved: 06/2019]

[18] “5G to Accelerate the Realization of Autonomous Cars” http://www.5gamericas.org/en/newsroom/press-releases/5g-accelerate-realization-autonomous-cars/ [Retrieved: 06/2019]

[19] “A 5G V2X Ecosystem Providing Internet of Vehicles” https://www.mdpi.com/1424-8220/19/3/550/htm [Retrieved: 06/2019]

[20] C. Campolo, A. Molinaro, A. Iera, R. R. Fontes, and C. E. Rothenberg, "Towards 5G Network Slicing for the V2X Ecosystem," *2018 4th IEEE Conference on Network Softwarization and Workshops (NetSoft)*, Montreal, QC, 2018, pp. 400-405. doi: 10.1109/NETSOFT.2018.8459911 URL: http://ieeexplore.ieee.org/stamp/stamp.jsp?tp=&arnumber=8459911&isnumber=8458492 [Retrieved: 06/2019]

[21] V. Vukadinovic et al., (2018). 3GPP C-V2X and IEEE 802.11p for Vehicle-to-Vehicle communications in highway platooning scenarios. Ad Hoc Networks. 74. 10.1016/j.adhoc.2018.03.004. URL: https://www.researchgate.net/publication/323843658_3GPP_C-V2X_and_IEEE_80211p_for_Vehicle-to-Vehicle_communications_in_highway_platooning_scenarios [Retrieved: 06/2019]

[22] D. Sabella et al., “Toward fully connected vehicles: Edge computing for advanced automotive communications,” [Online]. Available: http://5gaa.org/news/toward-fully-connected-vehicles-edge-computing-for-advanced-automotive-communications/ [Retrieved: 06/2019]

Interference Classification in a Factory Environment Based on Semi-supervised Deep Learning

Su Yi, Hao Wang, Wenqian Xue, and Lefei Wang
Fujitsu Research and Development Center
Beijing, China
Email: {yisu, wangh, xuewenqian, wanglefei}@cn.fujitsu.com

***Abstract*—The steadily growing use of license-free frequency bands requires reliable coexistence management and therefore proper wireless interference identification. This paper provides a realtime interference source classification method based on semi-supervised deep learning. It uses Received Signal Strength Indicator (RSSI) samples collected by an 802.15.4-based wireless sensor for formulating training data as well as online test data in a factory environment. To address the issue of laborious process on labeling the training data, a Fast Fourier Transform (FFT)-based algorithm is used to help labeling the sample data. We have trained a deep neural network with two hidden convolutional layers using raw RSSI samples as inputs. The whole realtime management system with the classifier is implemented on IEEE 802.15.4 System on Chip (SoC) and Linux-based system.**

Keywords–Interference classification; Semi-supervised deep learning; RSSI sampling.

I. Introduction

The Internet of Things (IoT) is one of the most important, exciting, and transformational technology developments today. IoT is global in impact, multi-disciplinary in nature, and spans virtually all industry segments. Recent trends to introduce IoT devices, such as sensors and cameras into factories have been accelerated by a strong demand for improving productivity, reducing labors and cost. For this reason, the digitalization of the factories, as well as the connection of information on production process and supply chain management within a factory and across factories are becoming important.

There are several system applications, e.g., preventive maintenance, management of materials and products, monitoring of movements and machine monitors, which are integrated in the network. More efforts will be required for wireless communication because of its limited and shared radio resources and the sensitive nature of the environment in which it will operate in. One of the most common and frequent wireless issues is related with interference, which is common to all wireless short range networks operating in unlicensed frequency band, such as IEEE 802.11, 802.15.4, 802.15.1, etc. Interference issues are critical since multiple systems may interfere with each other, and the number of nodes in the unlicensed spectrum is increasing rapidly.

When deploying a sensor network in a factory, it has been found that there exists different levels of interference, during different times, and at different positions. This paper aims to identify different interference sources in a factory environment. By diagnosing different interference sources, either at the network provisioning phase or during operation, IoT service providers can do better network planning, take countermeasures to solve the problem or avoid potential problems. Therefore, realtime state monitoring and automated trouble detection are required for efficient operation and management services. For instance, with the help of the resulting knowledge, the system can adapt its communication by choosing a better channel or other mitigation strategies.

The key idea is to use a low power, narrow band IEEE 802.15.4 wireless module to sample radio frequency (RF) energy and identify the interference source by learned interference patterns. The IEEE 802.15.4 standard defines that an Energy Detection (ED) value must be measured for the Clear Channel Assessment (CCA) and channel selection [1]. It is an estimate of the received signal power within the bandwidth of an IEEE 802.15.4 channel. No attempt is made to identify or decode signals on the channel. The ED time shall be equal to 8 symbol periods. This ED value is also widely known as the Received Signal Strength Indicator (RSSI). By setting the sampler on different ZigBee channels, it can detect Wi-Fi, ZigBee, Bluetooth, Bluetooth Low Energy (BLE), microwave oven, and other magnetrons, which use the spectrum overlapped with the sampler's channel.

Many efforts have been made to classify interference in wireless networks, such as in Wi-Fi systems or sensor networks. Airshark [2] leverages powerful Wi-Fi hardware to get the spectrum information to detect and classify non-Wi-Fi interference. In [3]–[5], the authors propose methods to classify interference by the observation that different interferences will result in different corruption patterns on received packets. The authors in [6]–[9] study and extract features purely from the time-domain RSSI sequence, and design a classification approach to identify the existence of different sources of interference. In recent years, deep learning has been introduced to analyze the spectral data for signal identification. In [10]–[12], spectral samples over frequency and time span are collected for training using convolutional neural networks.

Most previous works face the problem of labeling the interference source effectively. They often use human experience to label the training data or test data. Labeled data is always very hard to get since human annotation is boring and time-consuming. In our previous work [13], we study the interference effect on the link condition and the network performance and design a machine learning method to classify the wireless channel errors into different categories. We also conduct extensive experiments in office to study the RSSI patterns and use deep learning to identify different patterns for major wireless scenarios [14]. In this paper, we develop a semi-supervised deep learning mechanism to identify interference types with focus on a factory scenario. Compared with our previous work, one novel point is an auto-labeling algorithm which can be done using training data collected from natural environment instead of a controlled environment.

The rest of the paper is structured as follows. Section II gives an overview of deployment of the interference identification. In Section III, we describe the semi-supervised deep learning with an auto-labeling method. Section IV provides the test results. Finally, we conclude the work in Section V.

II. Deployment Scenario

The interference identification framework we propose in this work can be deployed in industrial IoT where some example IoT applications include miniaturized sensors integrated into critical equipment that monitor performance parameters to proactively diagnose maintenance issues, enable trend analysis of equipment performance, and optimize overall system operations.

Inspired by recent advances and the remarkable success of deep learning in a broad range of problems such as image or speech recognition and machine translation, we use similar approaches in interference classification with a high rate RSSI sampler to get RSSI traces as input. As a measurement of the RF power level at the input of the transceiver, RSSI is an important parameter to reflect a wireless channel condition. When there is interference, the RF energy increases so it can be used to detect the occurrence of interference.

In our implementation, a $95\mu s$ sampling interval (10.5kHz sampling rate) is achievable. We use a TI CC2530 802.15.4 module and program it to read the built-in RSSI register continuously to get the RSSI sampling data. The RSSI sampler captures the energy in the channel due to the interferers' emissions. It continuously reads the RSSI register of the sensor nodes' radio chip.

The interference analysis is done in a very short period to reflect the fast-changing channel condition. We use the training data collected from different channels to train a unified data model, then this data model becomes channel-independent. That is to say, when we run the online classification algorithm, we use the same model for any sampling channel. The end user, such as the network administrator or a network management application, can generate a detailed report for every diagnosis window or a report with statistical results over a longer period.

Figure 1 illustrates our deployment scenario where these samplers are placed in the intended locations in a factory environment. The RSSI sampler is connected to a small single-board computer Raspberry Pi (RPi) 3 with an USB to serial interface. The sampling results are easily accessible by the interference analysis engine on the RPi. One or more samplers can be placed in a certain area to get the channel information of that area. The Network Management System (NMS), usually implemented with a graphical user interface (GUI), or a Web service, can remotely access the analysis engine on the RPi through Internet. This management system can configure the setting of the interference diagnosis and read the results of the interference source classification.

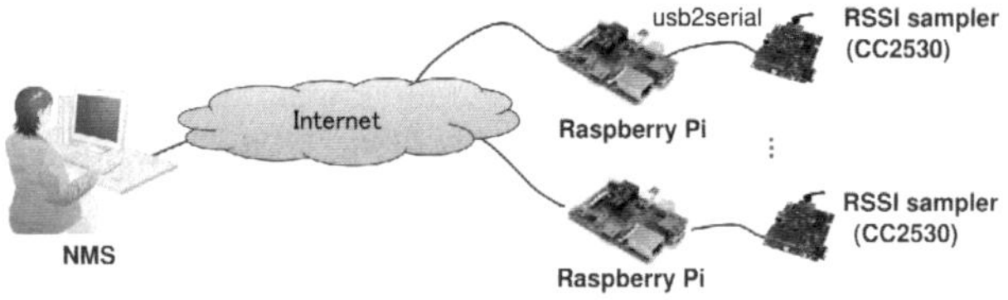

Figure 1. Deployment scenario of the interference classification system.

Another implementation choice is to implement RSSI sampling function on a sensor node. In this case, there is no dedicated node for sampling. The sampling function may be activated during provisioning phase, analyzing phase, or as all-time monitoring.

In the investigated factory, we find out that the interference sources mainly come from electromagnetic radiation caused by the operating machines, and interference caused by the sparse wireless communication signals from the sensor network deployment, such as beacons and sensor data. It has been shown in many studies that industrial and factory equipment produces electromagnetic interference (EMI) that causes a great deal of damage on wireless performance [15].

Figure 2 shows four typical RSSI traces for different interference scenarios in our factory, as well as a *Normal* scenario (Figure 2a) meaning that channel is relatively idle and clear of interference. Sometimes there will be a mix of different patterns of these four.

The RSSI pattern in Figure 2b is a waveform with a cycle of 20ms, which means the energy pattern is periodic with a frequency cycle around 50Hz. Figure 2c has a similar pattern, only that the period is about 10ms, leading to a frequency cycle of 100Hz.

Figure 2d is the RSSI pattern for pulse-shaped wireless communication signals. In factories where there is very sparse traffic, the pulse-like signal pulses are mostly from beacons (Wi-Fi, Bluetooth, BLE, etc.), or sensor data transmitting measurement results. These energy peaks also exhibit a periodic pattern (with a 60+ms period in the figure). We define this pattern as the result of wireless communication signals.

III. Interference Classification with Deep Learning

Traditional machine learning has been used in error diagnosis or interference source identification in the wireless systems in literatures while the results are not so promising. Deep learning may be utilized to automatically extract more low-level and high-level features and has been used in complex applications [16]. It normally requires large amount of training data, which can be achievable by the high rate RSSI sampling.

The RSSI samples in a detection window (20ms) form an N-element input vector. Since a sampling rate $95\mu s$/sample is used, $N = 20\text{ms}/95\mu s \approx 210$. This N-element input vector is passed to a deep learning classification model to generate an $M \times 1$ output vector. M represents the number of classes defined. In this paper, $M = 4$ representing *Normal* and 3 types of interference sources.

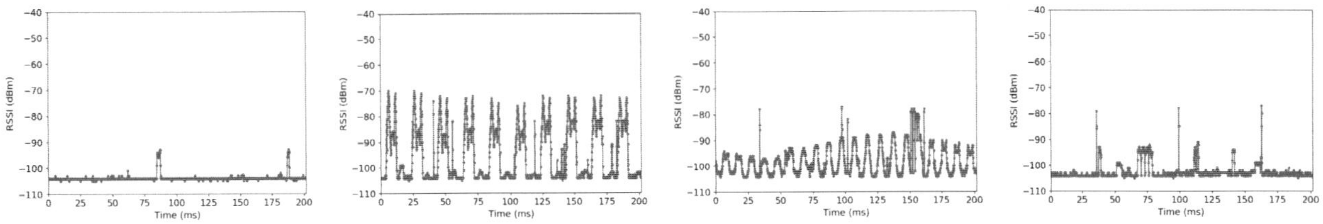

(a) Normal (b) Magnetron with 20ms cycle (c) Magnetron with 10ms cycle (d) Wireless communication signal

Figure 2. Typical RSSI traces of difference cases.

A. Auto-labeling

Training data is collected on a 24-hour basis in a factory. Several days of data are used to formulate the training data set. Before training, we need to prepare all the input vector data composed of RSSI samples together with their labels. This is specifically challenging since it is unfeasible to find out what is actually happening over the air on a 24-hour basis. This paper uses Fast Fourier Transform (FFT) to automatically label the training data to avoid human annotation.

Due to the fact that all interference patterns in our factory are found to be periodic, the proposed automatic labeling utilizes FFT to find the spectrum characteristics of the RSSI samples. Magnetron patterns and wireless communication signal patterns are quite different in that wireless communication signals cover a much shorter time period and are very easy to be overwhelmed by magnetrons or other noises. It happens that magnetrons mostly happen in daytime, since they come from machine noises. We collect sample logs for several days and nights and separate them into daytime training data and night training data. Daytime training data are used to find magnetron patterns and night training data are for wireless communication signals.

Firstly, we use FFT to find the ideal patterns for magnetrons and for normal state. We use daytime training data and label selected data automatically by FFT method. In detail, the sample log is divided into sample sequences of length N_F corresponding to a period of time T_F. T_F can be considered as a hyper-window size (multiple of detection window size) used for FFT algorithm. For each hyper-window, N_F-point FFT is applied to find the fundamental frequency. N_F is large enough to guarantee the frequency resolution but not too large to have a mixed RSSI pattern in a hyper-window. In our experiments, $N_F = 5250$, so $T_F = N_F \times 95\mu\text{s} \approx 500\text{ms}$. Sampling frequency $f_s = 1/95\mu\text{s} = 10.526\text{kHz}$. The frequency resolution $d_f = f_s/N_F = 2\text{Hz}$.

We group these hyper-windows by their fundamental frequencies, and count the number of hyper-windows for each group over these sample logs. The number of hyper-windows for each fundamental frequency is given in Table I. Hyper-windows with DC (direct current) component (0Hz) as fundamental frequency indicate samples in these hyper-windows represent a normal state, so these hyper-windows belong to *Normal*. It is useful to choose fundamental frequencies (except DC component) with obviously higher number of hyper-windows than others. It implies that the interfering magnetron waveform has a cycle with the corresponding fundamental frequency. As a result, two fundamental frequencies (50Hz and 100Hz) with the most numbers of hyper-windows are selected, which exactly matches our observation on Figure 2b and 2c. Note here 50Hz or 100Hz frequency means that the interference is a waveform with 50Hz or 100Hz cycle (20ms or 10ms period). The carrier frequency of the interference source is the same as that of the sampler. We label hyper-windows with 50Hz fundamental frequency as *Interference #1* and hyper-windows with 100Hz fundamental frequency as *Interference #2*. Other hyper-windows are unlabeled for now.

TABLE I. NUMBER OF HYPER-WINDOWS WITH LENGTH T_F GROUPED BY FUNDAMENTAL FREQUENCY

Fund. freq. (Hz)	0	4	6	8	10	12	16	20
# hyper-windows	**11879**	63	9	3	3	7	2	2
Fund. freq. (Hz)	22	24	26	30	34	36	38	40
# hyper-windows	4	18	4	1	1	1	2	2
Fund. freq. (Hz)	42	44	46	48	50	54	80	88
# hyper-windows	3	17	15	38	**236**	1	1	1
Fund. freq. (Hz)	98	100	136	142	150	188	200	250
# hyper-windows	8	**87**	1	1	40	3	18	2

We break up each labeled hyper-window into multiple (500ms/20ms = 25) detection windows and label each 20ms-detection window using the same label of hyper-window it belongs to. Now we have three types of labeled training data: *Normal*, *Interference #1* and *Interference #2*.

Secondly, we use FFT to find the ideal patterns for wireless communication signals using night training data. Unlike the magnetron, the pulse-like wireless communication signal only covers very short time. Due to the background noise, the energy of the signal pulse cannot be identified by directly using FFT. To identify pulse-like wireless signal, a filter (Figure 3) is used to filter out noises before using FFT.

In our experiments, RSSI_THRESHOLD = -80dBm, NOISE_FLOOR = -108dBm.

The new filtered RSSI trace is used to do FFT and automatic labeling. For each hyper-window with length T'_F, FFT is used to find the fundamental frequency. $N'_F = 52500$, $T'_F = N'_F \times 95\mu\text{s} \approx 5\text{s}$ and thus $d'_f = 0.2\text{Hz}$. T'_F is larger than T_F since wireless communication signals normally have a period longer than that of the magnetrons. The fundamental frequencies are rounded down to the nearest integer and the count of hyper-windows for each rounded-down fundamental frequency over these sample logs is listed in Table II. Similarly, one or more fundamental frequencies which have obviously highest number of hyper-windows are selected. Hyper-window

```
Input: A sequence of RSSI values: {rssi_0, rssi_1, ..., rssi_{n-1}}
Output: New sequence of RSSI after filtering: {rssi_filt_0,
    rssi_filt_1, ..., rssi_filt_{n-1}}
for (i = 0; i < n; i++) do
    if rssi_i < RSSI_THRESHOLD then
        rssi_filt_i = NOISE_FLOOR
    else
        rssi_filt_i = rssi_i
    end if
end for
```

Figure 3. Pseudo codes for RSSI filtering

```
Input: Labeled data (X_l, Y_l), unlabeled data X_u.
Output: CNN model f : X → Y
f ← train using (X_l, Y_l)
for x ∈ X_u do
    Predict using y = f(x)
    if y! = Normal then
        (X_l, Y_l) ← (X_l + x, Y_l + y)
        f ← train using (X_l, Y_l)
    end if
end for
```

Figure 4. Semi-supervised learning algorithm

with selected fundamental frequency means that the samples in this hyper-window indicate the existence of a periodic, pulse-like wireless signal. Frequency 15Hz (actually ranging from 15Hz to 16Hz) has the maximum number of hyper-windows, which corresponds to the ~64ms period signal shown in Figure 2d. These hyper-windows are labeled as *Interference #3*. Then all the RSSI samples are replaced by their original pre-filter values.

TABLE II. NUMBER OF HYPER-WINDOWS WITH LENGTH T'_F GROUPED BY FUNDAMENTAL FREQUENCY

Fund. freq. (Hz)	0	5	6	7	8	9	10	11
# hyper-windows	2548	874	139	38	534	55	59	34
Fund. freq. (Hz)	12	13	14	15	16	19	20	...
# hyper-windows	18	15	7	**2582**	46	9	13	...

We split the labeled hyper-window with length T'_F into multiple prediction windows. Only the prediction windows which have samples with value greater than RSSI_THRESHOLD are chosen and labeled as *Interference #3*. We put these new labeled data into training data. Other data are left unlabeled and will be used in later semi-supervised learning.

Finally, this auto-labeling process results in the initial training data, each in a length of a detection window, with four different labels. It's necessary to balance the amount of training data for each class before training.

One may ask why not apply the same labeling technique to the test samples without learning process. The main reason for using deep learning is that FFT can only find the typical patterns of these interference source. There are large number of unlabeled data due to FFT resolution errors, non-ideal RSSI patterns, or mixed scenarios in a hyper-window. These data cannot be solved by using FFT alone. Besides, most labeled data are actually *Normal*. Semi-supervised learning is used to utilize larger amounts of unsupervised labels, specifically non-normal labels to improve the accuracy.

B. Semi-supervised Learning

When auto-labeling is done, there are data left unlabeled. To make use of unlabeled data for training as well, each unlabeled hyper-window is partitioned into multiple windows in 20ms. We use a conventional semi-supervised learning algorithm – self-training – to learn the deep model [17]. The basic procedure is shown in Figure 4. We first train a deep model using labeled data, then predict on unlabeled data and get a classification output. After each prediction, we add the wanted input-output pair to the labeled data to form a new set of training data and then train again until all unlabeled data are checked.

Slightly different from Figure 4, in real implementation, unlabeled data are put into iteration in batches for higher efficiency. A final deep model can be achieved in the end. By using semi-supervised learning, the training data amount has been increased from 70,000+ to 100,000+.

C. Convolutional Neural Network

Convolutional Neural Network (CNN) is used in the semi-supervised deep learning since it is applicable to array data where nearby values are correlated, and it greatly reduces number of parameters for deep networks. CNN performs feature learning via non-linear transformations implemented as a series of nested layers. The raw RSSI samples organized into data vectors are pipelined as input for classification. Traditionally CNN is used mostly for 2-dimensional inputs, such as in image recognition. In our case we just use one dimension – a vector – as input. This can be considered as a special case and the other properties for the network remain the same.

The goal of deep learning or more generally, machine learning is to find a mathematical function f, that defines the relation between a set of inputs $\mathbf{X}$, and a set of outputs $\mathbf{Y}$, i.e.

$$f : \mathbf{X} \rightarrow \mathbf{Y} \quad (1)$$

The inputs, $\mathbf{X} = [\mathbf{x}_1, \mathbf{x}_2, ..., \mathbf{x}_K]^T$, present a number of distinct data points, samples or observations, where K is the sample size, while $\mathbf{x}_i$ is a vector of N measurements of features for the ith observation called a feature vector. $\mathbf{x}_i = [x_{i1}, x_{i2}, ..., x_{iN}]^T, i = 1, ..., K$. The outputs, $\mathbf{y}$, are all the outcomes, labels, or target values corresponding to the K inputs $\mathbf{x}_i$, denoted by $\mathbf{y} = [y_1, y_2, ..., y_K]^T$. Then the observed data consists of K input-output pairs, called the training data or training set $\mathbf{S}$.

We use three main types of layers to build CNN architectures: convolutional layer, pooling layer, and fully-connected (FC) layer (exactly as seen in regular neural networks). After investigation on relevant literatures and numerous experiments, we have settled with LeNet model, a CNN with two convolutional layers [18]. The configurations for the network architecture are given in Figure 5, with a 210-element vector as input and a 4-class output. The last FC layer $[4 \times 1]$

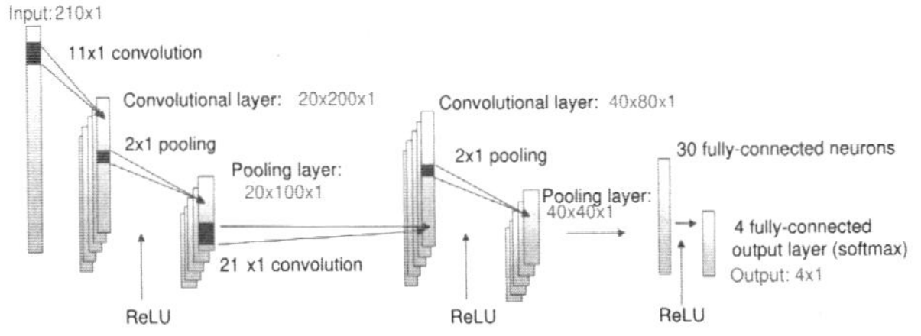

Figure 5. CNN architecture.

will compute the class scores where each of the 4 numbers corresponds to a class score, among the 4 types of classes. The very last layer is a Softmax classifier, which computes the *posterior* probability of each class label over 4 classes as

$$\hat{y_i} = \frac{e_i^z}{\sum_{j=1}^{4} e_j^z}, i = 1, ..., 4 \tag{2}$$

That is, the scores z_i computed at the output layer are translated into probabilities.

A cost function, C, is calculated on the last fully-connected layer that measures the difference between the estimated probability vector, $\hat{\mathbf{y}}_i$, and the index encoding of the true class label, y_i. The CNN parameters, Θ, are obtained by minimizing the cost function on the training set $\{\mathbf{x}_i, y_i\}_{i\in\mathbf{S}}$ of size K,

$$\min_{\Theta} \sum_{i\in\mathbf{S}} C(\hat{\mathbf{y}}_i, y_i) \tag{3}$$

where $C(\hat{\mathbf{y}}_i, y_i) \equiv -\ln(\hat{\mathbf{y}}_i[y_i])$ is the negative log-likelihood cost function. Note that $\hat{\mathbf{y}}_i[y_i]$ means the y_i-th element of the vector $\hat{\mathbf{y}}_i$.

All the RSSI samples are normalized to range [-1, 1] as CNN inputs. In the training process, stochastic gradient descent (SGD) is used with backpropagation with a mini-batch size of 500 and a learning rate 0.1, as well as L2 regularization to avoid overfitting.

One advantage of this framework is that our data inputs for learning and testing do not need feature extraction as most prior arts do. Feature extraction may have a chance to lose some hidden features in the data. We use raw RSSI samples as input so that all information is conveyed to deep learning.

IV. RESULTS

We have implemented the off-line training on a Linux based server, and an online realtime detection system with a RPi, a ZigBee sampler, and a GUI on a PC.

With regard to the implementation on the off-line training, Python 2.7 in combination with computation library Theano 0.9 is utilized. The CNN is trained and validated on a high computation platform with 24-core CPU Intel(R) Xeon(R) E5-2620 v2 @ 2.10GHz, with 128GB RAM and the Cuda enabled GPU Nvidia Tesla K80.

When the model is trained, the calculation for classifying a test instance into one of the classes is very fast since each test instance needs to be compared against the pre-computed model. The computation time for a single test data is around 8ms on RPi. If test data are input to the classifier in batches the average computation speed will be even faster. Therefore, the RSSI samples can be fed into the trained CNN model to get the diagnosis result in realtime with a RPi.

To evaluate proposed interference source identification scheme, extensive experiments are conducted in a factory for several days. Test data and training data are collected at different time to reduce the dependency of the data. The RPi is used as a sample data collector, as well as a predictor during online test phase. This system basically only consists of 'listening' radio devices, which do not interfere with the current wireless communication system.

Due to security and other reasons, any change of the operating machines or change of the wireless system in the field is not allowed. This leads to the difficulty to obtain the ground truth of the environment. Nevertheless we have randomly picked some RSSI traces from different times and checked with the prediction result using human's knowledge, and the detailed prediction results (%) are compared with observed results in Table III. As introduced in Section III-A, three types of interference sources are: *Interference #1* – magnetron with 50Hz frequency cycle, *Interference #2* – magnetron with 100Hz frequency cycle, *Interference #3* – wireless communication signal. Note that some RSSI patterns are unidentifiable by humans, so there is an additional observed class named *Unknown*.

TABLE III. THE CONFUSION MATRIX OF IDENTIFIED CLASSES

Observed class	Predicted class (%): *Normal*	*Intf. #1*	*Intf. #2*	*Intf. #3*
Normal	**100**	0	0	0
Intf. #1	0	**100**	0	0
Intf. #2	1.3	16.4	**82.3**	0
Intf. #3	15.8	10.5	0	**73.7**
Unknown	25.5	16.4	58.2	0

The predictions for selected time periods are plotted in Figure 6 with each plot having a duration of about 12 minutes. The ratio of outputs for each of the 4 classes is calculated every 10 seconds. Only ratios of non-*Normal* results are plotted in colored bars. Predictions for different time periods from two days are compared. In early morning (6:00~6:12), the predictions of all interference types are low for both days. During 10:00~10:27, probability of *Interference #2* increases for some time on both days. Around noon (12:30~12:42), predictions for *Interference #1* become dominant and show a very high probability for both days. In the afternoon (17:00~17:12), the predictions for interference decrease while the results for Day1 and Day2 are slightly different.

Generally, the magnetron cycle is a combination effect of the machine model, AC (alternating current) power cycle, transformer type, switching type, inverter type, etc. This prediction can help manage, locate, or mitigate interference caused by magnetron leakage or wireless systems in deployment scenarios.

V. CONCLUSION

In this paper, we collect extensive sample data from a factory to study the RSSI trace patterns which are sampled by IEEE 802.15.4 nodes for different interference sources. A semi-supervised deep learning utilizing RSSI samples is

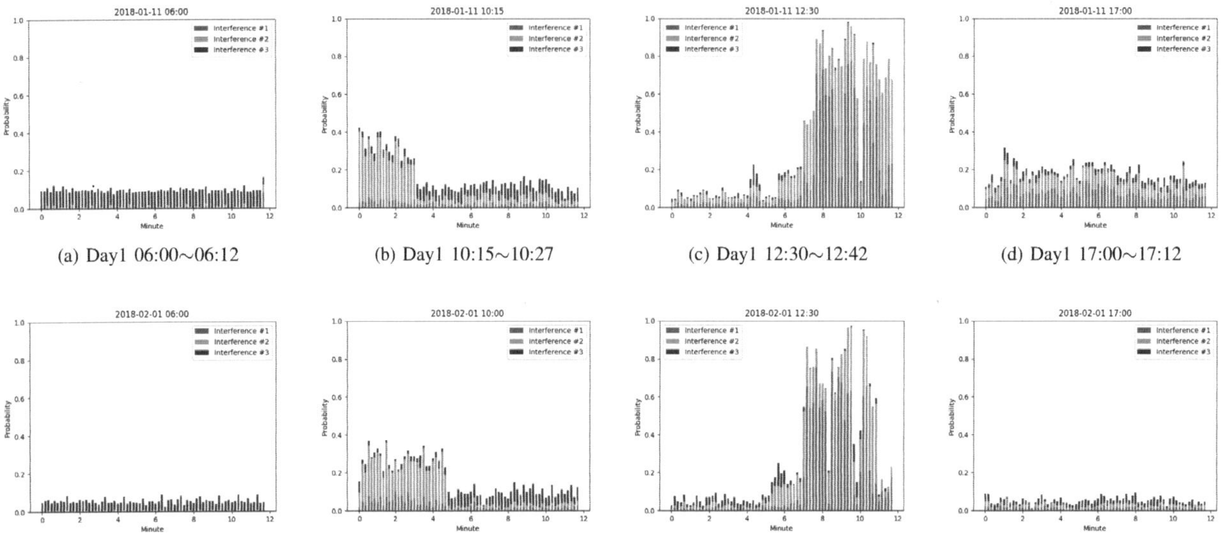

(a) Day1 06:00∼06:12 (b) Day1 10:15∼10:27 (c) Day1 12:30∼12:42 (d) Day1 17:00∼17:12

(e) Day2 06:00∼06:12 (f) Day2 10:00∼10:12 (g) Day2 12:30∼12:42 (h) Day2 17:00∼17:12

Figure 6. Selected predictions on factory data.

proposed to infer the interference type. Automatic labeling of training data is achieved taking advantage of the periodicity of the interference patterns. Sample collection and the classification algorithm are implemented on RPi 3 to monitor the wireless channel condition in a realtime fashion. Compared with the spectral data from a spectral analyzer, RSSI samples on the working channel are much easier to obtain.

The training procedure has to be performed when used in different environments and must be validated in the field to become a viable option as a classifier. This interference source identification scheme opens up numerous other possibilities. There can be a dedicated device or it can be embedded in a sensor to do external interference avoidance mechanisms based on the input from the sampling. Finally, the classification result of a channel is not only informative, but can be used to adapt the transmit parameters. Thus, an interference-aware communication protocol that adapts its parameters to the class of interference is a potential application for this algorithm. Further validation of these prediction results in a factory deployment and how to utilize these results remain for our future research.

ACKNOWLEDGMENT

The authors would like to thank Yuki Nishiguchi, Ai Yano, Takeshi Ohtani, and Ryuichi Matsukura from Fujitsu Laboratories Ltd., Kawasaki, Japan for providing experimental data in factory and all the fruitful discussions on the topic.

REFERENCES

[1] IEEE Std 802.15.4-2015, "Part 15.4: Wireless medium access control (MAC) and physical layer (PHY) specifications for low-rate wireless personal area networks (WPANs)," 2015.

[2] S. Rayanchu, A. Patro, and S. Banerjee, "Airshark: Detecting non-WiFi RF devices using commodity WiFi hardware," in Proceedings of the 2011 ACM SIGCOMM conference on Internet measurement conference, Berlin, Germany, November 2011, pp. 137–154.

[3] F. Hermans, O. Rensfelt, L.-Å. Larzon, and P. Gunningberg, "A lightweight approach to online detection and classification of interference in 802.15.4-based sensor networks," ACM SIGBED Review – Special Issue on the 3rd International Workshop on Networks of Cooperating Objects (CONET), vol. 9, no. 3, July 2012, pp. 11–20.

[4] F. Hermans, O. Rensfelt, T. Voigt, E. Ngai, L.-Å. Nordén, and P. Gunningberg, "SoNIC: Classifying interference in 802.15.4 sensor networks," in Proceedings of ACM/IEEE IPSN, Philadelphia, PA, USA, April 2013, pp. 55–66.

[5] K. Wu, H. Tan, H.-L. Ngan, Y. Liu, and L. M. Ni, "Chip error pattern analysis in ieee 802.15.4," IEEE Transactions on Mobile Computing, vol. 11, no. 4, April 2012, pp. 543–552.

[6] X. Zheng, Z. Cao, and J. Wang, "ZiSense: Towards interference resilient duty cycling in wireless sensor networks," in Proceedings of the 12th ACM Conference on Embedded Network Sensor Systems (SenSys), Memphis, TN, USA, November 2014, pp. 119–133.

[7] S. Zacharias, T. Newe, S. O'Keeffe, and E. Lewis, "Identifying sources of interference in rssi traces of a single ieee 802.15.4 channel," in Proceedings of the Eighth International Conference on Wireless and Mobile Communications (ICWMC), Venice, Italy, June 2012, pp. 408–414.

[8] ——, "A lightweight classification algorithm for external sources of interference in ieee 802.15.4-based wireless sensor networks operating at the 2.4 GHz," International Journal of Distributed Sensor Networks, vol. 10, no. 9, August 2014, pp. 265–286.

[9] V. Iyer, F. Hermans, and T. Voigt, "Detecting and avoiding multiple sources of interference in the 2.4 GHz spectrum," EWSN 2015, LNCS, vol. 8965, 2015, pp. 35–51.

[10] M. Schmidt, D. Block, and U. Meier, "Wireless interference identification with convolutional neural networks," CoRR, 2017. [Online]. Available: http://arxiv.org/abs/1703.00737

[11] K. Longi, T. Pulkkinen, and A. Klami, "Semi-supervised convolutional neural networks for identifying Wi-Fi interference sources," in Proceedings of the Ninth Asian Conference on Machine Learning, ser. PMLR 77, Seoul, Korea, November 2017, pp. 391–406.

[12] M. Kulin, T. Kazaz, I. Moerman, and E. de Poorter, "End-to-end learning from spectrum data: A deep learning approach for wireless

signal identification in spectrum monitoring applications," IEEE Access, March 2018, pp. 18 484–18 501.

[13] S. Yi et al., "Machine learning based channel error diagnostics in wireless sensor networks," in Proceedings of IEEE VTC Spring, Sydney, Australia, June 2017, pp. 1–5.

[14] S. Yi et al., "Interference source identification for ieee 802.15.4 wireless sensor networks using deep learning," in Proceedings of IEEE PIMRC, Bologna, Italy, September 2018, pp. 1–7.

[15] J. Chilo, C. Karlsson, P. Ängskog, and P. Stenumgaard, "EMI disruptive effect on wireless industrial communication systems in a paper plant," in Proceedings of IEEE International Symposium on Electromagnetic Compatibility (EMC), Austin, TX, USA, August 2009, pp. 221–224.

[16] M. A. Nielsen, Neural Networks and Deep Learning. Determination Press, 2015.

[17] X. Zhu, "Semi-supervised learning tutorial," in Tutorial of International Conference on Machine Learning (ICML), Corvallis, OR, USA, June 2007.

[18] Y. Lecun, L. Bottou, Y. Bengio, and P. Haffner, "Gradient-based learning applied to document recognition," Proceedings of the IEEE, vol. 86, no. 11, November 1998, pp. 2278–2324.

Performance Evaluation of Named Data Networking Based Ad Hoc Network Focusing on Node Moving

Ngo Quang Minh, Ryo Yamamoto, Satoshi Ohzahata, and Toshihiko Kato
University of Electro-Communications, Tokyo, Japan
e-mail: mingus@net.lab.uec.ac.jp, ryo-yamamoto@uec.ac.jp, ohzahata@is.uec.ac.jp, kato@is.uec.ac.jp

***Abstract*—We have been studying on applying the named data networking technology to mobile ad hoc networks. We suppose a type of ad hoc networks that advertise versatile information in public spaces such as shopping mall and museum. The proposed approach is a hybrid one where a proactive routing is used in the producer side network, and a reactive routing is used in the consumer side network. The proactive routing here has a feature that only the name prefix advertisement is focused on. In the reactive routing, only the first Interest packet is flooded and the corresponding Data packet creates a routing entry. Although we reported some results of the performance evaluation of the proposed method previously, they are still insufficient. In this paper, we show the results of performance evaluation focusing on the node moving in the consumer side network. The results indicate that our proposal has little overhead both for Interest packet transfer and routing control.**

Keywords- Ad Hoc Network; Named Data Networking; Hybrid Routing; Proactive Routing; Reactive Routing.

I. INTRODUCTION

Recently, the Information Centric Network (ICN) is widely studied as a future Internet architecture well suited for large scale content distribution. The Named Data Networking (NDN) [1] is adopted widely as a platform for ICN research activities. The fundamental concept in NDN is the name of required content, not the address of hosts containing content. A consumer requesting a content sends an Interest packet containing the content name. A producer providing the corresponding content data returns a Data packet to the consumer. NDN routers transferring the Data packet cache the packet for future redistribution.

Originally, NDN is designed for wired network topology, but it can be effectively applied to wireless multi-hop ad hoc network topology. In wireless ad hoc network, the routing mechanism is more important research topic than wired fixed network, because network nodes move around. In NDN, the purpose of routing is how to construct Forwarding Information Base (FIB) for name prefixes, which specifies the correspondence between a name prefix and an interface called face (or a neighbor identifier) to the content with this name prefix.

In the previous papers, we proposed a new NDN ad hoc routing scheme [2][3], which is targeting at ad hoc networks providing various useful information in public spaces, such as station, shopping mall and museum. Content providers advertise helpful information for users, such as location map, advertising catalog, and exhibition details. The proposed scheme adopts a hybrid approach, which has the following features. First, in the type of ad hoc networks we suppose, a content producer side has a stable network where producers and intermediate routers are located in fixed positions. On the other hand, consumers are mobile nodes which change their locations quite often. Therefore, a proactive routing is adopted in a producer side network, because of its in-advance route setting, and a reactive routing is adopted in a consumer side network, because of its flexibility for mobility. The second is about the procedure of proactive routing. The NDN proactive routing procedures proposed so far [4]-[8] are focusing on advertising both the network topology and the name prefix. On the other hand, the proactive routing adopted in our proposal is focusing on just the name prefix advertisement. The third is about the procedure of reactive routing. The reactive routing of our proposal uses both FIB and PIT. Although the first Interest packet for a specific name prefix is flooded, the corresponding FIB entry is created by the returning Data packet and the following Interest packets for the name prefix are transferred by this FIB entry.

Although the basic idea was presented in our previous papers, the performance evaluation results described in those papers and another paper [9] are limited, because they only provide rather simple theoretical analysis and do not evaluate detailed behaviors of routing protocols.

This paper describes the detailed results of the performance evaluation for the routing control and Interest transfer overheads focusing on moving consumer side nodes. The performance evaluation is conducted with ndnSIM [10], a widely used NDN simulator implemented over the ns-3 network simulator [11]. The rest of this paper consists of the following sections. Section 2 shows the related work on NDN routing. Section 3 describes our NDN ad hoc routing protocol. Section 4 shows the implementation of the proposed protocol over ndnSIM and the results of the performance evaluation. Section 5 concludes this paper.

II. RELATED WORK ON NDN ROUTING

There are several proposals on the routing in NDN. For the wired NDN topology, the proposed named OSPFN [4] and NSLR [5] are examples introduced in an early stage. Both of them are based on the link state routing protocol, which maintains and advertises link statuses between neighbors, shares the topology information, and creates routing tables from it. The protocol in [6] is a relatively new proposal based on the link state routing considering multipath routing.

In the case of the NDN based wireless ad hoc network, both the proactive and the reactive approaches are proposed [12]. This trend is the same as the IP based ad hoc network. MobileCCN [7] and TOP-CCN [8] are examples of the proactive routing mechanism. MobileCCN can be said an

NDN version of Routing Information Protocol (RIP) [13]. TOP-CCN is an NDN version of Optimized Link State Routing (OLSR) [14]. On the other hand, E-CHANET [15] and REMIF [16] are examples of reactive routing mechanism, which are designed based on Ad Hoc On-Demand Distance Vector routing (AODV) [17]. In these reactive routing mechanisms, FIB is not used at all, but Interest packets are flooded to find producers or cached Data packets. Only Pending Interest Table (PIT) is used for forwarding Data packets.

The proactive routing can create FIB responding to an up-to-date network topology, but has some overhead of routing control message exchange. On the contrary, the reactive routing has no overhead of routing, but has some overhead of Interest packet transfer.

III. HYBRID ROUTING PROTOCOL FOR NDN AD HOC NETWORK

A. *Overview of Proposed Routing Protocol*

We have adopted the following design principles for our hybrid NDN based routing mechanism.

- As described above, we divide a whole NDN network into the producer side and the consumer side. In the producer side, NDN nodes including producers and intermediate routers have their location fixed. So, a proactive routing mechanism is introduced in this part. On the other hand, the consumer side includes mobile nodes working as consumers or intermediate routers. Those nodes move around and the network configuration often changes. In this part, a reactive routing mechanism is introduced.
- For the producer side, our proactive routing focuses only on name prefix advertisement. It constructs a Directed Acyclic Graph (DAG) starting from each producer. An FIB entry for a specific name prefix is given by pointing upstream nodes traversing the corresponding DAG in a reverse direction. If there are more than one upstream nodes, both of them are registered in the entry and used for multipath forwarding [18].
- In order to create a DAG for a specific name prefix, the corresponding producer issues a *Name Prefix Announcement Request* (*NPAreq*) packet. It is broadcasted, and if any receiving NDN nodes are on the corresponding DAG, they return a *Name Prefix Announcement Reply* (*NPArep*) packet by unicast.
- As for the consumer side, NDN nodes do not use any control packets for routing. Instead, the FIB entry is created by the first Interest packet for a name prefix. The first Interest packet is flooded throughout the consumer side, and after it reaches some node in the producer side, this Interest packet is transferred to the producer. When the corresponding Data packet returned, a temporary FIB entry is created at the nodes in consumer side. For the following Interest packets for the same name prefix, this FIB entry is used.

B. *Communication Sequence of Proposed Protocol*

Figure 1 shows an example of communication sequence of the proposed protocol focusing on the consumer side behavior. Figure 1(a) is an example network, where the producer side nodes construct a DAG whose root is producer *node 2*. As shown in Figure 1(b), when consumer *node p* starts the content retrieval for name prefix *name*, the first Interest packet is flooded among the consumer side nodes. The Interest packet arriving at *node 6* is transferred according to the DAG, via *node 5* to *node 2*. When the corresponding Data packet returns, the corresponding FIB entry is created at *nodes q* and *p*. The following Interest packets will be transferred using these FIB entries.

IV. PERFORMANCE EVALUATION

In this section, we describe the results of performance evaluation using the ndnSIM simulator version 1.0.

A. *Simulation conditions*

Figure 2 shows the network configuration used in the simulation. In the fields of 300 m by 200 m, four producer side nodes are located in a grid configuration with 100 m distance. The location of these nodes are fixed through a simulation. In addition, ten consumer side nodes are deployed

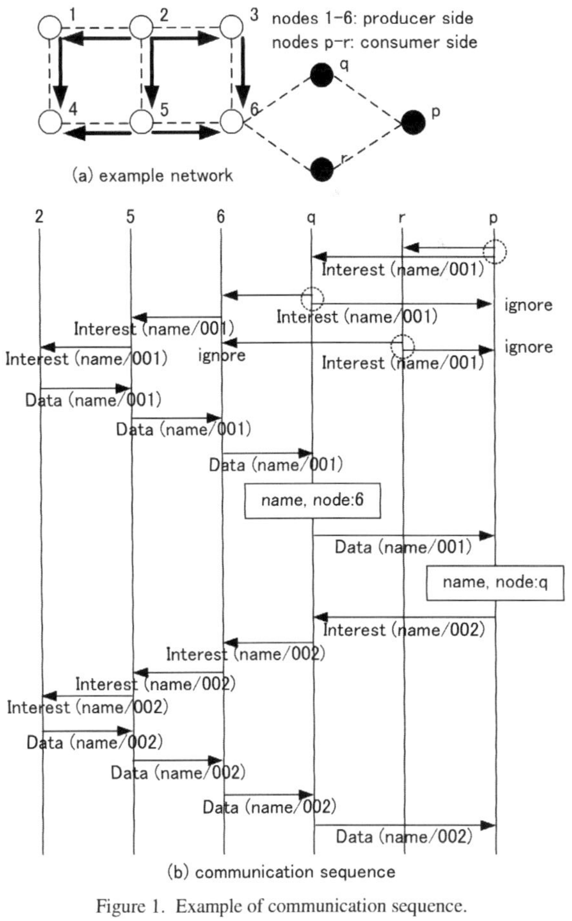

Figure 1. Example of communication sequence.

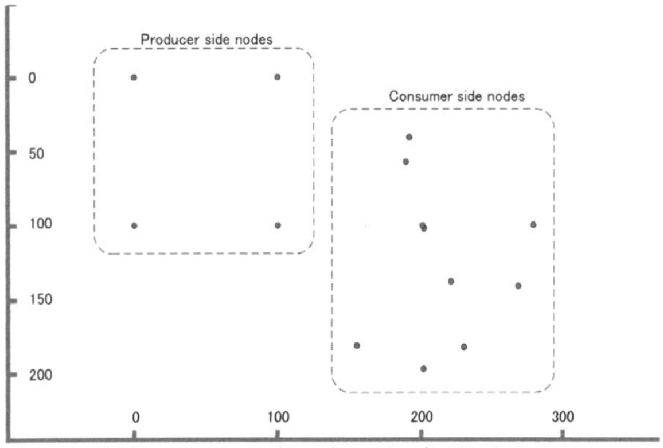

Figure 2. Network configuration for simulation.

TABLE I. SIMULATION PARAMETERS.

Radio propagarion	constant speed propagation delay model; three log distance / Nakagami propagation loss model
Wifi data mode	OFDM rate 24 Mbps
Mobility model	Random work 2D model; course change at every 2 second; mobility speed = 40 m/s, 20 m/s, or 10 m/s
Consumer	Randomly selected two, four, six and eight nodes; request different content/the same content; 10.0 through 10.3 Interests/s
Producer	node at (0, 0); Data packet size = 1200 bytes
Cache size	1000 packets at each node
Evaluation	15 seconds for each simulation run; 10 seconds for Interest packet origination, and 5 seconds just for timeout retransmission

randomly with the center of (200, 100). These nodes move around according to a random walk model. All nodes communicate with each other through ad hoc mode IEEE 802.11a protocol.

The details of simulation condition are given in Table I. As for the radio propagation, we used a setting used commonly in the ns-3 simulator. The data rate in IEEE 802.11a is 24 Mbps constant. The consumer side nodes move around according to the 2 dimensional random walk model with the constant mobility speed, where nodes change their direction at every 2 second. We adopted the mobility speed of 40 m/s, 20 m/s, and 10 m/s. Those values are large as a moving speed of human, but they are adopted for changing the wireless connection during a 15 second simulation run. Among the producer side nodes, the node located at the position (0, 0) works as a producer. As for the consumer side, two, four, six, or eight nodes work as consumers requesting different content or the same content. If each consumer requests different content, the Data packet caching is not effective in the simulation. If the same content is used for all consumers, the caching will be used effectively.

B. Evaluated methods and their implementation details

The methods evaluated in this paper are the proposed method, REMIF (simplified version), and NDN over UDP/IP ad hoc network with OLSR routing (OLSR based NDN). OLSR based NDN is used in order to estimate the performance of TOP-CCN, because the exchange of Hello and TC (Topology Control) messages corresponds to that of CA packets in TOP-CCN. On the other hand, OLSR based NDN uses the IP based routing in intermediate nodes as shown in our previous paper [19], and even if all consumers request the same content, the Data packet caching is not effective. So, when the same content is used, OLSR based NDN can be used to estimate an IP based ad hoc network.

The following describe the details of the implementation of three evaluated methods.

(1) REMIF

FIB is not specified, and Interest packets are always transferred with the destination address set to broadcast MAC address ("ff:ff:ff:ff:ff:ff"). On the other hand, PIT is used for returning Data packets to consumers. When a new Interest packet is received, the incoming face and the source MAC address of the Interest packet is stored in a new PIT entry. Since it is possible that the identical Interest packet is received via a different path, the duplication is detected by the Interest nonce stored in this PIT entry. A retransmitted Interest packet from a consumer contains the same nonce as the original Interest packet. In order to handle retransmitted Interest packets properly, a PIT entry for which a Data packet is not returned needs to be discarded when its lifetime expires. The lifetime of a PIT entry is set to the lifetime of Interest packet, 500 msec in this evaluation.

Since REMIF uses the broadcast in transmitting Interest packets, we observed a mis-ordering problem. The details are described in our previous papers [9][19]. In order to avoid this problem, we took the following way. In the PIT handling in the *ForwardingStrategy* class, when a Data packet is received, the records for incoming faces and outgoing faces are cleared, and then the PIT entry is erased by setting the PIT entry pruning timer. In the default, this value is set to 0 and the PIT entry is removed instantly. In this evaluation, we set this timer value to 50 msec. This means that our implementation ignores duplicate Interest packets received during 50 msec from the Data packet handling.

(2) Proposed method

In the performance evaluation here, we focus on the protocol behavior and the routing overhead when consumer side nodes move around. So, as for the routing protocols for producer side nodes, we set the FIB by hand before simulation runs start.

We implemented the FIB handling behavior in consumer side nodes by extending the REMIF program described above. At first, when a consumer side node receives an Interest packet, it looks for an FIB entry matching the name prefix included in the Interest packet. If there are no entries, it creates a new entry for the name prefix with the default face and the broadcast MAC address. A consumer side node transmits s the received Interest packet according to the corresponding FIB entry.

When a consumer side node receives a Data packet, it registers the face from which the packet is received and the source MAC address of the data frame containing the Data packet in the corresponding FIB entry, if the MAC address in the entry is the broadcast MAC address.

When the network configuration of consumer side nodes changes, the FIB needs to be reconstructed. We implemented this mechanism in the following way.

- In order to detect the route change in consumer side nodes, we use the PIT entry pruning timer described above. When this timer is expired, the incoming and outgoing faces in the PIT entry examined. If they remain in the entry, we can decide that the Data packet corresponding to an Interest packet is not returned. These checks are executed in the PIT related class (the *PitImpl* class, specifically).
- If this timeout occurs consecutively (three times in our implementation), we decide that the route change occurs. Then, the outgoing face in the PIT entry is checked and, if the outgoing face has a unicast MAC address, the routine for clearing FIB entry in the *ForwardingStrategy* class is called.
- In the clearing FIB entry routine, the MAC address is set to the broadcast MAC address.

(3) OLSR based NDN

The OLSR based NDN method is implemented the approach using the TCP/IP protocol stack under NDN. We can use the *OlsrHelper* class supported in the ns-3 simulator and the *IpFaceHelper* supported in the ndnSIM simulator. It should be noted that the calling of "Bing()" in the "*CreateOrGetUdpFace*()" method in the *IpFaceStack* class needs to be commented out, in ndnSIM version 1.0.

C. Evaluation results

(1) Overview

We conducted three kinds of performance evaluation. The first is that using two consumers by changing the mobility speed. The second is that changing the number of consumers from two to eight with 20 m/s mobility speed. In these evaluations, individual consumers retrieve their own content, that is, no cache mechanisms are used. The third one is that where all consumers request the same content. In this case, cache mechanism is effective for REMIF and the proposed method. The conditions of the third evaluation is similar with that of the second evaluation.

In the evaluation for REMIF and the proposed method, we evaluated the following features, by changing the mobility speed of consumer side nodes or the number of consumers:

- the total number of Interest packets originated from consumers,
- the total number of Interest packets actually sent from consumers (including retransmissions),
- the total number of Data packets consumers received,
- the total number of forwarded Interest packets by all nodes, and
- the total number of forwarded Data packets by all nodes.

In the evaluation for OLSR based NDN, we evaluated the following features:

- the total number of Interest packets originated from consumers,
- the total number of Interest packets actually sent from consumers (including retransmissions),
- the total number of Data packets consumers received, and
- the total number of Hello and TC messages used in OLSR.

As for the sending interval of Hello and TC messages, we selected 0.5 sec and 1 sec, respectively. In order to establish routing information in the evaluation of OLSR based NDN, we introduce 5 second period before starting the content retrieval. In other word, simulation runs for OLSR based NDN take 20 seconds, consisting of 5 seconds for routing information setting, 10 seconds for Interest packet origination, and 5 seconds for timeout retransmission.

(2) Results of evaluation by changing mobility speed

Figures 3 through 5 show the results of the first performance evaluation. In the following figures, we normalize the number of packets by the total number of Interest packets originated from consumers. By adopting this normalization, the number of Data packet received by consumers shows the data delivery ratio.

Figure 3 shows the total numbers of Interest and Data packets that consumers sent and received actually. The number of Interest packets is one through four times of that of the original Interest packets. The three methods have a similar tendency. Similarly, the number of Data packets that consumers received, i.e., the data delivery ratio, is 1 except the case of OLSR based NDN with 40 m/s speed, in which case the value is 0.99. With the 5 second retransition period, almost all Interest packets are satisfied by the corresponding Data packets.

Figure 4 shows the numbers of Interest and Data packets forwarded by all nodes in the network. Except the Interest packets in REMIF, the numbers are several times of the original Interest packets. The number of forwarded Interest packets in REMIF is more than twenty times of that of the original Interest packets.

Figure 5 shows the overhead of OLSR, i.e., the numbers of Hello and TC messages during the Interest origination and retransmission period. From this result, it can be said that the overhead of OLSR routing messages is not very large.

Those results with two consumers show that although the number of forwarded Interest packets in REMIF is large, the data delivery rate is high for three methods, and that the mobility speed examined here does not affect the performance so much.

(3) Results of evaluation by changing number of consumers

Figures 6 and 7 show the results of the second performance evaluation. Here, we changed the number of consumers, which request their own content, from two to eight. The mobility speed is set to 20 m/s. It should be noted that the vertical axis is logarithmic in those graphs.

Figure 6 shows the total numbers of Interest and Data packets that consumers sent and received actually. The proposed method and OLSR based NDN have a similar tendency, but the data delivery ratio is high for the proposed method. When there are eight consumers, the ratio of the proposed method is 0.85 and that of OLSR based NDN is 0.52. On the other hand, the performance of REMIF is worse than the others. In the case of eight consumers, the number of Interest packets actually sent by consumers goes to as high as

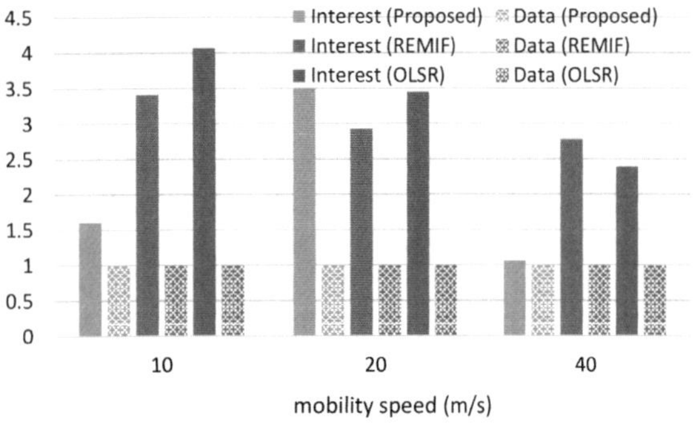

Figure 3. Numbers of Interest packets actually sent from consumers and Data packets received by consumers (normalized by originated Interests; changing mobility speed).

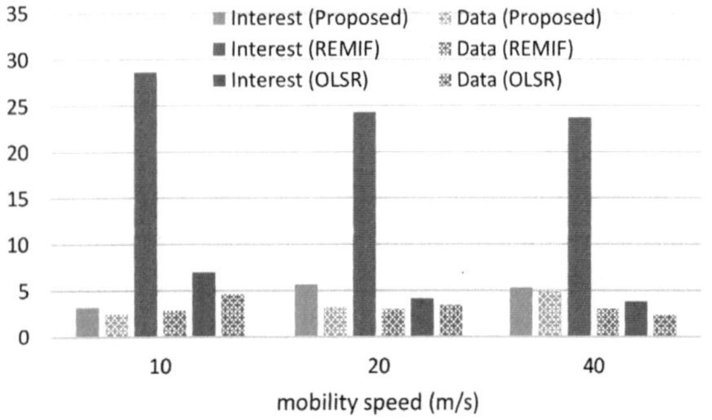

Figure 4. Numbers of Interest and Data packets forwarded by all nodes (normalized by originated Interests; changing mobility speed).

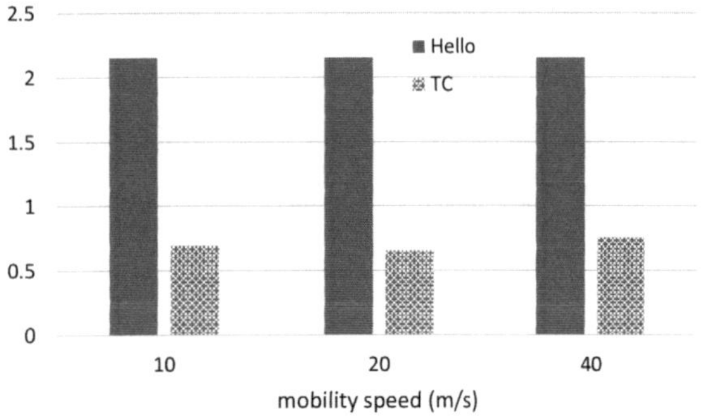

Figure 5. Numbers of OLSR Hello and TC messages (normalized by originated Interests; changing mobility speed).

32.7 times that of original Interest packets, and the data delivery ratio goes down to 0.27.

Figure 7, giving the total numbers of Interest and Data packets forwarded through the network, shows similar results. In the case of eight consumers, the total number of forwarded Interest packet is 242 times of the number of original Interest packets. The proposed method and OLSR based NDN also give similar tendency in this figure.

From the results with changing the number of consumers, it can be said that the performance of REMIF is worse than the others according to the increase of consumers requesting different content. It should be noted that the REMIF used in this paper is a simplified version, which does not include the

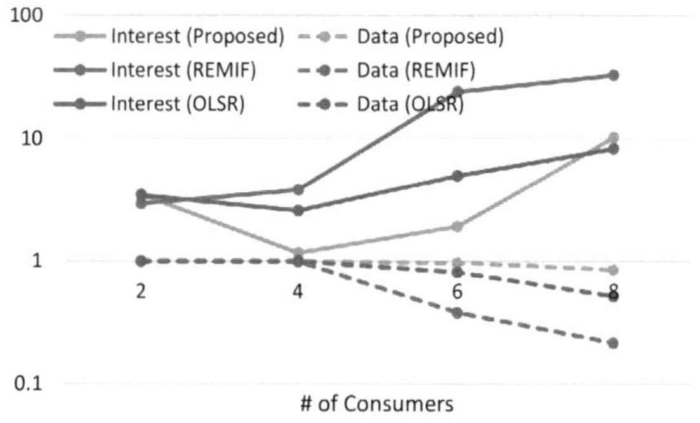

Figure 6. Numbers of Interest packets actually sent from consumers and Data packets received by consumers (normalized by originated Interests; changing number of consumers).

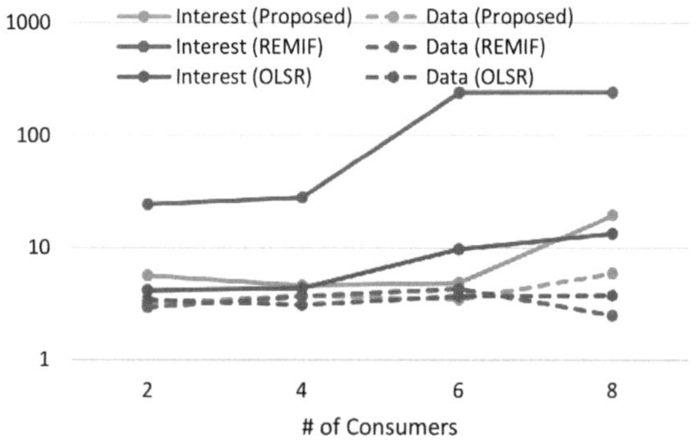

Figure 7. Numbers of Interest and Data packets forwarded by all nodes (normalized by originated Interests; changing number of consumers).

Interest suppression with deferring the Interest packet flooding randomly. But, we believe that the Interest flooding without FIB may be a problem when the number of consumers is large.

(4) Results of evaluation with Data packet caching

Figures 8 and 9 show the results of the third performance evaluation. Here, all consumers request the identical content, and therefore the Data packet cache is expected to work effectively. The cache size of each node is 1,000 packets and the other conditions are the same as in the second evaluation. As described in Section 4, the caching does not work in OLSR based NDN, and so, it indicates the performance of IP based ad hoc network in this evaluation.

Figure 8 shows the total numbers of Interest and Data packets that consumers sent and received actually. In this figure, the results of the proposed method and REMIF changed largely compared with Figure 6. The number of actually sent Interest packets is up to around twice of the original Interest packets. That of REMIF becomes less than 10 % of Figure 6 in the case of eight consumers. The data delivery ratio of the proposed method and REMIF is 1 through this evaluation. On the other hand, the result of OLSR based NDN is similar with that shown in Figure 6. In the case of eight consumers, the data delivery ratio is 0.59.

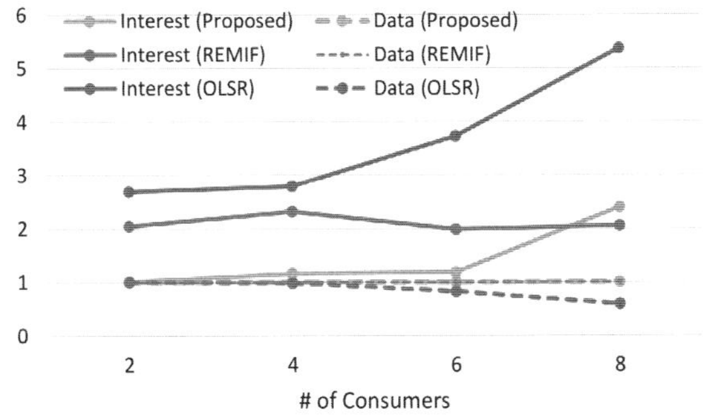

Figure 8. Numbers of Interest packets actually sent from consumers and Data packets received by consumers (normalized by originated Interests; consumers requesting same content).

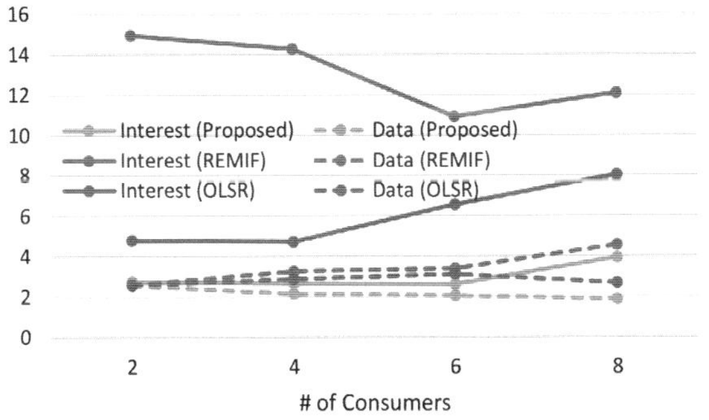

Figure 9. Numbers of Interest and Data packets forwarded by all nodes (normalized by originated Interests; consumers requesting same content).

Figure 9 shows the total numbers of Interest and Data packets forwarded through the network. In this figure, the result of REMIF changed largely from that in Figure 7, although the number of forwarded Interest packets is still largest among the three method. In the case of eight consumers, the number was 242 times of that of original Interest packets, but it decreases to 12 times when the caching works well.

From those results, it can be said that the Data packet caching can reduce the traffic largely and that the performance can be increased compared with IP based ad hoc network.

V. CONCLUSIONS

This paper showed three kinds of performance evaluation with mobile nodes which move around according to the random walk model. The results of the performance evaluation show the followings.

When the number of consumers is small, the proposed method, a simplified reactive routing (simplified REMIF), and a proactive routing (OLSR based NDN) have a similar data delivery ratio, although the number of flooded Interest packets is large in simplified REMIF. The mobility speed of consumer side nodes did not affect the delivery ratio so much. Secondly, when the number of consumers requesting different content increases, the performance, i.e., the data delivery ratio and the routing overhead, of REMIF becomes worse. The data delivery ratio of the proposed method is better than that of OLSR based NDN supposing TOP-CCN. Thirdly, when the Data packet caching works effectively, the performance of the proposed method and REMIF is improved largely. The OLSR based NDN, which does not use the caching and therefore emulates IP based ad hoc network, has poor data delivery ratio than NDN based method. So, it can be said that the data caching is effective.

REFERENCES

[1] V. Jacobson, et al., "Networking Named Content," Proc. of CoNEXT '09, pp.1-12, Dec. 2009.

[2] N. Minh, R. Yamamoto, S. Ohzahata, and T. Kato, "A Routing Protocol Proposal for NDN Based Ad Hoc Networks Combining Proactive and Reactive Routing Mechanism," Proc. of 13th Advanced International Conference on Telecommunications (AICT 2017), pp. 80-86, Jun. 2017.

[3] N. Minh, R. Yamamoto, S. Ohzahata, and T. Kato, "Proposal and Performance Analysis of Hybrid NDN Based Ad Hoc Routing Combining Proactive and Reactive Mechanisms," International Journal on Advances in Networks and Services, vol. 11, no. 1&2, pp. 1-10, Jul. 2018.

[4] L. Wang, A. Hoque, C. Yi, A. Alyyan, and B. Zhang, "OSPFN: An OSPF Based Routing Protocol for Named Data Networking," NDN, Technical Report NDN-0003, pp.1-15, Jul. 2012.

[5] A. Hoque, et al., "NLSR: Named-data Link State Routing Protocol," Proc. of ICN '13, pp.1-6, Aug. 2013.

[6] E. Hemmati and J. Garcia-Luna-Aceves, "A New Approach to Name-Based Link-State Routing for Information-Centric Networks," Proc. of ICN '15, pp.29-38, Sep. 2015.

[7] S. Yao, X. Zhang, F. Lao, and Z. Guo, "MobileCCN: Wireless Ad-hoc Content-centric Networks over SmartPhone," Proc. of ACM International Conference on Future Internet Tech. (CFI '13), pp.1-2, Jun. 2013.

[8] J. Kim, D. Shin, and Y. Ko, "TOP-CCN: Topology aware Content Centric Networking for Mobile Ad Hoc Networks," Proc. of ICON '13, pp.1-6, Dec. 2013.

[9] N. Minh, R. Yamamoto, S. Ohzahata, and T. Kato, "Performance Evaluation of MANET Based on Named Data Networking Using Hybrid Routing Mechanism," Proc. of 2nd International Conference on Information, Networks and Communications (ICINC 2019), pp. 1-7, Mar. 2019.

[10] A. Afanasyev, I. Moiseenko, and L. Zhang, "ndnSIM: NDN simulator for NS-3," NDN, Technical Report NDN-0005, pp. 1-7, Oct. 2012.

[11] "ns-3," https://www.nsnam.org/ [retrieved: Jun. 2019].

[12] X. Liu, Z. Li, P. Yang, and Y. Dong, "Information-centric mobile ad hoc networks and content routing: A survey," Ad Hoc Network, Available online, pp.1-14, Apr. 2016.

[13] G. Malkin, "RIP Version 2," IETF RFC 2453, Nov. 1998.

[14] T. Clausen and P. Jacquet, "Optimized Link State Routing Protocol (OLSR)", IETF RFC 3626, Oct. 2003.

[15] M. Amadeo, A. Molinaro, and G. Ruggeri, "E-CHANET: Routing, forwarding and transport in Information-Centric multihop wireless networks," Computer Communications, vol.36, pp. 792-803, 2013.

[16] R. Rehman, T. Hieu, and H. Bae, "Robust and Efficient Multipath Interest Forwarding for NDN-based MANETs," Proc. of WMNC '16, pp. 1-6, Jul. 2016.

[17] C. Perkins, E. Belding-Royer, and S. Das, "Ad hoc On-Demand Distance Vector (AODV) Routing," IETF RFC 3561, Jul. 2003.

[18] C. Yi, et al., "A Case for Stateful Forwarding Plane," NDN, Technical Report NDN-0002, pp. 1-16, 2012.

[19] T. Kato, N. Minh, R. Yamamoto, and S. Ohzahata, "How to Implement NDN MANET over ndnSIM Simulator," Proc. of IEEE ICCC 2018, pp. 451-456, Dec. 2018.

Securing Perception System of Autonomous Vehicle

Mariam Faied, Kevin Daimi, Samar Bayan
Department of Electrical and Computer Engineering, and Computer Science
University of Detroit Mercy
Detroit, Michigan, USA
Email: {faiedma, daimikj, bayansa}@udmercy.edu

***Abstract*—The sophisticated internal communication of the autonomous vehicle together with the various external communications will greatly increase the attack surface and widely open the door for even more security threats as compared to the non-autonomous vehicle. This requires further strict security measures and protection. This paper attempts to secure the communications within the Perception System. It aims to protect both the Environment and Location Perception modules. Both symmetric and asymmetric cryptography will be used depending on the size of the exchanged messages. Cryptographic protocols will be provided.**

Keywords*— *Autonomous vehicle; Cryptography; Perception system security; Security protocol.

I. INTRODUCTION

Vehicle accident statistics showed about six million average car accidents per year occurring in the United States [1]. Those that resulted in death were caused by driver's faults, such as alcohol drinking (40 %), speeding (30 %) and reckless driving (33 %). According to the National Highway Traffic Safety Administration (NHTSA), the financial cost of crashes reached 242 billion dollars in 2010 [2]. For this reason, scientists nowadays are more oriented towards how to minimize the role of the driver. As a result, it should be no surprise that the autonomous vehicle idea became a reality. The autonomous vehicles are divided into five levels of autonomy ranging from level 1 (low level driver assistance) to level 5 (full automation) [3]. The autonomous vehicle provides various benefits including reduced human stress, improved productivity and mobility, traffic safety, and reduced accidents costs [4]. In 2007, about six autonomous vehicles (level 3) completed 90 Km test drives [5]. The improvements resulting from these tests will definitely contribute to having even more autonomous vehicles on the roads during the years to come.

Autonomous vehicles are anticipated to provide safer transportation with well-planned techniques to avoid these large numbers of accidents. Undoubtedly, they will improve human safety and reduce the accident costs. The way that the autonomous vehicle functions could be compared to the way humans analyse the environmental signals. In other words, humans possess an action-perception reaction to the environment. This process is handled by three systems: the perception system (sensing the environment), the cognition system (analysing the data and making decisions) and finally the action system (implementing the decisions resulted from the cognitive system) [6]. An autonomous vehicle is supposed to function in a similar pattern.

The work of the autonomous vehicle is basically dependent on three technologies: the embedded processors, the sensors, and the communication systems [7]. The communication technologies can be categorized into inter- and intra-vehicle. The first category allows for outside communications and the second is defined by different communication techniques allowing data transmission within the vehicle [8]. These increased levels of communications of the autonomous vehicle make it more vulnerable to security attacks [9].

In the past, vehicles were initially made to be isolated mechanical devices [10]. This means that the attacks were targeted to a specific vehicle because every vehicle was operating independently. However, with the introduction of connected and autonomous vehicles, inter-vehicle communication increases the risk over multiple vehicles. Hence, part of autonomous vehicle safety relies in providing deterministic techniques to improve cybersecurity and prevent cyber-attacks. Physical safety is the other part of the autonomous vehicle's security which ensures that pedestrians and people in the vehicle are safe [11]. This is achieved through well-designed navigation algorithms.

The use of various processors and networks by autonomous vehicles opened the door wide for several possible vulnerabilities. These include spoofing, sender/receiver related errors, segmented network related errors, and communication corruption [12] – [15]. Weaknesses of the Control Area Network (CAN), such as the susceptibility to Denial of Service attacks (DoS), and the absence of authentication, contribute to the majority of these vulnerabilities. To avoid security attacks based on these vulnerabilities, security requirements should have been enforced prior to the actual design of these vehicles [16]. Message encryption techniques alone do not impose data integrity and confidentiality [17]. To help with the protection efforts, researchers have introduced a number of tools to enrich the security of data transmission in both inter-vehicle and intra-vehicle communications [18]. To this end, Schlatowe et al. [19] suggested relying on trust management and control. In a similar fashion, the use of polices to govern the access to these resources was proposed in [20]. Further attempts to enrich the security of the autonomous vehicles included relying on the tamper proof microkernel, proxy, and network stack to augment the security of the vehicle networks [21]. Others suggested adding more sensors to the autonomous vehicle to monitor the chips' performance to provide integrity and availability [22].

As detailed in Section II, the autonomous vehicle relies on three major components: Perception, Planning and Control Systems. This paper aims at securing the Location and Environment Perception subsystems of the Perception System. Both symmetric and asymmetric cryptography will be employed. The proposed security protocols will be discussed. The reminder of the paper is organized as follows. Section II briefly presents an overview of the autonomous vehicle. Section III introduces the proposed Perception

System Security (PSS), and Section IV gives the security requirements of the proposed protocol. Finally, the paper is concluded in Section V.

II. AUTONOMOUS VEHICLE OVERVIEW

Autonomous vehicles are intended to transport passengers to their destinations without any human interference. The function of an autonomous vehicle is modelled by three major systems: Perception, Planning and Control [8] [23]-[26]. These components are illustrated in Figure 1.

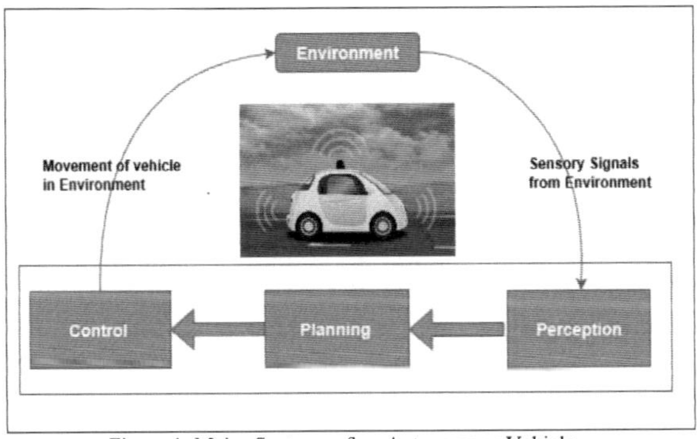

Figure 1. Major Systems of an Autonomous Vehicle.

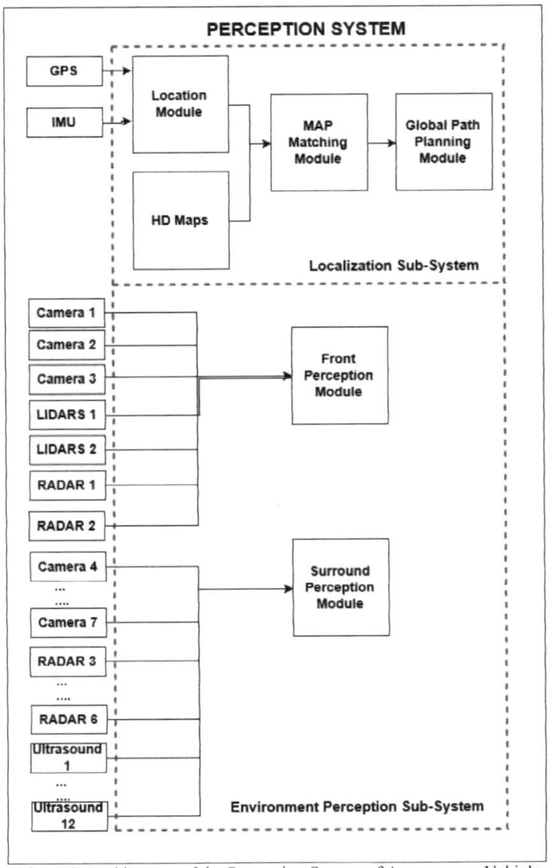

Figure 2. Architecture of the Perception System of Autonomous Vehicle.

The Perception System consists of the Localization and Environmental Perception Subsystems. The Environment Perception Subsystem collects information from the external environment to pilot the detection and identification of the vehicle surroundings. Its function is aided by four types of smart sensors: Camera, Light Detection and Ranging Device (LIDAR), Radio Detection and Ranging Device (Radar), and Ultrasound. Cameras execute detections of lane lines marking, road surface, and on-road objects. The LIDAR constructs a map of the environment to discover obstacles, and the Radar employs radio waves to detect obstacles. Together, LIDAR and Radar grant more accurate positioning of the obstacles on the road than each functioning alone. The Ultrasound Sensor perceives objects through ultrasound acoustic waves. The main purpose of the Perception Module is to blend data coming from the four sensors and prepare them for the next phase [24] [26].

The Localization Subsystem is in charge of determining the autonomous vehicle's position and planning the global path to the destination. An autonomous vehicle's location can be relative, absolute, or hybrid [23]. Relative location represents the location of the autonomous vehicle in relative to its initial position and the absolute location is determined by the Global Positioning System (GPS). The hybrid location refers to the combination of both relative and absolute locations for a more accurate position determination. This is the technique currently pursued in autonomous vehicles testing [23]. Once the hybrid location is identified by the Location Module, the Map Matching Module intermixes it with High Definition Mapping (HD). The HD map is a high resolution map [27] acting as a storage space within the Location Subsystem that saves various types of information including information about roads, traffic conditions, and traffic signs. This map is updated constantly by the manufacturers. Note that this reliance on high accurate maps stems from the fact that an autonomous vehicle operates precisely in 3D space [28]. The final step in the Localization Subsystem is carrying out global planning to the vehicle's final destination. The architecture of the overall perception system is illustrated in Figure 2.

The Planning System employs artificial intelligence to merge and analyse the data from the Environmental Perception Subsystem, Location Subsystem and the outer environment. It is similar to the way the cognitive system of human beings functions. Planning is divided into three stages: Mission Planning, Behavioural Planning, and Motion Planning. The mission planning is accomplished by implementing a search over the roads network connectivity. Behavioural planning deals with the behaviour of the autonomous vehicle based on road signs and traffic conditions, and the motion planning stamps the most important role that artificial intelligence plays in studying the local positioning and making decisions on driving the autonomous vehicle [26]. The control system of the autonomous vehicle receives decisions made by the planning system and implements them through many Electronic Control Units (ECUs) [8] [23]. An overall architecture of the autonomous vehicle is presented in Figure 3.

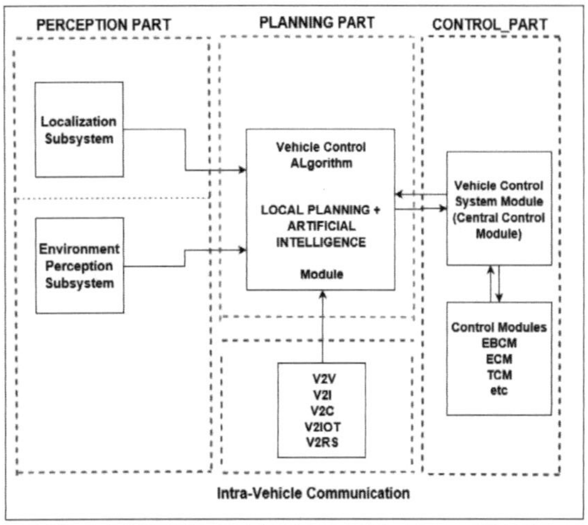

Figure 3. Overall Internal Architecture of Autonomous Vehicle.

III. PROPOSED PSS SECURITY APPROACH

The proposed security protocol will handle the communication between the components of the perception system in the autonomous vehicle. The perception system is made up of two subsystems: Location Subsystem and Environment Perception Subsystem. The parties involved in this protocol and the notations used are illustrated in Tables I and II. As mentioned above, the Environment Perception Subsystem includes the Camera, LIDAR, Radar, and Ultrasound sensors.

TABLE I. COMMUNICATION PARTIES

Party	Meaning
S_i	Environment Perception Sensors
GPS	Global Positioning System Module
IMU	Inertial Measurement Unit
iPM	Front/ Surround Perception Module
MMM	Map matching Module
LM	Location Module

TABLE II. NOTATION USED IN PROTOCOLS

Party	Meaning
PU_S, PR_S	Public and private keys of sender
PU_R, PR_R	Public and private keys of receiver
$PU_{S\text{-old}}$, $PR_{S\text{-old}}$	Old public/private key of sender
$PUR_{\text{-old}}$, $PRR_{\text{-old}}$	Old public/private key of receiver
K_{Old}	Old symmetric master key
K	Master key (symmetric)
K_{Sn}	Session key (symmetric)
$K_{Sn\text{-old}}$	Old session key (symmetric)
H	Hash
MAC	Message Authentication Code
K_{MAC}	MAC key
E	Encryption
D	Decryption
TS_i, where i=1 to 5	Time stamps
N_i	Nonce generated by sensor i
M_i	Message generated by sensor i
C	Cipher text

A. *Localization Subsystem Communication*

The communications between the modules in the Localization Subsystem of the Perception System (LSPS) are unidirectional (one-way communication). These include communication between GPS/IMU modules and the Location Module (LM), communication between the Location Module (LM) and the Map Matching Module (MMM), and communication between the Map Matching Module (MMM) and the Global Path Module (GPM).

In the GPS/IMU and LM communication, the GPS module sends the coordinates of the autonomous vehicle, known as GPS coordinates, to the Location Module. GPS coordinates represent unique identification of the location of the vehicle. They are expressed as a combination of latitude and longitude. GPS coordinates embody the absolute location of the autonomous vehicle. The IMU unit sends the velocity, altitude and the position of the vehicle. However, these represent the relative location of the autonomous vehicle. The LM will then calculate the hybrid location of the autonomous vehicle, which is the most accurate location based on the absolute and the relative locations. LM sends this hybrid location to the MMM. The MMM will match the location of the autonomous vehicle with the electronic map EM data. This matched location is sent to the GPM. The GPM is responsible for planning the global path from the starting point to the destination point. Hence, the message transmitted within the above three communications is converted into the real-time location of the autonomous vehicle. Table III lists the different types of messages that are exchanged between various components of the Location Subsystem in the Perception System. The exchanged messages, as represented in Table III, are small. This justifies the use of asymmetric encryption. In other words, since these messages are small, the communications within the Location Subsystem lead themselves efficiently to public key cryptography.

TABLE III. MESSAGES WITHIN LOCALIZATION SYSTEM

Operation	Message Type
GPS to LM	GPS coordinates (Absolute location)
IMU to LM	Altitude, Velocity (Relative location)
LM to MMM	Hybrid location
MMM to GPM	Hybrid location

Since the approach is similar for all of the above communications, this protocol will adopt S for sender and R for receiver. If LM is sending data to MMM, S is LM, and R is MMM, and if MMM is sending data to GPM, S is MMM, and R is GPM. The details of this protocol are presented below.

1) *Initialization and Key Distribution Stage*

Each component in the Location Subsystem has its own built-in public and private keys. In addition, components also have built-in public keys of the receivers. To clarify this, Figure 4 depicts the initialization phase once the vehicle starts. The built-in keys will be referred to as old keys because they will be replaced immediately with fresh new keys for security purposes. Therefore, 'old" will be added to suffix to denote that.

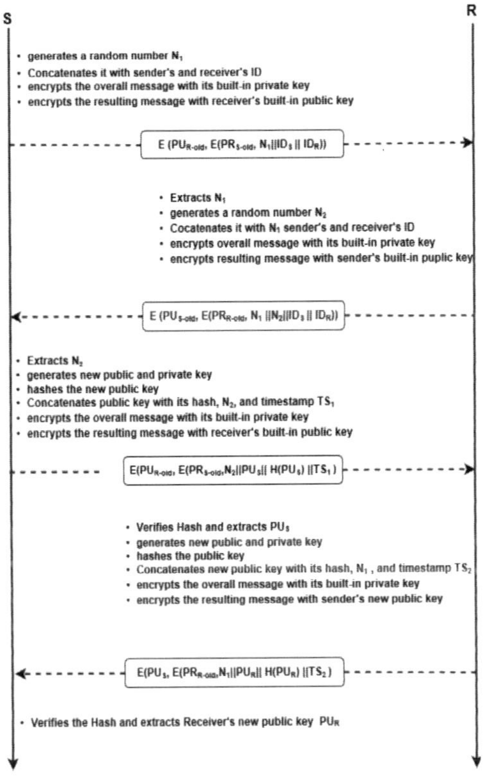

Figure 4. Initialization Stage of LSPS

The sender first generates a random number N_1, concatenates it with the ID of the receiver and its ID, encrypts the concatenated message with the built-in private key and then with the receiver's public key. This represents a request for communication. Note that || stands for concatenation.

$$S \rightarrow R: E\,(PU_{R\text{-old}}, E\,(PR_{S\text{-old}}, N_1 || ID_S || ID_R)) \quad (1)$$

$$\text{Let } X = E\,(PU_{R\text{-old}}, E\,(PR_{S\text{-old}}, N_1 || ID_S || ID_R)) \quad (2)$$

The receiver decrypts X with its private key. It then decrypts the resulting message with the sender's public key. This is done to extract the nonce N_1.

$$R: D\,(PU_{S\text{-old}}, D\,(PR_{R\text{-old}}, X)) = N_1 \;||\; ID_S \;||\; ID_R \quad (3)$$

The receiver generates its random number N_2 and concatenates it with N_1, ID_S, and ID_R. The resulting message is encrypted with its private key, then with the sender's public key to confirm the request received.

$$R \rightarrow S: E\,(PU_{S\text{-old}}, E\,(PR_{R\text{-old}}, N_1 || N_2 || ID_S || ID_R)) \quad (4)$$

Upon receiving the message, the sender decrypts it with its private key. The resulting message is then decrypted with the receiver's public key to get the concatenated nonce. The sender extracts the second nonce N_2 and generates its new public key (PU_S) and private key (PR_S). Furthermore, it concatenates the public key, hash of the public key, the time stamp TS_1, and the nonce N_2. The concatenated message is encrypted with its private key and then with the receiver's public key. Note that time stamp is used because S and R are synchronized.

$$S \rightarrow R: E\,(PU_{R\text{-old}}, E\,(PR_{S\text{-old}}, N_2 || PU_S || H(PU_S) || TS_1)) \quad (5)$$

The receiver decrypts the received message with its private key. It then decrypts it with the sender's public key. R then verifies the hash, ensure the time of the message is still valid, and extracts the sender's new public key (PU_S). The receiver follows the same procedure as the sender did to create its public (PU_R) and private (PR_R) and sends its new public key (PU_R) to the sender. It uses new time stamp TS_2.

$$R \rightarrow S: E\,(PU_S, E\,(PR_{R\text{-old}}, N_1 || PU_R || H(PU_R) || TS_2)) \quad (6)$$

The sender follows similar decryption steps to extract the receiver's new public key (PU_R).

2) LSPS Message Exchange

The sender first encrypts a message (Table III) with the receiver's public key and applies the hash function to the resulting message. Then, it encrypts it with its private key.

$$S \rightarrow R: E\,(PU_R, E\,(PR_S, M || H(M) || TS_3))) \quad (7)$$

The receiver, R, decrypts the received message with its private key. What is left from the original message is then decrypted with the sender's public key. The receiver, R, verifies the hash and the time, and extracts the message M. M could be the absolute location, relative location or hybrid location of the autonomous vehicle.

3) LSPS Keys Update

After exchanging a fixed number of messages or after a certain time, both parties will update their keys in a fashion similar to (1) above. The current key will be the old key.

B. Environment Perception Subsystem Communication

The protocol for the Environment Perception Subsystem of the Perception System (EPSPS) below is applied to the messages sent by perception sensors (Camera, LIDAR, Radar and Ultrasound) to the Perception Modules. There are two types of perception modules: Front Perception Module (FPM) and Surround Perception Module (SPM). The encryption details will be similar for both. For this reason, iPM will be used to refer to both.

The type of messages that are transmitted within the Environment Perception Subsystem depends on the smart sensor (LIDAR, Radar, Ultrasound or Camera) that sends the message. Table IV identifies the messages transmitted within this subsystem.

TABLE IV. MESSAGES WITHIN ENVIRONMENT PERCEPTION

Source	Message Type
Camera	Images
LIDAR, Radar, US	Vector of Distances to Obstacles

Since these messages are large, the communications within the Environment Perception Subsystem demands symmetric encryption. The protocol for these communications is as follows.

1) Initialization Stage

The components of the Environment Perception Subsystem have built-in master keys. They are preinstalled at manufacturing time. This means that the Front and Surround Perception Modules will have N built-in master keys, where N is the number of smart sensors connected to the Perception Module, whether front or surround perception module. Once the system becomes in service, the master keys need to be updated and the session keys need to be generated.

2) Master Key Management

The approach begins with a handshake procedure followed by key exchange. The detailed steps are represented in Figure 5.

Each smart sensor generates a nonce, N_1. This nonce with ID_{Si} and ID_{iPM} are encrypted with the old master key and sent to the corresponding perception module. Note that, initially, the old master key is the built in key. Once the new keys are created, the current keys will be old.

$S_i \rightarrow iPM: E(K_{old}, N_1 || ID_{Si} || ID_{iPM})$ (8)

The iPM confirms the request for communication. It generates another nonce, N_2, and concatenates it with N_1. The resulting value is encrypted with its master key.

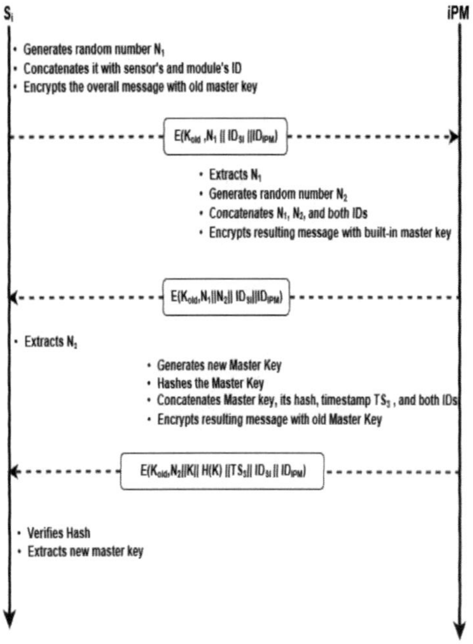

Figure 5. Initialization Stage of EPSPS

$iPM \rightarrow S_i: E(K_{old}, N_1 || N_2 || ID_{Si} || ID_{iPM})$ (9)

The smart sensor extracts the second nonce by decrypting the received message with the old master key. iPM then generates a new master key and concatenates it with the hash of this key, its nonce, N_2, and a time stamp. The resulting expression is encrypted its old master key.

$iPM \rightarrow S_i: E(K_{old}, K || H(K) || N_2 || TS_3 || ID_{Si} || ID_{iPM})$ (10)

The smart sensor decrypts the received message with the old master key, verifies the hash and time, and then extracts the new master key. The master key is changed periodically.

3) Session Key Generation

Once the master key is generated, the Perception Modules (whether front or surround) will generate the session key, concatenate it with its hash and time stamp, all encrypted with the old session key. The resulting message is encrypted with the master key.

$iPM \rightarrow S_i: E(K, E(K_{Sn\text{-}old}, K_{Sn} || H(K_{Sn}) || TS_4))$ (11)

The message is decrypted by the smart sensor using the master key. The resulting message is decrypted using the current session key. Having done that, the smart sensor then verifies the hash and extracts the new session key. The iPM then generates the MAC key, K_{MAC}.

4) EPSPS Message Exchange

The smart sensor generates the MAC of the message. It then concatenates the message, MAC of the message and the timestamp. The resulting message is encrypted with the session key and sent to the Perception Module.

$X = E(K_{Sn}, M_i || MAC(K_{MAC}, M_i) || TS_5 || ID_{Si} || ID_{iPM})$ (12)

$S_i \rightarrow iPM: X$ (13)

The received message (cipher text C) is decrypted using K_S. The result of this decryption represents the concatenation of the message, M_i, and its MAC, timestamp, ID_{Si}, and ID_{iPM}. The time stamp is checked to ensure that the message is current. The IDs are verified and the MAC of the message M_i is found and compared to the received MAC. If they are the same, the message will be considered by the Perception Module.

IV. Autonomous Vehicle Security Requirements

Within the LSPS, the message integrity is ensured through hashing the message. The hash typically provides integrity of the exchanged data. If the data is changed by even one bit, the hash will be invalid. This makes it hard for an attacker to disturb the data. To ensure that only the receiver will recover the exchanged message, messages are encrypted by the public key of the receiver to achieve confidentiality so that no one except the receiver can decrypt it. Message authentication is ensured by encrypting the overall result with the sender's private key. This authenticates the sender.

For the EPSPS, the message integrity and the authentication are enforced by applying the message authentication code. The use of the MAC confirms that the message received is coming from the sender without being modified [20]. Through this part of the protocol, symmetric key encryption guarantees the confidentiality of the message since no one, but the sender and receiver, know the symmetric key used within each session. Moreover, the use of the master key enhances the security level.

V. Conclusion

Autonomous vehicles are no more just ideas but are finding their way to implementation. The autonomous vehicle should be secured so that people can trust the use of these technologies. The autonomous vehicle is considered part of the Internet of Things (IoT). It works in a similar way to the human being, but with much more focus. Enforcing the security of the Perception System of the autonomous vehicle was the focus of this paper. Both Environmental Perception and Localization Subsystems were protected via cryptographical protocols to secure the data transmission within both subsystems of the perception system. The first subsystem, the Localization Module, consisted of short messages that caused the employment of public key cryptography, while the long messages of the Environment Perception Module necessitated private key cryptography.

This work concentrated on the security of the Perception System. Future work will include securing the Planning and Control Systems in addition to securing the communication between the three systems.

References

[1] Driver Knowledge, "Car Accidents in the United States," [Online]. Available: https://www.driverknowledge.com/car-accident-statistics/. Retrieved June 2019.

[2] N. H. T. S. Administration, "Traffic Safety Facts," Department of Transportation, United States, 2016, [online]. Available: https://cdan.nhtsa.gov/tsftables/tsfar.htm. Retreived June 2019.

[3] SAE, "Taxonomy and definitions for term related to on-road motor vehicle automated driving systems," Standard J3016, 2014, [online]. Available: https://www.sae.org/standards/content/j3016_201401/. Retreived June 2019.

[4] T. Litman,Victoria Transport Policy Institute, "Autonomous Vehicle Implementation Predictions: Implications for Transport Planning," Victoria Transport Policy Institute, March 2019. [Online]. Available: http://www.vtpi.org/avip.pdf, Retreived May 2019.

[5] A. Hars, "Autonomous cars: The next revolution looms," inventivio Innovative Briefs, 2010. [Online]. Available: http://www.inventivio.com/innovationbriefs/2010-01/index.html. Retreived June 2019.

[6] R. Shiffrar and M. Blake, "Perception of Human Motion," Annu. Rev. Psychol, 2007, [online]. Available: http://psych.annualreviews.org. Retreived June 2019.

[7] A. M. Wyglinski, X. Huang, T. Padir, L. Lai, T. R. Elsenbarth, and K. Venkatasbramanian, "Security of Autonomous Systems Employing Embedded Computing and Sensors," in Proc. IEEE Computer Society, 2013, pp 80-86.

[8] J. Wang, J. Liu, and N. Kato, "Networking and Communications in Autonomous Driving, A Survey," in Proc. IEEE Communication Surveys and Tutorials, Dec. 2018, pp. 1-1.

[9] V. L. L. Thing and J. Wu, "Autonomous Vehicle Security: A taxonomy of Attacks and Defences.," in IEEE International Conference on Internet of Things (iThings); IEEE Green Computing and Communications (GreenCom); IEEE Cyber, Physical and Social Computing (CPSCom), IEEE SmartData (SmartData), 2016, pp. 534-539.

[10] S. Abuelsamid, " Autonomous Vehicle Cybersecurity, The Need to Protect Automated and Connected Vehicles", 2016, https://www.karambasecurity.com/static/pdf/Autonomous-Automotive-Cybersecurity-Report.pdf. Retrieved June 2019.

[11] S. Brame, "The safety and Security of Autonomous Cars", August 2018, https://restechtoday.com/safety-security-autonomous-cars/. Retrieved June 2019.

[12] M. Gerla and P. Reiher, "Securing the Futurre Autonomous Vehicles: A Cyber-Physical Systems Approach," in Securing Cyber-Physical Systems, Ed. K. P. Al-Sakib, London, CRC Press, 2015, pp. 197-217.

[13] U. E. Larson and D. K. Nilsson, "Securing Vehicles Against Cyber Attacks", in Proc. The 4th Annual Workshop on Cyber Security and Information Intelligence Research CSIIRW'08, New York, USA, 2008, pp. 1-3.

[14] P. Thom and C. MacCarley, "A Spy Under the Hood: Controlling Risk and Automotive EDR". Risk Management Magazine, Feb. 2008; pp. 22–25.

[15] M. Wolf, M. Weimerskirch, and C. Paar, "Security in Automotive Bus Systems," in: Proc. the Workshop on Embedded Security in Cars, Bochum, Germany, 2004, pp. 1-13.

[16] E. Yagdereli, C. Gemci, and A. Z. Aktas, "A Study on Cyber-Security of Autonomous and Unmanned Vehicles," in Proc. Journal of Defense Modeling and Simulation: Applications, Methodology, Technology, 2015, Vol. 12, pp. 369-381.

[17] J. Yoshida, EE Times, "CAN Bus Can Be Encrypted, Says Trillium," [online]. Available: http: //www.eetimes.com/document.asp?doc id=1328081, Oct. 2015. Retrieved: May 2019.

[18] A. Lima, F. Rocha, M. Volp, and P. Esteves-Verissimo, "Towards Safe and Secure Autonomous and Cooperative Vehicle Ecosystems", in Proc. the 2nd ACM Workshop on Cyber-Physical Systems Security and Privacy CPS-SPC'16, Vienna, Austria, Oct. 2016, pp. 59-70.

[19] J. Schlatow, M. Moestl, and R. Ernst, "An Extensible Autonomous Reconfiguration Framework for Complex Component-Based Embedded Systems," in Proc. 12th International Conference on Autonomic Computing (ICAC), Grenoble, France, July 2015, pp. 239–242.

[20] V. Prevelakis and M. Hammad, "A Policy-Based Communications Architecture for Vehicles,' in Proc. International Conference on Information Systems Security and Privacy, Angers, France, 2015, pp. 155-162.

[21] M. Hamad, J. Schlatow, V. Prevelakis, and R. Ernst, "A Communication Framework for Distributed Access Control in Microkernel-Based Systems." In Proc. the 12th Annual Workshop on Operating Systems Platforms for Embedded Real-Time Applications (OSPERT16), Toulouse, France, July 2016, pp. 11–16.

[22] E. Villani, N. Fathollahnejad, R. Pathan, R. Barbosa, and J. Karlsson, "Reliability Analysis of Consensus in Cooperative Transport Systems," In Proc. 32nd International Conference on Computer Safety, Reliability and Security, SAFECOMP 2013 - Workshop ASCoMS (Architecting Safety in Collaborative Mobile Systems) of the, Toulouse, France, Sept. 2013, pp. 1-8.

[23] J. Zhao, B. Liang, and Q. Chen, "The key Technology toward the self-driving car," in Proc. The International Journal of Intelligent Unmanned Systems, vol. 6, issue 1, pp. 2-20, 2018.

[24] M. Mody et al., "Understanding Vehicle E/E Architecture Topologies for Automated Driving: System Partitioning and Trade-off Parameters," in Proc. Autonomous Vehicles and Machine Conference, 2018, pp. 358-1-358-5(5).

[25] S. Behere and N. Torngren, "A Functional Architecture for Autonomous Driving," in Proc. WASA'15, Montereal, Canada, 2015, pp. 1-7.

[26] S. D. Pendleton, H. Andersen, X. Du, X. Shen, M. Meghjani, Y. H. Eng, D. Rus, and M. H. Ang, "Perception, Planning, Control, and Coordination for Autonomous Vehicles," Machines, Vol. 5, issue 1, 2017, pp. 1-54.

[27] Nanalyze, "5 Startups Doing HD Mapping for Autonomous Vehile", November 2018, https://www.nanalyze.com/2018/11/hd-mapping-autonomous-vehicles/. Retrieved June 2019.

[28] H. Verdhan, "HD Maps: New age maps powering the autonomous vehicles", September 2017,[online]. Available: https://www.geospatialworld.net/article/hd-maps-autonomous-vehicles/. Retrieved June 2019.

Enterprise Estimation of Broadband Performance

Erik Massarczyk, Peter Winzer
Faculty of Design – Computer Science – Media
RheinMain University of Applied Sciences
Wiesbaden, Germany
Email: erik.massarczyk@hs-rm.de, peter.winzer@hs-rm.de

Abstract—**The worldwide broadband demand is increasing. However, often the research regards the demand for a better broadband availability and higher broadband connection speeds on the base of residential broadband demand, whereas the need for higher bandwidths and estimation of the broadband performance of enterprises are mostly unconsidered. Since only a few market analyses explicitly include the broadband requirements of companies, these requirements have been given little attention in Germany up to now. To deepen the research-based knowledge about the needs of enterprises regarding the usage of broadband connections, a survey of enterprises in Germany (with focus on the Rhein-Main area) has been performed. Based on the analysis, the broadband performance, which are available for enterprises, with special regard of the received broadband connection speeds and the price-performance ratio, this study, shows that the satisfaction of companies depends in particular on the extent to which broadband access covers their future needs and less on the current situation.**

Keywords-enterprise broadband demand; broadband connection speeds; broadband performance; price-performance ratio.

I. INTRODUCTION

On the base of the upcoming digitization of workflows and an increasing linkage between different enterprise locations and between enterprises and customers in the virtual world, the broadband provision and the availability of high broadband connection speeds get more and more important for enterprises in the business and industry sector [1]. Since the availability of broadband accesses is a key factor for enterprise and private household settlement, broadband accesses need to be stable, appropriate to the needs and comprehensively available [2]-[7].

Based on the economic significance of a sufficient broadband provision for enterprises, a situation analysis about the current broadband provision of enterprises is necessary. In this context, an online survey has been conducted to figure out how the enterprises in Germany (with focus on the Rhein-Main area) evaluate the performance and sufficiency of their current broadband provision. Here, information about the currently achieved broadband connection speeds, the perceived price-performance ratio and the satisfaction about the broadband performance has been also collected by the survey. The main intention was to identify how enterprises experience the performance of their current broadband access and if the performance will be sufficient for the future by satisfying the enterprise needs regarding the different kinds of business purposes and activities.

Therefore, the paper is structured as follows. After the introduction, the second section covers the literature review. Here, the first subsection contains an in-depth definition of broadband. The second subsection of the literature review regards the challenges by the consideration of the enterprise broadband demand. The following subsection compromises the conceptual model and the set hypotheses. Based on the structure of these three subsections, the next section presents the methodology and research approach of the study. Section 4 contains the data analysis and the main results of the survey. In the fifth section, the results will be briefly discussed.

II. LITERATURE REVIEW

A. Definition of Broadband

Broadband means an uninterrupted access to a great number of services, using fast connection speeds [7]. Since the access speeds and demand for Internet services are still increasing the definition of the speed at which a broadband connection is established must be adjusted from time to time, with this (lower) limit being adjusted from 0.5 Mbps to 4 Mbps in the period before 2011 [8]-[11]. This limit was increased to (up to) 25 Mbps downstream in the last update 2015 [12].

B. Challenges

In general, the studies and reports from the International Telecommunications Union (ITU) [13] and Organisation for Economic Cooperation and Development (OECD) [14][15] focus on the broadband provision of private households, whereas the broadband supply of enterprises is often unconsidered.

On the base that residential customers represent 80% of broadband users [16], the focus on the consideration of the broadband provision of private households is naturally. However, since companies, for example as employers, have a decisive influence on the (economic) importance of a region, the significance of broadband connections for business customers must be taken into account. In principle, it can be assumed that business customers have a higher demand for broadband and a higher willingness to pay than residential customers [17]. In Germany, for example, users of broadband access with at least 100 Mbps are mainly companies and a few private heavy users [18]. Generally, enterprises have a strong necessity to send and receive large amounts of data between different enterprise locations or in the enterprise-customer communication.

On the expectation that enterprises have a greater willingness to pay for higher broadband connection speeds (compared to private households), network operators believe that business customers have a significantly higher revenue potential per line (compared to residential customers).

However, the network operators can only benefit from the higher willingness to pay from the enterprises if they are able to satisfy the enterprises broadband needs. This study is intended to contribute to the question if the performance of the current broadband access is sufficient to satisfy the enterprise needs.

C. Conceptual Model

In this subsection, the conceptual model (see Figure 1) for the comprehension about the enterprise perceptions regarding the broadband access performance will be deepened.

The core problem is that enterprises see the own broadband access with connection speeds as one important economical location factor, which they need to keep their status in business competition [2]-[7]. From this point of view, the presence of high quality broadband infrastructures indicates a key factor for enterprises in their choice of location, economic success and future (international) competitiveness [19]. If the availability of broadband access in a specific region or area do not satisfy enterprise needs, the enterprises get directly limited by doing their business purposes and they may choose another location for doing their business activities. In this respect, a non-existent local broadband provision directly deters the enterprise productivity and service quality in the specific region.

In addition, the availability of broadband Internet builds the base for the collection of information and exploiting the potential of electronic markets in the digital world [10][20]. In this regard, a sufficient broadband access with high connection speeds is the base for the national competitiveness and profitability of enterprises [9][21]-[23].

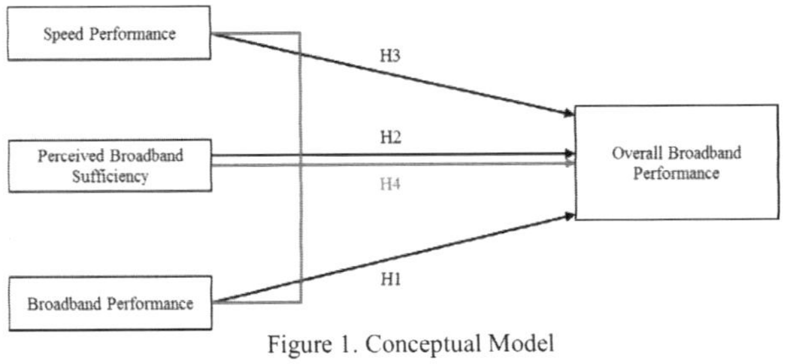

Figure 1. Conceptual Model

The technological progress of telecommunications infrastructures allows the achievement of broadband connection speeds of 100 Mbps and more. From the technological perspective, the network operators should be able to satisfy the bandwidth needs of the enterprises [24][25].

Besides the availability of a high quality broadband network, enterprises expect that the broadband access would be also cover the enterprise needs in future. Furthermore, the broadband access should have a (a) fair price-performance ratio, (b) availability in other enterprise locations, (c) guaranteed stable connections, and (d) appropriate lead times [26]-[28].

The evaluation of the performance of the current broadband access directly depends on the paid prices and the network availability [29]. For example, the evaluation of the perceived broadband access performance gives a direct feedback if the needs of the enterprise are fulfilled.

In this context, the authors assume that the overall broadband performance is rated as good if the broadband connection speeds are sufficient to meet companies' current and future broadband needs and if the price-performance ratio is perceived as fair.

Based on this, the hypotheses for this paper are:

H1: A positive assessment of the speed performance of the current broadband access by enterprises has a positive impact on the overall perceived broadband access performance.

H2: A positive assessment of the sufficiency of the current broadband access for future needs positively affects the overall perceived broadband access performance.

H3: A positive assessment of the price-performance-ratio of the current broadband access positively affects the overall perceived broadband access performance.

H4: A positive assessment of all the above-mentioned performance parameters positively affects the overall perceived broadband access performance.

III. METHODOLOGY

To verify appropriateness of the hypotheses, the authors have performed a survey about the current performance of enterprises' broadband accesses. Especially, the survey captures information regarding (a) the current broadband connection speeds in downstream and upstream, (b) the paid prices and the perceived price-performance ratio, (c) the level of Internet interruptions, as well as (d) the expected broadband demand. The main intention is here to figure out how the enterprises evaluate the total performance of the received broadband access and how the different indicators affect this evaluation.

As our university is located in the Rhein-Main area (Hesse) in Germany, the survey was mainly distributed via local multipliers located in the municipalities to reach all types of businesses (from micro to large). For the simplification of the data collection, a cross-sectional online-survey ("one-shot survey") have been prepared [30].

Although an online survey can in principle reach a wide range of potential respondents, the absence of a high participation rate and the completeness and accuracy of the answers cannot be guaranteed for such online surveys. In addition, the questionnaire was designed in such a way that individual questions can be skipped without ending the survey. The survey was distributed during the period from May to July 2018 and 364 companies had opened the questionnaire. However, only 81 of the 364 companies have completely passed the questionnaire.

In the first part of the survey, the enterprises were asked about their industry, enterprise size and degree of Internet usage in general. The second part covers questions about the Internet provider, broadband technology, and the broadband connection speed in downstream and upstream. The third part include questions about the importance of different Internet services. The following fourth part of the survey deals with the question to what extent the current broadband situation satisfies the needs of the company. These are supplemented in the fifth part by questions on service quality and fault frequency. The last part regards questions about the price of the current broadband access and the willingness to pay for a better broadband access.

The collected data were analyzed using quantitative research methods and the Statistical Package for the Social Sciences (SPSS) statistical program. To examine the reliability and validity of the data, the estimation of the Cronbach's Alpha and the Exploratory Factor Analysis were performed.

The questions regarding the broadband performance are determined on the base of 5-Point-Likert-scale questions [31]. Here, the measurement of the broadband performance follows the scale from a very strong to a very weak evaluation of the performance. Furthermore, the scope of disturbances gives an overview about fault frequency of the used broadband access (5-Point-Likert-scale: very rarely to very often) [31]. Lastly, the price-performance-ratio (5-Point-Likert-scale: very strong to a very weak performance) and the willingness to pay (5-Point-Likert-scale: fully disagree to fully agree) for a better broadband connection are queried.

As introduced above, the used approach for assessment the hypotheses partly deviate from the original model of the Unified Theory of Acceptance and Use of Technology 2 (UTAUT2).

IV. DATA ANALYSIS AND RESULTS

A. Result Conditions

The further analysis assumes that the participants of the survey will answer these from their position as business customers. In the following, first the descriptive results and the correlation analysis are presented. After a validation of the concepts used, the results of the validity and reliability analyses are briefly discussed. Finally, the results of the ordinary least square regressions of the hypothesis test are presented.

B. Descriptive Results

In the beginning of the analysis, the classification of the involved companies will be discussed. 23.5% of the responding enterprises are directed in the IT section, whereas 17.3% of the enterprises are situated in provision of services. The other participating companies are distributed almost evenly across the other 11 industrial sectors and each represents only a small proportion of the total distribution.

Regarding the classification of the enterprise size in Table I, it can be seen that micro enterprises and small enterprises take the biggest shares of the responding enterprises with 38.5% and 37.2%, respectively. On the base of the assumption that the distribution of the enterprises in Germany in regard to their size would be quite similar with the distribution of the enterprises in Hesse, it must be admitted that the shares of micro enterprises in the survey is underrepresented. Contrary, small, medium, and large enterprises are overrepresented.

Although the distribution of enterprises does not coincide with the distribution of enterprises in Germany and Hessen, the available data can provide detailed feedback on the broadband connections available to small, medium-sized and large enterprises.

It can be assumed that larger enterprises tend to require higher broadband connection speeds than small and medium-sized enterprises, in particular due to the connection of different business locations. On the base of evolving Internet services and applications and by linking these pieces of information in relation to the degree of Internet usage, it is not surprising that in over 60% of the companies surveyed, over 80% of employees have to use Internet connections to perform their daily business tasks (see Table II).

As shown in Table III, more than half of the companies surveyed have only one business location. The remaining approx. 45% of companies with more than one location depend on a good quality of links between these locations. Otherwise, problems could arise that lead, for example, to loss of information, longer work processes or a delay in processing business transactions.

The current broadband coverage of enterprises is described below. Figure 2 shows that 60% of companies use copper-based broadband connections. In second place are fiber optic lines with just over 20%. (In contrast, coax cable infrastructure is the second most important connectivity technology after copper for residential lines in Germany). Although fixed broadband connections are best able to secure stable broadband connections with a defined connection speed without frequency and weather interferences, 5.2% of the companies surveyed still access the Internet via mobile networks and 1.7% via satellite connections.

TABLE I. SIZE OF THE ENTERPIRSES
(EM = Employees) [33]

Size	Percentages in the Survey	Percentages in Germany
Micro Enterprises (below 10 EM)	38.5%	89.5%
Small Enterprises (10-49 EM)	37.2%	8.3%
Medium Enterprises (50-249 EM)	17.9%	1.8%
Large Enterprises (250 EM and more)	6.4%	0.4%

TABLE II. PERCENTAGE OF EMPLOYEES USING THE INTERNET

Percentage of EM using the Internet	Percentages of Enterprises in the Survey
0% to 20%	8.6%
21% to 40%	9.9%
41% to 60%	9.9%
61% to 80%	11.1%
More than 80%	60.5%

TABLE III. NUMBER OF ENTERPRISE LOCATIONS

Number of Locations	Percentages in the Survey
1	55.1%
2 to 5	32.1%
6 to 10	5.1%
11 to 15	1.3%
More than 15	6.4%

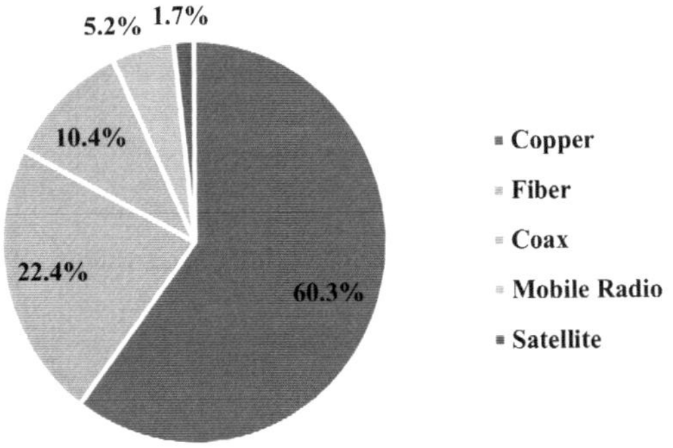

Figure 2. Distribution of the Broadband Access Technology

Only 20% of the companies have access speeds of 100 to 1,000 Mbps. Therefore, it is not surprising that about 70% of the queried enterprises companies assume that their current broadband connection speed will not be sufficient to provide the services and products of the future business life.

In this respect, 77.6% of the companies surveyed responded that they immediately needed higher bandwidths, which is in line with the previous studies [1].

Since, the main part of the copper infrastructures in Germany are provided by the incumbent, it is not wondering that 69.6% of the enterprises are connected to broadband Internet by the incumbent of the German broadband market.

As shown in Table IV, approx. 48% of the enterprises use broadband connection speeds of less than 30 Mbps in downstream. In earlier studies, for the German market, values of about 40% of companies with broadband connections of (up to) 16 Mbps are mentioned, which is compatible with the figures given in Table IV (27.3% less than 16 Mbps and 47.8% less than 30 Mbps) [1].

TABLE IV. DISTRIBUTION OF DELIVERED BROADBAND CONNECTION SPEEDS

Size	Percentages in Downstream	Percentages in Upstream
Less than 2 Mbps	2.7%	21.6%
Less than 6 Mbps	8.2%	12.2%
Less than 16 Mbps	16.4%	23.0%
Less than 30 Mbps	20.5%	14.9%
Less than 50 Mbps	5.5%	2.7%
Less than 100 Mbps	21.9%	10.8%
100 Mbps an more	24.7%	14.9%

The fact that over 50% (70%) of companies still have download (upload) speeds of less than 50 Mbps is critical. Especially in view of the increasing digitalization of society and business activities, it can be assumed that such bandwidths will not be sufficient in the near future [1].

The problems with broadband coverage are also illustrated by the fact that 58.8% of respondents have not changed their broadband contract in the last four years (see Table V). In this context, it needs to be assessed whether respondents could change their broadband access to improve broadband coverage. In addition to the performance of broadband access in terms of downstream and upstream bandwidth, quality also depends crucially on how often the service is unavailable. 44.3% of companies have stated that they have interruptions in Internet access at least once a month.

Although once a month sounds less dramatic, the duration of the failures could be a critical problem. 54.4% of the failures lasted at least 8 hours, which means that the company was cut off from the commercial world for one working day.

Although 77.6% of the queried enterprises are not satisfied with their broadband access, most of the enterprises are not able to change the current broadband provision, which are shown in Figure 3. Nearly 60% of the queried enterprises face the problem that a better broadband infrastructure is not available. Round about 15.5% of the queried enterprises do not want to change the broadband access in regard the current access satisfies the broadband needs. On the one hand, 22.4% of companies reply that they have no need to use higher bandwidths.

On the other hand, only 15.5% of companies surveyed said they did not want to change their broadband access because it covers their current access. This means that some of the respondents who do not need (directly) higher bandwidths still want to change their current broadband access as a precaution.

In the last step, the questions consider (a) the paid monthly subscription fees and (b) the enterprise perceptions regarding the price-performance ratio, as well as (c) the degree of the satisfaction with the whole broadband access.

TABLE V. DURATION OF BROADBAND ACCESS CONTRACT

Duration	Percentages in the Survey
Less than 2 years	23.5%
Less than 4 years	17.6%
4 years and longer	58.8%

Considering the monthly subscription fee in Table VI, it can be noted that 58.6% of the enterprises pay a monthly price below 100 Euro. 11.4% of the enterprises spend more than 800 Euro per month. With regard to the price-performance ratio perceived by enterprises, it can be noted that 80.8% of the enterprises are not satisfied with the price-performance ratio of their broadband access (see Table VII).

TABLE VI. DISTRIBUTION OF PAID MONTHLY SUBSCRIPTION FEES (EXCLUDED VAT)

Price Categories	Percentages in the Survey
Less than 25 Euro	2.9%
Less than 50 Euro	38.6%
Less than 100 Euro	17.1%
Less than 200 Euro	17.1%
Less than 400 Euro	7.1%
Less than 600 Euro	4.3%
Less than 800 Euro	1.4%
800 Euro and more	11.4%

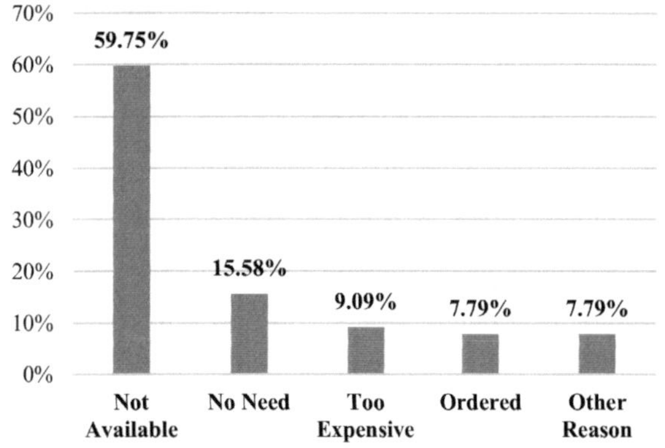

Figure 3. Reasons for the not performed Change of the Broadband Provision

Due to this high level of dissatisfaction, companies are increasingly willing to change the broadband infrastructure and/or the network operators as far as this is technically possible. The dissatisfaction is directly related to the fear of the companies that they may not be able to carry out their business activities in full scope due to the insufficient Internet connections [1]. The shortcomings can lead to e-mails (e.g., with large file attachments) not being processed at all or only very slowly, or video conferences with customers/business partners not being possible, which would have a negative effect on customer relations) [1].

Besides the consideration of the price-performance ratio, the focus of this study targets on the evaluation about the performance of the broadband access. In this regard, only 19.4% of the responding enterprises rates the overall satisfaction with their broadband access as good or very good (see Table VII).

One quarter of the queried enterprises rates the broadband performance on a medium ("neutral") level (see Table VII). In summarizing the whole estimation of the total broadband performance, it needs to be concluded that approx. 55% of the enterprises are not satisfied with their broadband access and rate the broadband performance as weakly or very weakly (see Table VII).

TABLE VII. EVALUATION OF THE PRICE-PERFORMANCE-RATIO AND THE TOTAL PERFORMANCE

Performance Evaluation	Price-Performance-Raito	Total Broadband Performance
Very Weak	16.4%	33.3%
Weak	23.3%	22.2%
Neutral	41.1%	25.0%
Strong	12.3%	12.5%
Very Strong	6.8%	6.9%

In addition, it can be noted that some companies notice large differences between the ordered/paid and the actual connection speeds provided, which further exacerbates their dissatisfaction

C. Correlation Analysis

Although a statistical analysis would normally begin with a review of reliability and validity, it exceptionally begins with a correlation analysis to find out which of the variables correlate with broadband access satisfaction. Based on the hypotheses, the authors assume that (a) the currently received connection speeds, (b) the degree of Internet usage in the company, (c) the failure rate, (d) the price-performance ratio, (e) the (monthly) price, (f) the demand for higher bandwidths, and (g) the estimate of whether the connection speeds will cover broadband demand in the future will influence the overall perception of the performance of the current broadband access.

Correlation analysis measures the degree of relationship between two individual variables. Here, it is necessary to distinguish that a correlation analysis would measure the proportionality between two variables instead of a degree of dependency. A correlation coefficient of 1.000 shows a 'perfect' relationship. A correlation coefficient higher than 0.500 is classified as a good correlation. Below the mark of 0.300, the correlation coefficients are weak [32][33].

As shown in Table VIII, most variables fulfill the assumption of significant linear proportionality (positive or negative) to the variable evaluation of total broadband performance. However, two variables, (1) the monthly subscription fee, and (2) the level of Internet usage, do not correlate significantly with the evaluation of total broadband performance. For this reason, the presented conceptual model in the second section will be adjusted and the two named variables will be excluded, since on the base of a missing significant correlation, an analysis regarding dependency does not make any sense.

In a further consideration of Table VIII, it can be seen that most of the other variables present strong correlations with the overall estimated broadband performance. Here, the assessment of the extent to which the connection speeds can cover the future demand shows the clearly highest correlation coefficients (downstream: 0.789; upstream: 0.800). The price-performance ratio (0.648) and the need for higher bandwidth (-0.669) also show high correlation coefficients with respect to the overall rating of broadband performance.

TABLE VIII. RESULTS OF THE CORRELATION ANALYSIS

Variables	Correlation Coefficients with the Evaluation of the Total Broadband Performance
Current Downstream Speed	0.631**
Current Upstream Speed	0.592**
Sufficiency of Downstream Speed	0.789**
Sufficiency of Upstream Speed	0.800**
Actual Monthly Subscription Fee	0.192
Price-Performance Ratio	0.648**
Degree of Internet Usage	-0.025
Need for Higher Bandwidth	-0.669**
Failure Frequency	-0.398**

**. Correlation p=0.01 (2-sided) significant. / *. Correlation p=0.05 (2-sided) significant.

Only for the frequency of failure, there is only a mean correlation with a correlation coefficient of -0.398. Overall, the variables appear to be good predictors for regression analyses with the overall rating of broadband performance. However, the correlation analysis cannot give any information about the degree of dependency or the direction of causality.

D. *Explanation fo the Research Concepts*

Before the results of the validity and reliability analyses will be introduced, the four research concepts will be explained. In general, all the research concepts include variables, which are used to analyze the stated hypotheses from the second section. The first research concept includes the downstream and upstream connection speed of the current broadband access. The second research concept covers the questions about the sufficiency of the downstream and upstream speeds and the need for higher bandwidths in the future. The following third research concept comprises the questions of the perceived price-performance ratio and the overall broadband performance. The subsequent last concept includes all correlating variables from Table VIII and the dependent variable of the perceived broadband performance. The following reliability and validity analysis will verify the truthfulness of the outcomes.

E. *Reliability and Validity Analysis*

Table IX and Table X illustrate the outcomes of the reliability and validity analyses to verify if all the concepts, which are used in the research model, stay valid and reliable.

To estimate the validity of the concepts and hypotheses, an exploratory factor analyses will be performed. Here, the factor analysis includes the examination of the Kaiser-Meyer-Olkin value (KMO), the significance test from Bartlett, the consideration of the communalities and the examination of the cumulative variance [34]-[38]. To achieve a good validity, the estimated concepts should reach significant p values below the mark of 5% in the Bartlett-Test and KMO values above 0.7 [34]-[38].

Further the communalities of the variables in the considered concept need to exceed in average the value of 0.6. To verify the validity in a further step, the variables will be split in so-called factors. Here, the validity would be given if the cumulative variance of all factors (with eigenvalue above 1), which show the degree of explained variance in the research concept, of the different possible factors achieve more than 50% [34]-[38].

It should be noted that the concepts are valid as they all meet the Bartlett-Test (see Table IX). With regard to the KMO values, only the concepts of perceived broadband usage and total broadband performance achieve satisfactory values (of at least 0.7). If (as recommended by some references [34]-[38]) less stringent KMO limits are applied and if it is assumed that KMO values from 0.5 are acceptable, the research concepts of speed performance (KMO value 0.677) and perceived broadband performance (KMO value 0.500) can be classified as acceptable.

If one considers the results to date together with the results of the municipalities and the cumulative variance, it can be seen that all research concepts have a cumulative variance above 50%, which indicates that the existing variance can be explained quite well. Regarding the communalities, only the concept with all included variables do not achieve an average of the variable communalities above 0.6. However, the average value of 0.593 is close to the mark 0.6 and therefore the communalities of this concept could be weakly accepted.

Overall, the stated research concepts describe a good validity.

TABLE IX. VALIDITY ANALYSIS

Research Concepts	KMO & Bartlett-Test	Communalities	Cumulative Variance
Speed Performance	0.677 $p < 0.000$	Ø Com. > 0.6	73.805%
Perceived Broadband Sufficiency	0.705 $p < 0.000$	Ø Com. > 0.6	81.799%
Perceived Broadband Performance	0.500 $p < 0.000$	Ø Com. > 0.6	82.385%
Broadband Performance – all Variables	0.860 $p < 0.000$	Ø Com. < 0.6	59.951%

TABLE X. RELIABILITY ANALYSIS

Research Concepts	Cronbach's Alpha
Speed Performance	**0.864**
Perceived Broadband Sufficiency	**0.445**
Perceived Broadband Performance	**0.781**
Broadband Performance – all Variables	**0.776**

Table X shows the results of the reliability analysis. Reliability is evaluated using Cronbach Alpha, whereby the Cronbach Alpha of a research concept for good reliability should be greater than 0.7 [39]-[41].

With the exception of the concept of the perceived broadband supply, for which good reliability could not be proven, all research concepts are to be classified as reliable, since these have Cronbach alpha values of over 0.7.

F. Regression Analysis

The regression analysis is performed on the base of the method of a multiple ordinary least square regression. Here, the regression analysis examines the degree of dependency and linear relationship between the dependent and independent variables For example, it will be examined, in which degree the predictor variables are able to explain the values of the dependent variable [42].

In the taken regression analysis, the following four indicators will be considered in deeply. Firstly, the r-square describes the explanatory power of the whole regression model. Here, the r-square presents the part of the dependent variable, which can be explained by the independent variables. Following Chin [43] and Cohen [44], the r-square should be at least 33%.

Secondly, the Analysis of the Variances (ANOVA) measures the model fit whereby the F-value needs to be higher than 3 and the probability needs to be significant. Thirdly, the regression coefficients of the independent variables need to be significant ($p<0.05$). Lastly, the test of multicollinearities by the Variance Inflation Factor (VIF) needs to be performed to figure out, whether the variables included in the regression analyses have an identical relation. In case of existing multicollinearities, the VIF values would exceed the mark of 10 (or in a stricter definition 3). In this case, it must be assumed that the outcomes of the regression analysis are biased [37][45][46].

Table XI identifies results of regression analysis of the different independent variables and their degree of dependency regarding the enterprise perceptions about the overall performance of their broadband access. The r-square of 78.3% describes a high explanatory rate of the dependent variable. For example, the independent variables are able to explain more than 3/4 of the result of overall perceived broadband performance. The ANOVA analysis shows a significant F-value higher than three, which indicates that a good model fit is given and the assumed model is better than a simple mean model.

The regression outcome shows that, three variables have a significant influence on the evaluation about the overall broadband performance. The price-performance have a positive significant regression coefficient of 0.266, which means if an enterprise perceives a good balance of price and performance, the overall performance of the broadband access will be also well rated.

The sufficiency of the upstream connection speed is also a significantly positive indicator for the estimation of the overall broadband performance. For example, if enterprises perceive that the upstream connection speed would be sufficient, the overall broadband performance would be rated positively.

Finally, it becomes clear that if companies find that they need a higher bandwidth (than they currently have), they will consider the overall performance of the (current) broadband connection to be weak.

TABLE XI. REGRESSION ANALYSIS (ENTER MODE) BROADBAND PERFORMANCE

Independent variables	Dependent: Estimation of the Overall Broadband Performance	
ANOVA = 29.313 p<0.05	**R-Square = 78.3%**	
	Regression Coefficients with Significance	**VIF**
Constant	**0.681**	
Downstream Speed	**0.078**	**3.416**
Upstream Speed	**0.040**	**3.154**
Sufficiency of Downstream Speed	**0.132**	**4.377**
Sufficiency of Upstream Speed	**0.253***	**4.686**
Failure Frequency	**-0.108**	**1.189**
Need for Higher Bandwidth	**-0.623***	**2.052**
Price-Performance Ratio	**0.266****	**1.686**

**. Correlation p=0.01 (2-sided) significant. / *. Correlation p=0.05 (2-sided) significant.

In other words, there is a "negative regressive correlation" (due to the binary coding of these variables) between (a) the need for higher bandwidth and (b) satisfaction with the performance of the (current) broadband connection.

However, it should be noted that the speed variable VIF values are above 3, suggesting that multicollinearities could influence the regression results.

In this respect, a stepwise regression analysis is carried out. The stepwise regression analysis implements systematically the significant independent variables in the regression outcome. On the base of this approach, the strength of the single independent variables as predictors for the dependent variable can be identified. In addition, this approach implies the exclusion of the insignificant variables. For the reason of the exclusion of variables, the bias problem of existing multicollinearities can be bypassed.

The results of the stepwise regression analysis in Table XII show a high r-square of 77.0%, indicating a strong model fit. Furthermore, four significant indicators for the explanation of the dependent variable of the overall broadband performance are presented. Since the stepwise regression implements systematically the significant indicators for dependent variables, the strongest predictor for the overall broadband performance would be the sufficiency of the upstream broadband connection.

Furthermore, the price-performance ratio and the need for higher bandwidth do also significantly explain the overall broadband performance in the same way as in the regression analysis on the base of the enter method displayed in Table XI. Compared to the previous regression analysis, the three indicators mentioned are slightly stronger in their impact on the evaluation of overall broadband performance.

However, in contrast to the previous regression analysis, the current downstream broadband connection speed would be also seen as predictor variable for the perceptions regarding the overall broadband performance. . The regression coefficient of 0.139 shows that companies achieving higher downstream speeds rate overall broadband performance more positively. In the consideration of the VIF values, all the significant parameters indicate VIF values below 3. For this reason, multicollinearities can be excluded.

TABLE XII. REGRESSION ANALYSIS (STEPWISE MODE) BROADBAND PERFORMANCE

Independent variables	Dependent: Estimation of the Overall Broadband Performance	
ANOVA = 50.253 p<0.05	R-Square = 77.0%	
	Regression Coefficients with Significance	VIF
Constant	0.481	
Sufficiency of Upstream Speed	0.343**	2.915
Price-Performance Ratio	0.303**	1.540
Need for Higher Bandwidth	-0.711**	1.949
Downstream Speed	0.139*	1.560

**. Correlation p=0.01 (2-sided) significant. / *. Correlation p=0.05 (2-sided) significant.

Other variables are excluded from the regression on the base of insignificance.

Given that broadband contracts contain fixed conditions for the speed of downstream and upstream connections, it is not surprising that these two speeds depend on each other and present precisely high multicollinearities. To avoid bias in the assumed regression models, the enterprise statements regarding the current downstream and upstream speed will be combined in the term of the access speed. This is done by a simple average of the two variables. The same procedure will be performed for the variables of the sufficiency of downstream and upstream speeds. Here, the resulting variable will be named sufficiency of access speed.

Table XIII presents the regression outcome regarding the estimated overall broadband performance on the base of a further model adjustment by the authors. The r-square with 78.1% presents a high explanatory rate of the dependent variable. The ANOVA analysis identifies a working model fit.

With the exception of default frequency, all the implemented independent variables are significantly. The results shown in Table XIII are quite similar to the results of the first regression analysis (Table XII), especially for the regression coefficients (a) price-performance ratio (0.264) and (b) need for higher bandwidth (-0.637). In this respect, reference can be made here to the explanations given above for Table XII.

Regarding the results of the "new combined" speed variables, it can be seen that both kinds of variables do significant positively influence the evaluation of the overall broadband performance. Here, the sufficiency of the access speed (regression coefficient: 0.385) has a greater impact on the satisfaction with the overall broadband performance than the current access speed of the companies (regression coefficient: 0.114).

From this point of view, it can be concluded that enterprises with a higher current access speed perceive a better broadband performance. Here, it is independently if the broadband connection speed mean the downstream or upstream speed. Since both kinds of speed have normally a (proportional) relation, it can be assumed if an enterprise gets a higher downstream speed, it also gets a higher upstream speed.

TABLE XIII. REGRESSION ANALYSIS (ENTER MODE) BROADBAND PERFORMANCE (COMBINED SPEED PARAMETER)

Independent variables	Dependent: Estimation of the Overall Broadband Performance	
ANOVA = 42.125 p<0.05	R-Square = 78.1%	
	Regression Coefficients with Significance	VIF
Constant	0.727	
Access Speed	0.114*	1.703
Sufficiency of Access Speed	0.385**	3.430
Failure Frequency	-0.110	1.176
Need for Higher Bandwidth	-0.637*	2.028
Price-Performance Ratio	0.264**	1.660

**. Correlation p=0.01 (2-sided) significant. / *. Correlation p=0.05 (2-sided) significant.

Furthermore, if enterprises perceive that the current access speeds would be sufficient to deliver the business services in future, they evaluate also broadband performance better. The same relation of access speeds and sufficiency of access speeds in regard to the evaluation of the broadband performance bases on the positive correlation of these both variables. If enterprises get currently a higher broadband connection speed, they perceive that the current access is sufficient for the provision of the business services in future.

Despite the significant results in Table XIII, it should be noted that the sufficiency of access speeds has a VIF value greater than 3. For example, it could be that the results in Table XIII are distorted by possible existing multicollinearities.

Nevertheless, all four hypotheses (presented in the second section) can be accepted.

V. CONCLUSIONS

The statistical analysis has shown which indicators are responsible for how companies evaluate their broadband access. In general, the satisfaction of enterprises about their broadband access depends in a larger degree on the perception about the sufficiency of the broadband access for the future business life, the price-performance ratio of the current broadband access and the need of the enterprise to use higher bandwidths in future. In a lower degree, the current access speeds in downstream and upstream would affect the satisfaction regarding the broadband access. Interestingly, the failure frequency of the broadband Internet access does not sustainably affect the satisfaction regarding the performance of the current broadband access.

Although further research will be necessary to get responses of more enterprises and to rise the quality of the results, it can be concluded that the enterprise satisfaction regarding their broadband access is mostly affected by the sustainability of their broadband access in future. In this respect, it is less important for companies how they currently assess their broadband access. Instead, it is much more important how the current broadband performance can meet future requirements from the companies' point of view. If this is the case, broadband performance will be assessed positively, otherwise it will be assessed negatively.

Network operators and government institutions should therefore primarily pay attention to what broadband services companies will need in the future in order to create the appropriate conditions. Otherwise, companies will be dissatisfied with their location and will think about moving to another location.

REFERENCES

[1] Vereinigung der Bayerischen Wirtschaft e. V., "Broadband demand of the Bavarian enterprises in 2017 – fixed and mobile," [German]: "Breitbandbedarf der bayerischen Unternehmen 2017 – leitungsgebunden und mobil", (Eds.) GMS Dr. Jung GmbH, Hamburg/München, 2018.

[2] W. Briglauer, "The Impact of Regulation and Competition on the Adoption of fiber-based Broadband Services: recent evidence from the European Union member states," Springer Verlag, pp. 450-468, 2014.

[3] M. Guenach, J. Maes, M. Timmers, O. Lamparter, and J.-C. M. Bischoff, "Vectoring in DSL systems: Practices and Challenges," IEEE Globecom, pp. 1-4, 2011.

[4] International Telecommunication Union/Broadband Commission, "The state of broadband 2014: broadband for all," Report from the broadband commission, pp. 16-23, 2014. [Online]. Available from: https://www.itu.int/dms_pub/itu-s/opb/pol/S-POL-BROADBAND.10-2014-PDF-E.pdf [retrieved 06.2019].

[5] P. Koutroumpis, "The Economic Impact of Broadband on Growth: A simultaneous approach," Elsevier Ltd Telecommunications Policy, vol. 33 (9), pp. 471-485, 2009.

[6] Monopoly Commission, "Special Report 61 – Telcommunication 2011: Strengthen investments and secure the competition," [German] "Monopolkommission "Sondergutachten 61 – Telekommunikation 2011: Investitionsanreize stärken, Wettbewerb sichern," pp. 24, 40-41, 55, 76-86, 2011. [Online]. Available from: https://www.monopolkommission.de/images/PDF/SG/s61_volltext.pdf [retrieved 06.2019].

[7] A. Picot and C. Wernick, "The Role of Government in Broadband Access," Elsevier Ltd. Telecommunications Policy, vol. 31, pp. 660-674, 2007.

[8] Federal Communications Commission (FCC), "FCC Releases New Census-Tract Level Data on High-Speed Internet Services," 2010. [Online]. Available from https://www.fcc.gov/document/fcc-releases-new-census-tract-level-data-high-speed-internet-services-0 [retrieved 06.2019].

[9] International Telecommunication Union (ITU), "Birth of Broadband – ITU Internet Reports," Geneva: ITU, p. 9, 2003.

[10] M. Jensen, R. H. Nielsen, and O. B. Madsen, "Comparison of Cost for Different Coverage Scenarios between Copper and Fiber Access Networks," IEEE Xplore, Advanced Communication Technology, ICACT 2006, The 8th International Conference, vol. 3, pp. 2015-2018, 2006.

[11] J.-H. Kim, J. M. Bauer, and S. S. Wildman, "Broadband Uptake in OECD Countries," 31st Research Conference on Communication, Information and Internet Policy, pp. 1-26, 2003.

[12] Federal Communications Commission (FCC), "2015 Broadband Progress Report," 2015. [Online]. Available from: https://www.fcc.gov/reports-research/reports/broadband-progress-reports/2015-broadband-progress-report [retrieved 06.2019].

[13] International Telecommunication Union, "Yearbook of Statistics 2014 – Telecommunication/ICT Indicators 2004-2013," 2014.

[14] OECD, "OECD Communications Outlook 2007 – Information and Communications Technologies," Organisation for Economic Cooperation and Development, 2007.

[15] OECD, "OECD Communications Outlook 2013 – Information and Communications Technologies," Organisation for Economic Cooperation and Development, 2013.

[16] Cisco, "The Zettabyte Era: Trends and Analysis," White Paper, 2014.

[17] Body of European Regulators for Electronic Communications (BEREC), "Challenges and Drivers of NGA Rollout and Infrastructure Competition," 2016.

[18] H. Deist, T, Proeger, and K. Bizer, "The market for broadband internet and political suggestions in Germany", [German]: "Der Markt für Breitbandinternet in Deutschland und Politikempfehlungen zu seiner Förderung", Studien zur Institutionsanalyse Nr. 16-1, pp. 22-23, 2016.

[19] F. Belloc, A. Nicita, and M. A. Rossi, "Whither Policy Design for Broadband Penetration? Evidence from 30 OECD countries," Elsevier Ltd Telecommunications Policy, vol. 36, (5), pp. 382-389, 2012.

[20] N. Economides, "Telecommunications Regulation: An Introduction,"NET Institute Working Paper No. 04-20; NYU Working Paper No. EC-04-10, pp. 48-76, 2004. [Online] Available from: https://ssrn.com/abstract=465020. or http://dx.doi.org/10.2139/ssrn.465020 [retrieved 06.2019].

[21] I. Cava-Ferreruela and A. Alabau-Munoz, "Evolution of the European Broadband Policy: Analysis and Perspective," pp. 1-17, 2005.

[22] J. Choudrie and H. Lee, "Broadband Development in South Korea: Institutional and Cultural Factors," European Journal of Information Systems. vol. 13, pp. 103-114, 2004.

[23] G. A. Woroch, "Open Access Rules and the Broadband Race," Review of Law 3, vol. 3 (1), pp. 1-23, 2002.

[24] Bundesministerium für Wirtschaft und Technologie (BMWI), "Third Report about the Broadband Strategy of the German Government," [German] "Dritter Monitoringbericht zur Breitbandstrategie der Bundesregierung", (Eds.) Goldmedia GmbH Strategy Consulting, pp. 18-21, 2013.

[25] U. Stopka, R. Pessier, and S. Flößel, "Broadband study 2030 – Prospective services, broadband adoption and demand," [German] "Breitbandstudie 2030 – Zukünftige Dienste, Adoptionsprozesse und Bandbreitenbedarf," pp. 42-50, 60, 166-164, 2013.

[26] W. Distaso, P. Lupi, and F. M. Maneti, "Platform competition and broadband uptake: Theory and Empirical evidence from

the European Union," Information Economics and Policy, vol. 18 (1), pp. 87-106, 2006.

[27] S. Sawyer, J. P. Allen, and H. Lee, "Broadband and Mobile Opportunities: a Socio-Technical Perspective," J. Information Technology. vol. 18, pp. 121-136, 2003.

[28] U. Stopka, R. Pessier, and G. Christofzik, "Liberalization of the Telecommunication Markets," [German] "Liberalisierung der Telekommunikationsmärkte – Revision liberalisierungsbedingter Wohlfahrtswirkungen auf Verbraucherseite," 2008. [Online]. Available from: https://tu-dresden.de/bu/verkehr/ivw/kom/ressourcen/dateien/forsch_berat/papers/liberalisierung_I.pdf?lang=de [retrieved 06.2019].

[29] M. Grosso, "Determinants of Broadband Penetration in OECD Nations," Regulatory Development Branch, Competition and Consumer Commission, pp. 1-31, 2006.

[30] A. Diekmann, "Empirical Social Research," [German]: "Empirische Sozialforschung," Rowohlt-Taschenbuch-Verlag., vol. 5, Reinbek bei Hamburg, 2011.

[31] R. Likert, "A Technique for the Measurement of Attitudes," Archives of Psychology, pp. 199-224, 1932.

[32] F. Brosius, "SPSS 8 Professional Statistics in Windows," [German] "SPSS 8 Professionelle Statistik unter Windows," International Thomson Publishing, vol. 1, chapter 21 Correlation, 1998.

[33] S. Hagl, "Quick Start in Statistics," [German] "Schnelleinstieg Statistik," Rudolf Haufe Verlag, vol. 1, München, 2008.

[34] A. Field, "Discovering Statistics Using SPSS," Sage Publications Ltd., vol. 4, 2013.

[35] S. Fromm, "Data Analysis with SPSS Part 1," [German] "Datenanalyse mit SPSS für Fortgeschrittene," VS Verlag für Sozialwissenschaften, GWV Fachverlage Arbeitsbuch, vol. 2, Wiesbaden, 2008.

[36] S. Fromm, "Data Analysis with SPSS Part 2," [German] "Datenanalyse mit SPSS für Fortgeschrittene 2: Multivariate Verfahren für Querschnittsdaten," VS Verlag für Sozialwissenschaften, Springer, Lehrbuch, vol. 1, Wiesbaden, 2010.

[37] J. F. J. Hair, R. E. Anderson, R. L. Tatham, and W. C. Black, "Multivariate Data Analysis," Macmillan, New York, NY, Macmillan, vol. 3, 1995.

[38] N. M. Schöneck and W. Voß, "Research Project", [German] "Das Forschungsprojekt – Planung, Durchführung und Auswertung einer quantitativen Studie," vol. 2. Springer Wiesbaden, 2013.

[39] L. J. Cronbach, "Coefficient Alpha and the Internal Structure of Tests," Psychometrika, vol. 16, pp. 297-334, 1951.

[40] C. Fornell and D. Larcker, "Evaluating Structural Equation Models with Unobservable Variables and Measurement Error," Journal of Marketing Research, vol. 18 (1), pp. 39-50, 1981.

[41] R. Hossiep, "Cronbachs Alpha," [German] "Cronbachs Alpha," (Eds.) M. A. Wirtz, Dorsch – Lexikon der Psychologie, Verlag Hans Huber, vol. 17., Bern, 2014.

[42] T. Schäfer, "Statistics 1 – Descriptive and Explorative Data Analysis," [German] "Statistik I. Deskriptive und Explorative Datenanalyse," VS Verlag für Sozialwissenschaften, p. 121, 2010.

[43] W. W. Chin, "The Partial Least Squares Approach for Structural Equation Modeling," (Eds.) G. A. Marcoulides, Modern Methods for Business Research. Lawrence Erlbaum Associates. Mahwah, NJ, pp. 295-336, 1998.

[44] J. Cohen, "Statistical Power Analysis for the Behavioral Sciences," Lawrence Erlbaum Associates, Hillsdale, edition 2, 1998.

[45] D. Lin, D. P. Foster, and L. H. Ungar, "VIF Regression: A Fast Regression Algorithm for Large Data," Journal of the American Statistical Association, vol. 106 (493), pp. 232-247, 2009.

[46] S. Petter, D. W. Straub, and A. Rai, "Specifying Formative Constructs in Information Systems Research," MIS Quarterly, vol. 31 (4), pp. 623-656, 2007.

Evaluating Streaming and Latency Compensation in a Cloud-based Game

Jiawei Sun, Mark Claypool
Worcester Polytechnic Institute
Worcester, MA, 01609 USA
email: {jsun|claypool}@wpi.edu

***Abstract*—The growth in cloud computing and network connectivity brings the opportunity for cloud-based game systems where players interact through a lightweight client that only displays rendered frames and captures input, while the heavyweight game processing happens on the cloud server. Compared to traditional game systems, cloud-based game systems present challenges in handling network latency and bitrate requirements. This work uses *Drizzle*, a custom cloud-based game system, to evaluate: 1) time warp to compensate for latency, and 2) graphics streaming to reduce network bitrates. A 30-person user study shows time warp mitigates the effects of latency on player performance, and system experiments show graphics streaming provides bitrate reductions compared to the video streaming typically used by commercial cloud-based game systems.**

***Keywords*–latency compensation; QoE; cloud-based games.**

I. INTRODUCTION

Although still an emerging commercial market, cloud-based games are growing rapidly with the increase in the number of gamers and the global penetration of the Internet and smart phones. Established companies like Sony and NVidia are already invested in cloud-based game services, but other big players such as Google and Microsoft are investing heavily and looking to capture market shares.

Cloud-based games differ from traditional games in that game clients are relatively lightweight, only sending user input (e.g., key presses and mouse actions) and receiving game output (i.e., images and sounds). The heavyweight game logic – applying physics to game objects, resolving collisions, processing Artificial Intelligence, etc. – and rendering are done at the server, with the game frames streamed to the client to display. A cloud-based game system offers advantages over traditional game systems including: modest client hardware requirements, no required client game installation, easier software piracy prevention, and fewer target platforms for developers.

While promising, cloud-based games face two major challenges when compared to traditional games: 1) *bitrates* – cloud-based games require significantly higher network bitrates from the server to the client [1] than do traditional network games; and 2) *latency* – cloud-based game clients cannot immediately act on player input but must instead send the input to the server, have it processed, the result rendered, and frame data sent back to the client for display [2].

Approaches to reduce bitrates can leverage innovations in image and video compression. However, the graphics-based nature of games present an opportunity for additional bitrate savings with only modest increases in client complexity by not necessarily streaming rendered game images but instead sending drawing information so the client can do the rendering [3].

Approaches to compensate for latency [4] have been widely used in commercial games. However, there has been limited scientific evaluation of their overall effectiveness and no specific evaluations covering the breadth of games and network conditions. Moreover, latency compensation techniques have not been studied with cloud-based game systems, which are more restrictive in the techniques they can use given the client's limited knowledge of the game state and reduced hardware capabilities.

This work makes three contributions to this area: 1) the evaluation of a latency compensation technique, *time warp*, in a cloud-based game system; 2) exploration of approaches to cloud-based game streaming to reduce network bitrates; and 3) evaluation using *Drizzle*, a cloud-based game system designed and developed from scratch using the Dragonfly [5] game engine.

Results of a 30-person user study show that time warp for projectile weapons can ameliorate the effects of latency on player performance, but with a cost in player perception of inconsistencies (i.e., visual glitches) in the rendered game world. Results of system experiments show graphics streaming can significantly reduce network bitrates over video streaming, but still has higher bitrates compared to traditional network games. Both time warp and game streaming have considerable CPU cost on the server, particularly as the number of game objects increases.

The rest of this paper is organized as follows: Section II describes related work; Section III presents our methodology and experiments; Section IV analyzes the results; and Section V summarizes our conclusions and possible future work.

II. RELATED WORK

This section describes research related to this work: architectures for cloud-based game systems (Section II-A), studies of latency and games (Section II-B), and work on latency compensation algorithms (Section II-C).

A. *Cloud-based Game Systems*

While there is no single agreed-upon cloud system architecture, a four-layer architecture defined by Foster et al. [6] has often been used by researchers, with cloud-based games (and Drizzle) at the application layer providing software as a service.

Cloud-based game systems can broadly be classified into graphics streaming and video streaming [7]. In graphics streaming, as done by de Winter et al. [3], instead of sending video, the server sends graphics commands to the client and the client renders the game images. In video streaming, as described by Shea et al. [8], the server is responsible for rendering the game scene, compressing the images as video, and then transmitting to the client. Both approaches reduce computation on the client versus a traditional network game architecture because only the server manages the entire game world. The video streaming approach is discussed the most in cloud gaming research [8], [9] and is currently used by most existing commercial cloud-based game systems since it reduces the workload on the client more than graphics streaming. Drizzle, our custom cloud-based game system, supports both graphics streaming and video streaming, each of which is evaluated in this paper.

B. Latency and Cloud-based Games

Chen et al. [2] discuss the effects of network latency (and other parameters) on the cloud-based game systems OnLive [10] and StreamMyGame [11]. However, the authors did not explicitly measure player performance with latency.

Jarschel et al. [12] conducted a user study in an emulated cloud game system, measuring the quality of experience for games users selected to play. Claypool and Finkel [13] present the results of two user studies that measured the objective and subjective effects of latency on cloud-based games. Sackl et al. [14] analyze the relationships between latency and player experience for cloud gaming. While more closely related to our work, these papers do not compare cloud-based games with and without latency compensation.

C. Latency Compensation

Bernier [15] describes methods game systems can use to compensate for network latencies, but does not provide scientific evaluation of the techniques.

Ivkovic et al. [16] carried out a controlled study of aiming in a first person shooter game with latency both with and without an aim assistance latency compensation technique. Lee and Chang [17] evaluated the effects of the latency compensation techniques time warp and interpolation on players in a commercial first person shooter game. Lee and Chang [18] continued evaluation of time warp with a custom first person shooter game, providing a guideline of 250 milliseconds as a limit for latency compensation.

While these papers are helpful in better understanding latency compensation, and some of the techniques are even used in traditional network games [19], latency compensation techniques have not been applied to cloud-based games. Our work applies a popular latency compensation technique, time warp, to a cloud-based game and evaluates it with a user study and system load measurements.

III. Methodology

This section presents our methodology to evaluate graphics streaming and latency compensation in cloud-based games.

A. Cloud-based Game Streaming

There are generally three approaches to cloud-based game streaming, depicted in Figure 1. At the top left is image streaming, where the game server renders the game frames to be displayed as individual images, compresses them (e.g., as a JPEG image) and sends them to the client for decoding and playing. Next down, is video streaming, where the server renders the game frames as images, then encodes them into a video stream and sends the stream to the client for decoding and playing. In video streaming, the server applies intra-encoding for each image as in image streaming, but also takes advantage of the temporal redundancy in adjacent images, applying inter-encoding for a higher compression rate. At the bottom is graphics streaming, where the server does not render individual images but instead sends graphics information for each frame to the client whereupon the client renders the images. Unlike in image streaming or video streaming, graphics streaming requires both the server and client to have *a priori* knowledge of how to render the image from the underlying image data.

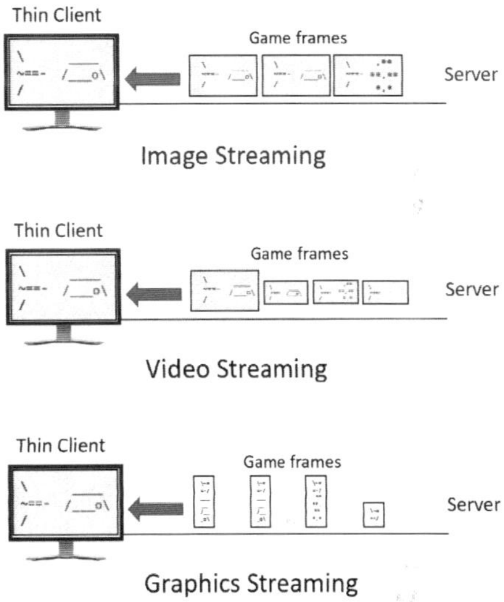

Figure 1. Cloud streaming approaches. Top: image streaming, Middle: video streaming, Bottom: graphics streaming.

The three approaches – image streaming, video streaming and graphics streaming – have tradeoffs depicted in Figure 2 in the bitrates required by the network and the decoding and rendering complexity needed by the client. At the top left is image streaming, the simplest for the client, but with the highest network bitrate owing to the only modest compression afforded to the individual images. Video streaming requires more client complexity in that both intra- and inter-image decoding is needed, but with a significant bitrate reduction attained by the inter-encoding. Graphics streaming requires somewhat more complexity than video streaming in that the client itself must render the images from graphics data, but there is significant potential for lower bitrates than in video streaming. For comparison, traditional games are at the bottom right, having fairly low bitrates (5 kb/s to 124 kb/s [1]) but require complex clients, capable of running a game engine and doing a full render of the game world from game data.

B. Time Warp

Time warp is a latency compensation technique deployed at a game server, as depicted in Figure 3. With time warp, the

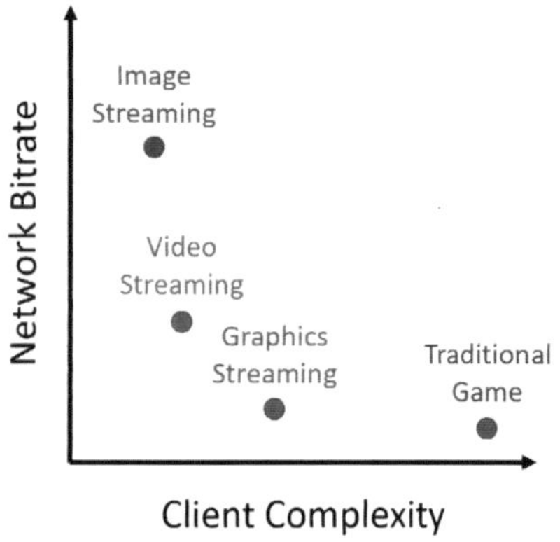

Figure 2. Cloud-based game streaming tradeoffs.

player acts (e.g., shooting) based on the opponent's apparent position, but when the server gets the input Δt later, the opponent's actual position has moved. To compensate for this latency, the server warps time (and the game world) back by Δt, determines the outcome, and rolls the game world forward to the present time.

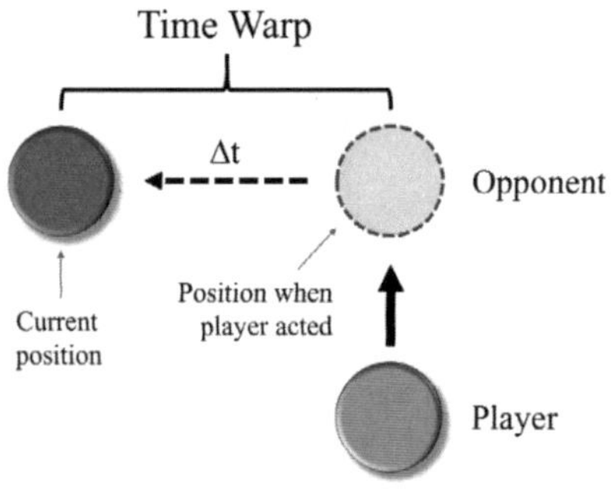

Figure 3. Time warp – server rolls back game world Δt.

C. Drizzle

Drizzle is based on *Dragonfly* – a text-based, 2d game engine, full-featured enough to make a wide variety of arcade-style games [20]. The core engine is written in C++ and includes graphics rendered with the Simple and Fast Multimedia Library (SFML), basic kinematics (velocity and acceleration), keyboard and mouse input, collision detection and resolution, and audio (sound effects and music).

We extended Dragonfly to support networking – specifically a network manager that uses Transmission Control Protocol (TCP) sockets. Drizzle uses the network manager in a heavyweight server that does the game computations and a "thin" client that displays frames and transmits user input.

The server starts up the game engine and gets ready for a client to connect by waiting on a well-known port. The client connects to the Drizzle server using the hostname provided by the player and the well-known port. Once the client connects, the server starts the game and does all the game computations – processing any game Artificial Intelligence, updating positions of game objects, detecting and resolving collisions, and composing frames. However, unlike in a traditional game, there is no player sitting at the console viewing the game and providing input. Instead, the server composes the game stream (depending on if it is using image streaming, video streaming or graphics streaming). The game stream data is streamed down the network socket to the client. The client receives the data and renders the frame depending on the type of streaming. The client also captures keyboard and mouse input from the player, sending all input back up to the server. The server receives the player input and applies it to the game as if the player were providing that input via the local keyboard and mouse on the server.

Drizzle can be configured to do image streaming, video streaming or graphics streaming. Image streaming is provided by using the SFML `capture()` method, sending the resulting image as a JPEG image. Video streaming is provided via the FFmpeg libraries. Graphics streaming is provided by sending the bare minimum information needed by the client to draw a game frame – the character to draw (1 byte), color (1 byte), and (x,y) location (4 bytes each).

D. Cloud Saucer Shoot

We created a Drizzle-compatible game called *Cloud Saucer Shoot* – an arcade-style shooting game set in space, where the player pilots a space ship against an endless, and ever increasing, horde of alien saucers. The player controls a ship using arrow keys to move up and down and green saucers automatically move right to left, spawning in greater numbers as time progresses. If the player's ship is struck by a saucer, both are destroyed. The player fires bullets from the ship by pressing the spacebar. Bullets When a bullet hits a saucer, both are destroyed and the player is awarded 10 points. The player also receives 1 point each second the ship is alive. The goal is to shoot as many saucers as possible before being destroyed.

E. Experiments

Our user study was conducted in a windowless computer lab with bright, fluorescent lighting.

Both the server and client ran on a laptop equipped with a 14" display, Intel i7 CPU 4 GHz processor, and 8 GB of memory running Windows 10. The system experiments were conducted on the same laptop. Given the lightweight nature of both the server, game and game client, the hardware was more than sufficient to provide a playout rate of 30 f/s.

Participants were volunteers solicited among graduate students in the game development program. First, the users heard a scripted brief about the study and signed an Institute Review Board (IRB) consent form. Next, they were asked to make themselves comfortable at the laptop by adjusting chair height and laptop screen tilt. Then users filled out an online demographics and gaming experience survey.

Users were told how to play the Cloud Saucer Shoot game and then played through a 15 second version of the game for practice. Results were not recorded for the practice session.

Immediately after the practice, users played 10 game sessions, each with an added latency selected from the range [0, 100, 200, 400, 800 milliseconds] using the network utility

Clumsy. Five of the sessions had time warp on and the other 5 had time warp off. The game sessions were shuffled and users were blind to the amount of added latency and time warp.

After each of the 10 game sessions, users were asked to rate the responsiveness and graphics consistency (i.e., absence of visual "glitches") from 0 (low) to 5 (high).

Playing through all game sessions typically took less than 15 minutes.

IV. ANALYSIS

This section summarizes participant demographics (Section IV-A), presents analysis of the user experience with time warp (Section IV-B), and analyzes system impact for the game streaming options (Section IV-C).

A. Demographics

Thirty users participated in the study. All users were 20 to 30 years old. Twenty-five identified as male and 5 as female. Sixty percent of the users played online games every day, 25 percent once per week, and 15 percent once per month or less.

B. User Experience

Figure 4 depicts user game performance, measured by game score, versus added latency, both with and without time warp. The x-axis is the added latency (in milliseconds) and the y-axis is the user score (a combination of Saucers destroyed and seconds alive). There are two trendlines, one for sessions with time warp on and the other for sessions with time warp off. Each point is the mean score for all users at that latency, shown with standard error bars. From the graph, user performance decreases with added latency, both with and without time warp. Without time warp, the trend is a clear exponential decay. With time warp, there is an initial decline in performance from 0 to 100 milliseconds of added delay, but then performance does not decline appreciably from 100 to 400 milliseconds, before decreasing again at 800 milliseconds. 800 milliseconds is about the time it takes a Saucer to travel completely across the screen in the game.

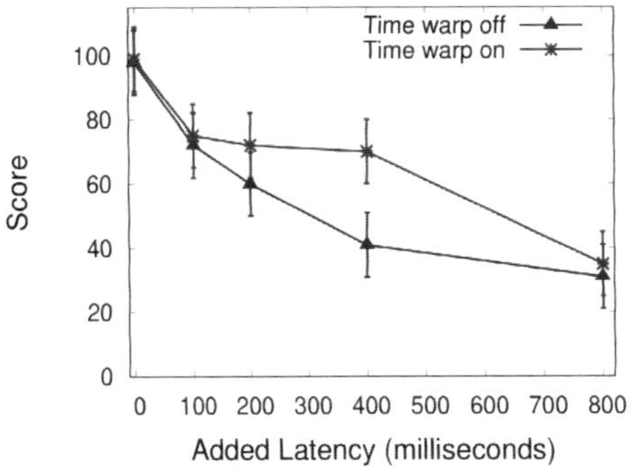

Figure 4. User game score versus added latency.

Figures 5 and 6 depict user opinions of the game sessions in the presence of latency – specifically, responsiveness and consistency, respectively. User opinions are on a 6 point scale, from 0 (low) to 5 (high). In both graphs, the x-axis, data points, error bars and trend lines are as for Figure 4. From the graphs, the responsiveness of the game is about the same with and without time warp, evidenced by the overlapping red and blue trend lines in Figure 5. The inconsistency in the game (i.e., presence of visual "glitches") with time warp is noticeable, however, seen by the clearly higher blue trend line in Figure 6. The absolute difference in consistency between time warp on and time warp off stays about the same (1 point) for all latencies.

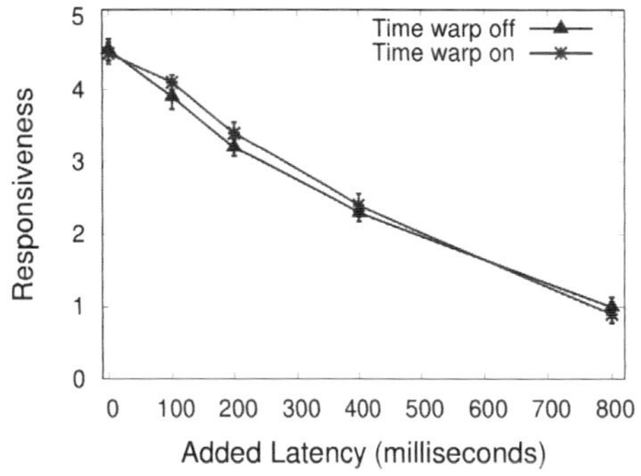

Figure 5. Responsiveness versus added latency.

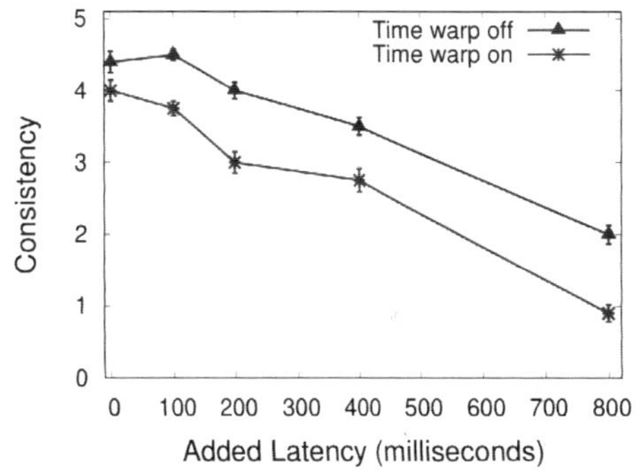

Figure 6. Consistency versus added latency.

C. System Impact

Figure 7 depicts the average downstream (server to client) network bitrate (the y-axis) for different Drizzle streaming approaches. Each bar shown is the average bitrate measured over a complete Cloud Saucer Shoot game session. From the graph, image streaming is network intensive, needing an average of almost 8 Mb/s. Video streaming has substantial bitrate savings, about 20% of that of image streaming. Graphics streaming has significantly reduced bitrates, about 20% that of video streaming and less than 5% that of image streaming.

In order to provide a perspective on Drizzle bitrates, Table I compares Drizzle bitrates to a commercial cloud-based game service, traditional network games and video conferencing. From the table, traditional network games have the lowest network bitrates since the heavyweight client runs a full copy of the game and only game object updates need to be sent over the network. Drizzle image streaming has the highest bitrate, but not substantially higher than commercial cloud-based game streaming. Drizzle image streaming has bitrates around that of video conferencing. Drizzle graphics streaming has bitrates

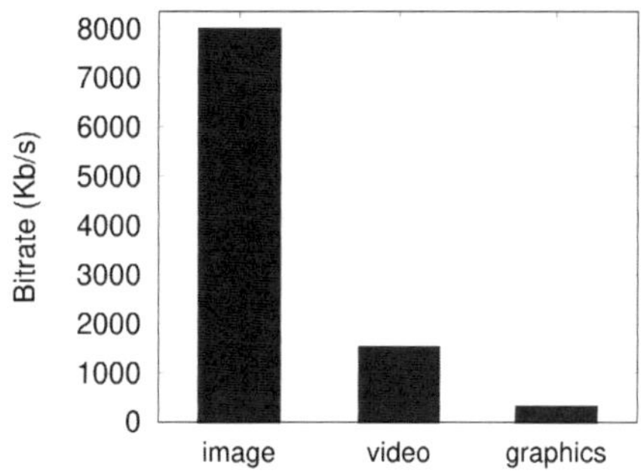

Figure 7. Network bitrates for Drizzle streaming approaches for Cloud Saucer Shoot.

between video conferencing and traditional network games, but closer to the latter.

TABLE I. NETWORK BITRATE COMPARISON

System	Bitrate (Kb/s)	Citation
Traditional network game	5 to 67	[21]–[23]
Drizzle graphics streaming	320	
Drizzle video streaming	1520	
Video conference	2222	
Commercial cloud-based game	6339	[1]
Drizzle image streaming	7950	

The game frames captured and sent by the server vary in size based on the game scene complexity. Game scenes with more game objects tend to be visually complex, not compressing as well for image and video streaming and requiring more commands for graphics streaming.

Figure 8 depicts the average network bitrate versus number of game objects for different Drizzle streaming approaches. The x-axis is the number of game objects and the y-axis is the network bitrate. Each point is the mean bitrate required for rendering a Cloud Saucer Shoot game frame with the indicated number of objects. From the graph, the bitrate requirements grow linearly with the number of objects. In all cases, image streaming has the highest bitrates by far, followed by video streaming and then graphics streaming.

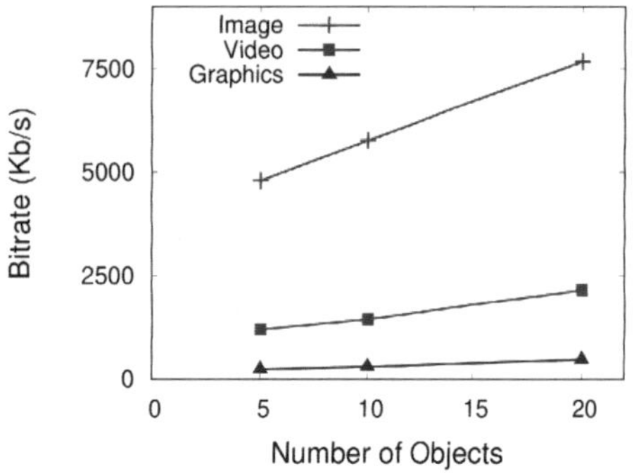

Figure 8. Network bitrates versus number of game objects with trendlines for each Drizzle streaming approach.

Supporting games with a lot of game objects can make the performance bottleneck the server instead of the network. Using the same computer as for our user study, we analyzed the CPU load for the Drizzle server for image streaming scenarios from Figure 9 with 200 milliseconds of added latency and time warp. The breakdown is as follows:

Time warp - each game loop (30 Hz), the server rolls back the game world 200 milliseconds to compensate for client latency, applies the user input, and (after Update) rolls the world forward again.

Update - the server updates the game world (moving game objects and resolving collisions).

Copy - the server copies the current game world, effectively replicating every game object in the game to preserve it for future time warping.

Stream - the server renders the game world and sends it to the client.

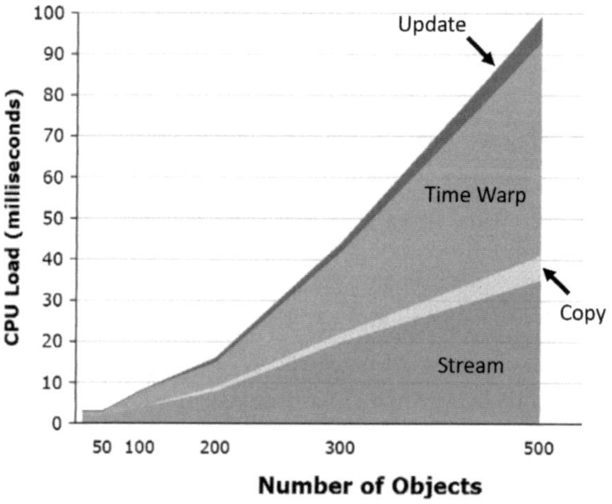

Figure 9. CPU load breakdown versus number of game objects.

From the graph, as expected, total CPU load increases with number of game objects. Once the CPU load exceeds 33 milliseconds (at about 260 game objects), the game engine can no longer keep up with the 30 Hz game loop rate. Under these conditions, the player experience would degrade from a reduced frame rate and overall sluggish performance. Time warp and streaming have the highest processing load by far. Many traditional game servers have latency compensation, but streaming adds an additional processing overhead unique to cloud-based game servers. This suggests the processing requirements for cloud-based servers are significantly higher than that of traditional game servers.

V. Conclusion and Future Work

The growth in games and networking has provided the opportunity for cloud-based games, where the server handles most of the game processing and rendering, streaming game frames to the lightweight client that primarily gathers and transmits player input. While cloud-based games have some advantages over traditional game architectures, the remote processing of gameplay presents challenges in accommodating latency and network bitrate requirements.

This paper presents *Drizzle*, a lightweight cloud-based game system that allows for the study of latency compensation and game streaming approaches. Drizzle is written in C++ using the Dragonfly [5] game engine, adding a networking component and a lightweight client for full cloud-based game system functionality.

Addressing network bitrates, Drizzle is used to evaluate different cloud-based game streaming approaches, comparing the bitrates required by image streaming, video streaming and graphics streaming. Results from our system experiments show video streaming, the state of the art for most commercial systems, provides a significant bitrate reduction over image streaming but graphics streaming can reduce bitrates even more.

Addressing latency, Drizzle is used to evaluate a well-known (but not well-evaluated) latency compensation technique – time warp – wherein the game server rolls back time to when the client provided input in order to accommodate the server-to-client latency. While time warp is often used by traditional game servers, e.g., Overwatch [19] (Blizzard, 2016), it has not been scientifically evaluated much nor has it been applied to cloud-based games. Results from our 30-participant user study show time warp with projectile weapons can mitigate some of the effects of latency in terms of player performance, but time warp has more visual inconsistencies than without time warp. Analysis of CPU load shows time warp and streaming dominate, suggesting cloud-based game servers need more resources than traditional game servers.

Future work might look to optimize the processing of streaming as well as latency compensation.

Future work could also evaluate time warp for hit scan (i.e., instant effect) weapons rather than for projectile weapons, as was done in this paper. Other latency compensation techniques such as aim assistance or time delay could be evaluated in a cloud-based game system (e.g., Drizzle).

While Drizzle shows graphics streaming has potential to reduce bitrates more than video streaming, future work could apply graphics streaming techniques to systems other game systems (e.g., Gaming Anywhere [7]) and explore the benefits for a wider range of games and game conditions.

REFERENCES

[1] M. Claypool, D. Finkel, A. Grant, and M. Solano, "On the Performance of OnLive Thin Client Games," Springer Multimedia Systems Journal (MMSJ) - Special Issue on NetGames, vol. 20, no. 5, 2014.

[2] K.-T. Chen, Y.-C. Chang, H.-J. Hsu, D.-Y. Chen, C.-Y. Huang, and C.-H. Hsu, "On the Quality of Service of Cloud Gaming Systems," IEEE Transactions on Multimedia, vol. 26, no. 2, Feb. 2014.

[3] D. D. Winter, P. Simoens, L. Deboosere, F. D. Turck, J. Moreau, B. Dhoedt, and P. Demeester, "A Hybrid Thin-client Protocol for Multimedia Streaming and Interactive Gaming Applications," in Proceedings of NOSSDAV, Newport, RI, USA, Jun. 2006.

[4] Y. W. Bernier, "Latency Compensating Methods in Client/Server In-game Protocol Design and Optimization," in Proceedings of GDC, San Francisco, CA, USA, Feb. 2001, https://tinyurl.com/yan2yvs2 (accessed 2019.6.14).

[5] M. Claypool, Dragonfly - Program a Game Engine from Scratch. Worcester, MA, USA: Interactive Media and Game Development, Worcester Polytechnic Institute, 2014, online at: http://dragonfly.wpi.edu/book/.

[6] I. Foster, Y. Zhao, I. Raicu, and S. Lu, "Cloud Computing and Grid Computing 360-Degree Compared," in Proceedings of Grid Computing Environments Workshop (GCE), Austin, TX, USA, Nov. 2008, pp. 1–10.

[7] C. Huang, C. Hsu, Y. Chang, and K. Chen, "GamingAnywhere: An Open Cloud Gaming System," in Proceedings of ACM Multimedia Systems (MMSys), Oslo, Norway, Feb. 2013.

[8] R. Shea, L. Jiangchuan, E. Ngai, and Y. Cui, "Cloud Gaming: Architecture and Performance," IEEE Network, vol. 27, no. 4, Jul-Aug 2013, pp. 16–21.

[9] I. Slivar, M. Suznjevic, and L. Skorin-Kapov, "Game Categorization for Deriving QoE-Driven Video Encoding Configuration Strategies for Cloud Gaming," ACM Transactions on Multimedia Computuing Communications and Applications, vol. 14, no. 3s, Jun. 2018, pp. 56:1–56:24.

[10] OnLive, http://onlive.com/.

[11] StreamMyGame, http://streammygame.com/.

[12] M. Jarschel, D. Schlosser, S. Scheuring, and T. Hossfeld, "An Evaluation of QoE in Cloud Gaming Based on Subjective Tests," in Proceedings of Innovative Mobile and Internet Services in Ubiquitous Computing, Seoul, Korea, 2011.

[13] M. Claypool and D. Finkel, "The Effects of Latency on Player Performance in Cloud-based Games," in Proceedings of NetGames, Nagoya, Japan, Dec. 2014.

[14] A. Sackl, R. Schatz, T. Hossfeld, F. Metzger, D. Lister, and R. Irmer, "QoE Management Made Uneasy: The Case of Cloud Gaming," in IEEE Conference on Communications Workshops (ICC), Kuala Lumpur, Malaysia, May 2016.

[15] Y. W. Bernier, "Latency Compensating Methods in Client/Server In-game Protocol Design and Optimization," in Proceedings of the Game Developers Conference, San Francisco, CA, USA, Feb. 2001, [Online] https://www.gamedevs.org/uploads/latency-compensation-in-client-server-protocols.pdf.

[16] Z. Ivkovic, I. Stavness, C. Gutwin, and S. Sutcliffe, "Quantifying and Mitigating the Negative Effects of Local Latencies on Aiming in 3D Shooter Games," in Proceedings of the Conference on Human Factors in Computing Systems, Seoul, Korea, 2015.

[17] W.-K. Lee and R. K. Chang, "Evaluation of Lag-related Configurations in First-person Shooter Games," in Proceedings of NetGames, Zagreb, Croatia, 2015.

[18] S. W. K. Lee and R. K. C. Chang, "On 'Shot Around a Corner' in First-Person Shooter Games," in Proceedings of NetGames, Jun. 2017.

[19] T. Ford and P. Orwig, "Developer Update - Let's Talk Netcode," Online, apr 2016, https://www.youtube.com/watch?v=vTH2ZPgYujQ (accessed: 1-17-2018).

[20] Dragonfly Game Trailers, https://tinyurl.com/df-trailers.

[21] J. Nichols and M. Claypool, "The Effects of Latency on Online Madden NFL Football," in Proceedings of NOSSDAV, Kinsale, County Cork, Ireland, Jun. 2004.

[22] T. Beigbeder, R. Coughlan, C. Lusher, J. Plunkett, E. Agu, and M. Claypool, "The Effects of Loss and Latency on User Performance in Unreal Tournament 2003," in Proceedings of NetGames, Portland, OG, USA, Sep. 2004.

[23] N. Sheldon, E. Girard, S. Borg, M. Claypool, and E. Agu, "The Effect of Latency on User Performance in Warcraft III," in Proceedings of NetGames, Redwood City, CA, USA, May 2003.

Sharing but not Caring – Performance of TCP BBR and TCP CUBIC at the Network Bottleneck

Saahil Claypool, Mark Claypool
Worcester Polytechnic Institute
Worcester, USA
Email: {smclaypool,claypool}@wpi.edu

Jae Chung
Viasat
Marlborough, USA
Email: jaeWon.chung@viasat.com

Feng Li
Verizon Labs
Waltham, USA
Email: feng.li@verizon.com

***Abstract*—Loss-based congestion control protocols, such as TCP CUBIC, can unnecessarily fill router buffers, adding delays that degrade application performance, particularly streaming video. Newcomer Transport Control Protocol (TCP) BBR (Bottleneck Bandwidth and Round-trip propagation time) uses estimates of the bottleneck bandwidth and Round-Trip Time (RTT) to try to operate at the theoretical optimum - just enough data to fully utilize the network without excess queuing. We present detailed experimental results showing that, in practice, BBR can misestimate the bottleneck bandwidth and RTT, causing high packet loss for shallow buffer routers and massive throughput variations when competing with TCP CUBIC flows. We suggest methods for improving BBR's estimation mechanisms to provide more stability and fairness.**

Keywords–TCP; congestion control; Raspberry Pi.

I. Introduction

TCP is the most commonly used Internet protocol and, for video, will account for 80% of all global traffic in 2019 [1]. Despite its prevalence, TCP is not optimized for video – video streaming has real-time constraints such that the next packet is often more important than a lost or in-flight packet. In contrast, TCP blocks sender window progression until each packet is delivered in order, possibly incurring playout delay at the client [2]. This is especially true when TCP is configured to use a loss-based congestion control protocol, such as CUBIC [3]. With TCP CUBIC, networks that would have Round-Trip Times (RTTs) of milliseconds when uncongested bloat buffers and can instead have RTTs of seconds. This increased RTT can reduce video streaming Quality of Service (QoS) because it can increase the time to detect and retransmit lost packets or to switch video to lower encoding rates [4].

TCP BBR, a new congestion control protocol developed by Google [5], aims to combat bufferbloat by estimating the minimum Round-Trip propagation time (RTprop) and the maximum Bottleneck Bandwidth (BtlBw) for a given connection to compute the Bandwidth Delay Product (BDP). BBR then caps its inflight packets to a small multiple of the BDP and paces its sending rate to match the estimated bottleneck bandwidth. In theory, having a single BDP of packets inflight is optimal for a network flow as it minimizes delay while maximizing a connection's throughput [6], and BBR's inflight cap is set to operate close to this optimal value.

In practice, BBR has been successfully deployed in Google's YouTube edge servers, increasing QoS [5]. Spotify AB, an audio streaming platform, has found that BBR helps reduce streaming stutters [7] and Dropbox, a file hosting service, has run preliminary BBR experiments that show an increase in file download speeds [8].

Despite promising performance, BBR may not operate well on pathways with shallow router buffers and when in direct competition with loss-based congestion controlled flows, such as TCP CUBIC [5], [9], [10]. In shallow buffers, BBR creates high loss due to its too-high Congestion Window (CWND) cap and persistence despite lost packets. This is especially problematic when it shares a bottleneck with loss-based congestion control protocols. Even when router queues are not shallow, BBR can induce significant throughput variation when sharing a bottleneck with CUBIC.

This study seeks to answer the following questions:

A) Can an inexpensive hardware testbed be effective for evaluating state of the art congestion control protocols?

B) Does BBR exhibit high loss rates when run over shallow router buffers?

C) Is BBR unfair when run with competing CUBIC flows?

We set up a hardware testbed for controlled experiments using the latest network OS code and create custom tools to conduct a wide variety of network performance tests. These tests vary: link capacities, network latencies, router queue lengths, TCP congestion control algorithms, and number of flows competing at a bottleneck.

Analysis of the results verifies prior work regarding BBR's performance in shallow buffers and in competition with CUBIC. It is crucial for experimental results to be reproduced by others within the scientific community in order to generalize the knowledge beyond the experience of the individual scientist. Our work goes further than previous research since our wide variety of tests allows us to more precisely define and identify BBR's behaviors over a range of network conditions. Specifically, we find that BBR's high throughput variation and high loss in shallow buffers are due to a static CWND cap and erroneous minimum RTprop estimates.

The contributions of this work include:

- Configuration, software framework and validation of an inexpensive testbed for conducting congestion control research using the latest Linux kernel code.
- Confirmation of base BBR performance under known, controlled conditions, validating Cardwell et al. [5].

- Extension to understanding BBR's behavior in shallow buffers, validating Hock et al. [11], with new observations on loss rate versus buffer size over a range of link conditions.
- Extension to understanding of BBR's cyclic behavior with deeper buffers and competing with CUBIC flows, validating Scholz et al. [9] and Miyazawa et al. [10], contributing new details on the BBR protocol features that cause this cyclic behavior, and quantification of fluctuation and unfairness versus buffer size.
- Suggestions for improving BBR by adjusting BBR's RTT estimation and adding a feedback loop to dynamically adjust BBR's CWND.

The rest of this paper is organized as follows: Section II discusses prior work in TCP congestion control and BBR; Section III describes our experimental setup to evaluate BBR in a hardware testbed; Section IV analyzes the experiment results; and Section V summarizes our conclusions and presents possible future work.

II. Related Work

This section defines the optimal network operating point (Section II-A), and describes recent TCP congestion control protocols (Section II-B), including BBR (Section II-C).

A. The Optimal Operating Point

Regardless of the number of hops, TCP views the network path as a single link characterized by its Bottleneck Bandwidth (BtlBw) and the minimum RTT (RTprop) it takes a packet to propagate through the network in the absence of queuing delay. The theoretical optimal operating point for a network flow using TCP is when exactly one bandwidth × delay (the Bandwidth-Delay Product, or BDP) of packets is in flight at all times, and the arrival rate of packets at the bottleneck router is close to the service rate (the limiting factor of the bandwidth) of that router [6], [12]. If these conditions are met, then the bottleneck router link is fully utilized with no extra queuing delay. This operating point has been coined *Kleinrock's operating point* after researcher Leonard Kleinrock.

This relationship can be seen in Figure 1, with the packets inflight depicted on the x-axes and the RTT (including queuing) on the y-axis of the top graph and the delivery rate on the y-axis of the bottom graph. The minimum RTT is labeled RTprop, achieved when the inflight is less than or equal to the BDP. When there is less than a BDP of packets in the network, the bottleneck link is underutilized, seen with a delivery rate less than the link capacity (labeled BtlBw). If there is more than one BDP of packets in the network, the delivery rate stays maxed out at the bottleneck link capacity, but the packets incur queuing delay and the RTT increases beyond the minimum. Thus, the optimal operating point achieves the maximum throughput *and* the minimum latency. Note that loss-based congestion control protocols, such as TCP CUBIC, operate at the right side of this graph, increasing the amount of inflight packets until the bottleneck router queue saturates and packets are dropped.

B. Recent Congestion Control Protocols

Unfortunately, Kleinrock's operating point has been proven to be practically impossible to converge to for a distributed algorithm [13]. Thus every congestion control protocol seeks a "good" operating point, often favoring throughput over delay. The different congestion control approaches include: loss-based protocols (Section II-B1) that maximize throughput, utility-based protocols (Section II-B2) that adjust their operating points based on measures of utility, and measurement-based protocols (Section II-B3) that explicitly set parameters in an attempt to match the theoretical optimal operating point.

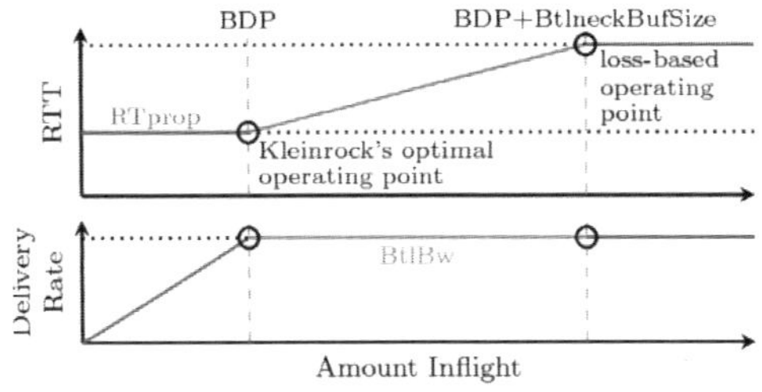

Figure 1. Optimal operating point [9].

1) Loss-based congestion control: Loss-based congestion control protocols treat lost packets as congestion signals, increasing the number of inflight packets until packet loss occurs (indicating the network is saturated) whereupon they decrease their inflight packets, and repeat the cycle. This behavior means loss-based protocols generally operate to the right of Kleinrock's operating point as depicted in Figure 1, resulting in high throughput, but also high latency.

TCP CUBIC [3], the de facto standard loss-based congestion control protocol, aims to maximize network utilization by controlling the Congestion Window (CWND) with a cubic function. The cubic function's convex nature allows the CWND to quickly grow to utilize available capacity. In the case of a congestion event (such as packet loss), the cubic function adjusts such that the CWND increases in a concave manner as it approaches the previous maximum, avoiding overshooting the maximum network capacity and excessive packet loss. In the absence of loss, the cubic function returns to the convex profile to rapidly fill available network capacity. Together, these two profiles seek high utilization and low loss.

2) Utility-based congestion control: Utility-based congestion control protocols evaluate their performance based on a utility function, and adjust parameters to maximize utility over time. Unlike loss-based congestion control protocols (such as TCP CUBIC), utility-based congestion control protocols do not have explicit responses for different congestion events, but rather have just a general set of actions to take to maximize their utilities. In general, using a utility function can simplify protocol design since not every condition needs to be explicitly handled, but rather only needs algorithm parameter adjustments to improve utility.

The utility-based Performance-oriented Congestion Control (PCC) [14] works under the assumption that networks are too complicated to deterministically predict the effects of a given action. The PCC premise is that it is infeasible for a protocol to tune performance with a predefined action for every congestion event, as does CUBIC. Thus, PCC treats the underlying network as a "black box" and empirically observes which actions provide better utility by continuously conducting mini experiments. In a mini experiment, PCC reduces or increases the sending rate and CWND and observes the utility

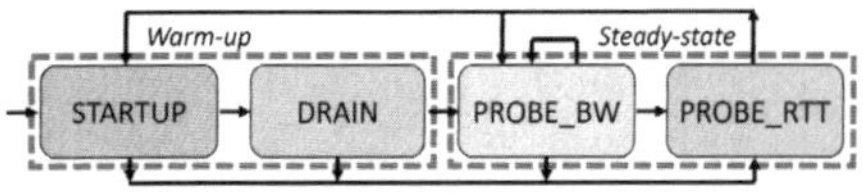

Figure 2. BBR state transition diagram.

for this action. The observation informs its next action through a gradient-ascent algorithm to adjust sending rates towards the optimal. This decoupling of congestion events and actions allows PCC to perform well even in networks with high random loss, such as in some wireless networks.

Copa [15], another utility-based congestion control protocol, uses a simple set of rules to update the sending rate and CWND towards an optimal utility value, creating little to no queuing at the bottleneck router if all flows are using a similar CWND updating method. Copa measures the queuing delay as the difference between the observed and minimum RTTs, and increases its sending rate until small queues are created at the bottleneck. Copa implements a "competitive mode" if it detects a competing buffer-filling flow. This addresses the problem with delay-based utility functions, such as in TCP Vegas [16], where full buffers cause a reduction in inflight packets to reduce congestion, leading to unfairness when competing with buffer-filling protocols.

3) Measurement-based Congestion Control: Loss-based congestion control protocols are reactive, waiting until loss is observed before taking an action to reduce congestion, and utility-based congestion control protocols treat the network as a black box, just taking actions to based on some utility function. Conversely, measurement-based protocols attempt to estimate the current network operating point and explicitly adjust protocol parameters to try to meet the optimal. Examples include TCP Vegas, discussed in this section, and TCP BBR, discussed in Section II-C.

TCP Vegas [16] measures the observed throughput and RTT to estimate how much bloat (excess queued packets) it has created in the network. Vegas sets the expected throughput to $CWND/RTprop$ and compares this value to the actual observed throughput. If the actual throughput is lower than the expected throughput by some threshold α, Vegas assumes it has too small a congestion window, and increases the CWND linearly for one RTT. Similarly, if the actual throughput is greater than the expected throughput by some threshold β, Vegas assumes the CWND is too large and decreases the CWND accordingly.

In theory, this scheme should let Vegas operate near Kleinrock's operating point, but in practice Vegas tends to be too conservative and cedes capacity to loss-based congestion control protocols such as CUBIC because Vegas decreases its CWND to minimize buffer bloat while loss-based protocols increase CWNDs until loss occurs.

C. Bottleneck Bandwidth and Round-trip Propagation Time

Bottleneck Bandwidth and Round-trip propagation time (BBR) [5] is a congestion control protocol designed to replace loss-based algorithms. BBR [5] aims to operate near Kleinrock's operating point (see Section II-A) by estimating the BtlBw and RTprop parameters and setting the sending rate and inflight packets accordingly. BBR operates using a series of states shown in Figure 2. After slow start, BBR looks for increases to the bandwidth during *PROBE_BW* every 8 RTTs, increasing the CWND and setting a rate multiplier to send at a rate greater than the current BtlBw. The new estimated BtlBw is set to the maximum delivery rate observed during this probe. The RTprop estimation expires after 10 seconds, causing BBR to enter *PROBE_RTT* to re-estimate the minimum RTT. In Probe_RTT, BBR briefly reduces its inflight packets, draining any queue that it had built up. The new RTprop estimate is set to the minimum RTT observed. BBR always paces its sending rate at the estimated BtlBw and caps its inflight CWND to two times the estimated BDP. The CWND inflight cap is set to two BDP rather than the theoretically optimal one BDP to accommodate delayed and stretched ACKs in wireless networks. However, as we show in Section IV, the larger CWND can cause high packet loss, instability, and unfairness.

Because BBR relies on an estimated RTprop and BtlBw, BBR has inconsistent behavior when it misestimates one or both of these values. Hock et al. [11] find that when multiple BBR flows share a bottleneck, BBR pathologically over-estimates its fair-share of the bandwidth since each flow measures the maximum available bandwidth over a time period. The sum of throughput's derived from these estimates is then *always* greater than the bottleneck's actual maximum bandwidth, causing persistent queues to build at the bottleneck router until the inflight cap of 2 BDP is reached [11]. This persistent queue is especially problematic when the bottleneck router queue is smaller than a single BDP, whereupon BBR attempts to build a queue of 1 BDP and ignores the massive packet loss caused by overwhelming the bottleneck queue.

Scholz et al. [9] and Miyazawa et al. [10] show that BBR also produces inaccurate RTprop estimates when it shares the bottleneck with buffer filling protocols, such as TCP CUBIC. When BBR over-estimates the RTprop, it drastically changes its CWND and thus creates large amounts of loss. This loss and mis-measurement leads to a cyclic behavior where BBR and CUBIC each have constantly fluctuating throughput.

We confirm these prior BBR results but in a broader range of network scenarios and provide additional explanations in Section IV. We incorporate these new insights into our suggestions to improve BBR's performance in Section IV-E.

III. EXPERIMENTS

We set up a hardware testbed and develop a set of custom tools that enable a variety of network experiments for evaluating TCP CUBIC and TCP BBR in a controlled environment. Because our testbed relies on off-the-shelf hardware and software, it provides an attractive environment for congestion control research that can be recreated at relatively low cost.

Our testbed, named "Panaderia" which translates to "bakery" or "bread shop" in Spanish, consists of 8 Raspberry Pi computers, two network switches, and one Linux PC named "Horno" (oven) functioning as a router. The use of hardware (versus simulation) allows us to run the mainline Linux kernel versions of BBR and CUBIC, thus ensuring adherence to implemented protocol behavior. Further, the low cost allows us to afford separate hosts for each flow, thus removing any confounding factors from multiple flows originating from a single machine.

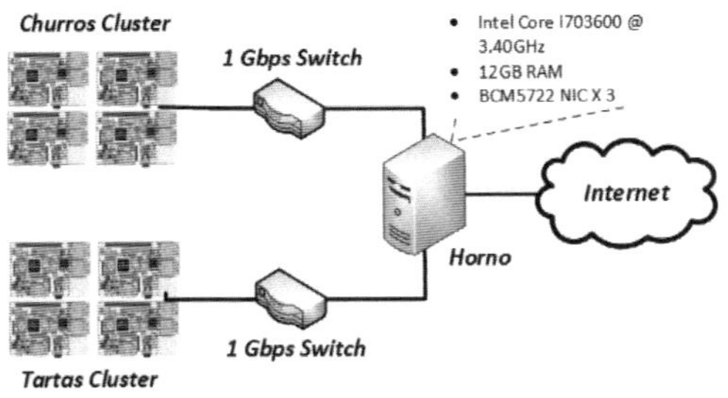

Figure 3. Hardware testbed topology.

TABLE I. EXPERIMENT PARAMETERS.

Parameters	Values
Number of Flows	2, 4, 8
Network Capacity	40, 80, 120 Mb/s
Congestion Control Protocol	CUBIC, BBR
Router Queue Size	0.25, 0.50, 0.75, 1.00, 1.25, 1.50, 1.75, 2.00, 4.00, 8.00 BDP

The hardware is configured in a traditional dumbbell topology shown in Figure 3 – the Raspberry Pis are split into two subnets of four machines ("churros" and "tartas" clusters).

Each Raspberry Pi is a model 3B+ running the Linux kernel v4.17. Pilot tests (not shown) reveal an individual Raspberry Pi has a maximum sending rate of about 225 Mb/s, limited by the USB 2.0 bus speed. Below this throughput, we verified that the network behavior of the Raspberry Pi performs similarly to the network behavior of a Linux PC. We developed a series of Python scripts to allow us to nimbly run experiments, vital for comparing BBR's behavior over a wide range of network conditions. Details on the setup specifics, as well as access to our configuration scripts, are available via our git repository [17].

The router is a Linux PC, configured with an Intel i7 CPU, 12 GB of RAM, and Broadcom BCM5722 Gigabit Ethernet PCI cards. The router uses NetEm [18] to add a fixed propagation delay of 24 ms giving a total round-trip propagation time of 25 ms to align with previous research [5]. The router also uses `tc-tbf` token bucket filters to control the bottleneck bandwidth [19]. Since accumulated tokens can cause bursts of traffic interfering with BBR's bottleneck bandwidth estimate, the router is configured with two token bucket filters with small buckets to limit instantaneous bursts [20]. Receiving and sending devices each collect `pcap` network traces, which are subsequently analyzed for RTT, throughput, and inflight packets. Additionally, the router records the number of bytes queued and number of packets dropped.

Our experiments vary flows, protocols, network capacities and router queue sizes, as shown in Table I.

Validation: When creating a novel testing environment, it is important to validate testbed behavior against known results. Similarly, for science, it is vital to confirm that prior work is reproducible to ensure a knowledge foundation before making improvements. We validate the Raspberry Pi's TCP networking by, among other methods, confirming that BBR follows the behavior seen by Cardwell et. al [5]. Specifically, we ensure that when multiple BBR flows share a single bottleneck, each flow converges to a fair share of the maximum bandwidth, and that the flows synchronizes during their PROBE_RTT phases.

Figure 4a depicts the throughputs of 5 simultaneous BBR flows with staggered start times competing for a 100 Mb/s bottleneck with a RTprop of 10 ms, as evaluated by Cardwell et al. [5]. Each of the flows obtains a fair share of the bottleneck capacity, 20 Mb/s, and after about 30 seconds, each flow enters PROBE_RTT at the same time, seen by the throughput dips at about times 30 and 40 seconds. Figure 4b depicts our Panaderia testbed's behavior in similar conditions with 4 simultaneous BBR flows with staggered start times competing for a 80 MB/s link. Similar to Cardwell et al., our BBR flows synchronize at a fair share of 20 Mb/s within about time 30 seconds, repeatedly doing so every 10 seconds. Further validation tests are not shown due to lack of space, but can be found in the full report [21]. In total, this both confirms Cardwell et al.'s measured BBR behavior (a first-class scientific contribution) as well as supports the validity of the Panaderia as a network testbed for evaluation of TCP congestion control protocols.

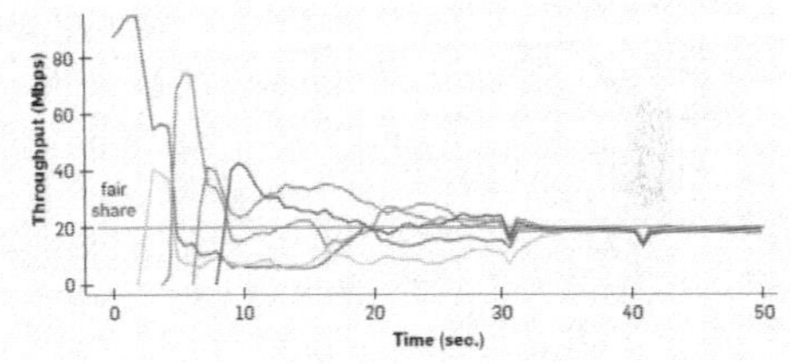

(a) Synchronization of BBR from Figure 8 of [5].

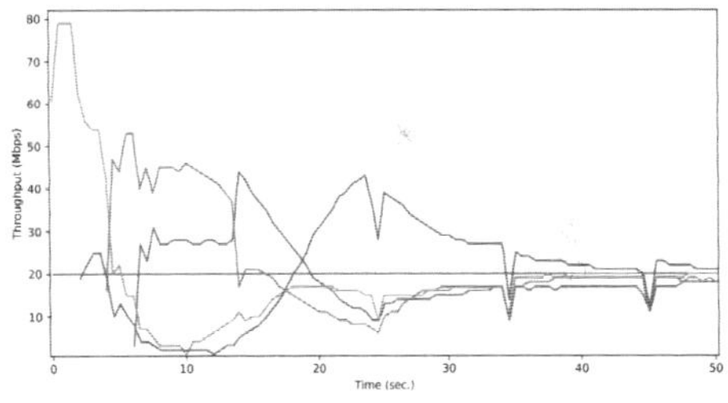

(b) Synchronization of BBR in the Panaderia.

Figure 4. Comparison of Cardwell et al. [5] to our Panaderia testbed.

IV. RESULTS

This section: validates BBR's behavior (Section IV-A); extends previous work in shallow buffers (Section IV-B) and router queue sizes (Section IV-C); evaluates BBR's interplay with CUBIC (Section IV-D); and proposes mechanisms to improve BBR's performance (Section IV-E).

A. Standard BBR Behavior

Prior work has shown that when there is more than one flow competing for the same bottleneck, BBR tends to create a 1 to 1.5 BDP standing queue [11]. We verify this by running 2, 4, and 8 BBR flows for 5 minutes at 40, 80, and 120 Mb/s with a 25 ms RTprop and a large bottleneck queue.

Figure 5 depicts 4 BBR flows competing for an 80 Mb/s link with the maximum router queue size set to 2 MBytes ($8BDP$). Only the steady-state behavior is analyzed (1 minute

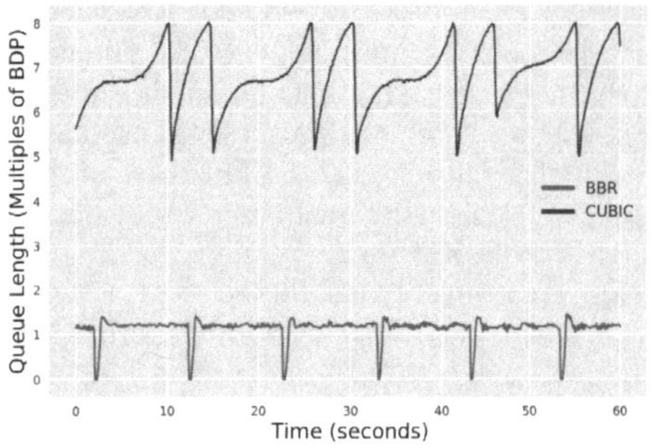

Figure 5. BBR and CUBIC in a large router queue.

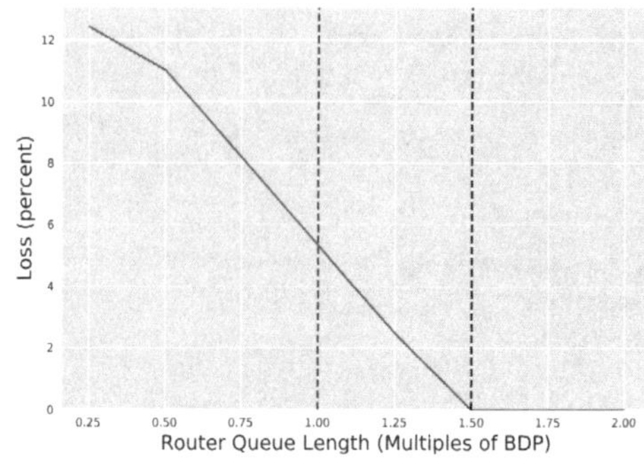

Figure 7. BBR's loss versus router queue size.

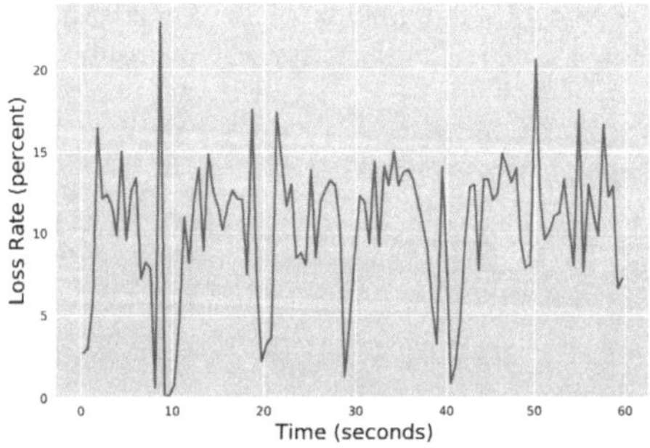

Figure 6. BBR's loss rate in a small router queue.

of a 5 minute trial). For reference, we independently ran and show on the same graph a TCP CUBIC flow to compare behaviors. CUBIC, as a loss-based protocol, continues to fill the queue until the 8 BDP maximum is reached. In contrast, BBR creates a persistent queue of about 1.1 BDP, increasing to roughly 1.5 BDP during bandwidth probing.

Over the full range of flows, capacities, and queue sizes listed in Table I, analysis confirms that BBR creates a standing queue of 1 to 1.5 BDP, similar to what is shown in Figure 5. Results are not shown due to lack of space, but can be found in the full report [21]. Note that while BBR's RTT is low (roughly 0.25 CUBIC's), it is around double the RTprop since the 1 BDP of packets queued at the router takes a full RTT to process ($BDP = BtlBw \times RTprop$).

B. BBR in Shallow Buffers

Since multiple BBR flows competing at a bottleneck create about a BDP queue at the bottleneck router, when routers have shallow buffers (i.e., a small router queue) BBR has the potential to saturate the queue and create loss.

We evaluate a shallow buffer scenario with a bottleneck bandwidth of 80 Mb/s and a RTprop of 25 ms, but with a bottleneck router queue of just 0.5 BDP. Figure 6 depicts the loss rate at the router averaged over 500 ms intervals. All further loss rate graphs are calculated in the same manner. From the graph, loss varies considerably over time, but persists and averages over 10 percent.

C. BBR over Different Router Queue Sizes

We evaluate BBR's loss rate over a range of router queue sizes. Specifically, we run 3 identical trials at 40, 80, and 120 Mb/s, all at 25 ms RTprop for 5 minutes for each given queue size: 0.25, 0.50, 0.75, 1.25, 1.50, 2.00, 4.00, and 8.00 BDP. The recorded packet captures at each host and the queue statistics at the bottleneck router determine the aggregate behavior of BBR given the bottleneck queue size.

Figure 7 depicts the results. The x-axis is the maximum router queue length in terms of the BDP and the y-axis is the loss rate during steady state (minutes 2 to 4 of a 5 minute connection) averaged over the 3 trials.

Since BBR causes an extra 1.5 BDP of packets to be enqueued at the bottleneck router, the loss rate is extremely high when the buffer size is less than a BDP and is high unless the router buffer size is at least 1.5 BDP. This result confirms the findings of Hock et al. that in practice BBR's inflight is 2.5 BDP [11], while providing specific analysis of the actual loss rates realized versus queue size.

Since BBR does not respond to loss as a congestion signal, the queue always grows to 1.5 BDP, even though BBR's throughput remains relatively high despite the loss (not shown due to lack of space, but shown in the full report [21]). From here on, we refer to buffers less than 1.5 BDP as shallow, buffers greater than 4 BDP as large and buffers in-between as medium. Note analysis of router queue size is relative to the BDP – with high throughput, high RTT, a shallow buffer of 1 BDP could have a lot of bytes.

D. BBR's Interplay with CUBIC

Another concern with BBR is when it competes with CUBIC and other loss-based congestion control. BBR's mechanism for controlling the bottleneck bandwidth is at odds with CUBIC's – CUBIC adjusts its CWND to minimize loss, while BBR mostly ignores loss as a congestion signal. This difference presents itself uniquely in each of the conditions discussed above – shallow, medium and large buffers.

1) BBR and CUBIC in Shallow Buffers: By itself in shallow buffers, BBR creates high amounts of ambient loss by growing its CWND beyond what the network can handle (see Figure 6). Because CUBIC treats such loss as congestion in the same scenario, CUBIC shrinks its CWND in response. Figure 8 depicts the relative throughputs of BBR and CUBIC competing over a shallow (0.5 BDP) buffer in an 80 Mb/s

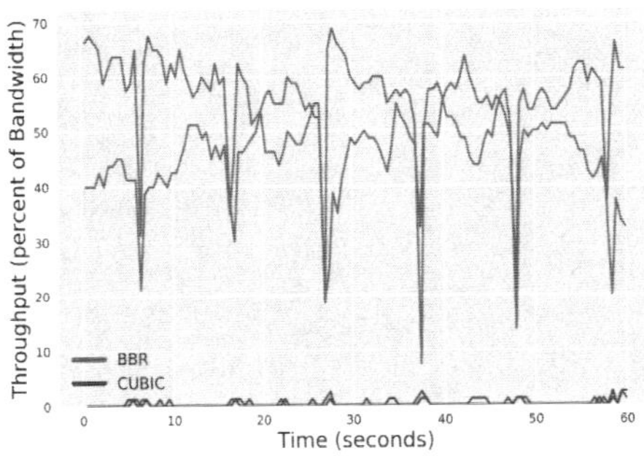

Figure 8. Throughput utilization.

and 25 ms bottleneck. The loss rates are similar to Figure 6, averaging about 10 percent. As seen in Figure 12, the relative throughput for CUBIC is *much* lower than BBR because, again, CUBIC responds to the loss whereas BBR does not. Similar trials with 40, 80 and 120 Mb/s and 2, 4 and 8 flows show similar results. These results are omitted due to lack of space, but can be found in the full report [21].

2) BBR and CUBIC in Medium to Large Buffers: In medium buffers, where BBR is *not* persistently inducing loss, BBR and CUBIC display a cyclic behavior. We evaluate this by running 2 BBR and 2 CUBIC flows through a 80 Mb/s capacity, 25 ms RTprop bottleneck and a router queue of 1.75 BDP. Figure 9 shows the results, annotated to match the explanations that follow. BBR and CUBIC exhibit cyclic performance – they alternate which flows dominate the connection over a regular 20 second period, confirming prior results by Scholz et al. [9] and Miyazawa et al. [10]. We build upon this work by explaining the factors that cause the cycles in detail.

CUBIC Dominates. When BBR has an accurate estimate for the BtlBw and RTprop, it caps its inflight at 2 $\widehat{BDP}$. This means that BBR allows just 1 BDP of packets to enqueue at the bottleneck router for 8 RTTs. During this time, CUBIC expands its CWND by an additional 0.75 BDP to fill the router queue before encountering loss.

Since a flow's throughput is proportional to the queue share at the bottleneck router, as CUBIC gets more packets enqueued, BBR observes a lower throughput and thus further decreases its CWND, which is derived from the observed throughput. This creates a positive feedback loop allowing CUBIC to continue to increase its CWND in response to BBR's decrease of its CWND as it observes a reduced throughput. This behavior can be seen from time 0 to 10 sec. in Figure 9.

BBR takes over. Every 10 seconds without observing a new minimum RTT ($\widehat{RTprop}$), BBR probes for RTprop by reducing its inflight packets to just 4 packets to drain the router queue [5] (e.g., time 28 seconds of Figure 9a). BBR uses the minimum observed RTT as the new $\widehat{RTprop}$. However, the queue length, shown in Figure 9b, does not change significantly because most of the packets in the queue are from the CUBIC flows. In other words, even when BBR decreases its inflight packets, the queue stays relatively filled. Figure 9d depicts the RTT over this period, where around time 28 seconds, the RTT is still much higher than the true RTprop – around 60 ms rather than 25 ms. This causes the $\widehat{RTprop}$ to

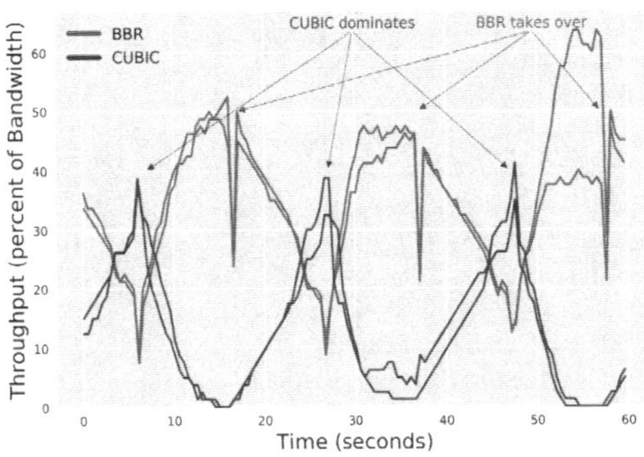

(a) Throughput for BBR and CUBIC. Cyclic.

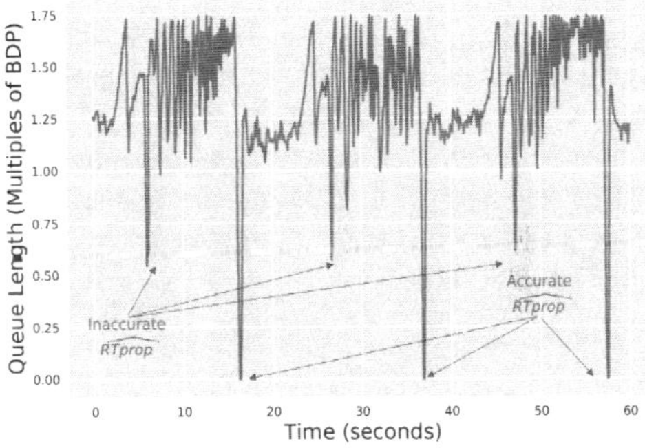

(b) Queue Length. Not always draining.

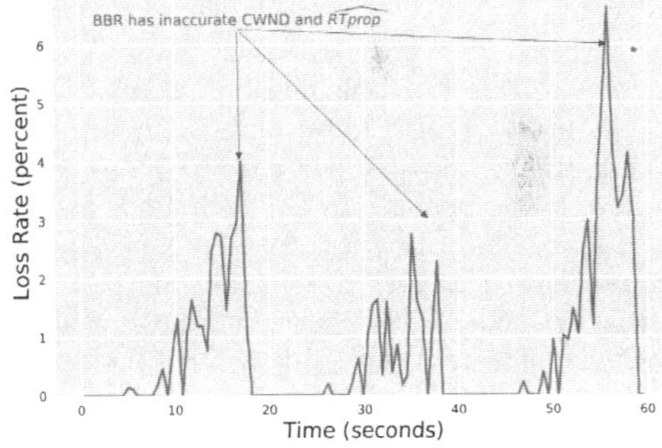

(c) Loss rate. High loss every 20 seconds.

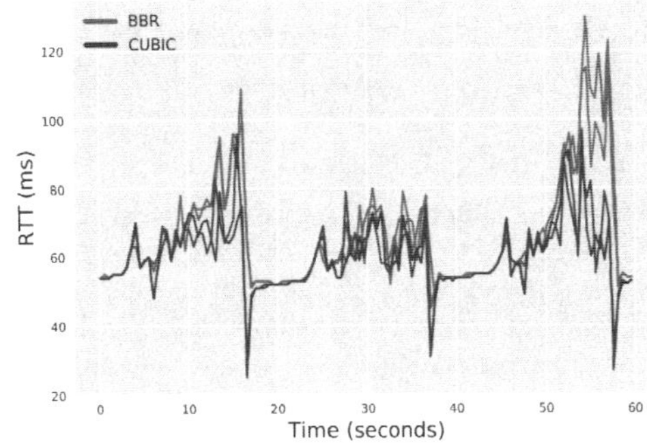

(d) RTT. Cyclic.

Figure 9. BBR and CUBIC show cyclic performance in medium buffers.

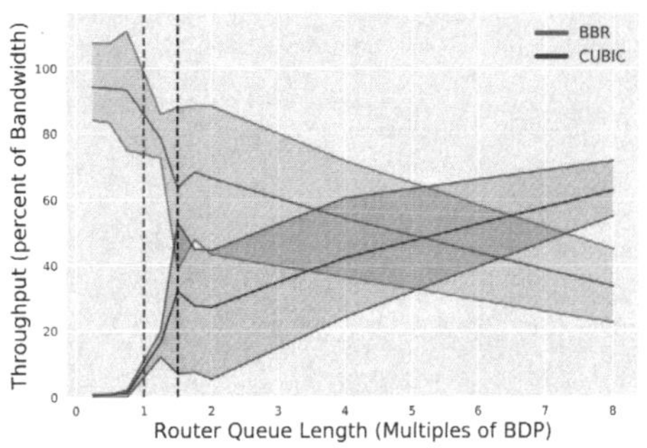

Figure 10. BBR and CUBIC's interplay versus router queue length.

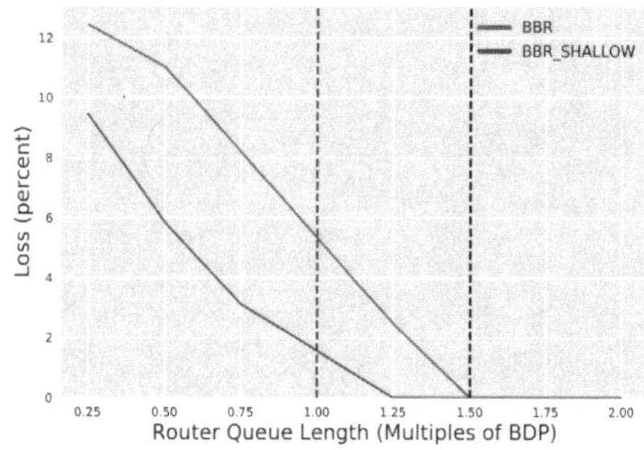

Figure 11. Modified BBR_Shallow's loss versus router queue length.

be too large, and, because BBR's $\widehat{BDP}$, and thus CWND, is derived from this RTprop, BBR greatly increases its CWND.

Because the router queue is already filled by CUBIC, BBR's increased CWND causes a large amount of packet loss for both CUBIC and BBR. BBR mostly ignores the loss, but CUBIC backs off, decreasing its inflight packets. This loss can be seen at around time 10, 30, and 50 seconds of Figure 9c, each of which corresponds to just after BBR increases its CWND after an inaccurate RTprop probe.

This continues for 10 seconds, whereupon BBR again probes for RTprop. This time, the probe obtains an accurate $\widehat{RTprop}$ of 25 ms, as seen at time 38 seconds of Figure 9b, because the queue is fully drained, and thus BBR reduces its CWND accordingly. This allows CUBIC to grow its CWND, as discussed above, and the cycle repeats.

We analyzed this behavior over the full range of test parameters in Table I, visualizing this interplay for 80 Mb/s, 25 ms, 2 BBR & 2 CUBIC flows with queue sizes: 0.25, 0.50, 0.75, 1.00, 1.75, 2.00, 4.00, and 8.00 BDP in Figure 10. The x-axis depicts the queue size for each trial, and the y-axis the throughput utilized by the flows grouped by congestion control protocol. The thick lines depict the mean throughput of BBR (red) and CUBIC (blue), with the thinner colored lines showing the 25th and 75th percentiles, averaged over half second intervals. From the figure, the behavior differs drastically for router queue sizes below 1.5 BDP where BBR creates persistent loss. Above 1.5 BDP, throughput spread greatly increases from the cyclic performance described earlier.

As the bottleneck queue gets larger, BBR becomes more limited by its 2 BDP CWND cap. This causes CUBIC to progressively obtain more of the throughput as its CWND grows beyond BBR's CWND limits.

E. *Improving BBR's Performance*

We have identified two performance weaknesses in BBR: BBR's static 2 BDP CWND, and BBR's inaccurate RTprop estimation. This section suggests fixes to these issues, with a limited proof of concept evaluation. Note that the evaluation is meant as an inspiration, not as a vigorous implementation.

1) CWND: Currently, BBR caps the inflight packets at 2 BDP, causing there to be 1 to 1.5 BDP of packets queued at the bottleneck router and a high amount of loss in shallow buffers. These results indicate that this 2 BDP CWND cap is sometimes too large to suit the network conditions. However, when the

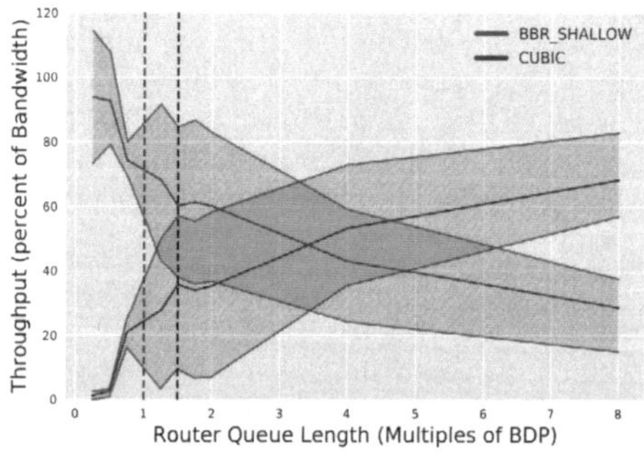

Figure 12. BBR_Shallow and CUBIC's interplay versus router queue length.

bottleneck router queue is large and BBR competes with a loss-based congestion control protocol, BBR's CWND cap limits its queue share, and, hence, it's share of the bottleneck bandwidth. These results indicate the CWND cap is sometimes too small to suit the network conditions. We suggest a feedback loop where BBR dynamically adjusts its CWND cap based on the loss, throughput and RTT measurements. This idea is similar to the approach of Copa [15] which generally keeps a small CWND, but increases it in response to competition from buffer-filling congestion control protocols.

When encountering persistent, high loss, BBR can infer that it is over saturating, and in response BBR can decrease the CWND cap. However, if the observed throughput is less than the measured bottleneck bandwidth (BtlBw), BBR can infer it is underutilizing its share of the bottleneck capacity (or that there are delayed and/or aggregated ACKs) and increase the CWND cap. When the measured RTT is greater than the RTT min, then the router queue must be saturated and the CWND cap should be decreased.

We demonstrate that BBR's inflight cap is responsible for its capacity and shallow buffer loss by manually adjusting BBR's inflight cap to 1.5 BDP down from 2 BDP. We then rerun our experiments with this modified "BBR_Shallow" [22].

Figure 11 depicts loss rate at the router calculated with a 500 ms sliding window as in Figure 7. BBR_Shallow induces less loss in buffers smaller than 1.5 BDP because it attempts to queue fewer packets at the bottleneck router, helping with inter-protocol fairness by reducing loss.

When competing with CUBIC, the router queue size that

provides for a fair share is smaller, as shown in Figure 12, following the format of Figure 10. Instead of having a fair share when the bottleneck router queue size is around 5 BDP, the fair share is instead when the maximum bottleneck router queue size is around 3 BDP. Thus, the CWND cap helps determine inter-protocol fairness by limiting throughputs.

2) Improving BBR's RTprop estimation: The RTprop should be nearly constant for the same network path, only changing after a route change. However, when BBR competes with CUBIC, BBR *increases* the estimated RTprop when it is unable to drain the queue, causing BBR to greatly overestimate the BDP, and thus create high queuing and loss.

BBR could instead always use the historical minimum RTT, basically never increasing the estimated RTprop. With this change, BBR would no longer be responsive to route changes that result in a higher RTprop. Either BBR could ignore route changes completely (since they are uncommon, and most flows are short) or BBR could only accept a higher RTprop if it is *consistently* higher for many RTprop probes or drastically higher for a single probe. This could allow BBR to detect a route change without increasing its CWND erroneously.

V CONCLUSIONS AND FUTURE WORK

As TCP BBR becomes more widely adopted in streaming audio and video applications, it is important that BBR provides consistent behavior alongside existing protocols, such as TCP CUBIC, and efficient behavior over a range of router queue sizes. Currently, BBR's high loss rates in shallow buffers and throughput variations with CUBIC in deeper buffers can be inefficient for throughput and disastrous for streaming audio and video applications that rely on a consistent network throughput for smooth playback.

Contributions of our work include: a) description and software for an inexpensive testbed for congestion control research; b) validation of base BBR performance [5]; c) validation of BBR performance in shallow buffers, with new contributions on loss rate versus buffer size; d) validation of cyclic behavior when BBR and CUBIC compete [9], [10], with new details on the BBR protocol features, and quantification of variation and unfairness versus buffer size; e) original analysis quantifying variation and unfairness of CUBIC and BBR versus buffer size; and f) contemporary improvement suggestions to BBR to address the above shortcomings.

In response to the questions posed in the Section I:

A) Raspberry Pi 3B+ end-hosts and a Linux PC configured as a router can be used for congestion control research, having the benefits of a controlled, network testbed and the latest Linux kernel code as is used on the Internet.

B) BBR induces packet loss on congested links with a router buffer sized smaller than 1.5 BDP, with loss increasing linearly with a decrease in buffer size. Loss rates are 5.5% for a router buffer size of 1 BDP, doubling to about 11% when the router buffer size is 0.5 BDP, caused by BBR's 2 BDP CWND cap.

C) BBR is extremely unfair when competing with CUBIC in shallow buffers since CUBIC responds to the packet loss by reducing rates while BBR does not. In deeper buffers, BBR and CUBIC exhibit large 20-second throughput cycles, with average throughput fairness achieved only for specific router queue sizes based on the BDP. These cycles are caused by BBR's inaccurate estimate of the minimum RTT, with the unfairness caused by the tension between the difference between the BBR and CUBIC operating points.

We suggest heuristics to improve BBR that include a feedback loop to adjust BBR's CWND and minimum RTT measurements based on the network conditions. Future work is needed to implement and test these proposed changes. Future work could also verify that BBR's unstable behavior is present in competition with any buffer-filling congestion control. Additionally, BBR evaluation over broader network conditions such as 4G, 5G and satellite is important.

REFERENCES

[1] Cisco, "VNI Global Fixed and Mobile Internet Traffic Forecasts," 2017.

[2] B. Wang, J. Kurose, P. Shenoy, and D. Towsley, "Multimedia streaming via TCP: An analytic performance study," ACM Transactions on Multimedia Computing (TOMM), vol. 4, no. 2, 2008, p. 16.

[3] S. Ha, I. Rhee, and L. Xu, "CUBIC: a new TCP-friendly high-speed TCP variant," ACM SIGOPS OS Review, vol. 42, no. 5, Jul. 2008.

[4] J. Gettys and K. Nichols, "Bufferbloat: dark buffers in the Internet," Communications of the ACM, vol. 55, no. 1, Jan. 2012, p. 57.

[5] N. Cardwell, Y. Cheng, C. S. Gunn, S. H. Yeganeh, and Van Jacobson, "BBR: congestion-based congestion control," Communications of the ACM, vol. 60, no. 2, Jan. 2017, pp. 58–66.

[6] L. Kleinrock, "Internet congestion control using the power metric: Keep the pipe just full, but no fuller," Ad Hoc Networks, vol. 80, Nov. 2018.

[7] E. Carlsson and E. Kakogianni, "Smoother streaming with BBR," Aug. 2018, Spotify Labs. Accessed: February 24, 2019. [Online]. Available: https://tinyurl.com/yyt5tbhd

[8] A. Ivanov, "Optimizing Web servers for high throughput and low latency," Sep. 2019, Dropbox Blogs. Accessed: April 7, 2019. [Online]. Available: https://tinyurl.com/y9qtt2yf

[9] D. Scholz, B. Jaeger, L. Schwaighofer, D. Raumer, F. Geyer, and G. Carle, "Towards a deeper understanding of TCP BBR congestion control," in Proceedings of IFIP Networking, Zurich, Switzerland, 2018.

[10] K. Miyazawa, K. Sasaki, N. Oda, and S. Yamaguchi, "Cycle and divergence of performance on TCP BBR," in IEEE 7th International Conference on Cloud Networking (CloudNet), 2018.

[11] M. Hock, R. Bless, and M. Zitterbart, "Experimental evaluation of BBR congestion control," in IEEE ICNP, Toronto, ON, Oct. 2017, pp. 1–10.

[12] L. Kleinrock, "Power and deterministic rules of thumb for probabilistic problems in computer communications," in ICC, Boston, MA, 1979.

[13] J. M. Jaffe, "Flow control power is nondecentralizable," IEEE Transactions on Communications, vol. 29, 10 1981, pp. 1301 – 1306.

[14] M. Dong, Q. Li, D. Zarchy, P. B. Godfrey, and M. Schapira, "PCC: Re-architecting congestion control for consistent high performance," in USENIX NSDI, 2015, pp. 395–408.

[15] V. Arun and H. Balakrishnan, "Copa: Practical Delay-Based Congestion Control for the Internet," in Proceedings of the Applied Networking Research Workshop. Montreal, QC: ACM Press, 2018, pp. 19–19.

[16] L. Brakmo and L. Peterson, "TCP Vegas: end to end congestion avoidance on a global Internet," IEEE Journal on Selected Areas in Communications, vol. 13, no. 8, Oct. 1995, pp. 1465–1480.

[17] S. Claypool, "The Panaderia," 2019. [Online]. Available: https://saahilclaypool.github.io/panaderia/

[18] S. Hemminger, "Network emulation with NetEm," in Proceedings of Linux Australia, Sydney NSW 2001, Australia, 2005, pp. 18–23.

[19] "tc-tbf (8): Token Bucket Filter - Linux man page," accessed: February 24, 2019. [Online]. Available: https://linux.die.net/man/8/tc-tbf

[20] "Dual Token Bucket Algorithms - TechLibrary," accessed: February 24, 2019. [Online]. Available: https://tinyurl.com/yy5owway

[21] S. Claypool, "Sharing but not caring - performance of TCP BBR and TCP CUBIC at the network bottleneck," WPI Major Qualifying Project MQP-CEW-1904, March 2019, (Advisor C. Wills). [Online]. Available: https://digitalcommons.wpi.edu/mqp-all/6728/

[22] S. Claypool, "BBR Shallow," 2019. [Online]. Available: https://tinyurl.com/bbrshallow-git

Phase Noise Effect on the Minimum Shift Keying Modulator

MohammaMahdi Asgharzadeh, Emil Novakov, Ghislaine Maury
Institut de Microélectronique, Electromagnétisme et Photonique (IMEP-LAHC)
University of Grenoble Alpes
Grenoble, France
Email: { mohammad-mahdi.asgharzadeh, emil.novakov, ghislaine.maury}@grenoble-inp.fr

Abstract— **It is essential to synchronize the receiver and the transmitter during any transmission. In a given receiver, the sensitivity of the synchronization system is usually higher than the sensitivity of the detection system. The performance of the synchronization system and the detection system in a given receiver depends on the signal to noise ratio at the input of the receiver. Phase noise must be carefully considered when applying any signal processing method, which involves synchronization. The effect of amplitude noise on the sensitivity of the receiver is a well-studied subject. On the other hand, the impact of phase noise on the phase synchronization process is not well-studied in literature. In this paper, the effect of phase noise on the Minimum Shift Keying (MSK) modulator is studied. The Bit Error Rate (BER) is used to demonstrate the impact of the different phase noise levels. Based on the simulation results we can conclude that the effect of phase noise on the synchronization system is negligible.**

Keywords- phase noise; synchronization; sensitivity; signal processing; time synchronous averaging; Internet of Things; Low Power Wide Area Network.

I. INTRODUCTION

The communication range and power efficiency are considered among the most critical issues for system design in the domain of Low Power Wide Area Networks (LPWAN) technologies dedicated to the Internet of Things (IoT) communication.

All LPWAN standards and technologies, such as SigFox [1], LoRa [2], Narrowband IoT (NB-IoT) [3], try to increase their efficiency in terms of both power consumption and data range. There are strict limitations by communication regulators like the Federal Communications Commission (FCC) [4] and the European Telecommunications Standards Institute (ETSI) [5]. These factors are related directly to the receiver sensitivity. Increasing the receiver sensitivity improves the link budget, which increases (under certain circumstances) the propagation distance.

A well-known technique to improve the receiver sensitivity is to increase the bandwidth, which can be viewed as a solution in the frequency domain. For example, in the spread spectrum technique, a narrow-band signal spreads over a wider frequency band. The power remains the same, but the power spectral density decreased as the signal spreads over a larger band and the receiver sensitivity improvement is related to the spreading factor.

Another solution to increase the sensitivity of the receiver is to decrease the data rate. Retransmitting the signal and process it later in the receiver is an example of this method. This can be viewed as spreading the signal over the time of the transmission (a time-domain solution).

In [6], the Time Synchronous Averaging (TSA) method is proposed to increase the sensitivity of a digital receiver based on the signal retransmission. It is shown that the synchronization system limits the performance of the TSA method. A new synchronization method was developed later. The performance of the TSA method with this new synchronization method is presented in [7]. Processing the signals and extracting the synchronization information from the transmitted signal with very low Signal to Noise Ratio (SNR) (even signals with SNR smaller than 1) is possible with this new synchronization method. TSA method is widely used in communications [8], medicine [9], mechanics [10], electronics and all scientific fields which treat periodic weak signals corrupted by noise [11].

Generally speaking, in the TSA method, the sampling is initiated by a trigger pulse as an input to the analyzer. These trigger pulses must be synchronized with the periodic signal. Time alignment is an essential parameter to the analysis of the repetitive signals, especially in the TSA method [12].

The efficiency of the TSA method is limited by the synchronization of the received data blocks. Synchronization is divided into synchronization in phase and frequency. Phase noise impacts the synchronization by varying the length of the repetitive data. The oscillator phase noise is presented briefly in Section II. Section III presents the applied method to study and simulate the effect of phase noise. In Section IV, the simulation results for the effect of the phase noise on the MSK modulator are presented. In this section, the phase noise effect is also simulated for a given transceiver, and the results are compared with other RF components. We conclude the work in Section V.

II. PHASE NOISE IN LOCAL OSCILLATOR

While an amplitude noise impacts the signal amplitude, any random fluctuation in the phase of a waveform in the frequency domain is presented by phase noise. Oscillator imperfection is one of the primary sources of phase noise. The noise in the local oscillator could be some multiplicative phase distortion during the up/down conversion at the transmitter and the receiver. The intensity of this noise depends on the quality of the RF component used in the transmitter/receiver.

Phase noise could be regarded as either natural phase noise caused by the local oscillator itself or "external" phase noise caused by vibration. In both cases, it is an essential problem for dynamic applications. The natural phase noise is mostly because of the oscillator's frequency instabilities. It is relevant for both static and dynamic applications. Any net changes in phase angle will result in an inaccuracy in the output frequency. The stability of the output frequency of the local oscillator is essential for any synchronization method. The output signal of a typical oscillator in the presence of the amplitude and phase noise is:

$$V(t) = A_0 \sin(2\pi f_0\, t + \Delta\emptyset(t)) \qquad (1)$$

A_0 is the nominal peak voltage and will establish the SNR and $\Delta\emptyset(t)$ represents the phase noise. Fig. 1 [13] presents the effect of phase noise on the oscillator output signal.

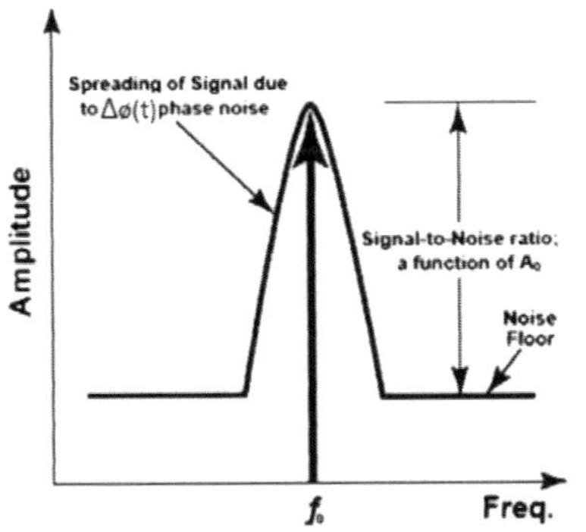

Figure 1. Oscillator output signal in the presence of phase noise

All oscillators have an amplitude limiting mechanism. The amplitude fluctuations are usually significantly attenuated and could be almost completely removed from the carrier at some frequencies [14]. Despite amplitude noise, the phase noise could not be reduced or filtered as it is very close to the carrier. However, phase noise in an oscillator can be reduced by various architecture choices and manufacturing technologies. The bipolar transistor and the Heterojunction Bipolar Transistor (HBT) are more efficient compared to the Field-Effect Transistors (FET), for example.

The Leeson model is essential to illustrate the phase noise spectrum concerning the carrier. The model is simple and effective and forms the theoretical basis of an oscillator phase noise. It is expressed as the following formula [15] and [16]:

$$S_{\Delta\emptyset}(f_m) = \frac{FkT}{2P_{si}}\left(1 + \frac{f_c}{f_m}\right)\left[1 + \frac{1}{f_m^2}\left(\frac{f_0}{2Q_L}\right)^2\right] \qquad (2)$$

$S_{\Delta\emptyset}(f_m)$ is the single-sideband output phase noise power spectral density, F is the noise figure, k is the Boltzmann constant and equals to 1.38×10^{-23} (J/K), T is the absolute temperature, P_{si} is the input signal power, f_m is the offset frequency, f_c is the corner frequency, f_0 is the carrier frequency, and Q_L is the loaded quality facture. The phase noise curve based on (2) is illustrated in Fig. 2 [16].

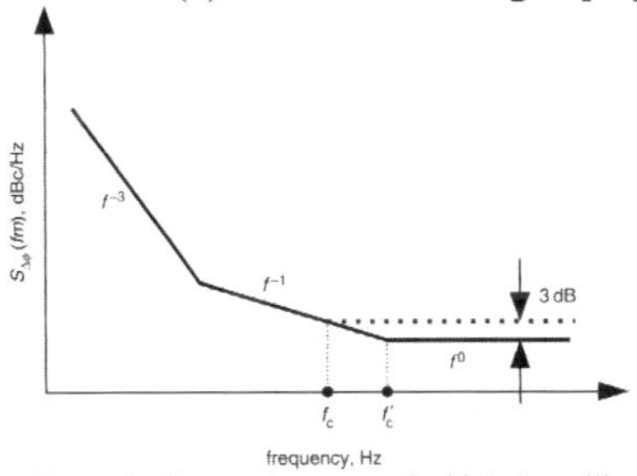

Figure 2. Phase noise curve of a high Q oscillator

The phase noise shows various behaviours depending on the frequency region and the distance from the carrier frequency. For example, a $1/f^3$ noise (30 dB per octave) is respected for the frequencies which are very close to the offset frequency. The Leeson model suggests increasing the resonator Q and signal amplitudes as a solution to reduce the phase noise. In this research, we are mostly focused on this region.

III. METHODOLOGY

Regarding the application goal (synchronization for the TSA method), the communication range, the receiver complexity as well as the energy efficiency, the MSK modulation technique was used in these simulations. The simulations were done in Matlab by generating the transmission data with time series. Amplitude noise and phase noise were added to the transmitted signal via Additive White Gaussian Noise (AWGN) channel and the phase noise block, respectively. The schematic of the simulation model is presented in Fig. 3. The simulation results are compared with theoretical BER for the MSK modulation to examine the accuracy of the proposed models.

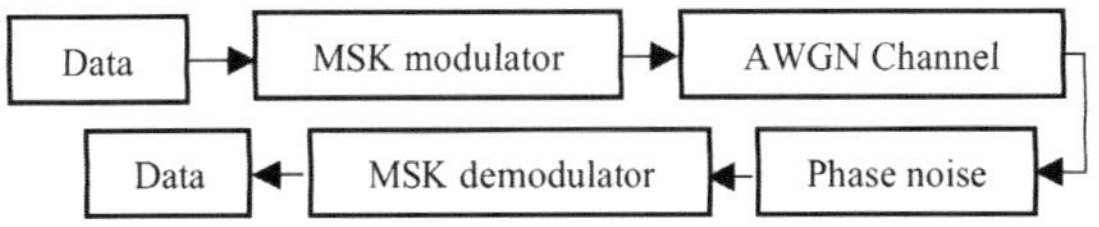

Figure 3. The presentation of the simulation model for the MSK modulation with Phase noise block in Simulink

BER graphs are used to demonstrate the results. The precision of the BER graph depends on the number of transmitted bits. The Monte-Carlo [17] method is a common technique for estimating the BER of a communication system. The number of required data symbols to achieve the desired accuracy is [18]:

$$N \approx \frac{1}{\sigma_n^2 p_e} \quad (3)$$

σ_n^2 is the normalized variance of the estimation error and P_e is the desired bit error rate. The small value of BER requires a considerable number of transmitted symbols. Otherwise, the estimation variation shall be significant when the error is too small. For example, $N \approx 100/p_e$ is needed while counting 100 errors for $\sigma = 0.1$. Therefore, at least 10^8 bits are needed to study a system with BER of 10^{-6}.

The BER was calculated by comparing the received and the transmitted signals. Fig. 4 presents the BER result with no additive phase noise in comparison with the theoretical BER graph of the MSK modulation. From this figure, the reliability of simulation models can be justified. The BER result from the proposed simulation method follows precisely the theoretical curve of the BER of the MSK modulation. To calculate the BER with higher precision, we need to transmit and process more bits, which will increase the time of calculation significantly. The difference between the two graphs of BER at the very low BER value is due to this issue.

IV. SIMULATION RESULTS

The BER graphs at different phase noise levels were traced for different values of the bit energy over the noise variance (E_b/N_0) to study the effect of phase noise on the efficiency of the communication systems in terms of BER for the MSK modulation. In each run of the simulation, E_b/N_0 varied from 1 to10 dB for a constant level of phase noise. In Fig. 5, the BER for different values of Phase Noise Level (PNL) from -96 to -80 dBc/Hz are presented. These results are compared with the BER for the MSK modulation in theory. By varying the phase noise level from -96 dBc/Hz up to -80 dBc/Hz, the bit error rate varies from almost the theoretical BER (for -96dBc/Hz) to the weakest BER result (at -80 dBc/Hz). The effect of phase noise on the MSK modulator is negligible for PNL equal or below -90 dBc/Hz,.

It is possible to simulate the phase noise effect for a specific RF component. In this case, a set of different phase noise levels are attributed to different frequencies. This information usually comes with the RF component datasheet. The precision of the simulation increases by having more data about the component phase noise level at different frequencies.

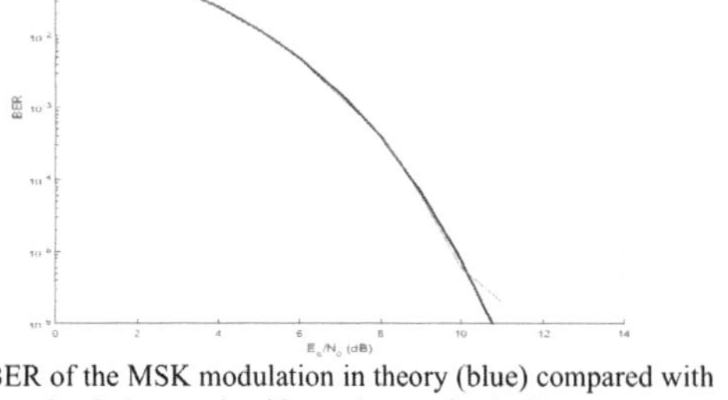

Figure 4. BER of the MSK modulation in theory (blue) compared with simulation result without phase noise (red)

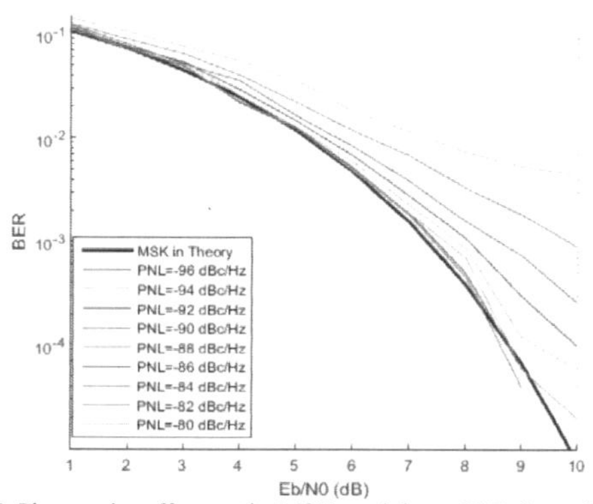

Figure 5. Phase noise effect on the MSK modulator, PNL from -96 to -80 dBc/Hz

Here, we consider the phase noise level for ADF-7021-V, which is a standard RF transceiver. The frequency offset were: [10Hz, 100Hz, 1000Hz] and the corresponding phase noise level for these frequencies were: [-71.5, -82, -92.5] dBc/Hz. Fig. 6 presents the result of the simulation in the presence of phase noise (in yellow) and without phase noise (in orange), in comparison with the theoretical BER for the MSK modulation (in blue).

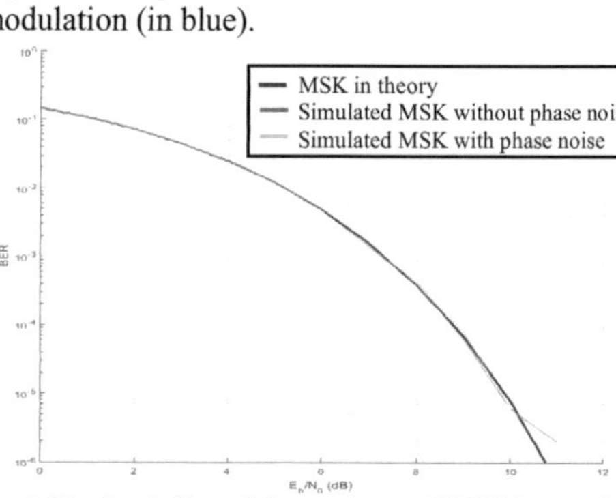

Figure 6. Simulated effect of phase noise on ADF7021 transceiver (without phase noise (red) and with Phase noise (orange))

The simulation results with and without phase noise are almost the same. As we can see, the phase noise does not have a significant impact on the BER of the MSK modulation.

These results should be compared with the phase noise level of other RF components. Tables I, II and III present the phase noise level for a standard RF transceiver, a mixer and a synthesizer, respectively. From these tables, we can note the maximum phase noise level of presented components and compare their phase noise level with the simulation results. The highest phase noise level in these tables is equal to -106 dBc/Hz for Si4464 at 460 MHz with ±10 kHz offset.

Respecting the simulation results, we conclude that the impact of the phase noise on the MSK modulator is negligible. This conclusion is proven with experimental tests for the transmission of a very noisy signal (SNR≈0.3dB). The results of experimental tests were published in [7].

TABLE I. PHASE NOISE LEVEL FOR A GIVEN RF TRANSCEIVER

Device number	Fabricant	Description	Frequency bands	Receiver Sensitivity	Phase noise in 460 MHz (dBc/Hz)	Phase noise in 169 MHz (dBc/Hz)
Si4464	Silicon Labs	high-performance, low-current transceivers	from 119 to 1050 MHz	–126 dBm at 500 bit/s	±10 kHz offset: -106 ±100 kHz offset:-110 ±1 MHz offset: -123	±10 kHz offset: -111 ±100 kHz offset:-116 ±1 MHz offset: -135

TABLE II. PHASE NOISE LEVEL FOR A GIVEN RF SYNTHESIZER

Device number	Fabricant	Description	Frequency bands	RF1 Phase Noise (dBc/Hz)	IF Phase Noise (dBc/Hz)
Si4123	Silicon Labs	Dual-band RF synthesizer with integrated VCO	RF1: 900 MHz to 1.8 GHz IF: 62.5 to 1000 MHz	100 KHz offset: -110 1 MHz offset: -132	100 KHz offset: -117 1 MHz offset: -134

TABLE III. PHASE NOISE LEVEL FOR A GIVEN RF MIXER

Device number	Fabricant	Description	LO Frequency	Phase noise level (dBc/Hz)
ADRF6655	Analog Devices	High dynamic range active mixer with integrated PLL and VCO.	1330 MHz	±100 kHz offset:-114 ±1 MHz offset: -138

V. CONCLUSION

LPWAN, as a novel communication paradigm, has been investigated as a solution which improves the communication range while enhancing power efficiency. These parameters can be enhanced by increasing the sensitivity of the receiver. Any variation in the frequency stability of the local oscillator has an impact on synchronization. In this article, the effect of phase noise was studied on the MSK modulator. The results of the simulation model were first compared to the theoretical result to verify the reliability of the proposed model. Various phase noise levels were analyzed and the results were compared with standard RF components. BER was used to compare the effect of phase noise for different signal energy levels. The simulation model was customized to study a specific RF transceiver (ADF7021).

By comparing the phase noise level for standard RF components and the simulation results, we can conclude that the effect of phase noise on the MSK modulator is negligible. Performing the TSA method during experimental tests on a very noisy signal (SNR around 0.3dB) presents the same results.

ACKNOWLEDGMENT

This work was financed by the EC-ENIAC project Things2Do, Grenoble, France.

[1] C. Gomez, J. C. Veras, R. Vidal, L. Casals and J. Paradells, "A Sigfox Energy Consumption Model", Sensors 19, no. 3, pp. 681.

[2] O. Khutsoane, B. Isong, and A. M. Abu-Mahfouz, "IoT devices and applications based on LoRa/LoRaWAN," IECON 2017 - 43rd Annual Conference of the IEEE Industrial Electronics Society, Beijing, 2017, pp. 6107-6112.

[3] Y. -. E. Wang, X. Lin, A. Adhikary, A. Grovlen, Y. Sui, Y. Blankenship, J. Bergman and H. S. Razaghi, "A Primer on 3GPP Narrowband Internet of Things", IEEE Communications Magazine, vol. 55, no. 3, pp. 117-123, March 2017.

[4] FCC, "Code of Federal Regulations", Title 47, Part 15, [retrieved Online: July, 2019]. Available: https://www.ecfr.gov/cgi-bin/text-idx?SID=0de4c456f009ac4e3b9c1df462296515&mc=true&node=pt47.1.15&rgn=div5

[5] ETSI, "Final draft ETSI EN 300 220-1" V2.4.1, 2012-01, [retrieved Online: July, 2019]. Available: https://www.etsi.org/deliver/etsi_en/300200_300299/30022001/02.04.01_40/en_30022001v020401o.pdf

[6] E. Novakov, M. Asgharzadeh and G. Maury, "Enhancement of the sensitivity of a digital receiver by time synchronous averaging," 2017 XXXIInd General Assembly and Scientific Symposium of the International Union of Radio Science (URSI GASS), Montreal, QC, 2017, pp. 1-4.

[7] M. Asgharzadeh, E. Novakov, and G. Maury, "Receiver Sensitivity Improvement for IoT," The Fourteenth Advanced International Conference on Telecommunications, Barcelona 2018.

[8] M. Sahmoudi, M. G. Amin and R. Landry, "Acquisition of weak GNSS signals using a new block averaging pre-processing," 2008 IEEE/ION Position, Location and Navigation Symposium, Monterey, CA, 2008, pp. 1362-1372.

[9] J. R. Jarrett, N. C. Flowers, and A. C. John, "Signal - averaged electrocardiography: History, techniques, and clinical applications," Clin Cardiol, NO14, pp.984-994.

[10] L. Zhu, H. Ding, and X. Y. Zhu, "Extraction of Periodic Signal Without External Reference by Time-Domain Average Scanning," IEEE Trans. on Industrial Electronics, February 2008, vol. 55, NO2, pp.918-92.

[11] D. Hochmann and M. Sadok, "Theory of Synchronous Averaging," 2004 IEEE Aerospace Conference Proceedings, pp.3636-3653.

[12] P. Laguna and L. Sörnmo, "Sampling rate and the estimation of ensemble variability for repetitive signals," Medical and Biological Engineering and Computing, September 2000, Volume 38, Issue 5, pp 540–546.

[13] R. M. Cerda, "Impact of ultralow phase noise oscillators on system performance," Crystek Corporation, [retrieved Online: July, 2019]. Available: https://www.crystek.com/documents/appnotes/ImpactUltralow.pdf

[14] T. H. Lee and A. Hajimiri, "Oscillator phase noise: a tutorial," IEEE Journal of Solid-State Circuits, 2000, vol. 35, Issue: 3, pp. 326 – 336.

[15] D. B. Leeson, "A simple model of feedback oscillator noises spectrum," Proc. IRE, February 1966, vol. 54, no. 2, pp. 329–330.

[16] G. Sauvage, "Phase noise in oscillators: a mathematical analysis of Leeson's model", Trans. Instrum. Meas., 1977, pp. 408.

[17] M. Jeruchim, "Techniques for Estimating the Bit Error Rate in the Simulation of Digital Communication Systems", IEEE Journal on Selected Areas in Communications, January 1984, vol. 2, no. 1, pp. 153-170,

[18] J. Dong, "Estimation of Bit Error Rate of any digital Communication System", Signal and Image Processing, Télécom Bretagne, Université de Bretagne Occidentale, 2013, English, tel-00978950.

Layered Network Domain Resource Management in Multi-domain 5G Slicing Environment

Eugen Borcoci, Andra Ciobanu, Cosmin Contu
University POLITEHNICA of Bucharest - UPB
Bucharest, Romania
Emails: eugen.borcoci@elcom.pub.ro, andratapu@elcom.pub.ro, cosmin.contu@elcom.pub.ro

Abstract – **Multi-domain and end-to-end (E2E) capabilities are major objectives in 5G slicing. A split is needed of the multi-domain slice capabilities between several technological and/or administrative domains while still preserving their individual independency. Admission control is also necessary when a new multi-domain slice is requested by an user/tenant, i.e., during the slice preparation and instantiation phase or at run-time when slice instances scaling is needed. The above tasks are solved by the Management and Orchestration (M&O) system for services, slices and resources (physical or virtual). The M&O is performed at two scopes (global and local in each domain) and can be organized using several layers depending on the business model (actors) considered. This paper contribution consists in the proposal and analysis of several architectural solutions to organize the domain-level management for a network segment of a multi-domain slice. In particular, the functions splitting and interactions among the layers of the domain management are studied in the context of Network Function Virtualization (NFV) and Software Defined Networks (SDN), technologies used in the system architecture.**

Keywords — 5G slicing; Multi-domain; Management and Orchestration; Resource management; Software Defined Networking; Network Function Virtualization.

I. INTRODUCTION

The slicing concept applied to 5G networks (based on virtualization and softwarization) enables the system to serve in a dedicated way various verticals/use-cases. It also allows programmability and modularity for network resources provisioning, adapted to different vertical service requirements (in terms of bandwidth, latency, etc.) [1-9]. A *Network Slice* (NSL) is a managed logical group of subsets of resources, *Physical/Virtual network functions* (PNFs/VNFs) in the architectural Data Plane (DPl), Control Plane (CPl) and Management Plane (MPl) [1][2].

Network Function Virtualization [6-8][10-12] and Software Defined Networks [13] architectures are used in cooperation [14-16], to manage and control in a flexible and programmable way the 5G sliced environment. Note that the general topics of the NFV framework and SDN are not detailed in this study; they are just used here in the 5G slicing architecture.

The layered structure of the M&O 5G sliced systems depends on the definition of business model and actors. Several business models aim to support multi-tenant, multi-domain end-to-end (E2E) and multi-operator capabilities. A basic and flexible model (see A. Galis, [9]) can be composed of four main actors:

Infrastructure Provider (InP) – owns and manages the physical infrastructure (network/cloud/data centre). It could lease its infrastructure (as it is) to a slice provider, or it can itself construct slices and then lease the infrastructure in network slicing fashion. An InP may include several technological domains (e.g., Radio Access Network (RAN), Core network, Transport network) and could be represented by a single Administrative domain.

Network Slice Provider (NSLP) – can be typically a telecommunication service provider. It could be the owner or tenant of the infrastructures from which network slices can be constructed. Generally, the NSLP can construct multi-domain slices, on top of infrastructures offered by different InPs. It should also support multiple tenants.

Slice Tenant (SLT) – is the generic user of a specific slice, including network/cloud/data centres, hosting customized services. The SLTs can request from a NSLP creation of new slices. The SLT can lease virtual resources from one or more NSLPs in the form of a virtual network, where the tenant can realize, manage and provide *Network Services* (NS) to its individual end users. A network service is a composition of Network Functions (NFs); it is defined in terms of the individual NFs and the mechanism used to connect them. A single tenant may have one or several slices in its domain.

End User (EU) - consumes (part of) the services supplied by the tenant, without providing them to other business actors.

The business model is recursive (see Ordonez et. al., [3]), i.e., a tenant can, in turn, offer parts of its sliced resources to other tenants. Other variants of business models are presented in [9].

The actual running slices are *Network Slice Instance*(s) (NSLI), i.e., specific, logically isolated, but full virtual networks created by the NSLP (based on NSL templates) at the request of an SLT or at NSLP's initiative. A *blueprint/template* is a logical representation of NFs and the resource requirements. It describes the structure, configuration and work flows for instantiating and controlling a NSLI. It includes particular network characteristics (e.g., bandwidth, latency, reliability) and refers to the required physical or logical resources and the sub-networks. A NSLI may be dedicated or shared across multiple *Service Instances*.

The 5G sliced networks M&O sub-system is usually organized in a hierarchical fashion on several layers [7]. The management can include the traditional functions; the orchestration consists in a coordinated set of activities to automatically select and control multiple resources, services and systems [14].

The *Life-Cycle Management* (LCM) of a NSLI comprises several phases performed by the Slice Provider: (1) *instantiation, configuration* and *activation*, (2) *run-time* and (3) *decommissioning* [6]. Actually, the LCM is preceded by a *preparation phase* (0) of the network for the future instantiation and support of a NSLI. Phase (1) is split into the instantiation/configuration sub-phase (the necessary shared/dedicated resources, including NFs, are configured and instantiated but not yet used) and the activation sub-phase (the NSLI handles traffic). The run-time phase focuses on data traffic transport, reporting the network service performance and possible NSLI re-configurations or scaling, if dynamic conditions impose that. Phase (3) includes the deactivation and termination of the NSLI and release of the allocated resources.

The specific contribution of this paper is the proposal and analysis of several architectural solutions, to organize the domain-level (InP) management for a network segment (controlled in SDN style) of a multi-domain slice (see Section IV). In particular, the function splitting and interactions among the SDN controller with an upper management layer (Virtual Infrastructure Manager – VIM or Wide area Infrastructure Manager – WIM) of the domain management are studied. The business model adopted will influence these interactions.

The paper structure is described below. Sections II and III are preliminary. They serve to introduce and clarify the 5G management and control framework, where the solutions of the main Section IV will be applied, in the context of NFV-SDN technologies. In particular, Section II presents a few relevant examples of related architectural work to emphasize the M&O elements for resources, slices and services in multi-domain context. Section III details the slice creation phase M&O interactions. Section IV proposes and compares several architectural variants for the interface between the domain controller (SDN-IC) and higher layer manager (V/WIM). This interface determines how the mapping can be done of the required slice segment resources upon the network domain owned by the InP. The work is still preliminary - at architectural level. Section V presents conclusions and a future work outline.

II. 5G MULTI-DOMAIN SLICING ARCHITECTURES

This section presents a few examples of relevant 5G slicing architectures, in order to outline the M&O entities roles in a multi-domain environment and *locate the individual domain levels as a zone of interest for this study.* Many studies, projects, pilots, define variants of 5G slicing multi-domain architectures in various contexts [4][6][7][14 - 17][18]. In all of them, the M&O functions are crucial for coordination of the components.

The document (The European Telecommunications Standards Institute (ETSI) NFV Evolution and Ecosystem (EVE) 012 [6]) and The 3rd Generation Partnership Project (3GPP) Technical Report (TR) 28.801 document [7] consider the ETSI NFV framework to which they added three new management functional blocks dedicated for slice management: *Communication Service Management Function* (CSMF) - to translate the service requirements into NSL ones; *Network Slice Management Function* (NSMF) - to manage (including lifecycle) the NSLIs (it derives network slice subnet requirements from the network slice related requirements); *Network Slice Subnet Management Function* (NSSMF) - to manage the *Network Slice Subnet Instances* NSLSIs. These three elements interact with the upper entity of the NFV *Management and Orchestration* (MANO), i.e., with NFV *Orchestration of the NFV* (NFVO).

The 5G Infrastructure Public Private Partnership (5GPPP) Working Group details the architecture by defining four planes [1]: *Service, M&O, Control* and *Data* planes. The architecture also includes a *Multi-Domain Network Operating System* containing different adaptors and network abstractions above the networks and clouds heterogeneous fabrics. It is responsible for allocation of (virtual) network resources and maintains network state to ensure network reliability in a multi domain environment.

The *Service* plane comprises the *Business Support Systems* (BSSs) and business-level Policy and Decision functions as well as applications and services operated by the tenant. This plane includes an *end-to-end orchestration* system.

The *M&O* plane includes a general *Service Management,* the *Software-Defined Mobile Network Orchestrator* (SDMO) and the ETSI NFV lower level managers (i.e., *VNF Manager* - VNFM and *Virtualized Infrastructure Manager* - VIM). The SDMO is composed of a *domain specific application management*, an *Inter-slice Resource Broker* and *NFV-NFVO.* The SDMO performs the E2E management of network services; it can set up slices by using the network slice templates and merge them properly at the described multiplexing point. The Service Management intermediates between the upper service layer and the Inter-slice Broker; it transforms consumer-facing service descriptions into resource-facing service descriptions and vice versa. The Inter-slice Broker handles cross-slice resource allocation. The domain-specific application management functions could be, e.g., for 3GPP: Element Managers (EM) and Network Management (NM) functions, including Network (Sub-) Slice Management Function.

The *Control* plane is "horizontally" separated in two parts: intra and inter-slice control functions. "Vertically", it is organized in SDN style, i.e., with three planes: *Control applications* (inter and intra-slice); *SDN controllers*; SDN nodes (these are actually slicing control function blocks realized as PNF/VNFs. Note here the flexibility of the SDN-NFV cooperation: some slicing control functions are seen and realized as SDN nodes. The SDN controllers are two types: *Software-Defined Mobile Network Coordinator* (SDM-X) and *Software-Defined Mobile Network Controller* (SDM-C). The SDM-C and SDM-X take care of dedicated and shared NFs, respectively; following the SDN principles, they translate decisions of the control applications into commands to SDN nodes, i.e., VNFs and PNFs. Note that also SDM-X and SDM-C, as well as other possible control applications could be implemented as VNFs or PNFs.

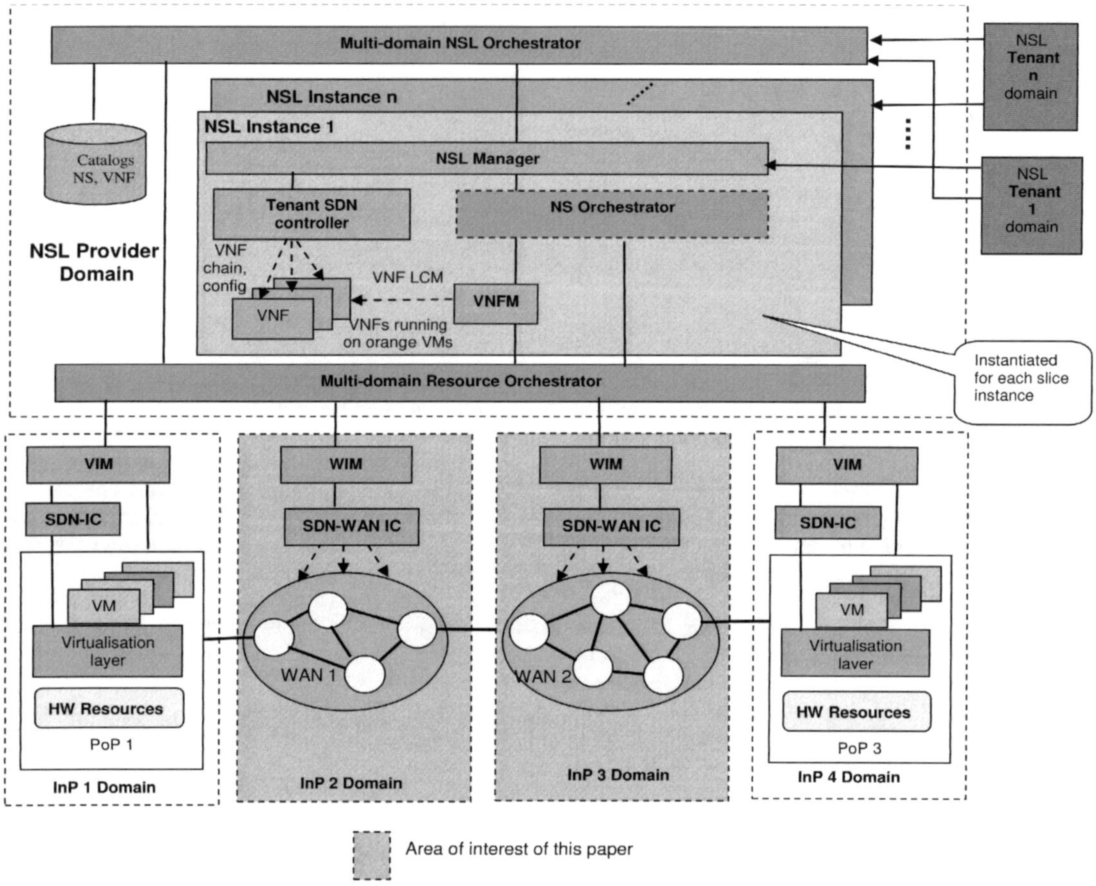

Figure 1. Run-time image of a multi-domain slicing architecture - example 1 (adapted from ETSI GR NFV-EVE 012 [6] and Ordonez-Lucena [3][18])

NS – Network Service; NSL - Network Slice; VNF – Virtualized Network Function; VNFM – VNF Manager; SDN Software Defined Networking; LCM – Life Cycle Management; VIM – Virtual Infrastructure Manager; WIM – WAN Infrastructure Manager; SDN-IC- Infrastructure SDN controller; HW-Hardware; WAN – Wide Area Network

The *Data plane* comprises the VNFs and PNFs needed to carry and process the user data traffic.

A relevant multi-domain slicing architecture, viewed at run-time phase, is presented in Figure 1 (adapted from ETSI GR NFV-EVE 012 [6] and J.Ordonez-Lucena et. al. [3][18]).

The specific contribution of this paper (Section IV) will be focused on the lower functional parts of such an architecture or a similar one.

A multi-domain slice instance can span several InPs and/or administrative or technological domains belonging to different providers. Figure 1 shows several domains upon which multi-domain slices can be constructed. Note also that this architectural picture focuses on the transport and core network domains, omitting the RAN domain.

The NSLP rents infrastructure resources owned by the underlying InPs to construct NSL instances. The *Resource Orchestration* (RO) manages the set of resources offered by different INPs (the resources are supplied under the control of the underlying VIMs/WIMs), and optimally dispatches them to the NSLIs aiming to satisfy their requirements but preserving their logical isolation. The RO *should have information on resource availability in each domain* whose resources will enter the multi-domain NSLI. To construct a multi-domain slice, some inter-domain interactions are also necessary.

The highest layer *NSL Orchestrator* (NSLO) has a main role in the *creation* phase of slices and also in the *run-time* phase. In the creation phase, NSLO receives the order to deploy a NSLI for a tenant (or the NSLP decides to construct a slice). The NSLO should have enough information (including on multi-domain resource availability) in order to check the feasibility of the order. To accomplish this, it interacts with RO (which aggregates resource information from several domains (InPs)), and also accesses the VNF and

NS catalogues. These catalogues contain VNF and NS descriptors, exposing the capabilities of all the VNFs and NSs that an NSL provider can select for the NSLs. If the slice is feasible, then NSLO triggers its instantiation.

At run-time, the NSLO performs policy-based inter-slice operations, e.g., it analyzes the performance and fault management data received from the operative NSLIs to check the fulfilment of their *Service Level Agreements* (SLAs). In case of SLA violations, the NSLO decides which NSLIs need to be modified and, if this is possible, sends corrective management actions (e.g., scaling, healing, etc.) to some specific NSL Managers.

Each NSLI has its own management plane (to get slice isolation) composed of: *NSL Manager, NS Orchestrator (NSO), Tenant SDN Controller* and *VNF Manager (VNFM)*. The VNFM(s) and the NSO perform the life cycle operations (e.g., instantiation, scaling, termination, etc.) over the instances of the VNFs and NS(s), respectively. Interactions between these functional blocks and the RO are necessary. The NSL Manager coordinates the operations on management data obtained from Tenant SDN Controller and the NS Orchestrator, to perform the fault, configuration, accounting, performance, and security management within the NSLI. Each tenant operates its NSLI instance (within the limits agreed with the NSL provider) through the NSL Manager.

Both in the preparation phase and at run-time the RO should interact with each domain management entities (e.g., VIM or WIM) in order to apply *Admission Control* (AC) before deciding on a new NSLI construction or later, on NSLI possible modification. Naturally, each domain should decide upon its resources availability. The specific contributions of this paper are focused on a domain resource management.

An SDN control is supposed to exist at domain level. The *SDN - Infrastructure Controller* (SDN-IC) manages and controls connectivity in its domain, under the directives of the corresponding VIM/WIM. The VIMs and WIMs can act as SDN applications, delegating the tasks related to the management of networking resources to their underlying ICs.

III. NETWORK SLICE CREATION

This section summarizes the general slice creation steps in order to clearly identify the scope and role of the management actions proposed in Section IV.

Before slice instantiation, preparation activities are necessary. Catalogues of available services and resources must be constructed in advance, usable by the tenants in order to select a slice model fitted to their needs.

The general typical set of steps coordinated by the NSLO and RO (see Figure 1) for a slice instance creation are [7][17][18]: a. Service ordering; b. Network slice resource description; c. Admission control; d. Optimization and Resource Reservation; e. Network slice preparation.

Service ordering: the NSLP should construct a *Service Catalogue* (business-driven), containing service offering (*service templates*). The catalogue contains NSLs specifications, optimized for different usage scenarios, like: enhanced Mobile Broadband (eMBB), massive Machine Type Communications (mMTC), ultra Reliable Low Latency Communications (uRLLC), or other vertical-specific applications. A service template includes all the information required to drive the NSL deployment, e.g., the NSL topology (technology-agnostic), NSL requirements (functional, performance, security), temporal, geo-location and other operational requirements [18]. The NSL provider offers application programming interfaces (APIs) to tenants, giving them access to the Service Catalogue, where the tenant can select the service template that best matches its requirements. Some parameters and attributes can be customized by the tenant. The result of this dialogue is a catalogue-driven NSL *service order* containing information to be mapped on technological segments (Radio Access Network (RAN), transport, and core network) and also over several administrative domains. The NSLO should process such information.

Network Slice Resource Description: this step creates a resource-centric view of the ordered NSL. For a higher flexibility and better adaptation to the tenant needs, different *Levels of Implementations* (NSL-IL) can be defined [18]. The NSLO extracts the relevant content from a resource viewpoint (e.g., the NSL topology, network requirements, etc.) and constructs an NSL-IL for the NSL instance. The NSL topology serves to identify which NS(s) need to be deployed for the NSL, retrieving the corresponding NS descriptor(s) from the NS Catalogue; the deployment option is selected for each descriptor (*NS descriptor ID, NS FlavorID, NS-IL ID*), that best matches the features and the performance level required for the NSL; an NSL-IL is constructed by referencing the selected triplet(s).

Admission Control (AC): the target NSL-IL specifies the resources needed for the tenant's demands. Now, the AC will be enforced on the ordered NSL-IL, from a resource viewpoint, to decide acceptance/rejection for deployment. Several types of information are needed in this process:

(1) NSLI resource requirements (resources to be allocated for each VNF instance and virtual link, affinity/anti-affinity rules applicable between VNF instances, reliability requirements for each VNF instance and virtual link);

(2) geographical region(s) where each VNF is needed;

(3) time intervals for activation of the NSL instance;

(4) information of the Points of Presence (PoPs) (and the WAN network(s) connecting them) to which the NSLP is subscribed. Such information is partially available at the NSLO and partially at RO; therefore, these two functional blocks need to interact within the AC actions.

Note that AC should be actually enforced at several levels: at a global multi-domain level and at each domain management level. This last aspect will be further analysed in Section IV.

Optimization and *Resource Reservation*: if several variants of NSL-ILs are found feasible by the AC, then RO can run an algorithm to select an optimal solution (note that this is a multi-criteria optimization problem). Afterwards, RO may proceed with resource reservation; it sends resource reservation requests to the underlying VIM(s)/WIM(s). The hard/soft nature of this reservation depends on the use case and NSL provider's policies.

Network Slice Preparation: it consists of setting up all that is required to manage the NSLI throughout its life cycle, i.e., from commissioning (instantiation, configuration, and activation) to decommissioning (de-activation and termination) (see for details, 3GPP TS 28.801 V.15.1.0 [7]). The preparation comprises: a. preparation of the network environment and b. designing and on-boarding the NSL descriptor.

For the step a., the NSLO (see Figure 1) performs the following tasks:

- negotiation with RO a priority level for the NSLI (this allows the RO to manage the cases when several NSLIs compete for the same resources, or to manage the case of resources shortage);
- instantiation of a NSLI specific management plane (NSL Manager, Tenant SDN Controller, NS Orchestrator, VNFM(s)); it configures these functional blocks, making them ready for the run-time phase.

In parallel to the network environment preparation, the NSLO builds up the NSL descriptor, which is a deployment template used by the NSL Manager to operate the NSLI during its life cycle. This descriptor includes the following parts: a set of policy-based workflows; the set of NSL-ILs available for use, constructed in the Network Slice Resource Description phase; VNF configuration primitives at application level and VNF chaining management instructions; information about management data, used for performance management.

IV. RESOURCE MANAGEMENT AT DOMAIN LEVEL

This section contains the specific contribution of the paper. The focus will be on network segments of a multi-domain NSL (e.g., InP2 and InP3 domains in Figure 1). However, the framework proposed could be applied also (with some modifications) for cloud-like segments like PoP1 or PoP3. The business model considered here will be flexible. The domain manager and controller (here it will be the SDN-IC) and the Virtual Infrastructure Manager (VIM/WIM) could belong to the same administrative entity of a domain. In this case, there is a clear separation between administrative domains and the InP could offer virtualized resources due to VIM/WIM capabilities. However, is it possible that an InP keeps the classical functions as equipment/infrastructure provider while virtualization tasks and management could be delegated to a third-party provider.

A. Function splitting between VIM/WIM and SDN-IC

An important architectural choice related to the slice mapping onto network resources in a network domain is the functional split among SDN-IC and WIM and consequently the interface/relationship between WIM and SDN-IC with respect to:

(1) the style used by SDN-IC to upload information to VIM/WIM, about its available resources: *on demand* (OD) or in *proactive* (P) style (at SDN-IC initiative);

(2) the amount and depth of information uploaded by SDN-IC on the network resources (graph, capacities, etc.). Table I presents the resulting *architectural variants* of the functional split and WIM/SDN-IC interface and Figure 2 presents *architectural variants* for mapping a slice on InP domain network resources.

It is assumed that the network domain resources can be represented by topology and Resource Availability Matrix information, collected by the SDN-IC from the domain network (e.g., ingress and egress points/routers, available paths and network resources per path, supported traffic classes to allow Quality of Services (QoS) enabled transport, etc.).

Note that for each variant, and depending on monitoring information at network level, a Resource Availability Matrix RAM can be uploaded to VIM/WIM and also adjusted by SDN-IC to improve the traffic engineering performances.

In turn, the VIM/WIM can express the requirements for this network domain in the form of a *Service order* (or, equivalent, *Server Level Specification* - SLS) request. The generation of this request is actually done by the RO (wanting to construct a new slice), after splitting the multi-domain slice requirements in sets of requirements for participating domains to the multi-domain slice. The details of such a split at RO level is out of scope of this paper. An example of connectivity set of requirements known by the VIM/WIM (to be mapped onto domain resources) is a matrix of *Traffic Trunks* (TT). Each VIM/WIM may have an abstract view of its network and output links towards neighbors in a form of a set of virtual pipes (called TTs). A set of such pipes can belong to a given QoS class; so, this approach allows a given multiple domain slice to belong to a specific QoS class.

To simplify the notation, in the following, only the WIM notation will be used.

Several variants of interactions and function splitting between WIM and SDN-IC are proposed and discussed below in terms of pros, cons and trade-off.

Proactive style: at the initiative of the SDN-IC, (periodically or event triggered) the information that is uploaded to WIM is: the Resource Availability Matrix (RAM), i.e., full connectivity graph and capacities, or only a summary called Overlay Network Topology – ONT [19].

- *Pros*: the SDN-IC is the most qualified to know when to deliver network information to WIM, e.g., every time when network re-dimensioning is performed; WIM has at every moment all the information about network resources.
- *Cons*: WIM can be overloaded with information that it does not really need at a given time; it may keep or discard some information, depending on its local policy at WIM level; signaling overhead appears.

On demand style: WIM asks the domain RAM from the SDN-IC when needed, in order to answer appropriately to service order requests.

- *Pros*: the WIM decides when it wants RAM information; this could lead to a better usage of WIM Data Base space; SDN-IC doesn't need to systematically inform the WIM anymore.

- *Cons*: higher delay in servicing the RO requests, because WIM should first acquire RAM in order to respond appropriately to RO, based on updated RAM information.

High WIM role (HR): SDN-IC uploads to WIM its full connectivity graph.

- *Pros:* WIM has deep control on the network resources. It becomes in this way a major factor in assuring efficient allocation and exploitation of network resources in the future slice; more seamless deployment, given the fact that mapping of the slice onto network resources is outsourced to WIM; therefore, not many changes have to be done in the traditional networking SDN-IC functionalities;SDN-IC is released of AC and mapping functions.
- *Cons:* overload at WIM level: it should make both *mapping* of the slice requested resources onto network nodes and perform AC*;* less clean architecture: actual network related tasks are moved at WIM layer.

Medium WIM role (MR): SDN-IC uploads to WIM an overlay RAM based on traffic trunks (similar to ONT):

- *Pros:* WIM has medium degree of control on the network resources; it is still capable to apply optimization techniques; routing tasks and mapping real-paths to TTs are done at network level (natural choice), where local SDN-IC policies can be considered; clean architecture – WIM works at overlay level only, making AC, thus being compliant with abstraction principles.
- *Cons:* AC is performed at WIM level; it is more difficult to consider the current status of the network load; optimization at WIM level is not "the best".

Low WIM role (LR): SDN-IC does not upload/disclose any topology and resources to WIM but only ingress-egress points IDs and answer Yes/No to an SLS request:

- *Pros:* WIM has simpler task to only download the SLS parameters to SDN-IC and then ask SDN-IC about the result; sophisticated optimization techniques could be applied at SDN-IC level, considering local policies and current network status; routing tasks and mapping real-paths to TTs are done at network level (natural choice), where local SDN-IC policies can be considered; clean architecture – WIM works at overlay level only, thus being compliant with abstraction principles.
- *Cons:* all mapping and local AC is performed at SDN-IC network level; SDN-IC is overloaded with additional functions.

In practice, one of the six variants can be selected, depending on the overall design objectives of the slicing system, general set of requirements and business model adopted.

TABLE I. VARIANTS OF COOPERATION BETWEEN WIM AND SDN-IC

		Amount of available information (on CND resources) from SDN-IC for V/WIM		
		High WIM role (HR): SDN-IC uploads to WIM its full connectivity graph	Medium WIM role (MR): SDN-IC uploads only an overlay availability matrix (similar to Overlay Network Topology -ONT)	Low WIM role (LR): SDN-IC does not upload/disclose any topology and resources to WIM but only ingress-egress points Ids and answer Yes/No to an SLS request
SDN-IC style to upload info to WIM about its available resources	Proactive (P) style	P-HR	P-MR	P-LR
	(OD) on demand from WIM	OD-HR	OD-MR	OD-LR

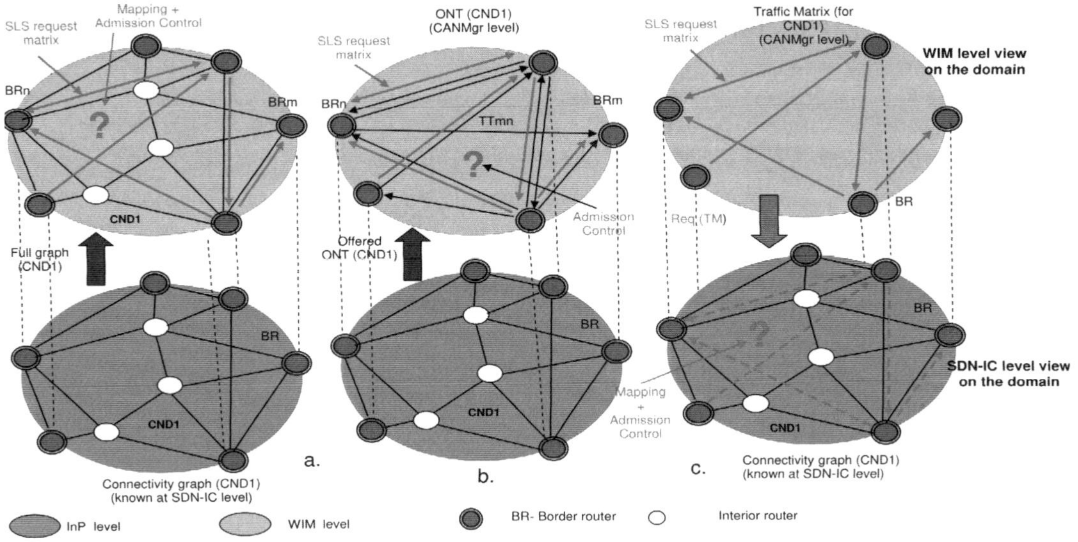

Figure 2. Architectural variants for mapping of a slice on InP domain network resources (WIM role: High, Medium, Low)

CND1-Connectivity Domain1; TM - Traffic Matrix; ONT – Overlay Network Topology

B. Local Resources Mapping

A design choice should be which entity has to perform the mapping of the RO requested resources (for the slice segment realized by this domain): WIM or SDN-IC? Two variants are proposed below.

WIM determines the mapping of SLS requested resources on the network resource matrix uploaded by the SDN-IC:

- *Pros*: SDN-IC does not need to run mapping algorithms but only to dimension its network conforming local policies; this way, a stronger control on mapping optimality is kept at the WIM level.
- *Cons*: more complexity at the level of WIM (AC for different levels of QoS guarantees are necessary); periodic or event-triggered updates are necessary to update the WIM vision on the network resources matrix, for the domain to which it is associated.

SDN-IC determines the mapping of SLS requested resources on its network resource matrix:

- *Pros*: SDN-IC has full knowledge on the network resource matrix, so the mapping can be optimized in a refined solution; SDN-IC will not disclose to the WIM any intra-domain topology; AC is enforced by SDN-IC, which decides upon the actual mapping.
- *Cons*: overloads the SDN-IC with additional functions.

C. Local Negotiation

An advanced solution could include a negotiation in the functionality of the WIM - SDN-IC interface. A negotiation protocol will be necessary here. The WIM could play the client role and SDN-IC the server role. Several variants can be considered and are discussed below in a comparative way:

Basic two-step negotiation session: "proposal followed by yes/no answer", started with a client proposal and then server accepting or rejecting it:

- *Pros*: simplest and fastest solution.
- *Cons*: non-optimal usage of resources; higher probability of negotiation failure.

Multi-step negotiation session: initial proposal from the client, revisions returned by the server, another proposal from the client and so on, up to the termination of the negotiation:

- *Pros*: higher probability of success for large network slices (several possibilities of SLS variants).
- *Cons*: lower speed wireless router two-step negotiation; medium complexity solution.

Optional enhanced negotiation based on several variants (alternatives) of negotiated objects values and selective acceptance or rejection of different alternatives:

- *Pros*: most refined way to negotiate due to selectivity of acceptance.
- *Cons*: high complexity and overhead; lowest speed.

V. CONCLUSIONS AND FUTURE WORK

This paper considered a 5G slicing system architecture based on NFV and SDN cooperation and selected some relevant layered examples, from those proposed in several standards and projects. The general architectural framework was described in Sections I-III.

Section IV developed the specific contribution, which was on studying the domain-level management for a network segment of a multi-domain slice.

The main management and control entities associated to an administrative domain were an SDN-Infrastructure Controller (SDN-IC) (playing also the role of an intra-domain network manager) and a Virtual Infrastructure Manager (VIM) (playing the role defined in ETSI-NFV MANO framework, plus some slice-specific new functions). Six variants of splitting the resource management functions (related to mapping of the virtual requested resources on the network domain ones) between two entities above, were proposed in the paper and comparatively analyzed with pros and cons comments. It has been shown that an additional flexibility can be added to the above cooperation if negotiations (related to resource availability) are introduced between VIM and SDN-IC.

Future work would be a continuation of this study, for a quantitative evaluation of the six variants in terms of complexity, performance, response time and seamless deployment capabilities. Also, refining the hierarchies and scope of admission control actions among the multi-domain Resource Orchestrator (higher level), VIM (middle level) and SDN-IC (lower level) is still an open research topic.

REFERENCES.

[1] 5GPPP Architecture Working Group, "View on 5G Architecture", Version 2.0, December 2017.

[2] NGMN Alliance, "Description of Network Slicing Concept, NGMN 5G P1 Requirements & Architecture, Work Stream End-to-End Architecture", Version 1.0, Jan. 2016.

[3] J. Ordonez-Lucena et al., "Network Slicing for 5G with SDN/NFV: Concepts, Architectures and Challenges", IEEE Communications Magazine, 2017, pp. 80-87, Citation information: DOI 10.1109/MCOM.2017.1600935.

[4] X. Foukas, G. Patounas, A. Elmokashfi, and M. K. Marina, "Network Slicing in 5G: Survey and Challenges", IEEE Communications Magazine, May 2017, pp.94-100

[5] P. Rost et al., "Network Slicing to Enable Scalability and Flexibility in 5G Mobile Networks", IEEE Communications Magazine, Vol.55, May 2017, pp.72-79.

[6] ETSI GR NFV-EVE 012 V3.1.1 (2017-12), Release 3 "NFV Evolution and Ecosystem; Report on Network Slicing Support with ETSI NFV Architecture Framework".

[7] 3GPP TR 28.801: "Telecommunication management; Study on management and orchestration of network slicing for next generation network". Rel. 15.0.0, September 2017.

[8] 3GPP TS 28.530, "Management of 5G networks and network slicing; Concepts, use cases and requirements", Rel.15, April 2018.

[9] A. Galis, "Network Slicing - A holistic architectural approach, orchestration and management with applicability in mobile and fixed networks and clouds",

http://discovery.ucl.ac.uk/10051374/ [retrieved January, 2019].
[10] ETSI GS NFV 002, "NFV Architectural Framework", Rel. 1.2.1, December 2014.
[11] ETSI GS NFV-IFA 009 "Network Functions Virtualisation (NFV); Management and Orchestration; Report on Architectural Options". Technical Report, Rel. 1.1.1, July 2016.
[12] ETSI GR NFV-IFA 028: "Network Functions Virtualisation (NFV) Release 3; Management and Orchestration; Report on architecture options to support multiple administrative domains" Technical Report, Rel. 3.1.1, January 2018.
[13] ONF TR-526, "Applying SDN Architecture to 5G Slicing", April 2016.
[14] K. Katsalis, N. Nikaein, and A. Edmonds, "Multi-Domain Orchestration for NFV: Challenges and Research Directions", 2016 15th Int'l Conf. on Ubiquitous Computing and Communications and International Symposium on Cyberspace and Security (IUCC-CSS), pp. 189–195, DOI: 10.1109/IUCC-CSS.2016.034, ttps://ieeexplore.ieee.org/document/7828601
[15] N. F. Saraiva de Sousa, D. A. Lachos Perez, R. V. Rosa, M. A. S. Santos and C. E. Rothenberg, "Network Service Orchestration: A Survey", 2018, https://arxiv.org/abs/1803.06596 [retrieved: February, 2019].
[16] I. Afolabi, T. Taleb, K. Samdanis, A. Ksentini, and H. Flinck, "Network Slicing & Softwarization: A Survey on Principles, Enabling Technologies & Solutions", IEEE Communications Surveys & Tutorials, Mar. 2018, pp. 2429-2453.
[17] T. Taleb, I. Afolabi, K. Samdanis, and F. Z. Yousaf, "On Multi-domain Network Slicing Orchestration Architecture & Federated Resource Control", http://mosaic-lab.org/uploads/papers/3f772f2d-9e0f-4329-9298-aae4ef8ded65.pdf [retrieved February, 2019]
[18] J. Ordonez-Lucena et al., "The Creation Phase in Network Slicing: From a Service Order to an Operative Network Slice", European Conference on Networks and Communications (EuCNC), 2018, https://arxiv.org/abs/1804.09642 [retrieved January, 2019]
[19] F. Verdi and M. F. Magalhaes, "Using Virtualization to Provide Interdomain QoS-enabled Routing", Journal of Networks, April 2007, pp. 23-32.

Studying Optical Frequency Comb-Based Fiber to Millimeter-Band Wireless Interface

Mikhail Belkin, Tatiana Bakhvalova
Scientific and Technological Center "Integrated Microwave Photonics"
MIREA - Russian Technological University
Moscow, Russian Federation
email: belkin@mirea.ru, bakhvalova@mirea.ru

Abstract—**Using off-the-shelf photonic computer-aided design tool VPIphotonics Design Suite, a detailed analysis of optical-frequency-comb-based fiber to millimeter-band wireless interface in actual base station for emerging 5G access networks of fiber-wireless architecture was carried out. The simulation experiments to study fiber transmission of 1.25-Gbit/s, 64-QAM signals in the bandwidth 37-43.5 GHz predict that the needed transmission quality is supported at a distance of optical cable between Central Office and Base Station up to 40 km, which is quite acceptable for an access network.**

Keywords-radio-over-fiber; base station; optical frequency comb; recirculating loop; suppressed carrier single sideband modulator.

I. INTRODUCTION

Within the recent decades, an explosion of researches and developments referring to the next-generation communication networks known as 5G New Radio (NR) has been observed [1]-[5]. Based on 4G Long-Term Evolution (LTE) progress [6], 5G NR is in principle a novel stage of unprecedented technological innovation with ubiquitous speed connectivity. As a result, it is expected that 5G NR will radically transform a number of industries and will provide direct, super-speed connections between any users and any sensors and devices.

At the present time, several reviews to analyze significant changes in the 5G NR approaches as compared to the existing 4G LTE networks have been published [7][8] denoting a series of milestones. Developing this topic, Table I summarizes the results of the advanced analysis adding the investigations of the last 5 years.

A review of the current Research and development (R&Ds) in 5G NR area convincingly demonstrates the consistent achievement of the milestones indicated in Table I, which is reflected in a vast number of publications and the emergence of commercial products. Among them, much attention is paid to radically expanding the available spectral bands (see point 1 of the Table I), which is associated with the absorption of the Millimeter Wavelengths (MMW). Following this tendency, currently, the local telecommunications commissions of various countries are proposing and harmonizing the plans of frequency allocation in MMW-band, which will be reviewed this year at the World Radio Conference (WRC-2019) [9]. Another milestone of great importance is the development of access networks (see point 3 of the Table I). In this direction, well-known Radio-over-Fiber (RoF) technology [10]-[12] is considered as the most promising approach, which is implemented based on Fiber-Wireless (FiWi) architecture.

TABLE I. THE MILESTONES IN THE WAY TO TRANSFORM 4G LTE TO 5G

No	Designation	Short Description
1	Radically expanding the available spectral bands	Some super-wide bandwidth cases in 5G access networks will require contiguous carrier bandwidths. To support them, additional carrier frequencies (below 6 GHz), as well as millimeter wave (mmWave) RF carriers will be required.
2	Increasing user densification	The answer is to use small-cell technology (from macro-cells to femto-cells) that enables carriers to provide more users with lower latency, better mobile device battery life, and expanded cellular coverage
3	Establishing optimized access network architecture	Following the milestones of the points 1 and 2, it is necessary to optimize the access network architecture so that at the same time provide high-quality communication with fixed and mobile users and low charges for the building and maintenance of networks. A promising candidate for solving the problem is a fiber-wireless architecture, already tested in 4G LTE systems.
4	Providing More Options with Fixed Wireless Access	Fixed Wireless Access provides users with more alternatives for connecting to the cloud using wireless broadband data communication to connect two or more fixed locations. In particular, the introduction of this type of service will be very feasible for the broad development of telemedicine.
5	Using a Mobile Phone as a Hub	A future people life is able to revolve around a new 5G smartphone. With high-speed mobile broadband access and truly ubiquitous coverage, it will enable devices to communicate directly with each other, without routing the data paths through a network infrastructure.
6	Using active antenna systems in mm-Wave communication	Following the tendencies of expanding the available spectral bands and increasing user densification, mm-Wave 5G wireless network infrastructure can be erected with a lot of small cell sites controlled by the corresponding remote (base) station (RS). In order to avoid inter-interference inside these cells, one of the promising approaches is to equip the RS with beam-steerable phased array antennas using hundreds of antenna elements to form directional beams.
7	Providing low latency	Mission-critical services requiring very high reliability, global coverage, and very low latency, which may be more important than throughput in some applications, will become more native to support 5G infrastructure.

A typical configuration of an RoF-based communication network including Central Office (CO), set of Base Stations (BS), and microwave or millimeter-wave band user radio terminals, have been discussed in detail in numerous publications (for example, in [10]-[13] and the papers cited there), so it is not considered in this paper. An important element of this network architecture is a base station, through which an interactive fiber-wireless interface is implemented. Taking part recent studies, we have proposed and previously investigated two design concepts of cost- and power-efficient base station for emerging FiWi networks [14][15], in which for a multi-frequency conversion of a Radio-Frequency (RF) carrier, an Optical Frequency Comb Generator (OFCG) based on microwave-photonic technology was used. Namely, it was designed on a long-wavelength Vertical Cavity Surface Emitting Laser (VCSEL) operating in the period doubling state in the first case, and on an Optical Recirculation Loop (ORL) technique using two Suppressed Carrier Single Sideband (SC-SSB) optical modulators in the second one.

Nevertheless, in the cited papers, as well as in the works of other authors referred to this direction, there is no analysis of the efficiency of the OFCG-based actual base station for emerging FiWi networks that supports high-speed multichannel digital RF-signal transmission. Meeting this shortcoming, the remainder of the paper is organized as follows. Section II demonstrates the models and setups for simulation of a recirculation-loop-based OFCG and fiber to MMW-band wireless interface using the well-known software tool VPIPhotonics Design Suit [16]. Leveraging the application of this OFCG for a realistic case, the simulation results by the same computer tool imitating multi-wavelength optical frequency comb generation and transmission of quadrature amplitude modulated RF signals through OFCG-based fiber-wireless interface of a FiWi-architected base station are discussed in Section III. Section IV concludes the paper.

II. DESCRIBING THE MODELS AND SETUPS FOR SIMULATION

A. Optical Frequency Comb Generator

Generally, the outstanding performance of OFCG has led to a revolution in a lot of radio-engineering fields, from radio-frequency arbitrary waveform generation to coherent optical communications. The key R&D achievements in this direction are summarized in [17]. In the paper, four layouts of OFCG suitable to achieve a comb with a spectrally flat envelope are reviewed consisting of cascaded intensity and phase modulators, dual-drive Mach Zehnder modulator (another name for the SC-SSB modulator), two-cascaded phase modulators with linearly chirped fiber Bragg grating, and three cascaded modulators: two intensity and one phase. As a result, it was concluded that the ideal optical frequency comb must be well conceived to target a particular application. Nevertheless, the above-mentioned paper does not consider the option of OFCG based on an optical recirculation loop, which has been studied for more than 10 years as a good candidate for designing microwave-photonics multichannel oscillators and frequency converters [18][19]. The undoubted advantages of this technique include simplicity of the scheme, stability, robustness, tunability, low RF driving voltage, etc. However, its important disadvantage is the relatively short comb length. For example, as follows from [18], the output comb of the device under study consists of only 5-9 teeth, that is, not enough for a realistic 5G application in MMW-band. The obvious way to create a multichannel fiber-to-wireless interface in such environment is to "compact" the comb by narrowing down the interval between frequency teeth.

Following this concept, Fig. 1 shows the VPI model and setup for simulation of the OFCG scheme under study. There are four units depicted in Fig. 1: the composed model of ORL includes library models of optical X-coupler, SC-SSB modulator, Optical Amplifier (OA), Optical Band-Pass Filter (OBPF), as well as library models of Continuous-Wave Semiconductor Laser (CW-SL) emitting at the frequency ν_0 as an optical source, RF Generator (RFG) as a RF signal source and library instrumental model of Optical Spectrum Analyzer (OSA). In order to close the ORL, output of OBPF through the service unit T and input of SC-SSB are connected to X-coupler's port 'input2' and port 'output2', correspondingly. During the simulation, RFG acts as a source of the reference RF signal (f_{ref}), while using the OSA, the output optical spectrum is recorded.

B. Optical-Frequency-Comb-Based Fiber-to-Wireless Interface

Fig. 2 shows the VPI model and setup for simulation of OFCG-based fiber to MMW band wireless interface while transmission of quadrature amplitude modulated RF signals is supported. The scheme represents the downlink channel of FiWi-architected RoF system and consists of three units imitating the operation of CO, BS, and 2-fiber optical cable between them. The CO includes the same laser model, the radiation of which is divided into two branches using a Y-coupler, library model of SC-SSB modulator with suppressing lower sideband, and library instrumental model of QAM RF Transmitter. The latter contains library models of QAM generator and output unit for power control following by electrical amplifier. This module generates an electrical M-QAM signal up-converted at a given RF carrier frequency. The Optical Cable includes two equivalent library models of single-mode optical fiber. Such a remote optical feed reduces

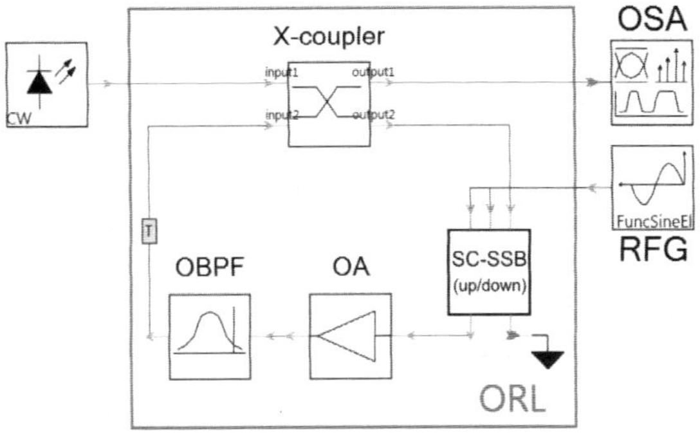

Figure 1. VPI model and setup for simulation of the OFCG.

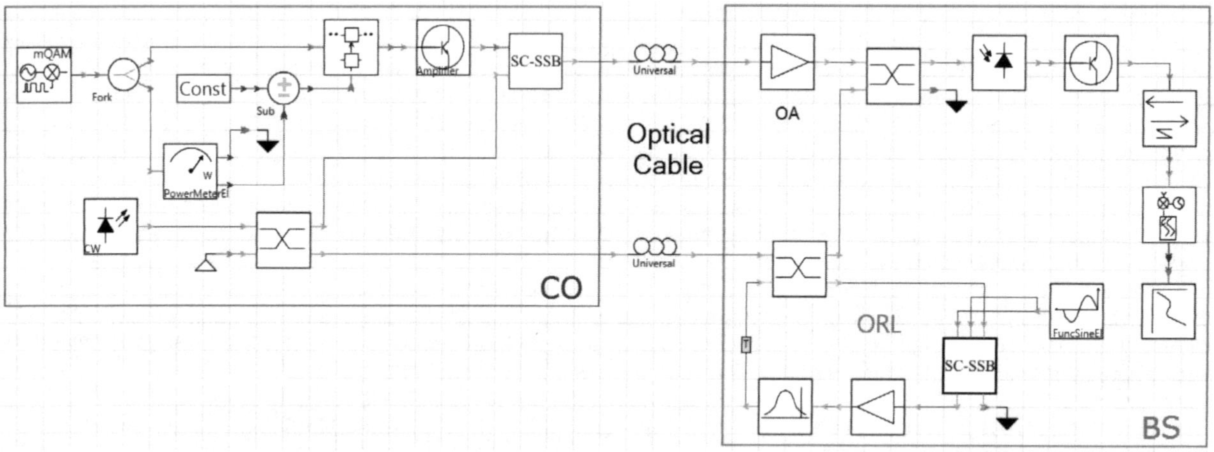

Figure 2. VPI model and setup for simulation of OFCG-based fiber to MMW band wireless interface.

the cost of the BS. Besides the OFCG model (see Fig. 1), the BS includes library models of optical amplifier, X-coupler, photodiode, and electrical post-amplifier outputted to the model of QAM RF Receiver. The latter detects the RF signal, decodes an electrical QAM signal and evaluates quantitatively the Symbol Error Rate (SER) and the Error-Vector Magnitude (EVM) of the output QAM signal. The model of Numerical 2D Analyzer is used for two-dimensional graphical representation of the data from the QAM RF Receiver output.

III. Simulation Experiments

A. Reference Data for the Simulation

In this work, the subject of the study is a fiber to MMW-band wireless interface and the device of the study is an OFCG based on a SC-SSB optical modulator. A tool for the computer simulation is the well-known commercial software VPIPhotonics Design Suit™. In the course of the research, first of all, the possibility of creating a multi-frequency OFCG with the closest arrangement of the teeth is checked. Then, the transmission quality of a digital RF signal with multi-position QAM through the downlink channel of the base station using fiber to MMW-band wireless interface is analyzed. Two limiting factors are taken into account during the simulation procedure: fiber chromatic dispersion and RF channel spacing. Table II lists the common reference data for the OFCG under study. In addition, Table III lists the reference data for the fiber to MMW-band wireless interface under study.

TABLE II. Reference Data for Optical Frequency Comb Generator

Parameter	**Value**
Laser Source Frequency (ν_0)	193.3 THz
Laser Linewidth	10 kHz
Reference RF frequency (f_{ref})	0.3 GHz
Type of modulator inside optical recirculating loop	SC-SSB (up/down)
Gain of Recirculating Loop (g)	0.8<g<1
Number of Up or Down Round Trips	Not less than 10
Level Non-Uniformity of Output Comb Teeth	Not more than 5 dB

TABLE III. Reference Data for the Fiber to MMW-Band Wireless Interface under Study

Parameter		**Value**
Length of PRBS*		2^{15}-1
Bitrate		1.25 Gbit/s
RF Carrier Frequency		40.2 GHz
Type of RF modulation		64-QAM
Optical Carrier		C-band
RF band		37-43.5 GHz
Type of optical modulation		SC-SSB (up)
PIN-Photodiode	Responsivity	0.92 A/W
	Dark current	100 nA
	3dB Bandwidth	50 GHz
	Optical Input Power	Near 3 mW
Post-amplifier	Gain	30 dB
	Noise Factor	2 dB
Optical Fiber	Type	SMF-28e+
	Length	Up to 50 km
	Attenuation	0.2 dB/km
	Dispersion	16e^{-6} s/m^2
	Dispersion Slope	80 s/m^3

* Pseudo Random Bit Sequence

B. Optical Frequency Comb Generator

Fig. 3 demonstrates an OSA's spectrum of multi-wavelength optical frequency comb output following the setup of Fig. 1. As one can see from Fig. 3, the OFCG under study includes 21 optical carriers with the spacing of 0.3 GHz and the level non-uniformity of less than 5 dB.

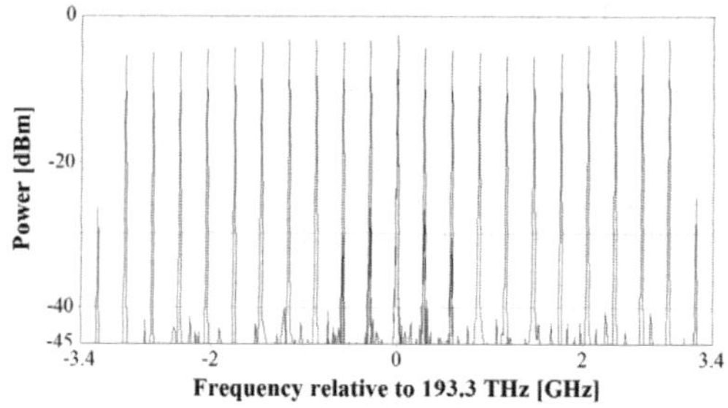

Figure 3. A spectrum of multi-wavelength optical frequency comb output.

C. Optical-Frequency-Comb-Based Fiber-to-Wireless Interface

Our further studies were related to EVM analysis depending on the length of the optical cable and the spacing between the RF channels in the setup of Fig. 2. The results of the simulations are presented in Fig. 4 and Fig. 5, respectively. For a clear view, there are some insets in Fig. 4 showing constellation diagrams in specific points. In particular, as one can see from Fig. 4, due to dispersion in the optical cable, the EVM values increase with a slope of near 0.17 %/km reaching a standard limit for 64-QAM of 8% [20] at the distance of 40 km.

Besides, Fig. 5 demonstrates EVM vs RF channel spacing characteristic at the fiber distance of near 12 km. As a result, as the co-channel spacing shrinks, the EVM remain at about 3% until 240 MHz. With a further reduction in the RF channel spacing, the slope of the EVM curve begins to increase reaching the standard limit at about 215 MHz.

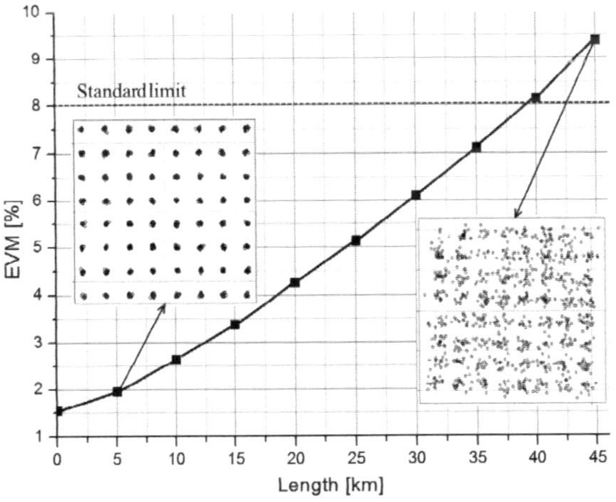

Figure 4. EVM vs Optical Cable Length.

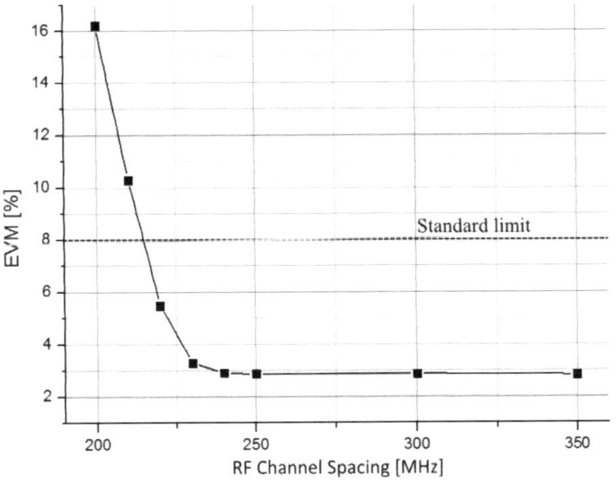

Figure 5. EVM vs RF Channel Spacing.

The following outputs can be derived from our study:

• When transmitting digital radio signals with 64-QAM on millimeter-wave RF carriers (37-43.5 GHz), even when using a single-sideband modulator with a suppressed optical carrier, dispersion in an optical cable has a significant impact on the quality of the received signal. However, the error is within the standard limit up to a distance of 40 km.

• With a fiber-optic link length of up to 12 km, it is acceptable to shrink the interval between RF channels from 300 to 215 MHz.

IV. CONCLUSION

In this paper, a detailed analysis of optical-frequency-comb-based fiber to millimeter-band wireless interface in actual base station for emerging 5G access networks of fiber-wireless architecture was carried out using off-the-shelf computer-aided design tool VPIphotonics Design Suite. The specific goal of the research was to assess the possibility and efficiency of creating a downlink channel of a multi-channel base station using a multi-wavelength optical frequency comb generator with a close arrangement of optical carriers based on a cost- and power-efficient optical recirculation loop including carrier-suppressed single-sideband optical modulator. Following this goal, firstly a computer model and a setup for simulation were proposed and described. Simulation experiment predicts that OFCG including 21 optical carriers with the spacing of 0.3 GHz and the level non-uniformity of less than 5 dB can be realized. Leveraging the application of this OFCG for a realistic case, the model and setup to simulate fiber to millimeter-band RF interface were proposed and described. The simulation experiment predicts that the needed transmission quality is supported at a distance of optical cable between Central Office and Base Station, which is quite acceptable for an access network. In the course of another simulation experiment evaluating the effect of RF co-channel interference, it was shown that the number of RF channels within the same frequency band could be increased 1.4 times.

ACKNOWLEDGMENT

This work was supported by the Russian Foundation for Basic Research, Grant No. 17-57-10002.

REFERENCES

[1] J. G. Andrews et al., “What Will 5G Be?” IEEE Journal on Selected Areas in Communications, vol. 32, no. 6; Jun. 2014, pp. 1065 – 1082.

[2] S. Chen and J. Zhao, “The requirements, challenges and technologies for 5G of terrestrial mobile telecommunication,” IEEE Commun. Mag., vol. 52, no. 5; May 2014. pp. 36–43.

[3] J. Munn, “Our 5G Future: In the Fast Lane with Numerical Simulation,” Microwaves & RF; Dec. 2016, pp. 48-50.

[4] L. Frenzel, “Making 5G Happen,” Microwaves & RF; Dec. 2017, pp. 1-5.

[5] J. Browne, “What Role Will Millimeter Waves Play in 5G Wireless Systems?” Microwaves & RF; Apr. 2018. pp. 38-42.

[6] R. Waterhouse and D. Novak, “Realizing 5G,” IEEE Microwave Magazine, vol. 16, no 8, pp. 84-92, Sept. 2015.

[7] F. Boccardi, R. W. Heath, A. Lozano, T. L. Marzetta, and P. Popovski, "Five Disruptive Technology Directions for 5G", IEEE Commun. Mag., vol. 52, no. 2, pp. 74-80, Feb. 2014.

[8] D. Novak and R. Waterhouse, "Emerging disruptive wireless technologies - Prospects and challenges for integration with optical networks", In Proceedings of Optical Fiber Communication Conference (OFC/NFOEC); 2013. pp. 1-3.

[9] https://www.itu.int/net/events/eventdetails.asp?eventid=14719 Online. Accessed July, 2019.

[10] D. Novak et al., "Radio-Over-Fiber Technologies for Emerging Wireless Systems", IEEE Journal of Quantum Electronics, vol. 52, no. 1, pp. 1-11, Jan 2016.

[11] H. Al-Raweshidy and S. Komaki, editors, Radio over Fiber Technologies for Mobile Communications Networks, Norwood: Artech House, 436 pp., 2002.

[12] M. Sauer, A. Kobyakov, and J. George, "Radio over Fiber for Picocellular Network Architectures," IEEE Journal of Lightwave Technology, 2007, vol. 25, no. 11, pp. 3301-3320.

[13] M. E. Belkin, D. Fofanov, V. Golovin, Y. Tyschuk, and A. S. Sigov, "Design and optimization of photonics-based beamforming networks for ultra-wide mmWave-band antenna arrays," Chapter in book IntechOpen "Antenna Array Optimization," 21 pp., 2018, DOI: 10.5772/intechopen.80899.

[14] M. E. Belkin, "The Building Principles of a Cost- and Power-Efficient Base Station for Emerging Fiber-Wireless Networks," International Conference on Microwaves, Communications, Antennas and Electronic Systems, COMCAS 2017, pp. 1-4, Tel Aviv, Israel, 13-15 Nov. 2017, DOI: 10.1109/COMCAS.2017.8244771.

[15] M. E. Belkin, T. Bakhvalova, S. Turitsyn, and A. Sigov, "The Design Principles of Reconfigurable Versatile Base Station for Upcoming Communication Networks". 26th Telecommunications Forum (TELFOR2018) – Belgrade, Serbia, Nov. 2018, pp. 180-182, DOI: 10.1109/TELFOR.2018.8611864.

[16] https://www.vpiphotonics.com/Tools/DesignSuite/ Online. Accessed July, 2019.

[17] V. Torres-Company and A. M. Weiner, "Optical frequency comb technology for ultra-broadband radio-frequency photonics," Laser & Photonics Reviews, p. 1-55, 18 December 2013 https://doi.org/10.1002/lpor.201300126.

[18] T. Kawanishi, T. Sakamoto, S. Shimada, and M. Izutsu, "Optical Frequency Comb Generator Using Optical Fiber Loops with Single Side-Band Modulation," IEICE Electronics Express, vol. 1, No 8, pp. 217-221, 2004.

[19] D. A. Fofanov, T. N. Bakhvalova, A. V. Alyoshin, M. E. Belkin, and A. S. Sigov, "Studying Microwave-Photonic Frequency Up-Conversion for Telecom and Measurement Equipment," 2018 IEEE Radio and Antenna Days of the Indian Ocean (RADIO), Mauritius, October 2018, 2 pp., DOI: 10.23919/RADIO.2018.8572474.

[20] ETSI, "Minimum requirements for Error Vector Magnitude," in Technical Specification, LTE; Evolved Universal Terrestrial Radio Access (E-UTRA); User Equipment (UE) radio transmission and reception (3GPP TS 36.101 version 14.3.0 Release 14), ETSI, 2017-04, p. 215.

Frequency Domain Equalization of CAZAC-OFDM with Transversal Filter using LMS Algorithm

Hiroyuki Yamano, Yoshitsugu Sugai and Masahiro Muraguchi
Department of Electrical Engineering, Tokyo University of Science
6-3-1 Niijuku, Katsushika-ku, Tokyo, 125-0051, Japan
E-mail: 4319579@ed.tus.ac.jp, murag@ee.kagu.tus.ac.jp

Abstract— **In wireless communications, signals are affected by multipath fading in the transmission channel, which causes amplitude fluctuation and phase fluctuation at the receiver front-end. Unfortunately, the Frequency Domain Equalization (FDE) using pilot subcarriers, which is ordinary used in conventional Orthogonal Frequency Division Multiplex (OFDM) systems, cannot apply the OFDM system with Constant Amplitude Zero Auto-Correlation (CAZAC) precoding, CAZAC-OFDM. In this paper, we propose a method to improve the negative effect of multipath fading by applying transversal filter using Least Mean Square (LMS) algorithm to CAZAC-OFDM systems. We have confirmed that the CAZAC-OFDM system with the proposed transversal filter maintains enough low Bit Error Rate (BER) performance under flat fading and frequency selective fading channels.**

Keywords-OFDM; CAZAC sequence; Frequency domain equalization; Transversal filter; LMS algorithm.

I. INTRODUCTION

In recent years, with the spread of smartphones, tablet terminals and PCs, the demand for wireless communication is expanding. Furthermore, with the advent of video distribution and streaming services, the amount of data has increased rapidly. Therefore, an Orthogonal Frequency Division Multiplex (OFDM) scheme is widely used in wireless communication, due to its great advantage of high spectrum utilization that is about twice spectral efficiency compared with single carrier scheme. Moreover, the OFDM scheme has resistance properties to multipath fading.

Unfortunately, OFDM scheme has high Peak-to-Average Power Ratio (PAPR). Many kinds of method have been proposed to solve this PAPR problem [1]. The OFDM scheme with Constant Amplitude Zero Auto-Correlation (CAZAC) precoding, CAZAC-OFDM, is a known modulation technique aimed at alleviating the PAPR problem [2][3]. It has been reported that one CAZAC sequence in cooperation with Inverse Fast Fourier Transform (IFFT) process converts the PAPR of the M-array Quadrature Amplitude Modulation (M-QAM) OFDM signal into the PAPR of an M-QAM single-carrier signal [4]-[7].

In wireless systems under multipath fading environment, interference between delayed waves makes amplitude fluctuation and phase fluctuation at the receiver front-end. The Frequency Domain Equalization (FDE) using pilot subcarriers, which is ordinary used in conventional OFDM systems, cannot apply the CAZAC-OFDM. In the CAZAC-OFDM scheme, IFFT input signal for each subcarrier includes all QAM signal components, and each subcarrier carries uniformly distributed QAM data. The CAZAC-OFDM has a nature of spread-spectrum just like a Code Division Multiple Access (CDMA) or convolutional coding. Therefore, the CAZAC-OFDM scheme cannot have any pilot subcarriers although it has a frequency diversity effect itself.

In this paper, we study a fading compensation technique by applying a transversal filter using Least Mean Square (LMS) algorithm to the CAZAC-OFDM. A waveform equalizer represented by a transversal filter equalizes the transmission channel characteristics by inserting it in front of the receiver. When the characteristics of the transmission channel are dynamically changing and not in the steady state, an adaptive equalizer must be used. In this case, the training signal should be sent periodically. The tap coefficients of the filter are iteratively updated so that the output signal converges to the transmission signal. One type of adaptive algorithm used in the adaptive equalizer is the LMS algorithm [8]-[10].

We have confirmed that the CAZAC-OFDM system with the proposed transversal filter maintains enough low Bit Error Rate (BER) performance under flat fading and frequency selective fading channels.

The rest of this paper is organized as follows: In Section 2, we describe the CAZAC-OFDM system. In Section 3, we describe the method of channel estimation. In Section 4, we describe the transversal filter. In Section 5, we describe LMS algorithm. In Section 6, we show how convergence is achieved by updating the tap coefficients of the filter. In Section 7, we describe the effect of the proposed transversal filter in the CAZAC-OFDM system. Finally, we conclude this paper in Section 8.

II. CAZAC-OFDM SYSTEM

A. OFDM System

OFDM system is a kind of multi-carrier modulation scheme that digitally modulates and multiplexes a number of orthogonal subcarriers in the frequency domain. In the OFDM system, data signals are mapped by digital modulation such as QAM or PSK. Then, it is converted from frequency domain signal to discrete-time domain signal by N size IFFT. The discrete-time OFDM signal $x[n]$ with N subcarriers is represented as follows.

$$x[n] = \frac{1}{N}\sum_{k=0}^{N-1} X[k]e^{j\frac{2\pi kn}{N}} \quad (1)$$

where $j = \sqrt{-1}$, n is the discrete-time index and $X[k]$ is the frequency domain signal [11].

In general, OFDM has high PAPR. PAPR is the ratio of peak power to average power and is defined by the following equation.

$$PAPR = 10\log_{10}\frac{\max_{0\le n\le N-1}|x[n]|^2}{\operatorname{mean}_{0\le n\le N-1}|x[n]|^2}\ [\mathrm{dB}] \quad (2)$$

The value of PAPR increases as the peak power increases compared to the average power. As PAPR increases, power consumption of the transmitter increases, so PAPR should be reduced as much as possible.

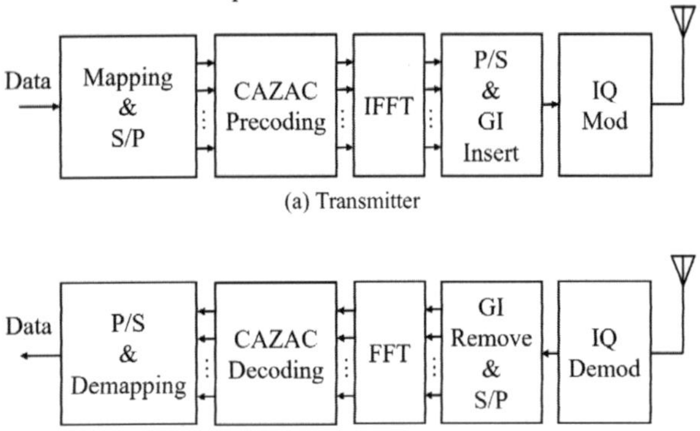

(a) Transmitter

(b) Receiver

Figure 1. CAZAC-OFDM system.

B. CAZAC Precoding

Figure 1 shows the configurations of CAZAC-OFDM transmitter and receiver. CAZAC-OFDM reduces PAPR by performing precoding using Zadoff-Chu sequence, which is a type of CAZAC sequence. The Zadoff-Chu sequence is expressed by the following equation.

$$c_k = \begin{cases} \exp\left(j\frac{\pi rk(k+1)}{L}\right) & (L \text{ is odd}) \\ \exp\left(j\frac{\pi rk^2}{L}\right) & (L \text{ is even}) \end{cases} \quad (3)$$
$$k = 0,1,\cdots,L-1$$

where L is the sequence length and r is the sequence number. Assuming that $r = 1$ and $L = N^2$ in the above equation, the Zadoff-Chu sequence is as follows.

$$c_k = \exp\left(j\frac{\pi k^2}{N^2}\right) \quad (4)$$

where N is the number of subcarriers. Using the above equation, CAZAC precoding generates an $N \times N$ square matrix $\boldsymbol{M}$.

$$\boldsymbol{M} = \frac{1}{N}\begin{bmatrix} c_0 & c_1 & \cdots & c_{N-1} \\ c_N & c_{N+1} & \cdots & c_{2N-1} \\ \vdots & \vdots & \ddots & \vdots \\ c_{(N-1)N} & c_{(N-1)N+1} & \cdots & c_{N^2-1} \end{bmatrix} \quad (5)$$

The transmission data sequence $\boldsymbol{X}$ with N subcarriers is expressed as follows.

$$\boldsymbol{X} = \begin{bmatrix} X_0 \\ X_1 \\ \vdots \\ X_{N-1} \end{bmatrix} \quad (6)$$

When the transmission data sequence $\boldsymbol{X}$ is multiplied by the square matrix $\boldsymbol{M}$, the output by CAZAC precoding $\boldsymbol{P}$ is expressed by the following equation.

$$\boldsymbol{P} = \boldsymbol{MX}$$
$$= \frac{1}{N}\begin{bmatrix} c_0 & c_1 & \cdots & c_{N-1} \\ c_N & c_{N+1} & \cdots & c_{2N-1} \\ \vdots & \vdots & \ddots & \vdots \\ c_{(N-1)N} & c_{(N-1)N+1} & \cdots & c_{N^2-1} \end{bmatrix}\begin{bmatrix} X_0 \\ X_1 \\ \vdots \\ X_{N-1} \end{bmatrix} \quad (7)$$

When IFFT is performed on the output by CAZAC precoding $\boldsymbol{P}$, the time signal of CAZAC-OFDM s_n is expressed by the following equation.

$$s_n = c_{\left(\frac{N}{2}-n\right)modN} \cdot X_{\left(\frac{N}{2}-n\right)modN} \quad (8)$$

Therefore, as shown in Figure 2, the time domain signal of CAZAC-OFDM is obtained by rotating the phase of the mapping data while maintaining the amplitude of the mapping data. As a result, CAZAC-OFDM has reduced PAPR compared to conventional OFDM.

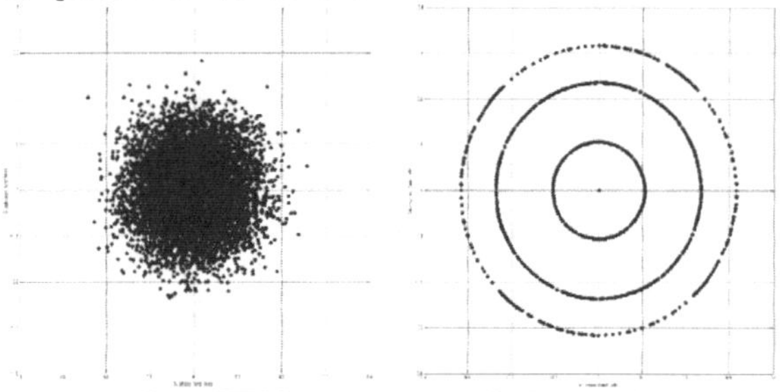

(a) Conv. OFDM (b) CAZAC-OFDM

Figure 2. Time domain signal.

In the conventional OFDM, the mapped value $\boldsymbol{X}$ is directly input to the IFFT. Therefore, in the frequency domain, each data is allocated to each subcarrier as shown in Figure 3a. On the other hand, in CAZAC-OFDM, $\boldsymbol{P}$ obtained by multiplying the mapped value $\boldsymbol{X}$ by the matrix $\boldsymbol{M}$ generated from the Zadoff-Chu sequence is input to the IFFT. In this case, the data loaded on the subcarrier is represented by the sum of the components of $\boldsymbol{X}$ with different phase rotations. Therefore, in the frequency domain, as shown in Figure 3b, all data are included in each subcarrier. This is the frequency diversity effect.

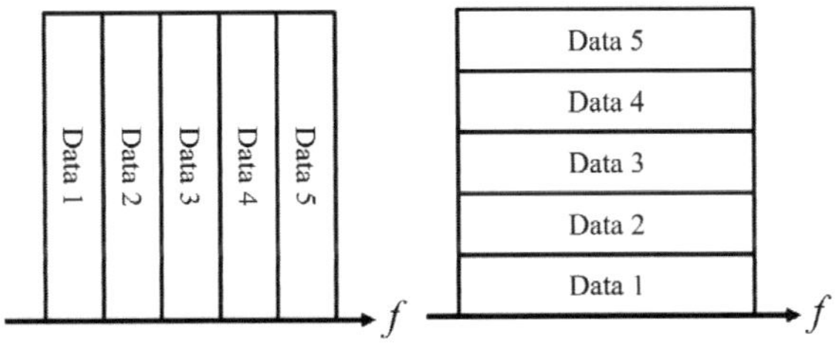

(a) Conv. OFDM (b) CAZAC-OFDM

Figure 3. State of data.

III. Channel Estimation

A. Channel Estimation in Conventional OFDM

In wireless communication, amplitude fluctuation and phase fluctuation occur in the transmission channel due to the influence of multipath fading. Therefore, the error rate of data becomes large. So, in the conventional OFDM, pilot subcarriers are used as a method to estimate the characteristics of multipath fading. The pilot subcarriers are known signals on the receiving side added for channel estimation, and is periodically inserted into the data subcarriers as shown in Figure 4. By examining how much the pilot subcarriers are fluctuated on the receiving side, it becomes possible to estimate the characteristics of multipath fading at that time.

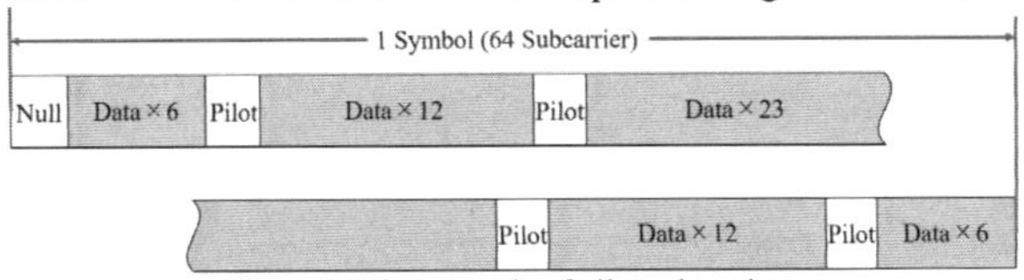

Figure 4. The example of pilot subcarriers.

B. Pilot Subcarriers in CAZAC-OFDM

As described above, in the conventional OFDM, the characteristics of multipath fading are estimated by inserting pilot subcarriers, and correction is performed accordingly. However, this method cannot be used in CAZAC-OFDM. This is due to the frequency diversity effect of CAZAC-OFDM. In the IFFT output after CAZAC precoding, all data in the time domain will be distributed to each subcarrier. Therefore, even if pilot subcarriers are inserted as shown in Figure 5, in the IFFT output, the information as the pilot subcarriers is dispersed to all the subcarriers, so that it cannot function as pilot subcarriers. Therefore, CAZAC-OFDM cannot correct the effect of multipath fading. Therefore, it is necessary to correct the influence of multipath fading without using pilot subcarriers.

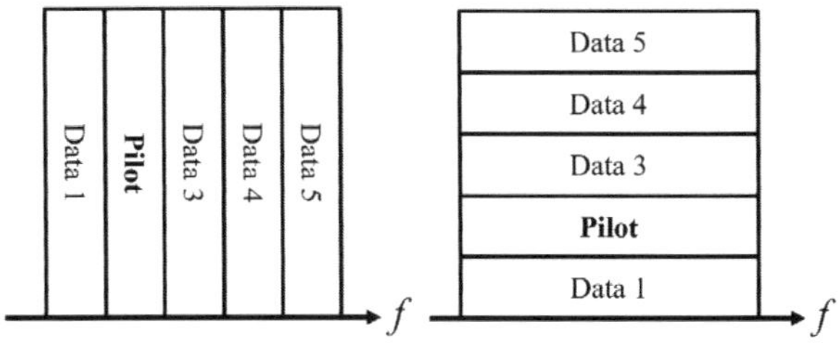

(a) Conv. OFDM (b) CAZAC-OFDM

Figure 5. Pilot subcarriers insertion.

IV. Transversal Filter

A. Structure

The model of the transversal filter is shown in Figure 6. The transmitted signal is received under the influence of multipath fading. Therefore, by inserting the transversal filter in front of the receiver on the receiving side, it is possible to estimate the transmission signal and correct the influence of multipath fading.

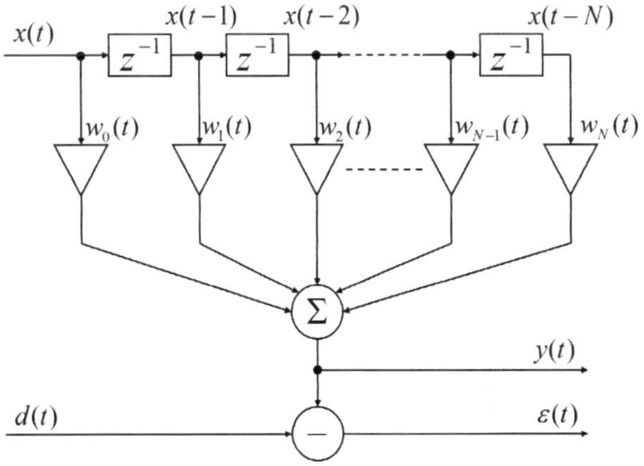

Figure 6. Transversal filter.

B. Principle

In the transversal filter of Figure 6, the output signal $y(t)$ is expressed by the following equation.

$$y(t) = \boldsymbol{x}^T(t)\boldsymbol{w}(t) \tag{9}$$

The input signal $x(t)$ and the tap coefficient $w(t)$ are respectively expressed as follows.

$$\boldsymbol{x}(t) = \begin{bmatrix} x(t) \\ x(t-1) \\ \vdots \\ x(t-N) \end{bmatrix} \tag{10}$$

$$\boldsymbol{w}(t) = \begin{bmatrix} w_0(t) \\ w_1(t) \\ \vdots \\ w_N(t) \end{bmatrix} \tag{11}$$

where the number of taps is $N+1$. The input signal is assumed to be in steady state. Here, let the training signal be $d(t)$. An error signal $\varepsilon(t)$, which is the difference between the output signal and the training signal is expressed by the following equation.

$$\varepsilon(t) = d(t) - y(t) \tag{12}$$

The tap coefficient $\boldsymbol{w}$ is set such that the error signal $\varepsilon(t)$ is minimized. As a result, the optimal tap coefficient $\boldsymbol{w_{opt}}$ is as follows [10].

$$\boldsymbol{w_{opt}} = \boldsymbol{R}^{-1}\boldsymbol{P} \tag{13}$$

where $\boldsymbol{R}$ and $\boldsymbol{P}$ are the following formulas, respectively.

$$\boldsymbol{R} = E[\boldsymbol{x}(t)\boldsymbol{x}^T(t)] \tag{14}$$

$$\boldsymbol{P} = E[d(t)\boldsymbol{x}(t)] \tag{15}$$

where $E[\cdot]$ is the ensemble average. This equation is the solution of the Wiener filter. From the above equation, the optimal tap coefficient can be determined by examining the autocorrelation of the input signal and the cross-correlation between the input signal and the training signal.

However, to determine the correlation of signals, it is necessary to collect the input signal for a long time, so it takes a long time to determine the tap coefficient. In addition, it is assumed that the signal is stationary, and it is decided to be the only optimal tap coefficient, so it cannot cope with the case where the characteristics of the transmission channel change dynamically. Therefore, these problems are solved by using an adaptive filter.

V. LMS ALGORITHM

In the adaptive filter, by iteratively updating the tap coefficient, it gradually approaches the optimal value. Therefore, if the change of the signal characteristics is slower than the convergence time of the adaptive filter, it can correspond to the change.

The steepest descent method is used as a method to update the tap coefficient iteratively so as to minimize the error. This is to update the tap coefficient in the direction of decreasing the gradient of $E[\varepsilon^2(t)]$ at a certain time t, and is expressed by the following equation.

$$\begin{aligned}\boldsymbol{w}(t+1) &= \boldsymbol{w}(t) - \frac{\mu \partial E[\varepsilon^2(t)]}{2\partial \boldsymbol{w}(t)} \\ &= \boldsymbol{w}(t) + \mu E[\varepsilon(t)\boldsymbol{x}(t)]\end{aligned} \tag{16}$$

where μ is the step size parameter, which is the parameter that determines the size of the slope down in one update. As the above equation shows, it requires ensemble average. Therefore, frequent updating of the tap coefficient cannot be performed. Therefore, LMS algorithm uses instantaneous estimates instead. As a result, the equation for updating the tap coefficient is as follows [9].

$$\begin{aligned}\boldsymbol{w}(t+1) &= \boldsymbol{w}(t) - \frac{\mu \partial \varepsilon^2(t)}{2\partial \boldsymbol{w}(t)} \\ &= \boldsymbol{w}(t) + \mu \varepsilon(t)\boldsymbol{x}(t)\end{aligned} \tag{17}$$

The convergence condition of the LMS algorithm is as follows [10].

$$0 < \mu < \frac{2}{N^*} \tag{18}$$

where N^* is the maximum value of the eigenvalues of the correlation matrix of the input signal. When the step size is increased, the convergence speed becomes faster but the steady-state error after convergence is increased. On the other hand, when the step size is reduced, the steady-state error after convergence is decreased but the convergence speed becomes slower. Therefore, it is necessary to decide the step size in consideration of the tradeoff between the convergence speed and the steady-state error.

VI. CONVERGENCE BY UPDATING TAP COEFFICIENTS

We simulated the convergence of constellation and time domain signals on the receiving side by updating the tap coefficient using MATLAB / Simulink. The simulation results are shown in Figures 7 and 8, respectively. Note that as the constellation and the time domain signals progress from Figure 7a to 7d, it indicates that time has elapsed.

The following figure shows that the constellation and the time domain signals converge as the tap coefficients are updated iteratively. As a result, communication becomes possible as usual only after convergence.

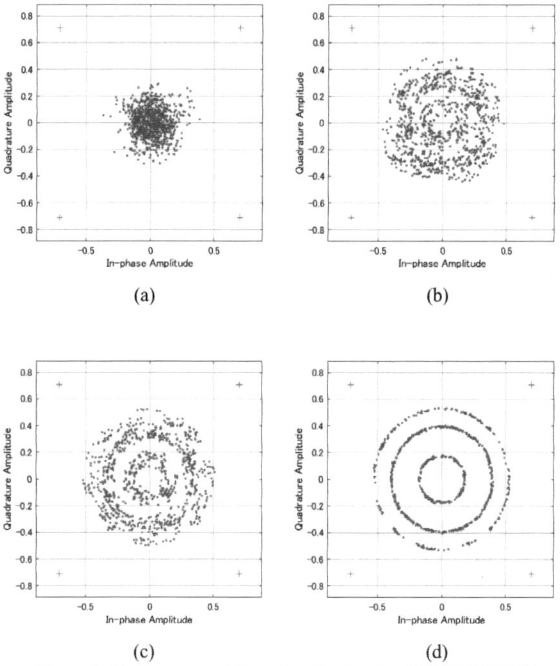

Figure 7. Convergence of time domain signals of CAZAC-OFDM.

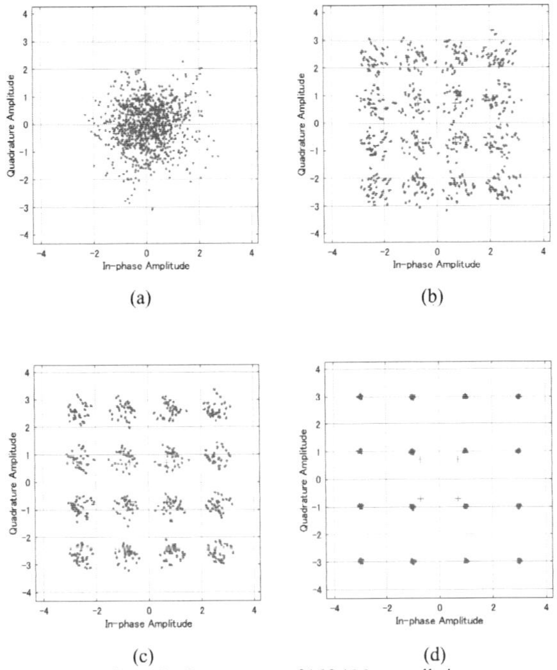

Figure 8. Convergence of 16QAM constellation.

VII. Performance Evaluation by Simulation

A. Simulation Specification

In this paper, in order to confirm how much the error rate of the signal is improved by using the transversal filter, the BER performance of CAZAC-OFDM and conventional OFDM are compared using MATLAB / Simulink.

Figures 9 and 10 show the configurations of CAZAC-OFDM transmitter and receiver, respectively. In addition, the transmitter and receiver configurations of the conventional OFDM, which does not use CAZAC precoding are structures, which removed the block of CAZAC precoding from Figures 9 and 10.

On the transmitting side, mapping (16QAM) is first performed on transmission data. Then, CAZAC-OFDM signal is generated by performing parallelization by serial-to-parallel conversion, CAZAC precoding and IFFT. At this time, if IFFT is performed without CAZAC precoding, a conventional OFDM signal is generated. After that, guard intervals are inserted, serialized by parallel-to-serial conversion, quadrature modulation is performed, and the signal is transmitted.

On the receiving side, fading in the transmission channel is corrected by passing through a transversal filter after quadrature demodulation. Then, received data is generated by serial-to-parallel conversion, removal of guard intervals, FFT, CAZAC decoding, parallel-to-serial conversion, and demapping.

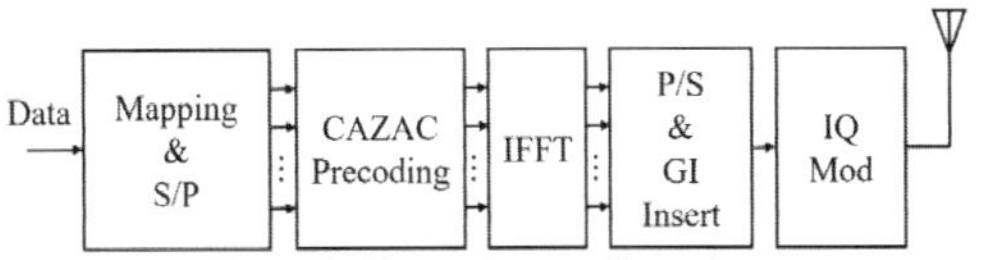

Figure 9. Transmitter configuration.

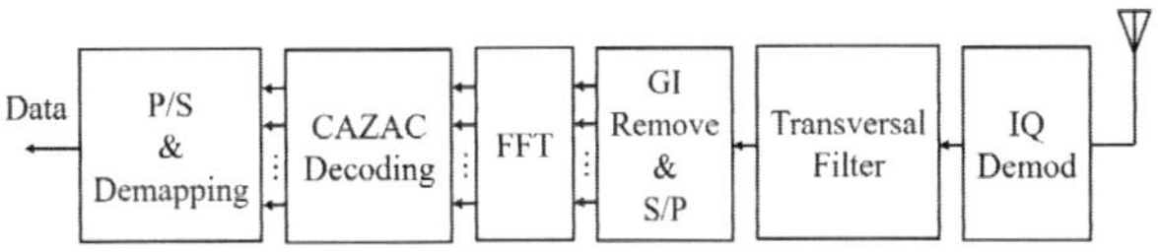

Figure 10. Receiver configuration.

Table I shows the simulation specification.

TABLE I. SIMULATION SPECIFICATION.

Mapping	16QAM
FFT Size	64
Carrier Frequency	120 MHz
Data Rate	32 Mbps
Number of Data Subcarriers	59
Guard Interval	16
Step Size	0.1
Channel Model	Flat Fading (Rayleigh)
	Frequency Selective Fading (Rayleigh)
	AWGN

B. Simulation Results

We compared the BER performance without fading channels. The simulation results are shown in Figure 11. From this result, it is proved that CAZAC-OFDM can obtain almost the same BER performance as conventional OFDM when the transversal filter is used.

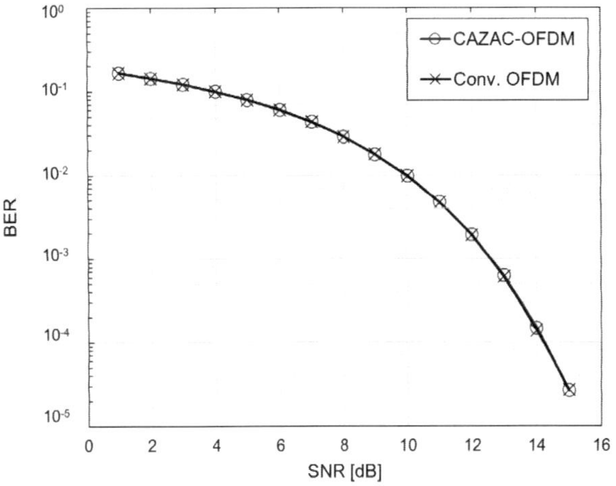

Figure 11. BER performance (without fading).

We compared the BER performance under flat fading and frequency selective fading channels. The simulation results are shown in Figure 12. From this result, it is proved that CAZAC-OFDM can obtain almost the same BER performance as that of the conventional OFDM by using the transversal filter even under fading environment. That is, it is concluded that CAZAC-OFDM is effective even under flat fading and frequency selective fading channels by using the transversal filter.

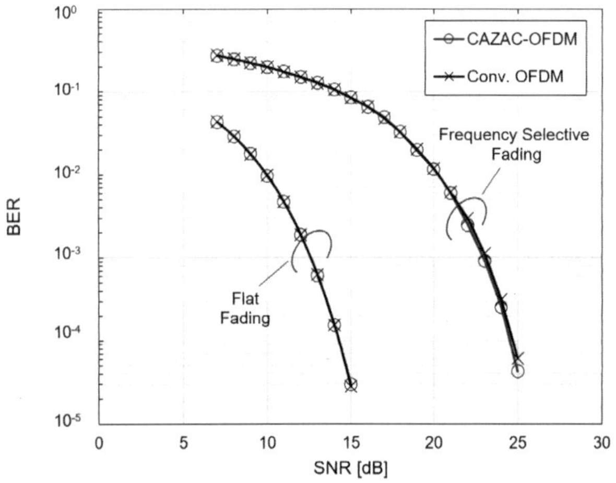

Figure 12. BER performance (with fading).

VIII. CONCLUSION

In this paper, we proposed a method to improve the negative effect of multipath fading by applying the transversal filter to CAZAC-OFDM system. Moreover, it has been confirmed by simulation that the CAZAC-OFDM system with the transversal filter maintains enough low BER performance under flat fading and frequency selective fading channels. The result shows that the CAZAC-OFDM system is effective under fading environment.

REFERENCES

[1] R. Ishioka, T. Kimura, and M. Muraguchi, "A Proposal for a New OFDM Wireless System using a CAZAC Equalization Scheme," Proc. AICT 2017, pp. 47-51, June 2017.

[2] Z. Feng, *et al.*, "Performance-Enhanced Direct Detection Optical OFDM Transmission With CAZAC Equalization," IEEE Photonics Technology Letters, vol. 27, no. 14, pp. 1507-1510, May 2015.

[3] I. Baig and V. Jeoti, "PAPR Reduction in OFDM Systems: Zadoff-Chu Matrix Transform Based Pre/Post-Coding Techniques," Second International Conference on Computational Intelligence, Communication Systems and Networks, pp. 373-377, July 2010.

[4] K. Miyazawa, T. Kimura, and M. Muraguchi, "Proposal of visible light OFDM system with CAZAC equalization," 23rd Asia-Pacific Conference on Communications (APCC), pp. 491-496, December 2017.

[5] Y. Sugai, Y. Shirato, T. Kimura, and M. Muraguchi, "PAPR and Spectral Control Procedure for OFDM Wireless Systems Using CAZAC Equalization," in AICT'2018, pp. 75-80, 2018.

[6] T. Onoda, R. Ishioka, and M. Muraguchi, "Proposal of Power Saving Techniques for Wireless Terminals," in AICT'2018, pp. 115-120, 2018.

[7] T. Kazama, K. Miyazawa, and M. Muraguchi, "Time-domain signal management for OFDM signals," 5th International Conference on Wireless and Mobile Network (WiMNeT 2018), pp. 23-35, November 2018.

[8] Z. Qingqing, Y. Xiao, H. Ling, and D. Sanlei, "The LMS channel estimation algorithm of low-voltage power line communication," Power Engineering and Automation Conference, pp. 541-544, September 2012.

[9] M. M. Rana, "Performance comparison of LMS and RLS channel estimation algorithms for 4G MIMO OFDM systems," Proceedings of 14th International Conference on Computer and Information Technology, pp. 635-639, December 2011.

[10] K. Elangovan, "Comparative study on the Channel Estimation for OFDM system using LMS, NLMS and RLS algorithms," Proceedings of the International Conference on Pattern Recognition, pp. 359-363, March 2012.

[11] H. Seung, Hee and L. Jae, Hong, "An Overview of Peak-to-Average Power Ratio Reduction Techniques for Multicarrier Transmission," IEEE Wireless Communications, vol. 12, no. 2, pp. 56-65, April 2005.

Symbol Synchronization Technique for Visible Light Communications using CAZAC-OFDM Scheme

Yuji Yoshihashi, Takuya Kazama, Masahiro Muraguchi
Department of Electrical Engineering, Tokyo University of Science
6-3-1 Niijuku, Katsushika-ku, Tokyo, 125-0051, Japan
E-mail: 4319582@ed.tus.ac.jp, 4318518@ed.tus.ac.jp, murag@ee.kagu.tus.ac.jp

Abstract— **Ordinary Orthogonal Frequency Division Multiplexing (OFDM) receivers acquire OFDM symbol synchronization in the preamble period and retain synchronization by using correlation of guard-intervals. In this paper, we propose a new technique of OFDM symbol synchronization for Visible Light Communication (VLC) using OFDM scheme with Constant Amplitude Zero Auto-Correlation (CAZAC) precoding, CAZAC-OFDM, which enables to avoid the use of the preamble and guard-intervals. Moreover, we can find out an accurate OFDM symbol timing after checking only two symbol size of Fast Fourier Transform (FFT) points with arbitrary start timing, even though those stride over two adjacent OFDM symbols.**

Keywords-OFDM; FFT; CAZAC; VLC; Synchronization.

I. INTRODUCTION

In recent years, with the rapid development of wireless communication technology, various communication services are deployed, but as the communication traffic volume increases, frequency bands available for communication are being exhausted. Therefore, studies on VLC technology using Light Emitting Diodes (LED) are under way [1][2]. This is because LEDs have features, such as high-speed responsiveness, low power consumption, and ease of dissemination due to low cost [3].

However, depending on the frequency characteristic of the LED, the usable bandwidth is limited, and it is difficult to obtain enough communication speed. Therefore, a VLC technique utilizing an OFDM scheme capable of improving frequency utilization efficiency has been studied. Here, the OFDM scheme is commonly adopted in wireless systems, Wireless Fidelity (WiFi), Long Term Evolution (LTE), Digital Video Broadcasting - Terrestrial (DVB-T), etc., due to its great advantage of high spectrum utilization that is about twice the spectral efficiency of a single carrier scheme.

The OFDM scheme, however, requires highly accurate OFDM symbol synchronization, and if the synchronization is not performed accurately, demodulated data will be collapsed because of losing orthogonality between subcarriers. Therefore, ordinary OFDM receivers for burst packet transmission systems, such as the 802.11 Wireless Local Area Network (WLAN) systems, acquire symbol synchronization in the preamble period and retain synchronization by using correlation of Guard-Intervals (GIs). On the other hand, continuous (non-burst) transmission systems, such as Digital TeleVision (DTV) systems, acquire symbol synchronization mainly by using correlation of GIs, because those systems cannot employ preamble scheme [4].

As OFDM signal is essentially a sum of multiple subcarrier signals aligned in frequency domain, its probability density function in time domain resembles Gaussian distribution. The CAZAC precoding makes time-domain signal of M-ary Quadrature Amplitude Modulation (M-QAM) OFDM signal into time-domain signal of M-QAM single-carrier signal with some phase rotation [5] - [9]. This single-carrier wave-form in OFDM with CAZAC precoding, CAZAC-OFDM, enables superficially normal data output through the FFT and the CAZAC decoding even though the FFT processing executes by using sample points over two adjacent OFDM symbols, although the output data becomes a value of incorrect signal point in the M-QAM constellation. Among various input data, null data is still null at the output ports of the CAZAC decoder, and if we allocate null data at a fixed position in the OFDM symbols, we can estimate the deviation from the aureate symbol timing position by checking the null data port-number of the CAZAC decoder.

In this paper, we propose a new technique of symbol timing estimation for visible light communications using CAZAC-OFDM scheme, which enables to avoid the use of the preamble and guard-intervals. In the case of visible light communications, which is one of typical Line-Of-Sight (LOS) communications, it is not necessary to employ the GI aiming at preventing interference between adjacent OFDM symbols because we do not need to consider multipath channels. Moreover, the GI has a demerit of leading to a decrease in data rate.

By simulations, we have acquired an accurate OFDM symbol synchronization after checking only two symbol size of FFT points with arbitrary start timing, even though those stride over two adjacent OFDM symbols. Here, we used only one null data per one OFDM symbol, and did not use a preamble or guard interval. Therefore, our symbol synchronization technique makes it possible to maximize throughput of visible light OFDM systems.

The remainder of this paper is organized into sections as follows: Section 2 gives an overview of symbol synchronization in a conventional OFDM scheme and Section 3 gives an overview of CAZAC-OFDM. Section 4 presents the proposed scheme that makes use of the features of CAZAC-OFDM and Section 5 presents the performance evaluation and simulation results of the proposed scheme. Finally, we conclude the paper in Section 6.

II. VISIBLE LIGHT OFDM

A. *Visible Light Communication (VLC)*

Visible light communication is a communication technology utilizing light visible to the human eye. Communication is enabled by modulating this visible light. The transmitted light is received by a light receiving element, such as a photodiode, and the data is reproduced by demodulating. As a light source, LEDs are mainly used for their characteristics, such as high-speed responsiveness and low power consumption. Also, since LEDs are widely used as lighting in various places in everyday life, visible light communication using LEDs is expected because existing infrastructure equipment can be used for communication as it is.

B. *OFDM scheme*

The OFDM scheme is a type of multicarrier modulation and is a scheme in which data is divided into several subcarriers and transmitted in parallel.

On the transmission side, data is divided into N data by serial-parallel conversion, quadrature modulation is performed, and data is transmitted on different carrier waves. At this time, Inverse Fast Fourier Transform (IFFT) is performed after primary modulation of the data sequence. An input signal after mapping by primary modulation is defined as X (length N), and a nth OFDM time signal corresponding thereto as x[n] is defined as

$$x[n] = \frac{1}{N}\sum_{k=0}^{N-1} X[k]e^{j\frac{2\pi}{N}kn} \qquad (1)$$

where $X[k]$ is the frequency-domain signal, and N is the number of subcarriers. After IFFT, a guard interval is inserted and the OFDM symbol is generated.

On the receiving side, the data is restored by demodulating the signal by the reverse procedure of the transmitting side using the corresponding n subcarriers.

Also, in the frequency domain, since the peak values of the respective subcarriers are arranged to satisfy mutual orthogonality, it is possible to efficiently use the frequency band and send the data.

C. *Symbol synchronization*

In the OFDM scheme, when FFT processing is not performed at the correct position, the data collapses on the receiving side. Therefore, highly accurate symbol synchronization is indispensable for demodulating data.

There are mainly two symbol synchronization methods in the OFDM scheme [4].

As shown in Figure 1, by using the fact that the correlation value becomes maximum when the signal matches the known sequence, the head of the symbol is detected, and synchronization is enabled.

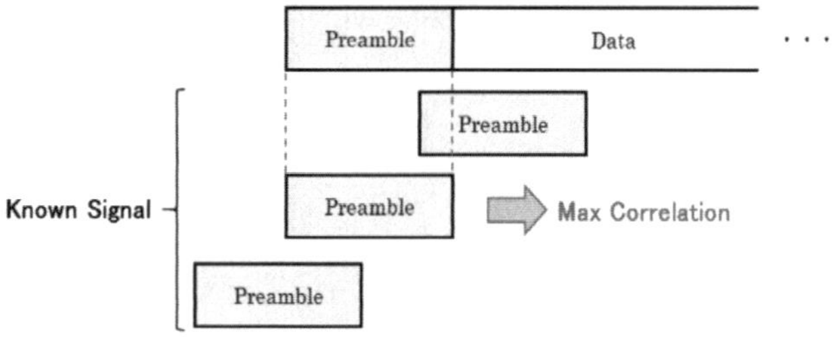

Figure 1. Symbol synchronization method using preamble

As shown in Figure 2, the other is a synchronization method that is performed by autocorrelation using guard intervals.

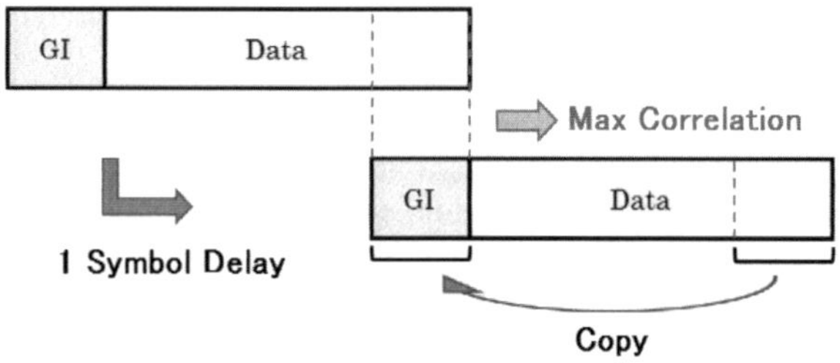

Figure 2. Symbol synchronization method using Guard Interval

This is since the rear part of the symbol is copied and added to the head and the correlation with the waveform delayed by the original one symbol length is maximized, the beginning of the symbol is detected, and synchronization can be performed.

III. CAZAC-OFDM

The CAZAC sequence is also called a constant amplitude zero auto-correlation sequence, and is a sequence having characteristics that the amplitude is constant in both the time domain and the frequency domain [5].

The OFDM scheme precoded using this CAZAC sequence is called CAZAC-OFDM. In the OFDM precoding process, a Zadoff-Chu sequence, which is one type of CAZAC sequence, is used.

The Zadoff-Chu sequence $C(k)$ is defined as

$$C(k) = \begin{cases} \exp\left(j\frac{\pi r k^2}{L}\right) & : L \text{ is even} \\ \exp\left(j\frac{\pi r k(k+1)}{L}\right) & : L \text{ is odd} \end{cases} \qquad (2)$$

$$k = 0,1,\dots,L-1$$

where L is the sequence length, r is the sequence number, and r takes an arbitrary integer value prime to L. In this case, when CAZAC precoding is used for OFDM, the sequence length L is a power of 2. The reason for this is based on the FFT size in OFDM.

Therefore, if r = 1 and $L = N^2$ in (2), since L is an even number, the Zadoff-Chu sequence $C(k)$ can be expressed as (3).

$$C(k) = \exp\left(j\frac{\pi k^2}{N^2}\right) \quad (3)$$
$$k = 0,1,\ldots,N-1$$

From (3), CAZAC precoding is expressed by (4) using Nth order complex square matrix M. Here, the matrix M is obtained by rearranging (3) in the row direction.

$$M = \frac{1}{N}\begin{bmatrix} c_0 & c_1 & \cdots & c_{N-1} \\ c_N & c_{N+1} & \cdots & c_{2N-1} \\ \vdots & \vdots & \ddots & \vdots \\ c_{(N-1)N} & c_{(N-1)N+1} & \cdots & c_{N^2-1} \end{bmatrix} \quad (4)$$

On the transmission side, precoding is performed by multiplying the matrix of (4) with the mapping data before IFFT, so that a time signal in CAZAC-OFDM can be obtained.

The signal X'after CAZAC precoding in the case where the data string to be transmitted is $X = [X_0, X_1, \cdots, X_{N-1}]$ is given by (5).

$$X' = M \cdot X = \frac{1}{N}\begin{bmatrix} c_0 & c_1 & \cdots & c_{N-1} \\ c_N & c_{N+1} & \cdots & c_{2N-1} \\ \vdots & \vdots & \ddots & \vdots \\ c_{(N-1)N} & c_{(N-1)N+1} & \cdots & c_{N^2-1} \end{bmatrix} \cdot \begin{bmatrix} X_0 \\ X_1 \\ \vdots \\ X_{N-1} \end{bmatrix} \quad (5)$$

Since IFFT processing is performed on this equation, the time signal $x(n)$ of CAZAC-OFDM of the nth sample after the IFFT can be finally defined as (6) [5].

$$x(n) = C_{\left(\frac{N}{2}-n\right)mod(N)} \cdot X_{\left(\frac{N}{2}-n\right)mod(N)} \quad (6)$$

Therefore, the signal point at this time is as shown in Figure 3.

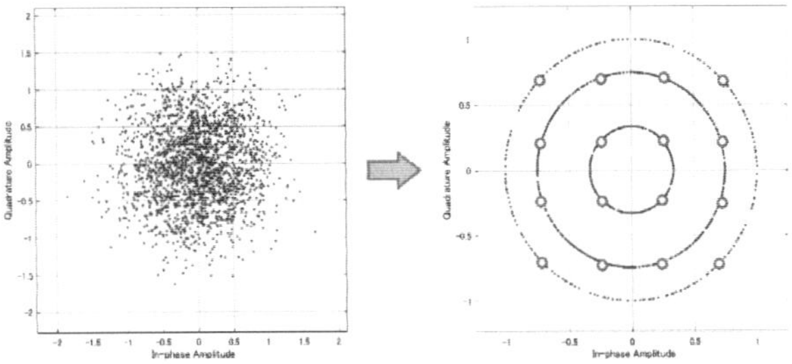

Figure 3. Time domain Signals of OFDM and CAZAC-OFDM

From Figure 3, it is confirmed that the waveform of the time signal of CAZAC-OFDM is obtained by phase-rotating the value of the mapping data, and the amplitude becomes constant as compared with ordinary OFDM.

Also, from (6), the relationship between the symbols before and after the CAZAC precoding and the IFFT processing on the transmission side is shown in Figure 4.

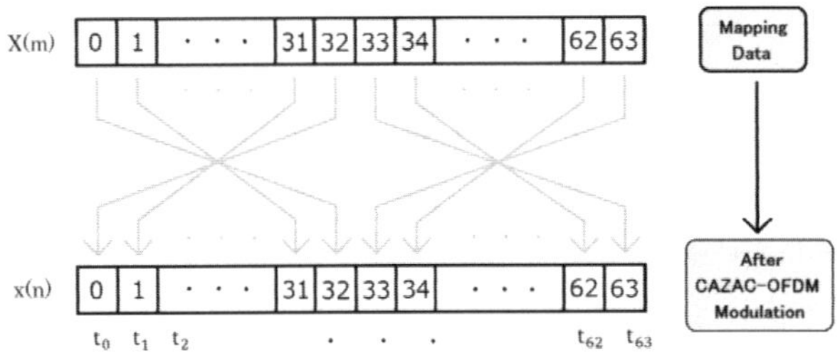

Figure 4. Symbol configuration before and after

From Figure 4, it is confirmed that the positions of the values before and after the CAZAC precoding and the IFFT processing are exchanged and uniquely determined. Also, before and after CAZAC decoding and FFT processing on the receiving side, they are exchanged in the same way.

In the symbol synchronization method proposed in this paper, we use the characteristics where this value is swapped.

IV. PROPOSED METHOD

A. Proposed symbol composition

In the ordinary OFDM scheme, symbol synchronization is performed by using correlation characteristics of preamble and guard-interval. However, we do not need to consider the multipath environment in visible light communication, so we assume that the guard-interval, which is originally intended to absorb delayed waves due to multipath, is unnecessary.

Therefore, utilizing the characteristics of the transmission waveform by CAZAC precoding, symbol synchronization is achieved by inserting null data instead of guard-interval on the transmitting side and detecting null on the receiving side. Therefore, the configuration of the symbol is as shown in Figure 5.

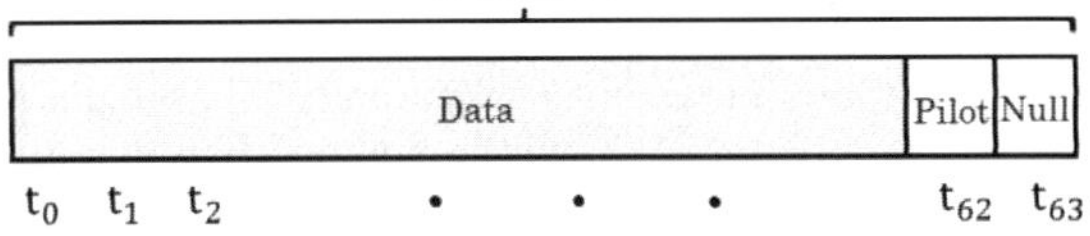

Figure 5. Proposed symbol composition

Here, one symbol is composed of 64 subcarriers, one null for synchronization and one pilot signal are inserted in the last part of the symbol in the time domain. We consider that at least one is enough to detect nulls, so the number of nulls inserted is one.

In the ordinary OFDM scheme in wireless communication, four pilot signals are inserted, but this time we have proposed one symbol configuration. The reason is that the main role of the pilot signal is phase correction and amplitude correction, and usually we do not consider that the amplitude and phase rotation abruptly change in a short period of symbol time, so we think that enough estimation and correction are possible by taking the moving average of the pilot signal.

Here, the symbol configuration before and after modulation on the receiving side is shown in Figure 6.

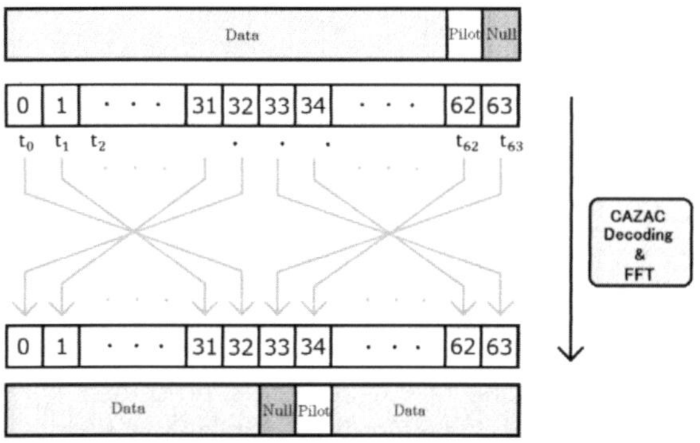

Figure 6. Symbol configuration before and after CAZAC decoding and FFT.

As shown in Figure 6, when CAZAC decoding and FFT processing are performed on the receiving side, the null data is outputted with the value being 0 being replaced with the center position.

By utilizing this fact, synchronization is enabled by detecting the null and correcting the position of the FFT processing.

B. Null detection and synchronization method

In the ordinary OFDM scheme, there is a problem with data collapsing when FFT points stride over two adjacent OFDM symbols. Even though we insert nulls on the sender side, we cannot detect nulls without accurate synchronization and FFT processing at the correct position. Therefore, highly accurate timing estimation is necessary, and FFT processing cannot be performed at an arbitrary timing.

However, in CAZAC-OFDM, even though FFT points stride over two adjacent OFDM symbols, data does not collapse, and the values of signal points at different points are output. Among them, null data is output as it is null and the direction and amount of deviation from the proper synchronous position can be accurately detected from the output port number.

Here, in FFT processing the received data, the case where it is performed at the correct position and at an arbitrary position are shown in Figure 7.

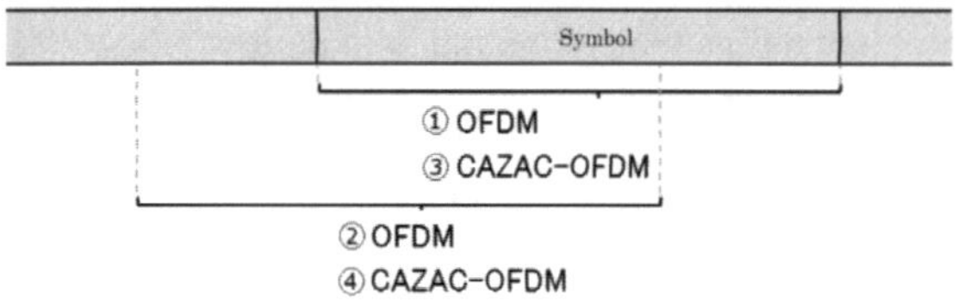

Figure 7. FFT points position

Here, ① and ③ are cases where FFT processing is performed at the correct position, and ② and ④ are cases where FFT processing is performed at an arbitrary position. Moreover, ① and ② are ordinary OFDM scheme without CAZAC, and ③ and ④ are CAZAC-OFDM with CAZAC. The output of two symbols after FFT processing at this time is shown in Figure 8. The waveform is the absolute value of the value of the data.

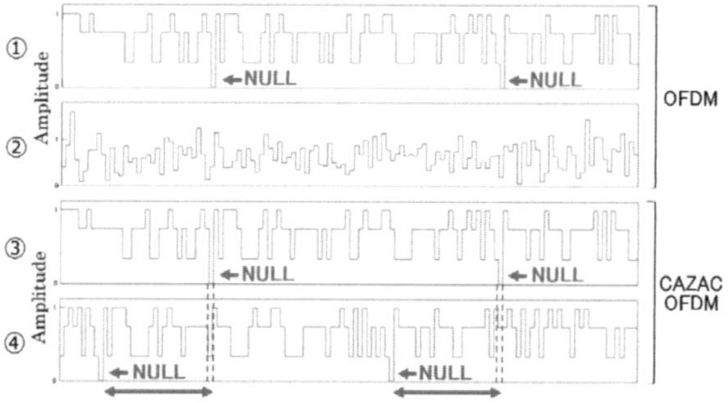

Figure 8. The contents of data in two symbols after FFT

As shown in Figure 8, since FFT processing is performed at the correct position in ① and ③, the output data does not collapse and outputs completely the same value, and the null is output to the place of X (33).

It can be seen that, if the FFT processing is performed at an arbitrary timing in the output of ② in the ordinary OFDM scheme, the data collapses and the magnitude of the amplitude becomes uneven. Also, the null inserted on the transmitting side is completely collapsed, it cannot be detected, and synchronization cannot be performed.

However, in the proposed method with CAZAC, even though FFT processing is performed at an arbitrary position that is not a correct position, the data does not collapse, and the data is exchanged between the symbols, but the null data is output as null. Also, from Figure 6, since the positions of the values before and after the CAZAC decoding and the FFT are uniquely determined, by comparing with the position of the null after performing the FFT processing at the correct position, we can estimate the deviation.

Here, in ④ in Figure 8, nulls are output at the location of X (10), so it is seen that the FFT points are shifted by 24 samples as compared with the place of null in ③.

Therefore, in the proposed CAZAC-OFDM, it is unnecessary to estimate the timing of highly accurate symbols before performing FFT processing, and even though FFT processing is performed at arbitrary timing, highly accurate synchronization is achieved.

Detection of null is done by minimum value judgment, as follows: perform CAZAC decoding and FFT processing at an arbitrary timing, and then take the absolute value and make the minimum value determination. Since null has a value of 0 and no data other than null has a value of 0, null can be reliably detected by performing the minimum value determination.

However, this is a case of a communication environment in an ideal state, and some noise occurs in actual communication. When noise is added, data other than null may be detected by the minimum value determination, making it difficult to detect the correct null.

Therefore, before the minimum value judgment is made, the system configuration is constructed in which the value of the flowing data is accumulated in the section where one symbol and the minimum value judgment is made for the cumulative sum. As a result, even though the detection of the null is mistaken for the data of one symbol, the accuracy of detection of the null can be improved by accumulating the data of the next symbol.

We provide an example to explain the minimum value judgment when two symbols are accumulated after adding noise. The waveforms of (a) and (b) of Figure 9 are obtained by dividing the received data for two symbols into data for each individual symbol. When the minimum value is determined for each piece of data, the position of the minimum value is detected. Here, the correct detection position of this null is assumed to be the 26th position. In (b), the position of the minimum value is the 26th position and the null detection succeeds, whereas in (a) the position of the minimum value is the 18th position, and the null detection is incorrect.

As described above, when noise is added, the detection of null may fail in the minimum value determination with only one symbol. To solve this, take the cumulative sum. Figure 10 shows a waveform of a data value obtained by taking the cumulative sum of two symbols.

When accumulating the data values of (a) and (b) in Figure 9, it becomes as shown in Figure 10, the minimum value clearly appears and the detection of null succeeds.

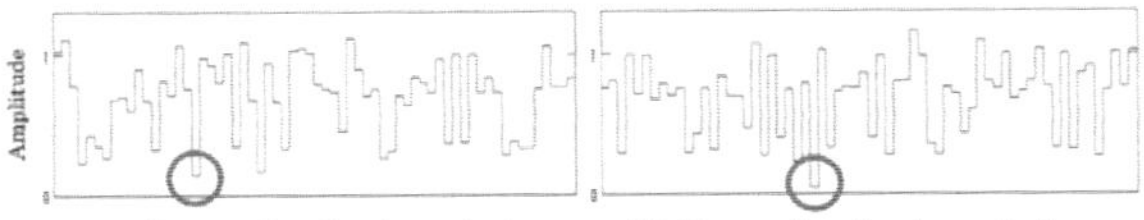

(a) Data value for 1 symbol (b) Data value for 1 symbol
Figure 9. Minimum value determination for one symbol

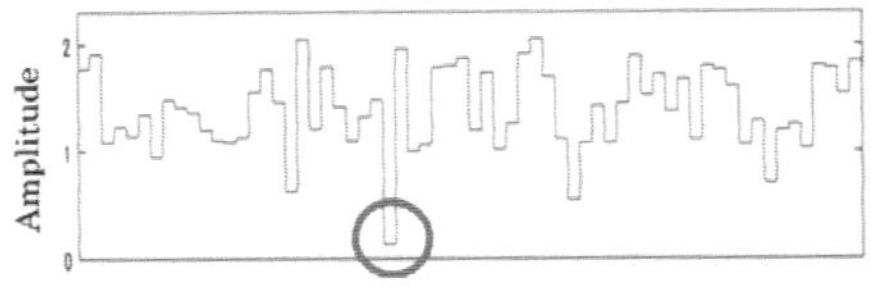

Figure 10. Minimum value determination with cumulative sum of 2 symbols

Therefore, even though the detection of the null is mistaken for the data of one symbol, the accuracy of detection of the null can be improved by accumulating the data of the next symbol.

V. PERFORMANCE EVALUATION BY SIMULATION

A. Simulation specification

To evaluate the performance of the proposed method, simulation was performed according to the specifications in Table I. The simulation is performed in MATLAB using communications system toolbox.

Also, the system configuration of the transmission and reception proposed in this paper is shown in Figure 11.

TABLE I. SIMULATION SPECIFICATION.

Primary modulation	16QAM
Secondary modulation	CAZAC-OFDM
Data Rate	58.125 Mbps
Bandwidth	15 MHz
Carrier frequency	15 MHz
Data size	62
Number of pilots	1
Null data length	1
FFT size	64

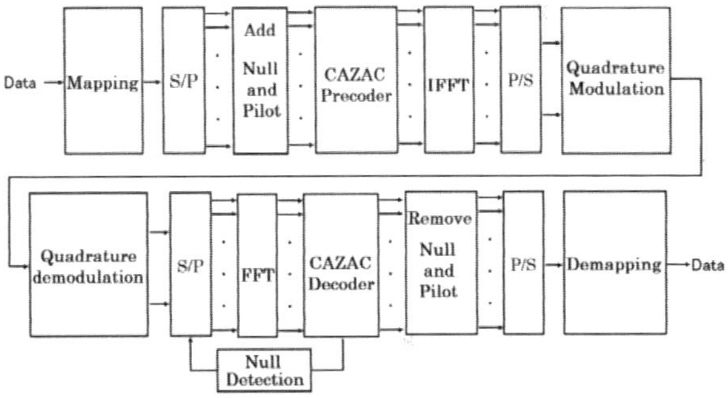

Figure 11. The proposed CAZAC-OFDM system

B. Simulation result (BER)

Figure 12 shows the BER characteristics when the proposed method is simulated with the specifications in Table 1.

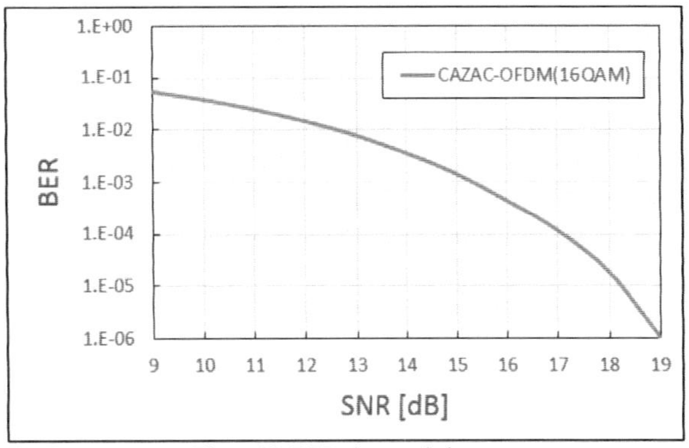

Figure 12. BER characteristics

Figure 12 shows the BER characteristics when a signal is received at the correct timing at which there is no synchronization deviation from the beginning by inserting one null and one pilot. From this result, it is understood that the error rate, which is the reproducible range, falls within the range of 10^{-3} or less when SNR is 16 or more.

Even though the receiving side performs FFT processing at an arbitrary timing, null is instantaneously detected by the minimum value judgment, and the cutout position of the FFT points is corrected. Therefore, it can be confirmed that the BER characteristic almost agrees with the value shown in Figure 12 regardless of the timing at which the FFT processing is performed.

C. Simulation result (Null detection success rate)

Figure 13 shows the detection success probability of null when simulated with the specifications in Table 1. Here, for detection, we compared the detection success probabilities of nulls when the minimum value judgment is performed on the cumulative sum for one symbol and two symbols, giving three symbols.

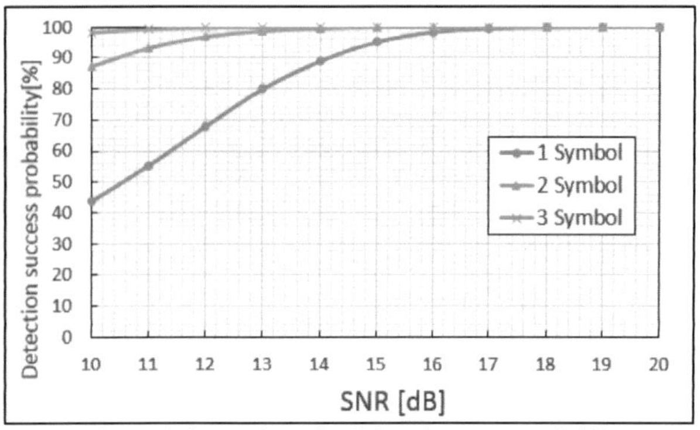

Figure 13. Comparison of null detection success probability

From the result of Figure 13, when null detection was performed only for one symbol, the probability of success became 100% when the SNR was 20 or more. Likewise, in the case of the cumulative sum of two symbols, the success probability became 100% when the SNR was 16 or more, and, in the case of the cumulative sum of 3 symbols, the SNR was 13 or more.

From this result, it is found that the detection success probability of null improves as the number of symbols to be accumulated increases. Therefore, it was confirmed that highly accurate synchronization can be achieved by increasing the number of symbols required for detection even in an environment with great influence of noise with low SNR.

Moreover, from the results in Figure 12, SNR was 16 or more in the proposed method where the error rate falls within the range of 10^{-3} or less. Therefore, when the SNR is 16 or more, the detection success probability becomes 100% when the number of symbols to be accumulated is at least two.

From the above results, it was confirmed that highly accurate symbol synchronization can be performed without failure by judging the cumulative sum of the two symbols by the minimum value.

VI. CONCLUSION

In this paper, we show that the amplitude of the OFDM signal is constant by using CAZAC precoding and inserted null data can be extracted as null. Also, we verified that null data can be extracted without corruption even though FFT points that stride over two adjacent OFDM symbols. We verified that, by using this characteristic, it is possible to perform synchronization with enough performance after checking only two symbol size of FFT points with arbitrary start timing.

REFERENCES

[1] A. Jovicic, J. Li, and T. Richardson, "Visible light communication: opportunities, challenges and the path to market", IEEE Communications Magazine, pp.26-32, Dec. 2013.

[2] H. Elgala, R. Mesleh, and H. Haas, "Indoor broadcasting via white LEDs and OFDM," IEEE Transactions on Consumer Electronics, pp.1127-1134, Aug. 2009.

[3] G. Cossu, A. M. Khalid, P. Choudhury, R. Corsini, and E. Ciaramella, "3.4 Gbit/s visible optical wireless transmission based on RGB LED," Opt. Exp., pp. B501-B506, Dec. 2012.

[4] T. M. Schmidl and D. C. Cox: "Robust frequency and timing synchronization for OFDM," IEEE Transactions on Communications, pp.1613-1621, Dec. 1997.

[5] R. Ishioka, T. Kimura, and M. Muraguchi, "A Proposal for a New OFDM Wireless System using a CAZAC Equalization Scheme," in AICT'2017, no. 1, pp. 47–51, 2017.

[6] K. Miyazawa, T. Kimura, and M. Muraguchi, "Proposal of visible light OFDM system with CAZAC equalization," 23rd Asia-Pacific Conference on Communications (APCC), pp.491-496, Dec. 2017.

[7] Y. Sugai, Y. Shirato, T. Kimura, and M. Muraguchi, "PAPR and Spectral Control Procedure for OFDM Wireless Systems Using CAZAC Equalization," in AICT'2018, pp. 75–80, 2018.

[8] T. Onoda, R. Ishioka, and M. Muraguchi, "Proposal of Power Saving Techniques for Wireless Terminals," in AICT'2018, pp. 115–120, 2018.

[9] T. Kazama, K. Miyazawa, and M. Muraguchi, "Time-domain signal management for OFDM signals," 5th International Conference on Wireless and Mobile Network (WiMNeT 2018), pp.23-35, Nov. 2018.

Implementation of Machine-Based Learning Solutions in Distance Education for Pathologists in Ophthalmic Oncology

Denis Garri
A.I. Yevdokimov Moscow State University of Medicine and Dentistry
Moscow, Russia
Email: ldenisl@inbox.ru

Svetlana Saakyan, Inna Khoroshilova-Maslova, Alexander Tsygankov
Helmholtz Moscow Research Institute of Eye Diseases
Moscow, Russia
Email: svsaakyan@yandex.ru
horoshilova@yandex.ru
alextsygankov1986@yandex.ru

Oleg Nikitin, Grigory Tarasov
Limited Liability Company "Artificial Networks and Technologies"
Moscow, Russia
Email: olegnikitin@mail.ru
grigoriy.tarasov.u@gmail.com

***Abstract* – Uveal melanoma is a malignant tumor originating from melanocytes of an eye vascular tract. Depending on the cellular composition, the tumor is classified as a spindle cell (A or B), epithelioid cell or mixed cell. The presence of epithelioid cells reflects an unfavorable vital prognosis. The study of the cellular composition of the tumor is subjective and results in disagreements about the type of individual cells in 13% of cases among qualified pathologists. The discrepancies in diagnoses are due to the use of different classifications, which can lead to an incorrect assessment of the vital prognosis and incorrect tactics of patient treatment. Machine learning can be used to objectify the criteria of pathomorphological study of uveal melanoma, but currently there are no published works on machine analysis of pathomorphological images of this type of tumors. Our solution is based on the use of conventional neural network for the classification of images of uveal melanoma cells. We obtained an average F-score value of 0.75 to differentiate spindle cells nuclei from epithelioid cells nuclei and developed a visualization interface to explain differences between various types of cells with color mark-up of cell nuclei, probability of belonging to a certain class and deconvolution maps.**

Keywords-E-learning; artificial neural networks; pathology; uveal melanoma.

I. INTRODUCTION

Uveal melanoma is the most common primary intraocular malignant tumor in the adult population [1]. Tumor cell dissemination is a frequent occurrence with uveal melanomas. Even with complete removal of the primary tumor, metastatic foci are detected in 50% of patients. In case of tumor metastasis, the vital prognosis is substantially worse, with the average survival rate during the first year falling to 20% [2].

The tumor cell type is an important prognostic factor. The McLean classification is used currently, including spindle-A, spindle-B, epithelioid and mixed tumors [3]. Studies have shown that spindle cell tumors offer the best vital prognoses, while for mixed cell tumors the outlook is intermediate, and epithelioid cell tumors present the most unfavorable prospects. A greater number of epithelioid cells in the field of view is associated with a worse vital prognosis [4]. The morphological characteristic of the tumor composition is subjective, and the quantity of epithelioid cells required to identify tumors as epithelioid or mixed type has not yet been universally defined. Disagreements among qualified pathologists regarding belonging of individual melanoma cells to a certain type are on average 13%, which is due to the lack of objectively measurable signs and the presence of intermediate-type cells that have signs of several cell types. McLean and co-authors found that differences in the classifications used led to differences in diagnosis in 32% of cases [3]. Machine learning can be used to objectify the criteria of pathomorphological study of uveal melanoma.

The article is organized as follows. In Section II, we present the state of art concerning machine learning use in digital pathology. Section III discusses our training set, method specification and performance metrics. In Section IV, the use of the trained network is discussed. Finally, the paper is concluded in Section V.

II. STATE OF ART

A. Machine Learning

Machine learning is applied in every field of human activity where digital data is used. Various articles have been published recently concerning the use of artificial intelligence for the purposes of classification, regression and segmentation in medicine and particularly in pathology.

Machine learning and deep learning are self-learning methods used to analyze complex data and find patterns and interdependencies without explicit programming. Due to this, they are sometimes called "artificial intelligence".

Machine learning includes models and algorithms that mimic the architecture of biological neural networks. Artificial neural networks are of great interest in the field of machine learning, particularly networks based on deep learning. This is due to their capacity for working effectively with complex and multidimensional databases, along with the increasing availability of databases and the performance of graphics processors.

B. *Digital Pathology*

Recent developments in the field of digital pathology, related to the access of medical institutions to digital microscopes and slide scanners, allow us to carry out scientific work with digital data, including gigapixel images of pathological specimens. The availability of such data allows the use of a range of machine learning methods to process it and to obtain new unified diagnostic criteria and prognoses for the passage of malignant diseases that are unavailable in a classical pathology study [5]. Recent studies have shown that convolutional neural networks reveal a high accuracy in the identification of pathological images of certain types of cancer, including the pathology of the prostate gland, lung, mammary gland, large intestine, and ovaries [6]-[10]. The unit of learning is usually a small image of about 100x100 microns or larger. This approach is convenient to identify tissue patterns in the images under study and can be used to determine the predominant cell population in the image, but to characterize individual cells, the size of one image should be comparable to the size of one cell – 10-20 microns.

No published articles devoted to the machine analysis of pathomorphological images of uveal melanoma are available at the moment. The articles that are the closest to our work in terms of purpose and methodology are devoted to the study of images of melanoma of the skin, which, despite the similarity of origin, has a different metastatic potential, responds differently to treatment and has different immunological and genetic characteristics. The primary tumor focus of melanoma of the skin lies in the depth of the tissues of epidermal origin, and uveal melanoma – in the tissues of mesodermal origin, which results in their different histological characteristics [11].

Effland et al. provided variational networks to differentiate tumor nuclei from the nuclei of immune cells. Tissue samples were tinted with immunofluorescent dyes, giving a different color signal while interacting with CD45 antigen of immune cells, gp100 protein antigen of tumor cells and adenine–thymine rich regions in nuclei, which allowed to form a training sample without using a manual marking process [12]. In [13], Rexhepaj et al. used Melan-A dye for immune staining of melanoma cells; they created training samples of tumor and non-tumor cells and analysed them using support vector machine. This experiment can not be used to differentiate different types of uveal melanoma cells due to the fact that there are no dyes specifically staining epithelioid or spindle cells.

Liu et al. used SetSVM – support vector machine modification – to solve a number of diagnostic problems, in particular, the differentiation of dysplastic nevus from malignant melanoma of the skin. The approach provided the use of cell nuclei features to categorize each case [14]. The method showed high accuracy in the classification of groups of homogeneous cells (up to 82.01%), but can not be used for mixed cell cases as well as to characterize individual cell elements.

Our contribution is to create and train an artificial convolutional neural network that would allow the less malignant cellular elements (spindle-shaped cells) to be distinguished from the most malignant (epithelioid cells). Determination of the cellular composition of a tumor is a routine event, but it is difficult to characterize individual cells, especially in mixed tumors. Our solution should help to improve the diagnostic skills of students and pathology specialists.

III. Artificial Neural Network Learning Process

The first stage of neural network training is the preparing of the training set. For this purpose, 52 patients who underwent enucleation from 2005–2006 were selected and their pathology reports and clinical records were studied. Being faced with the task of classification between two groups of cells, we selected for the training sample only those tumors that, according to the reports, were spindle or epithelioid. Inclusion in the training sample of mixed tumors would require labor-intensive process for marking various cells in the tumor site. The use of tumors with a homogeneous cell composition would allow the markup to be applied to the tumor site as a whole. According to current classifications, spindle cell tumors can contain up to 10% of epithelioid cells and vice versa, so we decided to evaluate the possibility of marking mainly homogeneous tumors after digitizing their histological slides.

By excluding mixed cell tumors from the training set, we had 23 patients and 37 histological slides for them. All samples were digitized using a Leica ScanScope CS2 slide scanner, producing 37 gigapixel images in .svs format. After reviewing the digitized images, we decided to use the following for further training set: 24 gigapixel images from 12 patients – spindle cell tumors; 4 gigapixel images from 3 patients – epithelioid cell tumors. In total, 28 images were used. Nine images from 8 patients could not be used in the training set since it proved impossible to isolate nodes of homogeneous cell composition. We plan to use the images not included in the training set for further control of the classifier.

Each gigapixel image was marked using Aperio ImageScope by a qualified pathologist. The marking was performed by complete encirclement of the tumor node with further exclusion from the marking area of non-tumor tissues and empty spaces. Convolutional neural networks require a large number of images in the training sample, so the problem of the small number of cases was solved by dividing the gigapixel images into smaller images of 240 x 240 pixels. The common term for such smaller images is a patch. One .svs image gave the output of a number of patches from 2,573 to 57,554; the total number of patches was 605,375, with the average number of patches per image of 21,620.

The original files in .svs or .scn format are a set of pyramidal images. The base layer is 240x240 pixel images compressed using the libjpeg application library. The top layers comprise 4–16 images combined of lower layers with lost pixel density, up to the topmost image of approximately 2000x2000 pixels. Such a composition allows prompt navigation due to simultaneous displaying of approximately 10 small images instead of a number of images from the lower layer. Individual patches are extracted from a pyramidal image file using the same library.

For further processing, we scanned individual 240x240 patches with a 48x48 pixel scanning window, in increments of 8 pixels, and with an overlay round mask. Neural network ResNet-101 was used for image cell identification. The weight for the neural network was taken from weights which produced the best results on 2018 Data Science Bowl for cell nucleus localization [15]. During training, 48x48 pixel images with a round mask containing one cell were fed to another neural network input. The second neural network had 18,490 parameters and used the Adam(lr=0.01) optimizer and categorical_crossentropy loss, as well as three Conv2D blocks:

- The first Conv2D block was composed of two foldings with 3x3 kernels, relu activation, BatchNormalization and dropout functions. The first Conv2D block had the convolution kernel size of 8, the first convolution stride of 2, and dropout rate of 0.2.
- The second Conv2D block had the convolution kernel size of 16, the first convolution stride of 2, and dropout rate of 0.4.
- The third Conv2D block had the convolution kernel size of 16, the first convolution stride of 2, and dropout rate of 0.4.

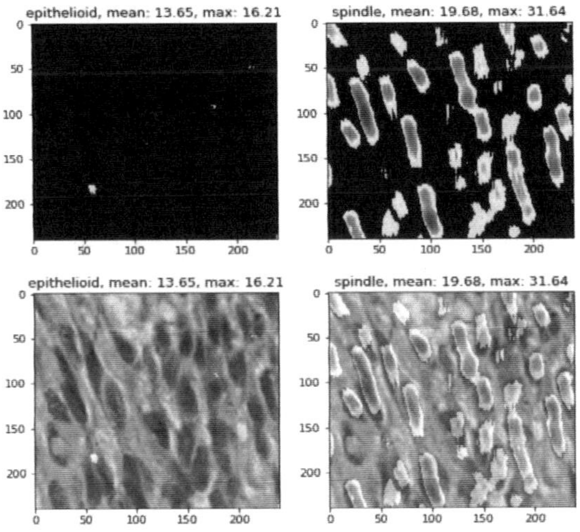

Figure 1. Mark-up of most and least probable nuclei location

Also, there are two fully connected layers with 32 parameters, relu activation, BatchNormalization and dropout functions. The last layer has two neurons and softmax activation.

To validate the results, a 4-fold approach was used, whereas the training set was randomly divided into 4 equal parts. Alternately, 3 parts were submitted to the training, and 1 was used for control.

When the training was complete, we calculated the F1-scores for 4 folds of this model and obtained the following values: 0.76, 0.82, 0.79, and 0.62, respectively. The mean F1-score for 4 folds of our model was 0.75.

I. USE OF TRAINED ARTIFICIAL NEURAL NETWORK

The marking in Aperio is stored for each gigapixel image as a file in .xml format. A trained neural network allows to mark each patch on a gigapixel image of uveal melanoma or on a selected part of the image and present such machine-aided marking as an .xml file. In the .xml file, each marking color corresponding to a single class (predominant cell elements) is represented as a list of polygons described as an enumeration of its boundary points.

This marking method is very similar to the method used by pathologists to assess the cell population ratios judging by predominant cells in a number of fields of vision in the light microscope (usually approximately 20), but it ensures rough assessment of the ratio, taking into account the tumor node as a whole.

The data to which the neural network responds may be presented as mark-ups to patches and gigapixel images. Mark-ups may be intensity maps, cells with their boundaries and the probability of belonging to a certain class, deconvolution maps with features marked which contributed to the decision to include a cell into a certain class.

As seen from Figure 1, the areas of most probable nuclei location are marked with red mark-up and those of least probable location with blue mark-up. Figure 2 shows another variant of a visual mark-up

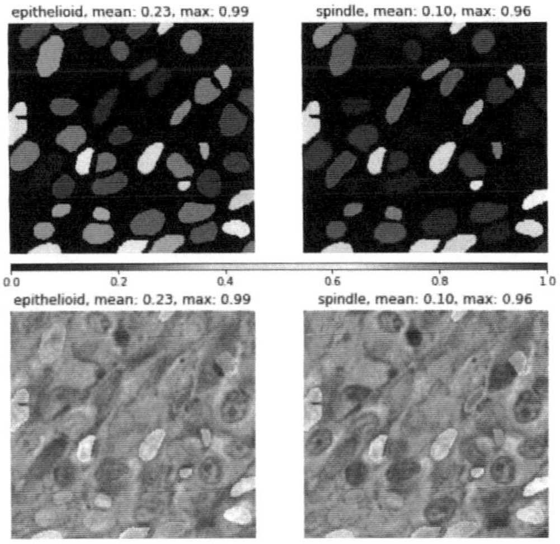

Figure 2. A color chart of the probability of cell belonging to a certain class

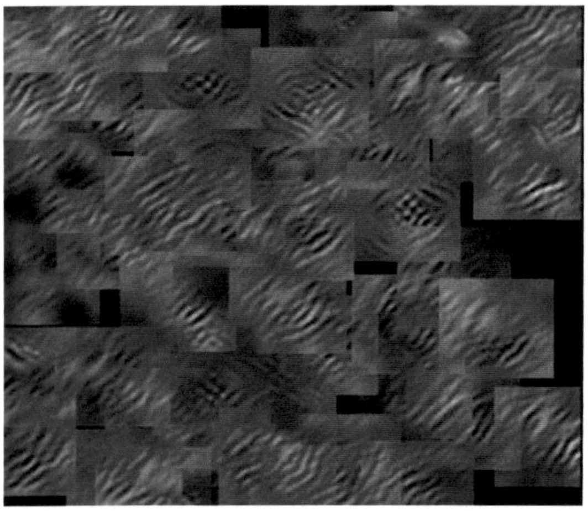

Figure 3. Deconvolution Map

presentation: a color chart of the probability of cell belonging to a certain class, where a bluish color represents the least probability and a reddish color corresponds to the highest probability. The last but the most diverse variant of data presentation is a map of contributions into the decision to include a cell into a certain class. Figure 3 shows an example of a deconvolution map for spindle-shaped and epithelioid cells. The patches show that spindle-shaped cells look like parallel folds rising above the plane of probability. Epithelioid cells are broken rounded folds. While comparing maps of contributions from parallel filters, it is obvious that higher probability folds for one class correlate with lower probability for the other. It can be assumed that this pair of filters mirrors inherent cell geometry, where epithelioid cells have a rounded nucleus and sphere-like shape and spindle-shaped cells have elongated nucleus and shape. A Web-based interface where anyone can upload a gigapixel image and see its machine-aided interpretation with a mentioned mark-up is being developed.

II. Conclusion and Future Work

Even small groups of patients may be used in digital pathology for training in convolution neural networks. This is possible due to the fact that each gigapixel image contains several thousand smaller images – patches, which in turn have two-three dozens of cells – training units. Our further work will be dedicated to training set extension and tests of images not included in the training sample.

The mean fold F1-score was 0.75. The result may seem unassertive if we do not take into consideration the fact that images in training sample very often had cells from another class. This aspect is very difficult to eliminate in pathology. The fact that machine-aided cell marking quite often contradicts the initial patches marking allows to assume that the classification accuracy is higher than this figure. Acquisition of more images with uniform cellular composition will allow us to assess more accurately the metrics of the classifier. In our opinion, the most appropriate mark-up to explain the differences between various types of cells is color mark-up with cell boundaries and the probability of belonging to a certain class. Even an experienced pathologist sometimes finds it difficult to differentiate between spindle-shaped and epithelioid cells. Thus, it can be assumed that there are a number of cell subtypes which are similar to cell classes. The presentation of each cell as corresponding to a certain class (with the probability indicated) allows us to visualize this trend.

Mark-ups in the form of contribution maps are more appropriate for a research work and advanced pathologists training. Their non-obviousness makes their use in specialist training possible only with explanations.

We assume that the best solution for processed data demonstration is a Web-based interface in a browser with two synchronized windows, where one window shows raw data and the other window demonstrates the results of the functioning neural network (predicted classes, cells with their boundaries and the probability of belonging to a certain class, maps of features which contributed to the decision to include a cell into a certain class).

Although our work is devoted to the visualization of cellular signs of uveal melanoma, this approach can be used for automated pathomorphological diagnosis of uveal melanoma, which requires further study of the material base and methodology.

References

[1] A. D. Singh, M. E. Turell, and A. K. Topham, "Uveal Melanoma: Trends in Incidence, Treatment, and Survival," Ophthalmology, Vol. 118(9), pp. 1881–1885, 2011, doi:10.1016/j.ophtha.2011.01.040

[2] D. Lorenzo et al., "Prognostic Factors and Decision Tree for Long-Term Survival in Metastatic Uveal Melanoma," Cancer Research and Treatment, Vol. 50(4), pp. 1130–1139, 2018, doi:10.4143/crt.2017.171

[3] I. W. McLean, W. D. Foster, L.E. Zimmerman, and J. W. Gamel, "Modifications of Callender's Classification of Uveal Melanoma at the Armed Forces Institute of Pathology," American Journal of Ophthalmology, Vol. 195, pp. lvi–lx, 2018, doi:10.1016/j.ajo.2018.08.025

[4] S. Kaliki, C. Shields, and J. Shields, "Uveal melanoma: Estimating prognosis," Indian Journal of Ophthalmology, Vol. 63(2), p.93, 2015, doi:10.4103/0301-4738.154367

[5] P. Khosravi, E. Kazemi, M. Imielinski, O. Elemento, and I. Hajirasouliha, "Deep Convolutional Neural Networks Enable Discrimination of Heterogeneous Digital Pathology Images," EBioMedicine, 2018, Vol. 27, pp. 317–328, doi:10.1016/j.ebiom.2017.12.02662.

[6] J. T. Kwak, S. M. Hewitt, S. Sinha, and R. Bhargava, "Multimodal microscopy for automated histologic analysis of prostate cancer," BMC Cancer, 2011, Vol. 11(1), pp. 1-16, doi:10.1186/1471-2407-11-6263.

[7] P. W. Hamilton et al., "Automated tumor analysis for molecular profiling in lung cancer," Oncotarget, 2015, Vol. 6(29), pp. 27938-27952, doi:10.18632/oncotarget.4391.

[8] L. W. Wang et al., "Computer-Based Image Studies on Tumor Nests Mathematical Features of Breast Cancer and Their Clinical Prognostic Value," PLoS ONE, 2013, Vol. 8(12), p. e82314, doi:10.1371/journal.pone.0082314.

[9] K. Bruno et al., "Deep learning for classification of colorectal polyps on whole-slide images," PLoS One, 2013, Vol. 8(12), p. e8231466, doi: 10.4103/jpi.jpi_34_17

[10] A. Janowczyk et al., "High-Throughput Biomarker Segmentation on Ovarian Cancer Tissue Microarrays via Hierarchical Normalized Cuts," IEEE Transactions on Biomedical Engineering, 2012, Vol. 59(5), pp. 1240–1252, doi:10.1109/tbme.2011.2179546

[11] C. Belmar-Lopez et al., "Uveal vs. cutaneous melanoma. Origins and causes of the differences," Clinical and Translational Oncology, 2008, Vol. 10(3), pp. 137–142, doi:10.1007/s12094-008-0170-4

[12] A. Effland et al., "Joint reconstruction and classification of tumor cells and cell interactions in melanoma tissue sections with synthesized training data," International Journal of Computer Assisted Radiology and Surgery, 2019, Vol. 14(4), pp. 587-599, doi:10.1007/s11548-019-01919-z

[13] E. Rexhepaj et al., "A Texture Based Pattern Recognition Approach to Distinguish Melanoma from Non-Melanoma Cells in Histopathological Tissue Microarray Sections," PLoS ONE, 2013, Vol. 8(5), pp. e62070, doi:10.1371/journal.pone.0062070

[14] C. Liu et al., "SetSVM: An Approach to Set Classification in Nuclei-based Cancer Detection," IEEE Journal of Biomedical and Health Informatics, 2019, Vol. 23(1), pp. 351-361, doi:10.1109/jbhi.2018.2803793

[15] L. Wang, W. Li, and Y. Kang, "Data Fusion Network for Instance Segmentation," Lecture Notes in Computer Science, 2018, pp. 175–182, doi:10.1007/978-3-030-01078-2

Telecommunications Services Selection Process Based on Analysis of Services Adoption

Višnja Križanović
J. J. Strossmayer University of Osijek
Faculty of Electrical Engineering, Computer Science and Information Technology
Osijek, Croatia
e-mail: visnja.krizanovic@ferit.hr

***Abstract*—Telecommunications operators continuously adapt their services offerings to new services usage trends in order to expand their customer base and enhance business models. With regard to existing services usage patterns, it is possible to select services that are suitable to users' needs and to create stronger business models. This is especially important given the fact that, despite numerous advantages arising from the new Internet of Things (IoT) solutions, a majority of operators still have not defined adequate IoT offers and related strategies for the deployment in the telecommunication markets. In this paper, the process of selection of telecommunications services is examined considering predictive modeling processes which are based on the time series data representing services adoption rates. The given forecasted results indicate an effective choice for creating adequate business models based on IoT services offerings and a reduction of modeling risks which are often related to the deployment of new services on the market.**

Keywords - telecommunications services; services usage; prediction models; business modeling.

I. Introduction

An overall boost in the volume of network traffic and the evolution towards the next generation networking based on advanced information and communication technologies (ICT) encourage telecommunications operators to consider and improve their existing business planning and modeling approaches according to market trends and services usage patterns in the existing network settings. Due to a vast number of possible options and existing requirements related to quality, efficiency, and performance of novel telecommunications services, an optimal selection of services becomes a very challenging task for operators. Although services quality will be additionally addressed by intelligent algorithms for adapting resource management and implementation of adequate techniques for content offloading, given accelerated trends in services development, there is often not a lot of time to closely consider customer requests related to services offerings before launching services on the markets. This last aspect is particularly important considering the fact that a vast number of operators are currently searching for the best solutions for positioning on the Internet of Things (IoT) services markets.

The prediction-based planning, services selection, and business modeling processes present significant challenges for operators under new market conditions. Therefore, the selection of adequate models for services offerings based on analytics of adoption of similar types of telecommunications services can effectively contribute to the optimization of business planning processes, as presented by analyses results gathered in this paper, as well.

Telecommunications services analytics usually takes into account time series data reflecting usage rates of particular services. That could point to valuable communication services, which reflect the specific needs of particular types of end users. If taking data representing services usage patterns into account to derive useful knowledge within a certain environment, suitable prediction models must be defined.

In this paper, the analytics of telecommunications services adoption processes is conducted using several predictive models which take into account only the cases with small sets of available time series data. In Section 2, an overview of current trends in telecommunication services adoption is presented. In Section 3, the importance of usage of the models for prediction of telecommunications services adoption in optimal business modeling is accentuated, and an overview of several common, as well as some additional predictive models, is presented. In Section 4, the defined models are applied to several collected data sets, and the collected results are presented and analyzed. In Section 5, in order to reduce the business modeling risks, optimal approaches in making decisions are indicated when short-term business planning is necessary under fast-changing market conditions.

II. Telecommunications Services Adoption Trends

The majority of current forecasts and market estimates reflect operators' high expectations for scale and scope arising from advanced telecommunications services offerings, and especially IoT services offerings. The positive expected results represent a major incentive for advanced services development and implementation processes. These expectations introduce new research challenges across different telecommunications settings.

The majority of businesses based upon usage of advanced telecommunications services monitor metrics that reflect improvements in supply levels and customer quality of experience rates. Higher levels of availability and quality of services could induce additional growth of services adoption, which is closely correlated with profitability gains, as presented in Figure 1 [1].

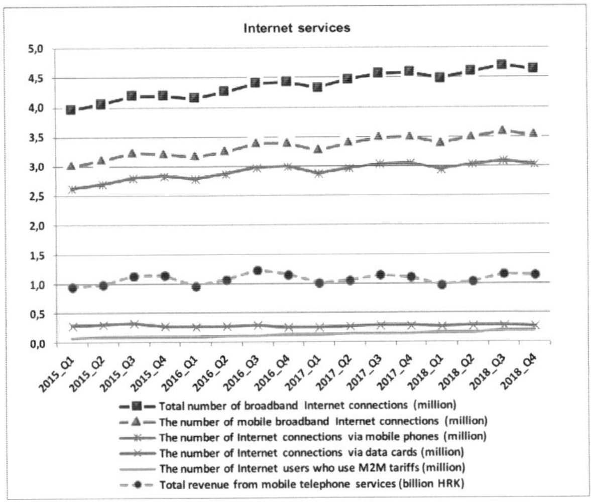

Figure 1. Internet services adoption rates and revenues.

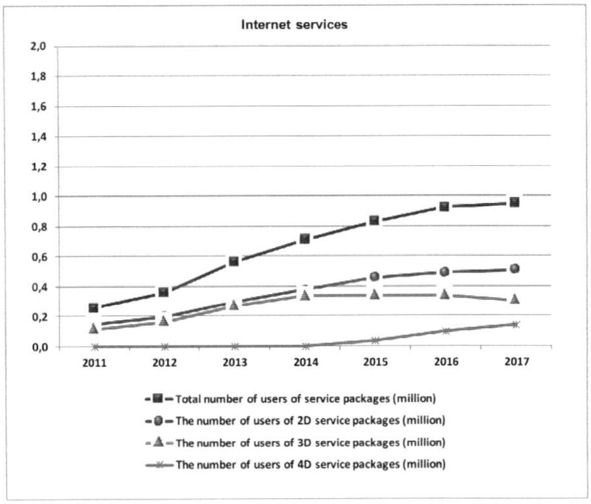

Figure 2. Internet services packages.

Therefore, the analyses and comparisons of possible business models involving various telecommunications services are important for the business planning processes of every telecommunications operator on the market since a timely application of relevant data and new knowledge represents an important advantage within every business modeling process, and can help in reducing churn rates.

Intensive adoption processes of a wide range of Internet services are currently taking place, as illustrated in Figure 1 [1]. One of the main drives behind the further anticipated traffic growth is the usage of audio and video-on-demand services and increase of the video content resolution [2]. So, audio-visual media streaming will account for the majority of overall network data traffic. In addition to these factors, other factors that are expected to impact the overall future traffic demand comprise an increase in the bit-rates and quality of experience. Moreover, the exchange of data traffic among end-user devices, terminal network equipment, servers and storage in the cloud will continue to grow.

The IoT solutions have the potential of becoming major contributors to the upcoming change in developing ICT business concepts. As part of the IoT solutions, Machine–to–Machine (M2M) services, which include automated communication and data transmission among two or more ICT entities, also have the potential of becoming one of the fastest growing segments for the Internet usage and increased mobile data demand. Although common characteristics of IoT and M2M are based on remote access to devices, IoT is expanding the concept of M2M because it can be integrated into comprehensive, scalable, and flexible business solutions. While IoT is focused more on software solutions and the IP network, M2M communication is predominantly oriented on embedded hardware and mobile networks. M2M communications are based on installing a SIM card or pulling a fixed line, but considering the fact that M2M with internet protocol represents a part of IoT, the common M2M/IoT services adoption trends can be closely analyzed.

As presented in Figure 2, many different forms of telecommunications services offerings are currently available in the markets [1]. Although the stand-alone service offerings have kept a strong position in the markets, services packages comprising more than one type of service have also achieved intensive adoption rates. These are, for example, any service packages where two (i.e., the 2D packages) or three (i.e., the 3D packages) electronic telecommunications services (e.g., the Internet, telephone or/and TV services) are provided to users jointly. The 4D packages, which have recently been introduced in the markets, mainly comprise a combination of telephone services in the fixed network, telephone services in the mobile network, Internet services, and TV services. As can be seen from the services adoption rates presented in Figure 2, the 4D packages note for fast adoption growth, mainly based on their total value. This goes in line with the concept which suggests the creation of all-inclusive services offerings for the end users, and a specific definition of the services' features [3].

Many advanced telecommunications networks implement necessary features that allow simultaneous management of various services, applications, and devices with different network and traffic requirements, and defined the quality of services. The methods that can be considered necessary for the selection of adequate services offerings to achieve optimal business models are based on the usage of predictive models and accurate forecast of services adoption rates.

III. PREDICTIVE MODELS

The models for prediction of telecommunications services adoption rates are increasingly important for optimal business modeling. The various predictive models whose implementation contributes to accurate business modeling are used [4].

An overall increase in network traffic has encouraged telecommunications operators to search for the best approaches to handle available data traffic, apply analytics over gathered data, and derive useful knowledge. Some efficient processes that can be used for the selection of adequate forecasting methods are described in [5].

For processing time series data, one of the most commonly used methods includes data classification. There are many examples of successful usage of data classification processes, some of which are used in adapting the mobility management mechanisms [6], prediction of applications' data consumption [7], and user activity [8].

In this paper, the several commonly used models for time series data analytics, described for instance in [9], and some additional models, described in more detail in [10], are taken into account. In [10], the analysis is conducted to point to the fact that the presented models enable an adequate forecast of the number of future service users.

However, the aim of the analysis conducted in this paper, unlike the one conducted in [10], is to demonstrate that the predictive modeling processes can also be used for selecting the best service offerings for chosen scenarios. This is particularly important for enhancing business planning processes and the selection of the most effective business models.

A. Common Models Used in Predictive Modeling

The scope of this paper covers the analyses of several common models [9], as well as additional predictive models [10], with the objective to compare their predictive accuracy.

1) Simple Logistic model

The simple Logistic model is a commonly used model for the forecasting of service market adoption, and is defined by the following expression:

$$L(t;M,a,b) = \frac{M}{1+e^{-a(t-b)}} \tag{1}$$

where L represents the number of broadband users per capita over period t. The model is defined by the following parameters: M, which reflects the market capacity; a, which reflects the speed of broadband adoption; and b, which positions the graph on the timescale.

2) Richards model

Richards model is called the Logistic model of four parameters, and is defined by the following expression:

$$R(t;M,a,b,c) = \frac{M}{\left[1+e^{-a(t-b)}\right]^{c}} \tag{2}$$

where R represents the number of broadband users per capita over period t. The model is defined by the following parameters: M, which reflects the market capacity; a, which reflects the speed of broadband adoption; b, which positions the graph on the timescale; and c, which positions the model's inflection point.

3) Bass model

The Bass model represents the most commonly used model for prediction of new services, and is defined by the expression:

$$B(t;M,p,q,t_s) = M \cdot \frac{1-e^{-(p+q)\cdot(t-t_s)}}{1+\dfrac{q}{p}\cdot e^{-(p+q)\cdot(t-t_s)}} \tag{3}$$

where B represents the number of broadband users per capita over period t. The model is defined by the following parameters: M, which reflects the market capacity; p, which reflects the coefficient of innovation ($p > 0$); q, which reflects the coefficient of imitation ($q \geq 0$); and t, which reflects the time when the service was introduced in the market ($t \geq ts$).

4) Gompertz model

The Gompertz model is a special case of a Logistic function, and is defined by the following expression:

$$G(t;M,a,b) = M \cdot e^{-e^{-a(t-b)}} \tag{4}$$

where G represents the number of broadband users per capita over period t. The model is defined by the following parameters: M, which reflects the market capacity; a, which reflects the speed of broadband adoption; and b, which positions the graph on the timescale.

B. Additional Predictive Models

In order to expand the analysis and compare features of additional models, combinations of some other parameters are taken into account and combined models are derived, as described in more detail in [10], using the following expression:

$$BB(t) = M \cdot \frac{e^{\left[1-e^{-a(t-b)}\right]^{d}}}{e^{\left[1+e^{-a(t-b)}\right]^{c}}} \tag{5}$$

where BB(t) denotes the number of broadband users, and M a total capacity. These modified forms take into account several additional combinations of parameters' values, previously defined in [10], as presented in Table I.

TABLE I. OVERVIEW OF ADDITIONAL PREDICTIVE MODELS

Models:	Parameters values: Parameter c:	Parameter d:	Notes:
Logistic (L)	1	0	
Bass (B)	1	1	
Richards (R)	$c \in \lvert 0,+\infty \rangle$	0	*For c*=1: R ≡ L
Gompertz (G)	0	1	Subcases of *c* for *d*=0 and *d*=1
	1	0	
GB	1	1	
GR	$c \in \lvert 0,+\infty \rangle$	0	Subcases: (*c*=0, *d*=0) and (*c*=1, *d*=0)
GBR	$c \in \lvert 0,+\infty \rangle$	1	Subcases: (*c*=0, *d*=1) and (*c*=1, *d*=1)

1) GB model

The GB model combines the features of the Gompertz (G) and Bass (B) models. Like the Gompertz model, it has a fixed inflection point and the three parameters, *M*, *a*, and *b*, respectively.

$$GB(t;M,p,q,t_s) = M \cdot \frac{e^{\left[1-e^{-(p+q)\cdot(t-t_s)}\right]}}{e^{\left[1+\frac{q}{p}\cdot e^{-(p+q)\cdot(t-t_s)}\right]}} \quad (6)$$

It models the fast growth. Moreover, this model can also be expressed by the parameters *p* and *q*, comprised within the Bass model.

2) GR model

The GR model combines the features of the Gompertz (G) and Richards (R) models and models fast growth. Like the Richards model, it has a flexible inflection point and the four parameters, *M*, *a*, *b* and *c*, respectively.

$$GR(t;M,a,b,c) = M \cdot \frac{e}{e^{\left[1+e^{-a(t-b)}\right]^{c}}} \quad (7)$$

3) GBR model

The GBR model combines the features of the Gompertz (G), Bass (B) and Richards (R) models. It has a flexible inflection point and the four parameters, *M*, *a*, *b* and *c*, respectively. It also models the fast growth.

$$GBR(t;M,a,b,c) = M \cdot \frac{e^{\left[1-e^{-a(t-b)}\right]}}{e^{\left[1+e^{-a(t-b)}\right]^{c}}} \quad (8)$$

The predictive models can be additionally modified using more explanatory parameters. Although certain generalizations of the existing models expand their features' description, additional parameters require larger sets of known data points used in the predictive modeling process, which limits their usage.

IV. Modeling of Services Adoption Process

All these models are suited for modeling of services adoption trends. For the given models, the analyses that point to the accuracy of fitting and forecasting processes are conducted. The estimated parameters can be used to generate the prediction of future values based on the known ones.

A. Fitting Process

As can be seen from the results presented in Figures 3-5, the fitting processes comprise the adjustments of models parameters to best describe the default time series values (denoted as '*Data*') representing the number of users and revenues, respectively. The results point to the fact that the Bass model can model faster growth, but its accuracy improves as the number of known data points, i.e., the ones used for training, increase. All other models show similarly good properties in the presented cases, despite somewhat scattered data set for quarterly periods presented in Figure 3.

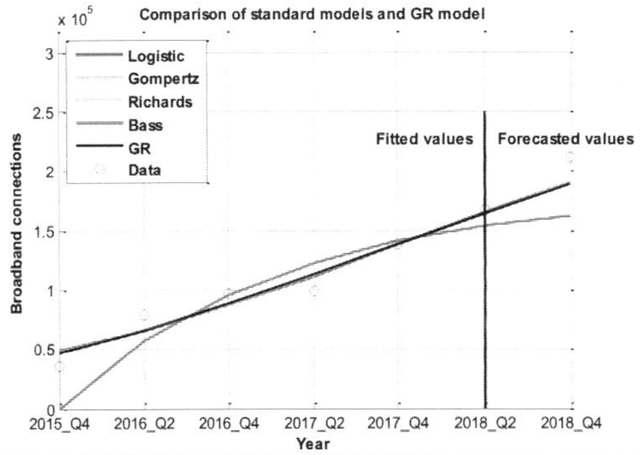

Time period:	2015_Q4	2016_Q2	2016_Q4	2017_Q2	2017_Q4	2018_Q2	2018_Q4
The nr. of users of the 4D service packages:	35.772	79.168	96.750	98.642	138.536	166.807	211.762

Figure 3. The number of users of the 4D services packages [1].

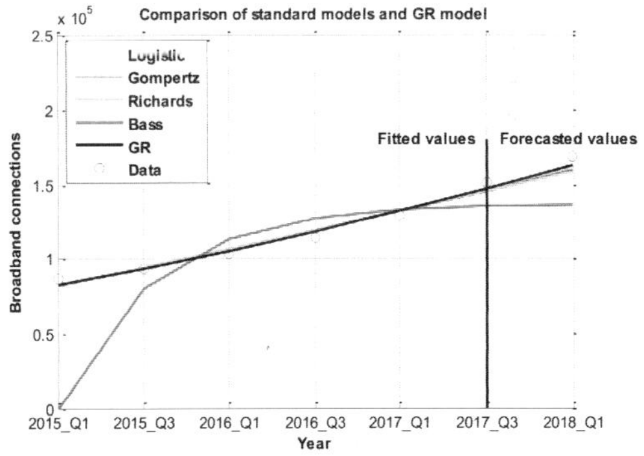

Time period:	2015_Q1	2015_Q3	2016_Q1	2016_Q3	2017_Q1	2017_Q3	2018_Q1
The nr. of users of the M2M/IoT services:	87.281	93.586	103.948	114.667	129.046	151.643	168.854

Figure 4. The number of users of the M2M/IoT services [1].

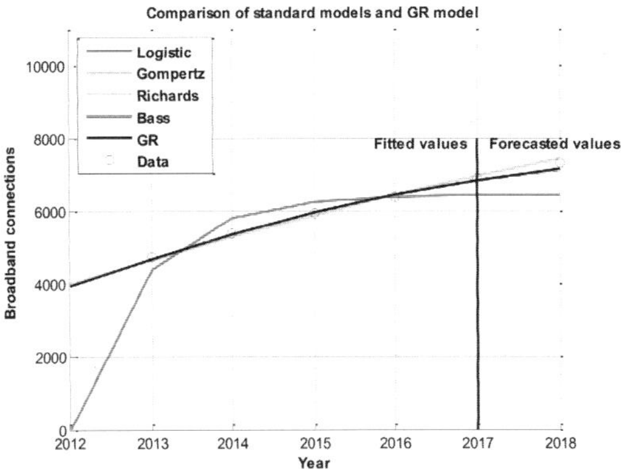

Time period:	2012	2013	2014	2015	2016	2017	2018
The global revenue of IoT (in mil. EUR):	3.900	4.750	5.400	5.950	6.400	6.900	7.350

Figure 5. The global revenue of IoT (in mil. EUR) [2].

B. Forecasting Process

A number of measures are used to determine the accuracy of forecasts [6]. Statistical criteria can be selected only after making the decision about the general type of forecasting method. There are mainly four types of forecast-error metrics: scale-dependent, percentage-error, relative-error, and scale-free error metrics. The chosen statistical metrics that describe the accuracy of forecasted time series values are the forecast error and the mean absolute deviation, as good metrics to use when analyzing the error for a single output, and considering the fact that the prediction errors are in the same unit as the original series. The Mean Absolute Deviation (MAD), also commonly called the Mean Absolute Error (MAE), is the measure of aggregate error defined by the expression:

$$MAD = \frac{\sum_{i=1}^{n} |E_i|}{n} \tag{9}$$

where n is the number of prediction errors which are used for the calculation, and forecast error, E, is the difference between the actual value and the forecasted value in the corresponding period t. A smaller value of the mean deviation denotes the model's better prediction performance.

The sample data set is divided into subsets which comprise the training data (shaded in Figures 3-5) - used for the model parameters fitting, and the testing data (all other) - used for determination of the accuracy of the forecasted values. The chosen available data sets comprise the number of users of the 4D services packages [1], the number of users of the M2M/IoT services [1], and the global revenue of IoT [2].

C. Overview and Analysis of Results

Considering the gathered results of the conducted fitting processes presented in Figures 3-5, and the conducted forecasting processes presented in Figures 6-8, the primary difference among the models' fitting and forecasting accuracy is caused by different positions of the models' inflection points.

As presented in Figures 3-8, the Bass model shows limitations both in fitting and in the forecasting of the initial short-term upper market capacity. All other models show good fitting properties, as presented in Figures 3-5. Moreover, the Logistic model is less accurate in the forecasting of accelerated growth, as presented in Figure 8, and is more suitable for modeling of slower growth. It can also be noticed that, in the slower growth phase, the simple Logistic model gives the most accurate forecasting results, as presented in Figure 7. Furthermore, the good forecasting properties of the Richards model within the growth phase are caused by its flexible inflection point, which can be accurately adapted to the given changes in the modeling values, as presented in Figures 6-8. Finally, the Gompertz model shows a good accuracy in forecasting within the growth phase since it adequately models the accelerated growth of values, as presented in Figures 6-8.

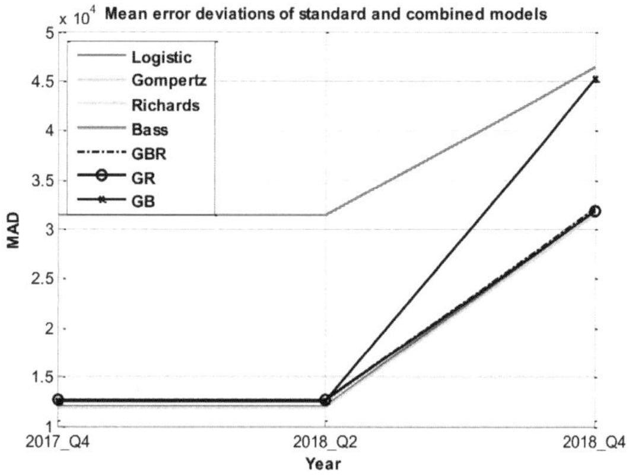

Figure 6. The number of users of the 4D services packages.

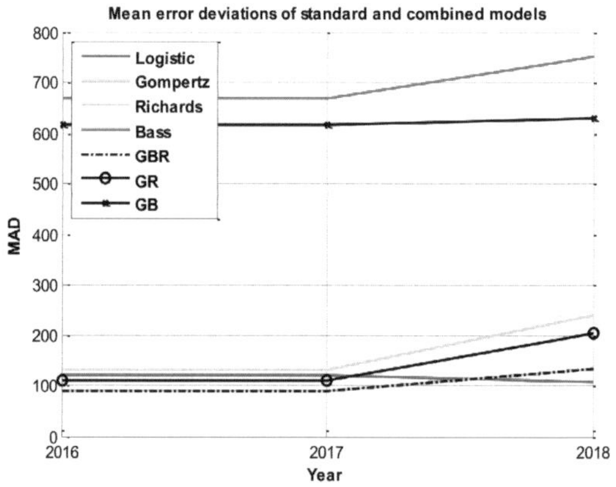

Figure 7. The global revenue of IoT (in mil. EUR).

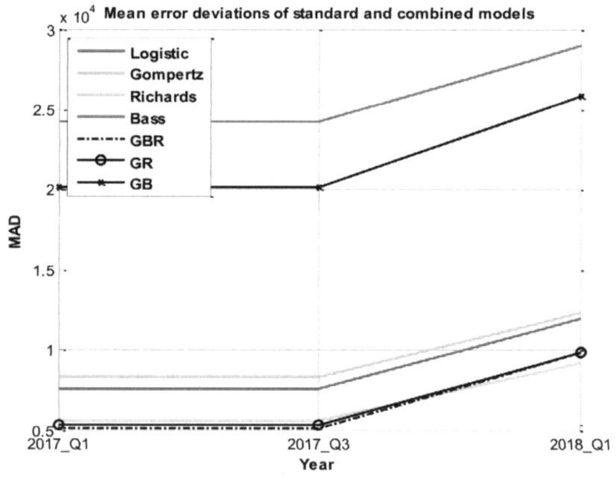

Figure 8. The number of users of the M2M/IoT services.

The additional GB, GR and GBR models combine the features of the Gompertz (G), Bass (B), and Richards (R) models. The combined models that have the features of the Gompertz model accurately predict the fast growth. However, the lack of the Gompertz model relates to the fact that it can not limit the excessive growth in the long run, and this can reflect the forecasting accuracy of the combined models, as well.

Since the Bass model has difficulties in assessing the exact upper market capacity limit in the initial growth phase, the forecasting accuracy of the Bass model combined solely with the Gompertz model, i.e., the GB model, is also not adequate, as presented in Figures 6-8.

However, the model that combines the features of the Bass model with the Gompertz and Richards models, i.e., GBR model, is more accurate for forecasting of the long-term adoption of the services since having a flexible inflection point which limits the accelerated growth in values, as presented in Figures 6-8.

The combined models that use the features of the Richards model, i.e., the GR and GBR models, generally show good forecasting properties even if the minimum number of values is used in fitting, as presented in Figures 3-5.

The Richards model accurately forecasts significant growth in the long run since it uses a flexible inflection point in order to adjust growth to the last existing training value, which can be seen for the GR and GBR models, as presented in Figures 6-8.

For a sum-up of the presented results, the models that combine the features of the Richards model with the Gompertz model achieve good fitting to fast growth and show good forecast results in all presented examples.

V. Conclusion

Since fast changes in the telecommunications markets around the world impact services development and adoption trends, users' demand for services features continuously changes. Advanced telecommunications services bring many advantages and added value to end users, so further growth in their adoption is inevitable. However, given the accelerated trends in services development, there is often not a lot of time to thoroughly consider users' requests related to services offerings before launching services in the markets. So, one of the challenges operators currently cope with is the way which makes it possible to select the best services offerings based on accurate forecasts of changes in market conditions and to estimate the adoption trends of novel telecommunications solutions. With regard to the presumption of usage patterns of novel services, it is possible to track usage patterns of similar services to create stronger business models.

In this paper, the analytics of telecommunications services adoption processes are conducted for the gathered smaller sets of time series data, i.e., for the short-term modeling period. For the chosen case study examples, the analyses of services adoption trends are compared based on the accuracy of forecasted model parameters. An overview and comparison of the accuracy of the predictive modeling of broadband services adoption using common adoption growth models are given. Alongside standard models, additional combined models are used to present their predictive capabilities, and to compensate for some lacks of the commonly used adoption models (for instance, of a Bass model which is not suitable for modeling of services adoption in the initial services' introduction on the market). The presented results point to fast expected growth in the number of services users.

Moreover, the presented results could be used to define adequate M2M/IoT services offerings. Based on the given results, the conclusion that can be taken as a guideline for the business modeling process is the fact that, despite their expected growth, and due to general risks related to slower demand for novel services, the M2M/IoT services can be offered within the packages combined with other types of services that already have their strong user base, which was presented as a good solution, considering the fast adoption growth of the package services.

Business models can be modified accordingly to enhance broadband adoption, boost revenue, or limit user churn rates in order to improve overall market dynamics.

References

[1] "Quarterly Electronic Communications Market Data," Reports 2010-2018, Croatian Regulatory Authority for Network Industries, 2018.

[2] "IMT traffic estimates for the years 2020 to 2030," Report, Mobile, radiodetermination, amateur and related satellite services, ITU-R M.2370-0, 07/2015.

[3] S. Moyer, "Networked Appliances: The Next Wave of Computing?," The Seventh International Workshop on Feature Interaction in Telecommunications and Software Systems, Ottawa, Canada, 2003.

[4] N. Meade and T. Islam, "Modelling and forecasting the diffusion of innovation – A 25-year review," International Journal of Forecasting, vol. 22, 2006.

[5] J. S. Armstrong, "Selecting Forecasting Methods," in Principles of Forecasting: A Handbook for Researchers and Practitioners, Ed. J. S. Armstrong, Kluwer, 2001.

[6] M. I. Sanchez, E. Zeydan, A. de la Oliva, A. S. Tan, U. Yabas, and C. J. Bernardos, "Mobility management: Deployment and adaptability aspects through mobile data traffic analysis," Comp. Communications, vol. 95, pp.3-14, 2016, ISSN: 0140-3664

[7] K.-W. Lim, S. Secci, L. Tabourier, and B. Tebbani, "Characterizing and predicting mobile application usage," Comp. Communications, vol. 95, pp.82-94, 2016, ISSN: 0140-3664

[8] Y. Leo, A. Busson, C. Sarraute, and E. Fleury, "Call detail records to characterize usages and mobility events of phone users," Comp. Communications, vol. 95, pp.43-53, 2016, ISSN: 0140-3664

[9] M. J. Panik, "Growth Curve Modeling: Theory and Applications," John Wiley & Sons, 2014, ISBN: 9781118764046

[10] V. Križanović, D. Žagar, K. Grgić, and M. Vranješ, "Enhanced Predictive Modelling Process of Broadband Services Adoption Based on Time Series Data," Adv. Eng. Informatics, vol. 38, 2018.

Security Methods Implementation and Quality of Experience (QoE) for Web Applications Performance

Ustijana Rechkoska-Shikoska
University for Information Science and Technology UIST "St. Paul the Apostle"
Ohrid, Macedonia
e-mail: ustijana@gmail.com

Abstract— **Web apps have a big impact in most of our activities nowadays. Unfortunately, they are also a target for illegal actions. When attacking Web apps, a hacker will try several means of compromising the applications, paying special attention to the database driven Web apps. The Structured Query Language (SQL) Injection Attacks (SQLIAs) are one of the most common methods of data theft on Web apps. SQLIA is a hacking technique that attackers use to compromise the database in most of Web apps, by manipulating SQL queries to change their behavior. Concomitantly, the attackers get full access harvesting sensitive information and taking control over the application for their personal benefit. The aim of this work is to acknowledge multiple security methods, such as parameterized statements, parameterized stored procedures, customized error messages and input validation type as efficient means for preventing SQLIA simulated on an online-based database application, MoviesBox. The successful prevention of the attack was confirmed through conducting a series of performance tests after the injection of malicious codes and Quality of experience (QoE) methods implementation.**

Keywords-Web Application; SQL Injection; Cyber Security; Defense; Database Security.

I. INTRODUCTION

The growth of corporate Web applications (Web apps) provides many opportunities for e-businesses to grow faster. These have become a significant communication channel among different kinds of service providers and clients over the Internet. However, the beneficial opportunities of Web apps also increased the security issues of a third party interfering. Even though there are many approaches for us to test the flaws and vulnerabilities, Web apps demand a more technology-independent solution.

Web apps are frequently vulnerable to attacks due to time and financial constraints, poor programming skills and lack of security awareness. These flaws provide opportunities for accessing sensitive information data that can lead to serious consequences and great damage. Therefore, an attacker can compromise this configuration faults and gain a full illegal access to user sensitive data. For this reason, governments, as well as many corporations and research communities, are paying increased attention to this issue in order to prevent its progression [1].

One of the top ten most dangerous attacks on Open Web Application Security Project (OWASP) is the SQL Injection Attack. This type of attack can do serious damage to database-driven applications, such as manipulation of the user input data, silent spying and monitoring, even corrupt and delete an entire database and gain unauthorized access to other network servers. Normally, this attack is done by injecting some malicious SQL code to the actual query driven by the application program in order to traverse, insert, update or delete the data. Even though there are number of mechanisms to detect the SQL injection attack, serious research has to be carried out to reveal the hidden and unexploited paths of these mechanisms, which may strengthen the defense against SQLIA. Based on literature review, our research did not find sufficiently favorable results concerning coding flaws level. Thus, there is a solid need to provide additional "rules" to the developers to secure Web apps from attacks. Numerous organizations have spent a great deal of money on antivirus programs, data leakage prevention systems and network firewalls on the off chance that software engineers follow the appropriate guidelines, hopefully saving a considerable amount of cash on cyber-attack prevention. As mentioned earlier, the coding flaws are crucial and they can lead to serious vulnerabilities in Web apps simply because they are easy to discover and abuse [2]. Therefore, the purpose of this work is to serve as basic guidelines to programmers to write code in a more secure manner, with the end goal of shielding Web apps from cyber-attacks.

The rest of the paper is structured as follows. In Section II, there is a detailed overview of the latest studies published regarding the SQLIA and the preventive approach that will be established in contrast to the already proposed methods. Section III gives a general idea and benefits of using Web apps, a detailed description of security, as well as types of malicious attacks and a background detail of SQLIA. In Sections IV, V, VI and VII, a vulnerable Web app made for SQLIA testing is presented and a method is proposed for protection of the aforementioned attack, execution of the proposed method and a penetration testing [3] that will prove the effectiveness of the implemented prevention techniques. Section VIII includes a test of the performance of the proposed Web app conducted on thirteen people. Sections IX and X present the conclusions and future work.

II. RELATED WORK

Because of the significant impact of Web apps in modern networking, attempts must be made for ensuring their safety. Following this prospect, many computer engineers are constantly trying to establish new and improve the already used techniques for prevention of SQLIA. A detailed overview of the studies published concerning these attacks has shown that, so far, promising efforts have been made in these fields, which guarantee the safety of Web apps and serve as tools for decreasing the rates of data theft.

A. Input validation attack including SQLIAs and Cross Side Scrpting (XSS)

An application is considered vulnerable when it does not properly filter or validate the entered data by a user on a Web page [4].

B. Static analysys and automated reasoning

Static analysis is one of the most often used techniques for analyzing the code [5] [6]. These techniques are used to detect the vulnerable code by scanning the Web app with the use of heuristic or information flow analysis. Moreover, they can also produce a false positive and false negative result because of the conversion of suspicious input. A combination of static analysis and automated reasoning techniques is the most suitable for detection of queries that contain tautologies by the Web app.

C. Encryption of confidential data

Encryption of confidential data stored in a database will not allow an unauthorized user to read confidential data even if it gets access by employing any kind of malicious technique [7].

In contrast to other published papers regarding investigations of SQLIA techniques and concisely describing each one of them, in this paper, SQLIA will be described in detail supported by appropriate examples. Additionally, the exploited vulnerabilities used for injection of malicious queries will provide knowledge to Web developers about the most exploited vulnerabilities, at the same time briefly describing the impact of SQL Injection. As opposed to [8]-[12], this paper will also propose useful guidelines and will illustrate a different approach to differentiate types, techniques and tools of SQLIA.

III. WEB APPLICATION AND SECURITY

Web development is generally associated with building Web sites for the Internet. It includes the development of a wide range of applications from simple plain text Web pages to complex Internet applications, mostly intended for electronic businesses and social networks. In scientific terms, a Web application is any computer program which uses Web browsers or technology as means for performing various tasks on the Internet.

The security of Web apps is the most important component of any e-commerce corporation, but, when deployed online, it is in the Internet's nature to expose properties for attacking Web apps from various locations using different levels of scale and complexity. Therefore, Web application security is essential and it deals specifically with security surrounding Websites, Web apps and Web services. Common methods of attacks, or "vectors", range from targeted database exploitation to large-scale network disruption. Such methods are:

- Cross Site Scripting (XSS) – attack where the hacker attaches code at the end of the Websites URL or it posts directly onto a page with user content and that attack will mostly execute when the victim loads the Website. Moreover, XSS is a client-side code injection attack.
- SQL Injections Attacks (SQLIAs) – typically occur by sending malicious SQL queries to an Application Programming Interface (API) endpoint provided by a Website or service, allowing the attacker to gain root access to a machine.
- Denial-of-Service (DoS) and Distributed Denial-of-Service (DDoS) – type of cyberattack where the hacker is able to perform traffic attack on a targeted server. The server then will no longer process incoming requests effectively and eventually deny service to legitimate users' incoming requests.
- Memory Corruption- this happens when a memory location is unintentionally changed and attackers take advantage of it to perform code injections or buffer overflow attacks.
- Buffer Overflow – by injecting malicious code into the memory, the buffer's ability to overflow can be exploited, potentially creating faults in the target machine.
- Cross-Site Request Forgery (CSRF) – type of attack that accidently tricks a user to change passwords, emails or transfer funds, which allows attackers to take control of the Web application.

IV. SQL INJECTION ATTACK

In this paper, more details will be given about SQLIA. Right now, SQLIA stands among the most dangerous threats to databases and Web apps. It typically includes malicious updates, modification of the user SQL input, either by changing the structure of existing conditions or by including additional conditions. Figure 1 demonstrates how an SQL Injection Attack is performed.

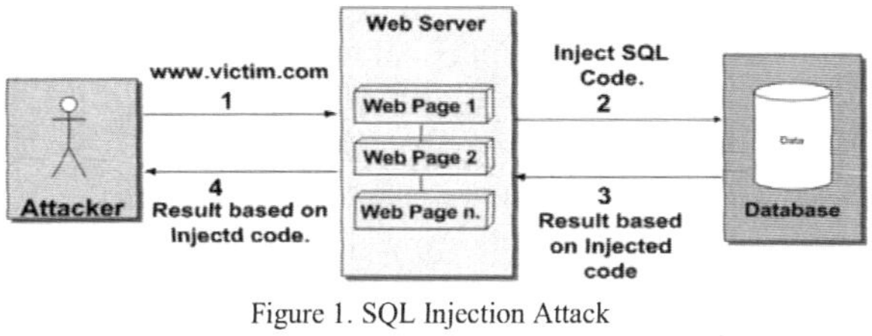

Figure 1. SQL Injection Attack

a) A user is accessing a Web application by typing the address in the URL.

b) The attacker injects malicious code to the Web application.

c) The malicious SQL-query is passed to the database server from the Web server.

d) The database management system sends the results based on the injected code back to the Web server. The results can be some data or error message or confirmation, depending on the injection type.

e) The Web server sends/shows the same result back to the attacker.

V. WEB APPLICATION AND SQLIA IMPLEMENTATION

MoviesBox is developed as an online database Web app, which is later used for SQLIA simulation. It contains three pages front-end written in Hypertext Markup Language 5 (HTML5), Cascading Style Sheet 3 (CSS3), Java Script and Bootstrap framework. For the server-side functionality, we used Hypertext Preprocessor (PHP) Language, MySQL-an Oracle-backed open source relational database management system (RDBMS) based on Structured Query Language (SQL), MySQL database and The Movie Database 3 (TMDb3) API. The application uses three types of authentication such as guest session, user and admin authentication.

In Figure 2, the Back End (Server side) and the Front End (Client Side) are presented.

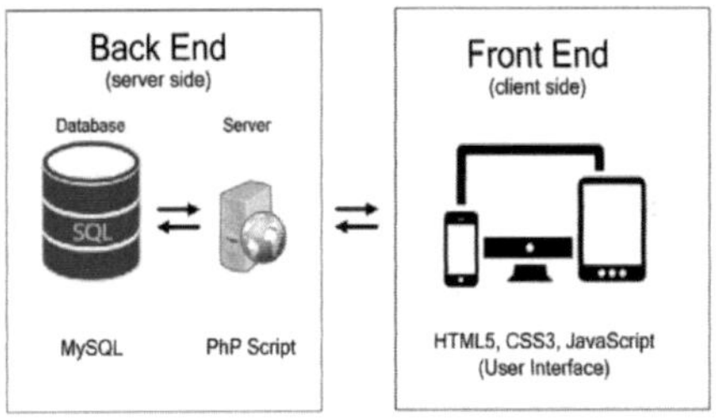

Figure 2. Back End (Server side) and Front End (Client Side)

A. Types of SQLIA

In order to prevent SQLIA, it is necessary to know the various techniques by which the attackers explore the vulnerabilities of the code and find the way to attack. They can be executed in the following ways:

1) Boolean-Based Blind: SQL injection technique that relies on statements that are always true. It is based on Boolean values (true or false), as suggested by the name, so the queries always give results by evaluating the condition WHERE.

SELECT * FROM users WHERE username = 'john' AND password = '1234';

In this scenario, it was assumed that the user had John as username and 1234 as password. This code can be exploited by adding a condition that is always true and just comment out the password part. By inputting the following, the attacker can easily gain access as user: `xxx@xxx.xxx'` OR 1=1 LIMIT -- '] for the username field; `xxx` as password. The new dynamic statement will be:

SELECT * FROM users WHERE username = 'xxx@xxx.xxx' OR 1=1 LIMIT -- '] ' AND password = 'xxx';

- xxx' ends with a single quote, which is a character limiter in SQL. With ' we delimit strings and we can test if the strings are properly escaped in the application or not.
- OR 1=1 LIMIT is a condition that is always true and limits the returned results to only one record.
- --'] is an SQL comment that removes the password part.

2) Union- Based Blind: type of attack that attackers use to obtain information from the database by extending the original query results. In other words, the attacker takes advantage of the UNION operator, which is used in SQLIA to join a query to the original, intentionally forged by the tester. The tester can access the values of columns of other tables by joining the results of the forged and original query. This means, the attackers are using this technique because they are not able to edit the original query to obtain what they want and this is the only way of running two or more SELECT statements into a single result.

SELECT username FROM userdata WHERE id='23';

The injected query will look as follows:

SELECT username FROM userdata WHERE id=' '
UNION
SELECT * FROM userdata.

This code will return all the detailed information of the table userdata.

3) Time-Based Blind: If there is a possibility when the hacker has no other way to retrieve information from the database server, the time-based blind method is used. The attacker uses an SQL statement which contains a particular database function to cause a time delay. The possibility of obtaining some information depends on the time it takes to get the server response. This kind of attack is not only used for determining the vulnerabilities, but also for extracting data from the server by integrating a time delay in a conditional statement. Consider the followin SQL statement:

SELECT * FROM users WHERE id=2;

By using time-based blind technique, the new injected query will be:

SELECT * FROM users WHERE id=2-SLEEP(20);

With the injected query, the attacker can only identify if the parameter is vulnerable to SQLIA. As mentioned before, time-based blind technique can not only check Web app's vulnerability, but also verify its database version and extract data from it. If the server responds in 20s, it can be concluded that the database is running on MySQL 5.0 server. This is done by using the malicious query:

```
SELECT * FROM users WHERE id=2-
IF(MID(VERSION(),1,1) = '5', SLEEP(20), 0);
```

4) Error-Based Blind: this technique is based on errors. Getting these errors indicates that the Web app is connected to a database and it is vulnerable to SQLIA. The injection of malicious code in the query that produces errors is done by sending or typing additional text to the server by Uniform Resource Locator (URL). After getting the error, it can be assumed what target is going to be next. To test whether the Web app is vulnerable, we can just put a single quote at the end.

VI. SQL INJECTION PREVENTION TECHNIQUES

1) Parameterized Queries

The use of parameterized statements, also known as prepared statements, can reduce the SQLIA by constructing the SQL-queries in a more secure way. If used exclusively, these statements completely remove the risk of all the SQLIA types such as tautology, timing attack, end of line comment and piggy backed attacks. Besides securing the Web app, prepared statements have another advantage because they help increase the work speed when executing the same or similar statements repeatedly.

```
$q = $conn->prepare("SELECT * FROM userdata WHERE
Username = ? && Password = ?");
$->bind_param("ss", $username, $password);
$q->execute();
```

In this code, implemented in MoviesBox, it is obvious that for the prepared statement we use a question mark (?) to substitute the parameters (integer, string, double or blob value). The second function binds the parameters and it is sending information to the database about what the parameters are. The "ss" informs the database server that the parameter is a string. The last function executes the parameters, where a dangerous SQL string will look as follows:

```
$q = "SELECT * FROM userdata WHERE Username =
'$username' && Pass = '$password'";
```

The main difference is the $q->execute(); method where the data is being passed. In the code with prepared statements, the parameterized string and parameters are passed to the database separately, enabling the driver to read them correctly, while the SQL statement in the second code is created before invoking the driver, meaning it is vulnerable to malicious parameters. This method can be very useful against SQLIA.

It is safe to say that these methods are currently the only and fundamental way to defend Web apps from this attack.

2) Parameterized Stored Procedures

Another prevention technique is using parameterized stored procedures. This includes a prepared SQL code that can be saved and reused as many times as needed without having to duplicate. Furthermore, they help reduce the network traffic between the database server and Web server just by sending the name of the stored procedure without having to send the SQL statement. As far as the security of the Web app is concerned, these procedures write the query in advance by placing parameter markers, so that data can be collected later.

```
/*!50003 CREATE DEFINER=`root`@`localhost`
PROCEDURE `validate_login`(
IN _username varchar(20),
 _pass VARCHAR(50)
)
BEGIN
SELECT * FROM userdata WHERE Username =
_username && Pass = _pass;
END */$$
DELIMITER ;
```

Second, in order to execute the stored procedure, a call function is used in the php code.

```
$q = $conn->prepare("CALL validate_login(?,?)");
$q->bind_param("ss", $username, $password);
$q->execute();
```

The main idea on how parameterized stored procedures work concerning security is that we can allow access to a stored procedure that updates a table, but forbid access to the table itself. This means, users would not have direct access to the database tables, but can only execute particular stored procedures.

3) Customized Error Messages

Error messages are also flaws that attackers use to gain access. Errors are visible when an invalid SQL statement is performed. This means, for any invalid SQL instruction that is identified when executing, the database will produce an error. By getting these messages, attackers gain information regarding the database and how to easily attack the Web app. It should also be noted that some powerful SQLIAs are entirely based on database errors such as unexpected quote, incorrect table name, etc. If these errors are completely removed, then attacking will become a difficult task. In order to prevent this, the use of customized error messages will reduce the possibility of SQLIA.

```
if ($conn->connect_error) {
  die("Error:    There    is    something    error".$conn->connect_error);
} else {
  echo "";
}
```

As mentioned before, error messages are retrieved from the SQL server as a response to any error query that is sent. The hacker can get important information about the target and retrieve table's name, stored procedure's name, etc. By using this method, we are not giving the attacker full access.

4) Input Data Type Validation

There are two ways on how SQLIA can be performed. The first is by injecting a command into a numeric parameter and the second into a string parameter. Programmers can avoid small attacks even if they do a simple input checks. The correct validation of the input data type such as string or numeric type plays a great role in the prevention of getting attacked. For example, if the user enters the input data incorrectly, then the incorrect input would be rejected due to the declared data type.

```
$q->bind_param("ss", $username, $password);
```

In the code above "ss" specifies the variable type, which is: "string, string".

VII. PENETRATION TEST AND RESULTS FROM PROPOSED TECHNIQUES

Penetration testing, also known as pen test, is an authorized simulated cyberattack on a computer system for its security evaluation. It identifies the weaknesses as well as strengths.

To execute the proof of demonstration, SqlMap and WebSpy Chrome plug-in were used for penetration testing. SqlMap is an open source penetration testing tools that automates the process of detecting and exploiting SQL injection flaws and taking database servers, while WebSpy monitors HTTP GET/POST requests of any Website and allows them to be viewed and to be tested.

Firstly, the penetration testing was made on vulnerable MoviesBox. After testing and analyzing the Web app MoviesBox, it can be concluded that most of the parameters in the pages are vulnerable to Boolean-based blind, Error-based, Time-based and Union-based blind injections (Table I). Besides, SqlMap was able to fetch the versions and type of the technology used. After more simulations, SqlMap obtained information not only about the database wanted, but all databases and tables on the server.

TABLE I. SQLMAP TEST RESULTS FROM VULNERABLE WEB APP

#	**SqlMap results on vulnerable pages of MoviesBox**			
	SQL Injection type	***Login Form***	***Register Form***	***Request Form***
1	Error-based Blind	√	√	√
2	Boolean-based Blind	√	√	
3	Time-based Blind	√	√	√
4	Union-based Blind			√

With implementing the abovementioned prevention techniques in MoviesBox, a penetration testing in SqlMap has been made by testing the login, register and request parameters; it showed great success (Table II).

TABLE II. SQLMAP TEST RESULTS FROM PROTECTED WEB APP

#	**SqlMap results on protected pages of MoviesBox**			
	SQL Injection type	***Login Form***	***Register Form***	***Request Form***
1	Error-based Blind	X	X	X
2	Boolean-based Blind	X	X	
3	Time-based Blind	X	X	X
4	Union-based Blind			X

The evaluation of the proposed techniques though the penetration testing showed that our preventive approach is effective. Table II shows that various SQLIA simulated on the Web app after implementing parameterized queries, stored procedures, customized error message and input validation. The SqlMap testing tool cannot exploit the parameters, which means that our approach is effective. Furthermore, extended security analysis was made through an entire Web app, not just the mentioned, and spotted a number of injectible points, which later on were corrected with the aforementioned techniques. Figure 3 presents various SQLIA simulated in the penetration test on the Web app after implementing the preventive methods. As it can be noticed from the tables, SQL Injection type, Login form, Register form, and Request form presented a suitable approach for this research.

For each of these issues, Error-based blind, Boolean based blind, Time-based blind and Union-based blind are included for testing. SqlMap test results on vulnerable pages of MoviesBox are performed and commented in Table I.

The SqlMap test results from the protected Web app are presented and commented in Table II. The Error-based blind concept enhances the Login Form, Register form and Request form in both scenarios. Additional testing will be done on this Web app once is in production to detect possible server or hosting failures. The evaluation of the proposed techniques though the penetration testing show that our preventive approach is effective.

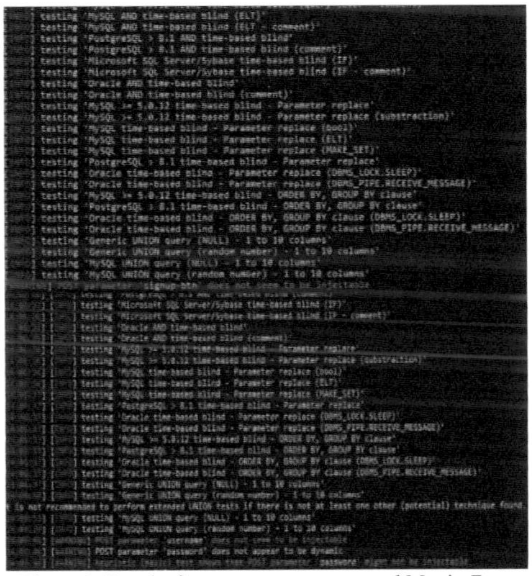

Figure 3. Results from pen test on protected MoviesBox.

VIII. Quality of Experience (QoE) for Web apps Performances

Performance testing is an important aspect when running a Web app. The main goal is to evaluate user experience on the Web app.

Quality of Service (QoS) refers to the technical and operational aspects of a service, such as time to support services, capacity, and transport. Quality of Experience (QoE) measures the difference between what users expected and what they actually received. Using the QoE is beneficial to estimate the perception of the user about the quality of a particular service and it depends on the customer's satisfaction in terms of usability, accessibility, retaining ability and integrity of using a specific service. QoE means overall acceptability of an application or service, as perceived subjectively by the end-user and represents a multidimensional subjective concept that is not easy to evaluate. In this work, QoE evaluation is used in order to measure the quality of the Web apps performances.

This test establishes whether the App meets user expectations such as: speed, usage, security, etc. Similarly, a test has been performed among 100 users from our university in order to evaluate the performance of the Web app MoviesBox. The results for testing the Usability, Load Time, GUI and Security, are presented in the following figures. The results were obtained according to a survey sent to university staff and students. As it can be seen later on, the concept of Security gives the best results based on Quality of Experience Analysis and tests performed.

A. *Usability Test*

The usability performance for MoviesBox showed that 87.0% of the people (Figure 4) answered that the Web application is easy to use.

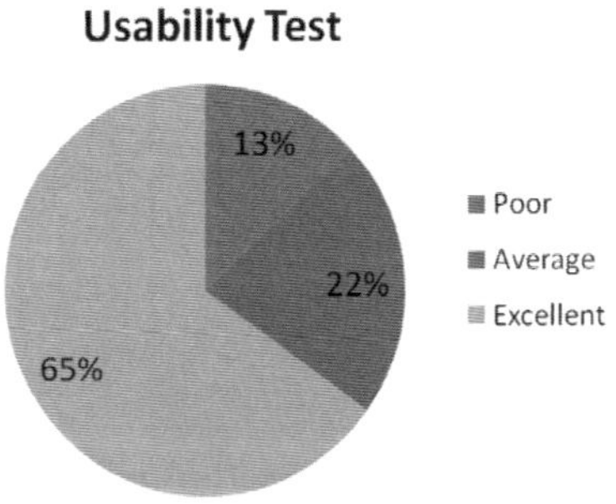

Figure 4. Usability Test

The instructions provided in the Web app are clear and satisfy its purpose. As far as user task analysys is concerned, MoviesBox showed excelent results regarding efficiency and accuracy. The provided main menu on each page was graded as user friendly, as well as the content. 13.0% of the people where not satified and proposed that more content will improve the Web app.

B. *Graphic User Interface (GUI)*

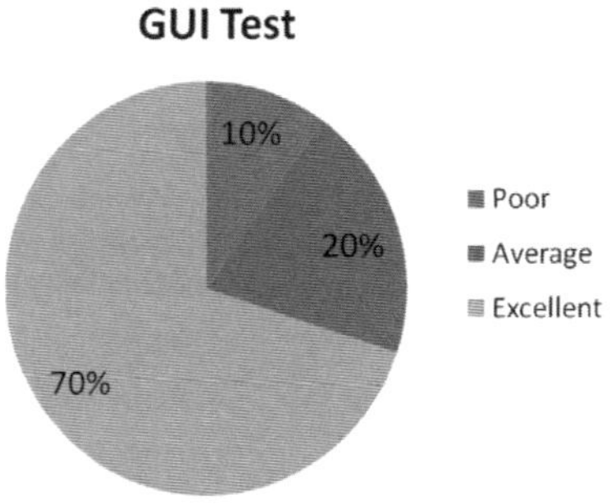

Figure 5. Graphic User Interface Test

GUI test showed favorable results since 90.0% of the people answered that the font used is readable, the alignment of the text is proper, as well as the color of the font (Figure 5). Regarding the GUI elements such as size, position, width, length and acceptance of characters and numbers in the inputs fields in MoviesBox, users were satisfied. GUI is an important concept of great interest for a large number of users. That is why this concept was tested for this application as well.

Interfaces are an important part of each application performance. The graphic display of the interface is important, especially with users' experience of this kind of applications.

Tests have also shown that the images used in MoviesBox had good clarity and error messages were displayed correctly. 10.0% of the people did not like the font and the colors used, as well as the error messages.

C. Load Time Test

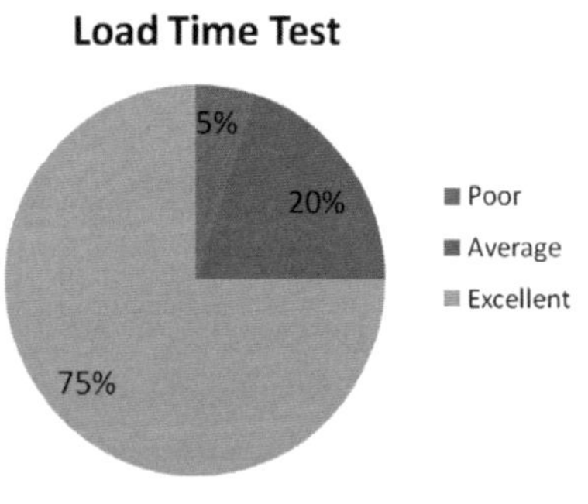

Figure 6. Load Time Test

After simultaneous usage by thirteen different accounts, this Web app showed huge rates of success. As shown in Figure 4, to 95.0% it took 3000 ms to load the Web page and it showed no error. It is known that usually users wait 10s and give up. Users were also satisfied with the short time for login (2505 ms). 5.0% were not satisfied and suggested implementation of a cache buster parameter to the URLs, which will make the request to bypass any full page.

D. Security Test

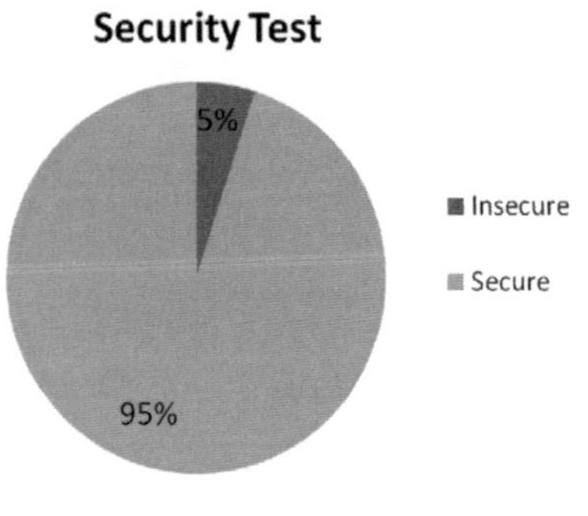

Figure 7. Security Test

Besides automatic penetration testing, a manual security test was done on MoviesBox among several people. The security test showed unauthorized access was not permitted and sessions were killed after prolonged user inactivity due to the aforementioned methods that were implemented. The threats were identified and showed that there were no potential vulnerabilities. As shown in Figure 7, 5.5% suggested captcha codes in the registration form and restriction of use of special characters, as well as proxy based application firewall, which is useful for detecting and blocking anything malicious.

IX. Conclusion

Web apps, as some of the most important "means of modern life", are still highly vulnerable to cyberattacks, mostly coming from unknown sources capable of inflicting serious damage. SQLIA is one of the most often used ways of compromising Web apps and since it is not enabled by technological flaws, it cannot be solved by the technology itself. Generally it is caused by the naive coding habits of developers, which make Web app firewalls or cloud computing powerless in resolving the security question against SQLIA, even though they can provide some level of protection. Therefore, this paper provides simple mechanisms, such as prepared statements, stored procedures, customized error messages as well as input data validation that showed a successful prevention of SQLIA on Web apps. Furthermore, the separate evaluation of these approaches showed that prepared statements are really the ones that are protecting the Web app. Without these, using just the rest of the methods still leaves the Web app vulnerable to SQLIA. Therefore, it is necessary to combine the right hardware together with multiple security approaches and more efficient coding in order to make the modern database systems safer.

X. Future Work

For future work, this application is planned to be working on Cloud of Things (CoT), due to many benefits including a small amount of disk storage, memory and resources necessary for execution of the app itself. Also, it can be approached by different users regardless of location and device with full support on different platforms and operating systems. There is independence of the app's upgrades from those of the machine software. Moreover, migrating this app on CoT will contribute to the reduction of the inconveniences (cost and other complexities) of direct hardware management. One major concern is that the CoT environment is susceptibility to cyberattacks. Therefore, the implementation of the aforementioned methods for SQLIA prevention is inevitable.

References

[1] R. K. Knake, C.o.F.R.I. Institutions, and G. G. Program, Internet Governance in an Age of Cyber Insecurity. 2010: Council on Foreign Relations.

[2] M. van Steen and A. S. Tanenbaum, Distributed Systems. 2017: CreateSpace Independent Publishing Platform.

[3] T. O'Connor, Violent Python: A Cookbook for Hackers, Forensic Analysts, Penetration Testers and Security Engineers. 2012: Elsevier Science.

[4] X. G. R Chaudari and M.V. Vaidya, A Survey on security and Vulnerabilities of Web Application. 2014 IJCSIT, (IJCSIT) International Journal of Computer Science and Information Technologies, Vol. 5 (2) , 2014, 1856-1860.

[5] Y. Xie and A. Aiken, Static detection of security vulnerabilities in scripting languages, in Proceedings of the 15th conference on USENIX Security Symposium - Volume 15. 2006, USENIX Association: Vancouver, B.C., Canada.

[6] V. B. Livshits and M.S. Lam, Finding security vulnerabilities in java applications with static analysis, in Proceedings of the 14th conference on USENIX Security Symposium - Volume 14. 2005, Jul 31, 2005 - SSYM'05 Proceedings of the 14th conference on USENIX Security Symposium Baltimore, MD — July 31 - August 05, 2005.

[7] U. S. M. Agarwal and K. S. Rana, "A Survey of SQL Injection Attacks". International Journal of Advanced Research in Computer Science and Software Engineering. Vol.(3): pp. 286-289, 2015.

[8] S. Sarasan, "Detection and Prevention of Web Application Security Attacks". International Journal of Advanced Electrical and Electronics Engineering. Vol.(3): pp. 29-34, 2013.

[9] R. Johari and P. Sharma, "A Survey on Web Application Vulnerabilities (SQLIA, XSS) Exploitation and Security Engine for SQL Injection". 2012 International Conference on Communication Systems and Network Technologies, 2012. pp. 453-458.

[10] M. R. Borade and N. A. Deshpande, "Extensive Review of SQLIA ‘ s Detection and Prevention Techniques", 2013.

[11] D. A. Kindy and A. S .K. Pathan, "A Detailed Survey on Various Aspects of SQL Injection in Web Applications: Vulnerabilities, Innovative Attacks, and Remedies". IJCNIS, 2013.

[12] D. A. Kindy and A. K. Pathan, "A survey on SQL injection: Vulnerabilities, attacks, and prevention techniques". 2011 IEEE 15th International Symposium on Consumer Electronics (ISCE), 2011. pp. 468-471.

The Influence of Energy Saving Strategy on Loss Probability in 3-stage Clos Switching Network

Mariusz Głąbowski*, Maciej Sobieraj* and Michał Stasiak†
*Poznan Univeristy of Technology
Chair of Communication and Computer Networks, Polanka 3, 60-965 Poznań, Poland
Email: mariusz.glabowski@put.poznan.pl, maciej.sobieraj@put.poznan.pl
†Poznan University of Economic and Business
Department of Investment and Real Estate, Al. Niepodległości 10, 60-875 Poznań, Poland
Email: michal.stasiak@ue.poznan.pl

***Abstract*—This article discusses the influence of an effective energy management strategy in nodes of elastic optical networks on the loss probability for calls of individual traffic classes. The structure of the network node is based on the architecture of a 3-stage optical Clos switching network. A key feature of the energy management strategy consists in switching off unused switches of the middle stage of the switching network.**

Keywords–Optical switching network; Energy saving; Loss probability; Clos switching network.

I. INTRODUCTION

Backbone networks are comprised of multiple facilities that transmit large amounts of data between the network access points over long distances through interconnected smaller networks, such as local or metropolitan networks. Typically, backbone networks offer large transmission speeds. For example, one fiber optic link is capable of transporting up to 560 channels in a C-band or 360 channels in the L-band. The possibility of effective use of such a large number of available channels to achieve high bitrates (along with different bitrates depending on different demands by users) is provided by a successful implementation of the concept of Elastic Optical Networks [1]–[3]. For competitive provision of services with high bitrates backbone networks demand huge amounts of energy necessary for sustainable transmission of signals in the optical fiber. The bulk of network devices that serve as backbone network nodes are designed with the assumption that traffic offered to inputs of devices has constant value. The reality is, however, that this traffic is changeable in time. This, in turn, leads to a situation where the system does not need as much network resources to service a given traffic intensity. When this is the case, constant power supply to all elements of a device/network node is not necessary. With the application of an appropriate energy management strategy, that can be based on temporary disabling of elements of active network nodes, we are in position to decrease the amount of supplied energy to devices when traffic load offered to them is slight). Then, in a situation where network traffic offered to the nodes increases, additional active elements of a device can be activated.

The issues of energy saving in network devices, as well as in systems/elements used in constructing nodes of the network are highly topical, while the increasing number of relevant publications that have been published over the years clearly testifies the interest in this innovative field [4]–[9].

In this article, the authors show the influence of the applied energy management strategy in a 3-stage Clos switching network on the loss probability for calls in this network. The structure of a large number of present-day network devices that serve as network nodes is based on the Clos structure. The investigated energy-saving management strategy will be based on switching-off individual switches of the middle stage in a 3-stage Clos switching network. Then, the influence of the number of active switches of the middle stage of the optical network on the values of loss probabilities for individual call classes that are offered to the network will be investigated.

The article is structured as follows. Section 2 presents the method for allocating network resources in elastic optical networks and proposes a definition of the frequency slot unit. Section 3 discusses the structure of the optical switching network and the structure of traffic offered to the network and presents a description of the path choice algorithm used to find an optimal sequence of choices to reach a certain connection in optical switching networks. Section 4 includes a description of the simulator (input data, simulation algorithm and the condition of termination). Section 5 shows the results of the simulation experiments for the optical switching networks in which the switches of the middle stage were switched off. Section 6 concludes the article.

II. ELASTIC OPTICAL NETWORKS

According to the information given in [2], fixed and flexible Dense Wavelength Division Multiplexing (DWDM) frequency grids are available. The advantage of the flexible grid architecture, that forms the basic underlying structure for Elastic Optical Networks (EON), is the possibility of using elastic allocation of network resources. The optical spectrum (e.g., C-band or L-band optical spectrum) available for EONs is divided into frequency slots with fixed spectral width equal to 12.5 GHz [2]. In thus defined slots optical connections are allocated, while the number neighboring frequency slots occupied by them depends on the demanded bitrate and on the applied modulation technique. According to the elastic frequency grid, standardized by the ITU-T [10], channel bands are allocated following a given nominal center frequency f_{nom} and the channel width ω which is the multiple of 12.5 GHz:

$$\omega = 12.5 \times m, \tag{1}$$

where m is a positive integer number, whereas 12.5 GHz is the so-called Frequency Slot Unit (FSU) [11]. The center frequency for particular channels (slots) is determined on the basis of the following formula:

$$f_{\text{nom}} = 193.1 + n \times 0.00625, \tag{2}$$

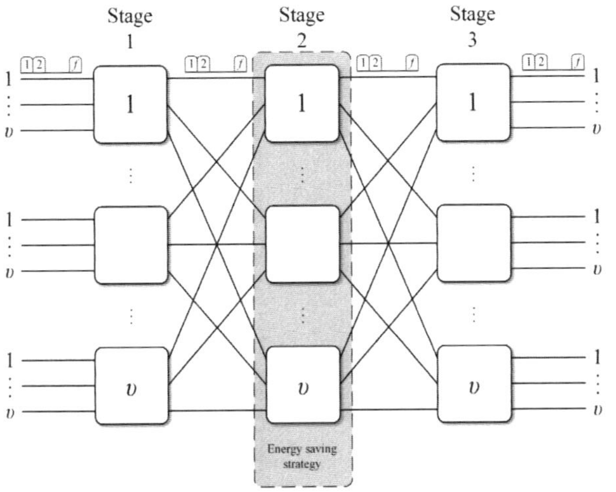

Figure 1. Structure of 3-stage optical Clos network

where n is an integer number, whereas 0.00625 is a fixed frequency shift, expressed in THz. To sum up, in order for an optical channel to be created in an EON network, beside the allocation of the value of the central frequency f_{nom} (similarly as in the allocation of wavelength in Wavelength Division Multiplexing (WDM)), the spectrum ω occupied by it should be also allocated.

III. STRUCTRURE OF SWITCHING NETWORK

A. *Structure of 3-stage optical Clos network*

Figure 1 shows a 3-stage Clos switching network. The network is composed of square $v \times v$ switches. The switches of the first and third stages make it possible for both the frequency slot (wavelength) and the output of a switch (optical fiber) to be changed, whereas the switches of the middle stage allow a change to be introduced in the output only. Each link in the switching network has the capacity equal to f FSUs. In addition, one link from each of the switches of the last stage belongs to one of v directions. The energy management strategy introduced in the switching network allows us to switch off unused middle stage switches.

B. *Structure of offered traffic*

The switching network (Figure 1) is offered m independent Erlang call streams with the intensities: $\lambda_1, \lambda_2, ..., \lambda_i, ..., \lambda_m$. The demanded FSUs related to particular traffic classes are: $t_1, t_2, ..., t_i, ..., t_m$, respectively. Service times for calls of all classes have exponential distributions with the parameters: $\mu_1, \mu_2, ..., \mu_i, ..., \mu_m$.

C. *Path choice algorithms*

Two algorithms for the point-to-group and point-to-point connection path choice can be used in the switching network. One of the two path choice algorithms in the switching network should be selected prior to the activation of the simulation program.

The point-to-group algorithm performs the following steps [12]:

Step 1: The counter of the attempts of setting up a connection is set to $l = 1$.

Step 2: Determination of the switch of the first stage at the input of which a call of class i appeared.

Step 3: Finding the switch of the last stage that has a free output link and has t_i free (consecutive) FSUs in the demanded direction. If none of the switches of the last stage have free t_i FSUs in the demanded direction, the call is lost due to the external blocking. In the instance where there are more than one switch of the last stage that have a free output link in the demanded direction, one of them is chosen randomly.

Step 4: An attempt to set up a connection between the selected switch of the first and last sections.

- If successful – the connection is set up. The operation of the algorithm is terminated. When there are more than one connection paths between the switches of the first and third stages, then one connecting path is chosen randomly.
- If unsuccessful, and the counter of attempts is $l < v$, the algorithm returns to Step 3 and the number of attempts is increased $l = l + 1$.
- If unsuccessful, and the counter of attempts is $l = v$, the call is lost due to the internal blocking. The operation of the algorithm is terminated.

The point-to-point algorithm works as follows [13]:

Step 1: Determination of a switch of the first stage at the output of which a call of class i appeared.

Step 2: Finding a switch of the last stage that has a free output link and has t_i free (consecutive) FSUs in the demanded direction. If none of the switches of the last stage have free t_i FSUs in the demanded direction, the call is lost due to the external blocking. In the case where more than one switch of the last stage have a free output link in the demanded direction, one of them is chosen randomly.

Step 3: An attempt to set up a connection between the selected switches of the first and last stages.

- If successful – the connection is set up. The operation of the algorithm is terminated. When there are more than one connection paths between the switches of the first and third stages, then one of them is selected randomly.
- If unsuccessful, the call is lost due to internal blocking. The operation of the algorithm is terminated.

IV. OPERATION OF THE SIMULATION PROGRAM

A. *Input data*

The simulator was written by the authors in C++ language using process interaction method. The input data for the simulator are the capacity and structure of the switching network. For each traffic class, the number of demanded FSUs and service time are given. The average value of traffic offered to a single FSU in the system is also given. To perform simulation tests in the switching network composed of the switches with $v \times v$ links in which the capacity of a single link is f FSUs, the values of the following parameters are to be introduced:

- the number m of offered traffic classes,

- the number t_i of demanded FSUs necessary to set up a connection of class i and average service time μ_i^{-1} for a call of class i,
- average traffic a offered to a single FSU in the output direction,
- the number of first-stage, middle-stage and last-stage switches.

On the basis of these parameters, the intensity λ_i of calls generated by sources of a given type of traffic stream can be determined in the simulator. Therefore, the parameter λ_i, depending on the average traffic offered to a single FSU, can be determined on the basis of the following formula:

$$\sum_{i=1}^{m} \lambda_i/\mu_i t_i = afvv. \quad (3)$$

The parameter determined on the basis of Formula (3) can be treated as the exponential distribution parameter that describes the process of the occurrence of new calls of individual traffic classes.

B. General simulation algorithm

The general algorithm according to which the simulation program is performed can be illustrated in the following steps that are in line with the process interaction method:

Step 1: Initial configuration of a simulation model – creation of a list of all sources generating calls of different traffic classes.
Step 2: Resetting the count of system time to zero.
Step 3: Activation of traffic sources and placement of events (*occurrence of a new call*) in the list.
Step 4: Checking the condition of termination for the simulation. If the condition of termination is satisfied, the simulation is terminated and the results are stored in a file.
Step 5: Updating system time to the time of the occurrence of the first event from the list (*occurrence of a new call, termination of call service*).
Step 6: Execution of the first event from the list.
Step 7: Removal of the first event from the list and return to Step 4.

Two events are then identified and defined for the switching network simulation model: *occurrence of a new call* and *termination of call service*. According to the process interaction method these events are serviced by one function. Thus described approach allows us to define a large number of traffic classes in the system.

Consider then a system in which m Erlang traffic classes have been defined. In the initial configuration of the system, it is necessary to plan (predict) the occurrence of a call of class i. The function that executes events related to Erlang traffic sources for the point-to-point selection (in the case of the point-to-group selection step 2(b) has to be repeated for each free link of the demanded output direction, if the earlier attempt failed to execute the connection) can be described as follows:

Step 1: Planning (prediction) of the occurrence of a new call of class i according to exponential distribution, where the parameter is the intensity λ_i. Placement of the event in the list.
Step 2: Checking if the system has enough resources for the call to be admitted for service:
a) Checking if any of the links in the demanded output direction have at least t_i free (neighboring) FSUs. If not - the call is lost due to the external blocking.
b) Checking if there is a connecting path between the input link at which a call has occurred and an output link in the demanded output direction that has at least t_i free (consecutive) FSUs, where free FSUs are meant to be finding the same frequency slots between switches of the first and the second stages and switches of the second and the third stages. If not – the call is lost due to the internal blocking.
If any of the conditions a) or b) are not satisfied, the next steps are not executed.
Step 3: Occupancy of the resources demanded by a call of class i.
Step 4: Planning of the termination of service according to the exponential distribution, where the parameter is the intensity λ_i. Placement of the event in the list.
Step 5: Service termination and release of resources.

C. The condition of termination in the simulation

The condition of termination for the simulation experiment is, with a determination of the loss probability, the counted appropriate number of generated calls of the least active class (typically, it is the class with the highest number of demanded FSUs). The mean result is calculated on the basis of 5 series. In practice, to obtain 95%-confidence intervals of not more than 5% of the mean value of the results obtained on the basis of simulation experiments, about 1,000,000 calls of the least active class are necessary to be generated. Confidence intervals are determined in the following way:

$$\left(\bar{X} - t_\alpha \frac{\sigma}{\sqrt{r}}; \bar{X} + t_\alpha \frac{\sigma}{\sqrt{r}}\right) \quad (4)$$

where $\bar{X}$ is the arithmetic mean calculated from r results (simulation courses), t_α is the value of the t-Student distribution for $r-1$ degrees of freedom. The parameter σ that determines standard deviation is calculated from the following formula:

$$\sigma^2 = \frac{1}{1-r}\sum_{s=1}^{r} x_s^2 - \frac{r}{r-1}\bar{X}^2, \quad (5)$$

where x_s is the result obtained in the s-th course of the simulation.

V. RESULTS

The simulator makes it possible to investigate switching networks with any number v of inputs/outputs in a single switch and any number v of outer-stage and arbitrary number of middle-stage switches in the switching network.

The number of demanded FSUs necessary to set up a connection of individual traffic classes not only depends on the required transmission speed, but also on the type of applied modulation format or range. For example, using the data given in [3], Table I shows the number of FSUs demanded by calls of traffic classes in relation to the type of modulation and range.

TABLE I. NUMBER OF FSUs IN DIFFERENT CONNECTIONS DEPENDING ON REQUIRED BITRATES AND MODULATION FORMAT [3].

Number of FSUs	Bitrate (Gb/s)	Maximum distance (km)	Modulation format
1	40	685	64-QAM
1	40	1024	32-QAM
1	40	1677.9	16-QAM
2	40	2585.2	QPSK
2	100	546	64-QAM
2	100	847.2	32-QAM
3	100	1342.5	16-QAM
5	100	2007.3	QPSK
3	160	475	64-QAM
4	160	756.5	32-QAM
4	160	1170.5	16-QAM
8	160	1710.9	QPSK
7	400	335	64-QAM
8	400	579.6	32-QAM
10	400	835.1	16-QAM
20	400	1133	QPSK
10	600	274	64-QAM
12	600	501.4	32-QAM
15	600	686.7	16-QAM
30	600	877.3	QPSK

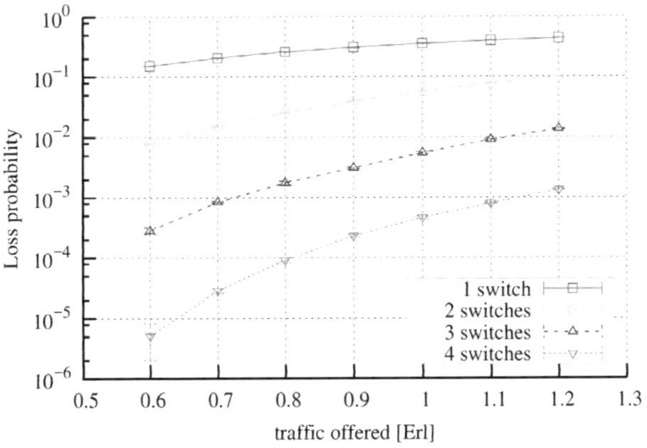

Figure 2. Loss probability for class 1 calls in System 1 with point-to-group selection and given number of middle stage switches

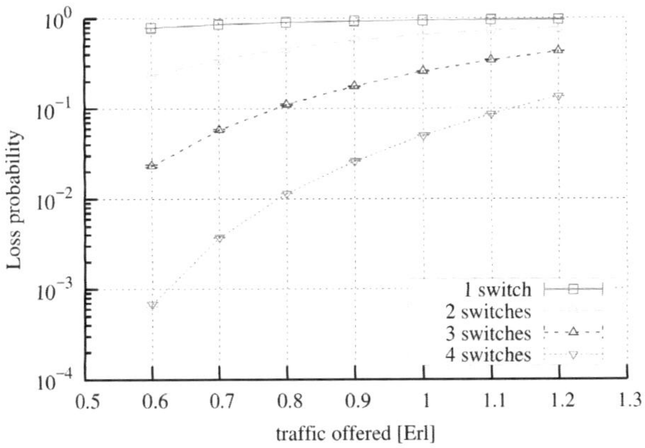

Figure 3. Loss probability for class 2 calls in System 1 with point-to-group selection and given number of middle stage switches

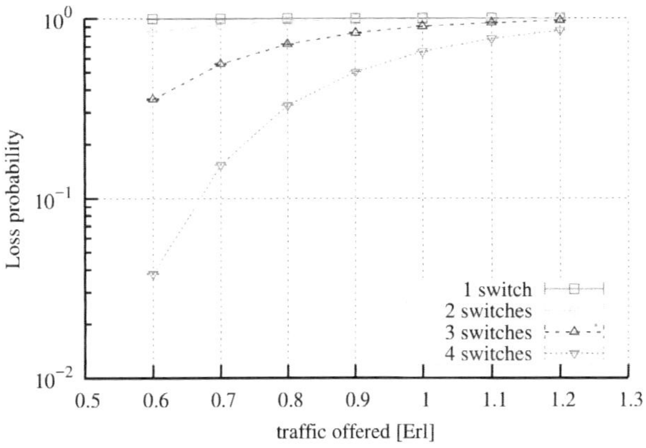

Figure 4. Loss probability for class 3 calls in System 1 with point-to-group selection and given number of middle stage switches

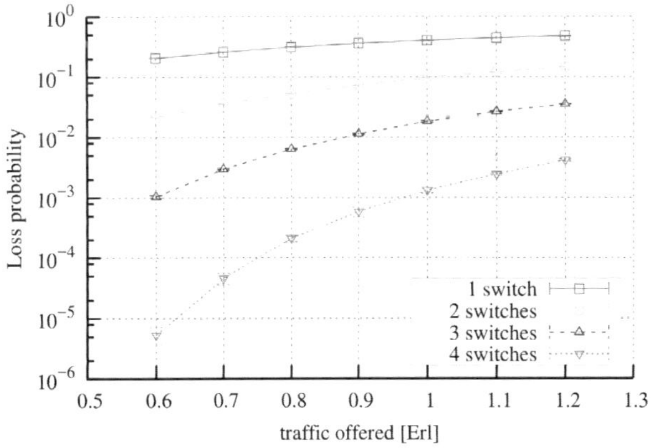

Figure 5. Loss probability for class 1 calls in System 2 with point-to-point selection and given number of middle stage switches

The findings presented in the article represent data referring to the investigations related to the influence of applied energy saving strategy in optical switching networks on the loss probability in individual call classes offered to the network. The following systems were investigated:

System 1:
- Structure of offered traffic: $t_1 = 5$ FSUs, $\mu_1^{-1} = 1$, $t_2 = 10$ FSUs, $\mu_2^{-1} = 1$, $t_3 = 20$ FSUs, $\mu_3^{-1} = 1$,
- Structure of switching network: $\upsilon = 4$, $f = 120$ FSUs,
- Path choice algorithm: *point-to-group*.

System 2:
- Structure of offered traffic: $t_1 = 4$ FSUs, $\mu_1^{-1} = 1$, $t_2 = 8$ FSUs, $\mu_2^{-1} = 1$, $t_3 = 12$ FSUs, $\mu_3^{-1} = 1$,
- Structure of switching network: $\upsilon = 4$, $f = 120$ FSUs,
- Path choice algorithm: *point-to-point*.

Figures 2-7 show the results for the loss probabilities in relation to traffic a offered to a single FSU in the switching network for individual traffic classes. In each of the figures the results for a different number of switches of the middle stage (from the minimum number 1 to the maximum number $\upsilon = 4$)

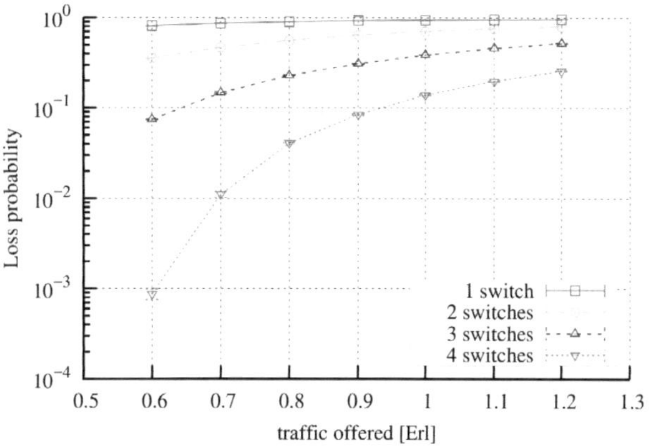

Figure 6. Loss probability for class 2 calls in System 2 with point-to-point selection and given number of middle stage switches

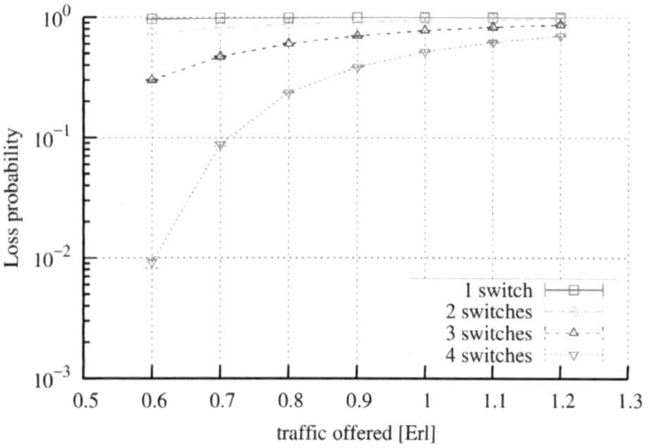

Figure 7. Loss probability for class 3 calls in System 2 with point-to-point selection and given number of middle stage switches

are indicated with a separate line in the graph. Figures 4 and 7 show the loss probability for the classes that demand the highest number of FSUs to set up a connection. It is easily noticeable that with a decrease in the number of switches of the middle stage to 3, the loss probability increases significantly. A different situation occurs with the case of the classes that demand the least number of FSUs (Figures 2 and 5). Here, switching off one or two switches in the middle stage is obviously followed by an increase in the loss probability, even though the obtained values for low loads of the system are still acceptable from an engineering point of view. Decreasing the number of middle stage switches has less impact on the increase in the blocking probability for classes requiring a smaller number of FSUs. For classes requiring a larger number of FSUs, the impact is already significant.

VI. CONCLUSION

This article presents the results of a study on the influence of energy management strategies on the loss probability in optical Clos switching networks. The simulation program presented in the article makes it possible to determine the loss probability in optical switching networks to which Erlang traffic is offered. The program can be applied to evaluate and assess when and with what load switches of the middle stage can be switched off in order to save energy. In future, the program can be used to verify analytical models of elastic optical switching networks in which an energy saving strategy is used.

ACKNOWLEDGMENT

This research was supported by the Ministry of Science and Higher Education in Poland.

REFERENCES

[1] W. Kabaciński, M. Michalski, R. Rajewski, and M. Żal, "Optical datacenter networks with elastic optical switches," in: IEEE International Conference on Communications (ICC), pp. 1-6. Paris 2017. doi:10.1109/ICC.2017.7997410

[2] X. Yu et al., "Migration from fixed grid to flexible grid in optical networks," in: IEEE Communications Magazine, vol. 53, no. 2, pp. 34-43, Feb. 2015. doi:10.1109/MCOM.2015.7045389

[3] C. T. Politi et al., "Dynamic Operation of Flexi-Grid OFDM-based Networks," Optical Fiber Communication Conference and Exposition, Los Angeles, CA, March 2012, pp. 1-3

[4] R. S. Tucker, "Scalability and Energy Consumption of Optical and Electronic Packet Switching," in Journal of Lightwave Technology, vol. 29, no. 16, pp. 2410-2421, Aug.15, 2011. doi: 10.1109/JLT.2011.2161602

[5] S. Zhang, W. Hu, W. Sun, and H. He, "Optimizing electrical power consumption in SOA based optical packet switching nodes," Asia Communications and Photonics Conference and Exhibition (ACP), Shanghai, 2011, pp. 1-6. doi: 10.1117/12.905434

[6] S. Aleksić, "Analysis of Power Consumption in Future High-Capacity Network Nodes," in IEEE/OSA Journal of Optical Communications and Networking, vol. 1, no. 3, pp. 245-258, August 2009. doi: 10.1364/JOCN.1.000245

[7] V. Eramo, A. Germoni, A. Cianfrani, M. Listanti, and C. Raffaelli, "Evaluation of Power Consumption in Low Spatial Complexity Optical Switching Fabrics," in IEEE Journal of Selected Topics in Quantum Electronics, vol. 17, no. 2, pp. 396-405, March-April 2011. doi: 10.1109/JSTQE.2010.2053350

[8] H. Yu, J. Zhang, M. Tornatore, and Y. Ji, "Energy-Efficient Lightpath Reconfiguration in a Decomposed-AWGR-Based Passive WDM Fronthaul," European Conference on Optical Communication (ECOC), Rome, 2018, pp. 1-3. doi: 10.1109/ECOC.2018.8535445

[9] C. Lea, "A Scalable AWGR-Based Optical Switch," in Journal of Lightwave Technology, vol. 33, no. 22, pp. 4612-4621, 15 Nov.15, 2015. doi: 10.1109/JLT.2015.2479296

[10] ITU-T Recommendation G.694.1. Spectral Grids for WDM Applications: DWDM Frequency Grid. Interna-tional Telecommunication Union – Telecommunication Standardization Sector (ITU-T) 2012.

[11] W. Kabaciński, M. Michalski, and R. Rajewski, "Strict-Sense Non-blocking W-S-W Node Architectures for Elastic Optical Networks," in Journal of Lightwave Technology, vol. 34, no. 13, pp. 3155-3162. July 1, 2016. doi:10.1109/JLT.2016.2560624

[12] M. Głąbowski and M. Sobieraj, "A Modified Method for Point-to-Group Blocking Probability Calculation in Switching Networks with Call Admission Control Mechanisms," in 11th International Symposium on Communication Systems, Networks and Digital Signal Processing (CSNDSP), pp. 1-6. July 18-20, 2018, Budapest, Hungary. doi:10.1109/CSNDSP.2018.8471832

[13] M. Głąbowski and M. Sobieraj, "Modified Direct Method for Point-to-Point Blocking Probability in Multi-service Switching Networks with Resource Allocation Control," in Quality, Reliability, Security and Robustness in Heterogeneous Systems : 14th EAI International Conference, Qshine, pp. 109-118. December 3-4, 2018, Ho Chi Minh City, Vietnam.